# THE
# TESTAMENT
# OF
# JESUS-SOPHIA

## A Redaction-Critical Study of the Eschatological Discourse in Matthew

Fred W. Burnett

UNIVERSITY
PRESS OF
AMERICA

LANHAM • NEW YORK • LONDON

**Library of Congress Cataloging in Publication Data**
Burnett, Fred W.
    The testament of Jesus-Sophia.

    Includes index.
    1. Bible. N.T. Matthew XXIV–Criticism,
interpretation, etc. 2. Eschatology–History of doctrines–
Early church, ca. 30–600. I. Title.
BS2575.2.B87            226'.206            80–67211
ISBN 0–8191–1743–9                      AACR2
ISBN 0–8191–1744–7 (pbk.)

To
John R. Donahue

## ACKNOWLEDGMENTS

Acknowledgment is made to the following for permission to use copyrighted material:

The Westminster Press for excerpts from: Daniel: A Commentary, by Norman W. Porteous. Published in the U.S.A. by The Westminster Press, 1965. Copyright © SCM Press, Ltd., 1965. Used by permission; Tradition and Interpretation in Matthew, by Günther Bornkamm, Gerhard Barth, and Heinz Joachim Held. Published in the U.S.A. by The Westminster Press, 1963. Copyright © SCM Press, Ltd., 1963. Used by permission; and, The Gospels: Portraits of Christ, by Wayne G. Rollins. Copyright © MCMLXIII W. L. Jenkins. Used by permission of The Westminster Press.

SCM Press, Ltd., for excerpts from: Promise and Fulfillment, by Werner Georg Kümmel, copyright © 1966 by SCM Press, Ltd., used by permission; Tradition and Interpretation in Matthew, by Günther Bornkamm, Gerhard Barth, and Heinz Joachim Held, copyright © 1963 by SCM Press, Ltd., used by permission; The Sayings of Jesus as Recorded in the Gospels According to St. Matthew and St. Luke, by T. W. Manson, copyright © 1957 SCM Press, Ltd., used by permission; and, Daniel: A Commentary, by Norman W. Porteous, copyright © 1965 SCM Press, Ltd., used by permission.

Columbia University Press for material from: Gnosticism and Early Christianity, by R. M. Grant, copyright © 1958 by A. R. Mowbray & Co., Ltd., copyright © 1959 by Columbia University Press, used by permission of Columbia University Press.

Jack Dean Kingsbury for excerpts from: The Parables of Jesus in Matthew 13, by Jack Dean Kingsbury, Published by John Knox Press, 1969, copyright © 1969 by Jack Dean Kingsbury, used by permission.

E. J. Brill for excerpts from: The Jewish Leaders in Matthew, by Sjef van Tilborg, copyright © 1972 E. J. Brill, used by permission E. J. Brill;

TABLE OF CONTENTS

xiii

## PREFACE

The material in this work was presented as a dissertation for the degree of Doctor of Philosophy at Vanderbilt University, and it was accepted in December, 1979. It appears here in substantially the same form as approved by my committee.

This dissertation could not have been completed without the aid and encouragement of many persons. I owe a special debt of gratitude to my director Fr. John R. Donahue, S.J. It was not only his initial suggestion which prompted me to work on the eschatological discourse in Matthew, but his constant encouragement and availability for critical suggestions enabled me to complete the task with enthusiasm. However, I am indebted to Fr. Donahue for more than routine committee work; he has provided me with a model of what it means to be an excellent teacher, a meticulous scholar, and a compassionate person. Others who graciously consented to serve on my committee were Professor Walter Harrelson, who served as chairperson, Professor Daniel Patte, whose interest in hermeneutics has provided an exciting eschatological direction for my research, Professor Charles H. Hambrick, who also guided my minor area of concentration in History of Religions, and Professor William H. Race, whose perspective as a classicist was welcomed by the entire committee. Although all of these persons made many helpful suggestions, the responsibility for the present work is, of course, my own.

My special thanks must also go to my wife and children, who accepted the roles of dissertation "widow and orphans" until this work was completed. I would also like to acknowledge the encouragement given by many persons simply by listing them, though the lack of comment in no way implies less gratitude on my part: my mother

and father, Mr. and Ms. A. F. Burnett, Rev. and
Ms. R. W. Struthers, Ms. Dorothy Bates, Professor
George Kufeldt (Anderson School of Theology),
Professor Delwin Brown (Arizona State University),
Professor Gary Phillips (College of the Holy
Cross), Professor Willard K. Reed, Jr. (Anderson
College, Indiana), Professor L. David Lewis
(Anderson College), Mr. Ronald W. Moore, Ms.
Janet Moore, Professor M. Eugene Miller (Anderson
College), Ms. Irene Miller, Rev. George Newton,
Ms. Edie Newton, Anderson College (especially
Dean Duane Hoak), and Ms. Helen Hudson (University
Press of America).

Although I have scrupulously reworked the manu-
script, it is inevitable that some errors will
remain.  It would be greatly appreciated if the
readers would call any errors to my attention.

Washington Square Park          Fred W. Burnett
New York, N.Y.
August, 1980

# ABBREVIATIONS

| | |
|---|---|
| ATANT | Abhandlungen zur Theologie des Alten und Neuen Testaments |
| BibZeit | Biblische Zeitschrift |
| BJRL | Bulletin of the John Rylands Library |
| BL | Bibel und Leben |
| Bl-D | F. Blass and A. Debrunner, A Greek Grammar of the New Testament, 1961 |
| CBQ | Catholic Biblical Quarterly |
| EThL | Ephemerides Theologicae Lovanienses |
| EvTh | Evangelische Theologie |
| FRLANT | Forschungen zur Religion und Literatur des Alten und Neuen Testaments |
| HThR | Harvard Theological Review |
| IDB | The Interpreter's Dictionary of the Bible |
| JAAR | Journal of the American Academy of Religion |
| JBL | Journal of Biblical Literature |
| JSNT | Journal for the Study of the New Testament |
| JThC | Journal for Theology and the Church |

| | |
|---|---|
| JThS | Journal of Theological Studies |
| LavThéol Phil | Laval Théologique et Philosophique |
| LXX | The Septuagint |
| NovTest | Novum Testamentum |
| NTS | New Testament Studies |
| RevExp | Review and Expositor |
| SANT | Studien zum Alten und Neuen Testament |
| SBT | Studies in Biblical Theology |
| STh | Studia Theologica |
| Str-Bill | Hermann L. Strack and Paul Billerbeck, Das Evangelium nach Matthäus Erläutert aus Talmud und Midrasch, Vol. 1 |
| TDNT | Theological Dictionary of the New Testament |
| ThS | Theological Studies |
| ThZ | Theologische Zeitschrift |
| TI | G. Bornkamm, G. Barth, and H. J. Held, Tradition and Interpretation in Matthew |
| USQR | Union Seminary Quarterly Review |
| WMANT | Wissenschaftliche Monographien zum Alten und Neuen Testament |

ZNW          Zeitschrift für die neutesta-
             mentliche Wissenschaft

ZThK         Zeitschrift für Theologie und
             Kirche

# INTRODUCTION

## The Problem

This is a study of Matthean theology in general and of the christology of one section of the gospel in particular (24:1-31). E. P. Blair remarked on the former in his survey of the results of Matthean research up to 1960:

> The Gospel of Matthew has been particularly stubborn in yielding up its secrets. No sure conclusions have been reached by scholars concerning its authorship, date, place of writing, original readers, purpose, and general theological point of view.[1]

On our particular concern, the so-called "apocalyptic discourse" (24:1-31), Peter Ellis, writing in 1974, has concluded: "The central part of the last great discourse continues to resist adequate explanation and is acknowledged by all to be the most difficult section of the whole gospel."[2] Two questions continue to vex interpreters: (1) what is the purpose and function of the discourse in Matthew's gospel, and (2) what are the redactional keys by which to interpret the discourse?

## Aim and Scope of the Present Study

Our aim is to answer the question: what is the purpose and the function of the eschato-

---

[1]E. P. Blair, _Jesus in the Gospel of Matthew_ (New York: Abingdon Press, 1960), p. 7.

[2]Peter F. Ellis, _Matthew: His Mind and His Message_ (Collegeville, Minnesota: The Liturgical Press, 1974), p. 82.

logical discourse (24:1-31) within the First
Gospel as a whole?  In order to answer this
question, we plan to analyze the eschatological
discourse within its immediate context, but we
also plan to deal with Matthean christological
and discipleship motifs in order to understand
the function of the discourse in terms of the
whole gospel.  The task of this study is complete
whenever these motifs have been brought to bear
upon the exegetical results of the eschatological
discourse itself.

Method

There are very few detailed redaction-
critical studies (of monograph length) which deal
with Matthew's eschatological discourse.[1]  The
lack of redaction-critical studies on the eschatological discourse is not surprising since this
approach to Matthean theology only dates from 1948
with G. Bornkamm's classic essay.[2]  To put it
simply, a detailed, redaction-critical study of
Matthew's eschatological discourse is the task
undertaken in this present volume.

Redaction criticism is no longer a new
method, and, since there is ample discussion of
it available, it is not presumptuous to assume
some acquaintance with the broad features of the
method.  Our purpose will be to clarify the way

---

[1]Only one, which was unavailable to me,
came to my attention: S. Vandakumpadar, The
Parousia Discourse Mt 24-25: Tradition and Redaction, dissertation, Pont. Biblical Institute,
1976.

[2]Günther Bornkamm, "The Stilling of the
Storm in Matthew," TI (London: SCM Press, Ltd.,
1963), pp. 52-57; this first appeared in Wort und
Dienst (1948): 49-54.

in which we plan to utilize the method.[1]

Redaction criticism has been succinctly defined by Norman Perrin:

> It is concerned with studying the theological motivation of an author as this is revealed in the collection, arrangement, editing, and modification of traditional material, and in the composition of new material or the creation of new forms within the traditions of early Christianity. Although the discipline is called redaction criticism, it could equally be called 'composition criticism' because it is concerned with the composition of new material and the arrangements of redacted or freshly created material into new units and patterns, as well as with the redaction of existing material.[2]

We plan to use the method in both its narrower and broader senses, but we will use it primarily in the latter as "composition criticism."

---

[1]Some of the relevant literature on redaction criticism is: Robert H. Stein, "What is Redaktionsgeschichte?" JBL 88 (1969): 45-56; Joachim Rohde, Die redaktionsgeschichtliche Methode. Einführung und Sichtung des Forschungsstandes (Hamburg: Furche, 1966; ET Rediscovering the Teaching of the Evangelists, trans. Dorothea M. Barton [Philadelphia: Westminster Press, 1969]); and, Norman Perrin, What Is Redaction Criticism? (Philadelphia: Fortress Press, 1969).

[2]Perrin, What Is Redaction Criticism?, p. 1.

3

Although Perrin's definition includes composition criticism, he does not outline it in detail. However, this has been done by John R. Donahue in his pioneering work on the passion narrative in Mark. In contrast to redaction criticism narrowly defined, which seeks to distinguish primarily between tradition and redaction, composition criticism:

> . . . concentrates on modes of composition, literary devices, and the discovery of patterns and structures. . . . This has often been called composition criticism and its model is the way in which any literary critic would approach a text. The emphasis is on the final product as an integral self-contained work of the author and the previous states of the work and outside influences are not critical for interpretation. This type of redaction criticism uses two sets of categories: one, taken from an analysis of the gospel itself to discover compositional techniques which the evangelist uses; the other consists in the application of modes of interpretation taken from classical and contemporary literary criticism to the text . . . . (Italics mine.).[1]

We can briefly summarize the premises of the method as outlined by Donahue. First, the Evangelists have theological concerns which are discernible in their literary activity. The

---

[1]John R. Donahue, <u>Are You the Christ?</u>, SBL Dissertation Series, no. 10 (Missoula, Montana: Society of Biblical Literature, 1973), pp. 41-42.

status of the material prior to its incorporation
into a particular gospel is not the primary
focus, but what the Evangelist does with it is
the interpreter's concern.[1]  Secondly, the final
gospel is the product of one hand.[2]  We will use
"Matthew" as a convenient designation of authorship in this sense.[3]  Thirdly, any part of the
gospel must be studied in relation to the whole
gospel.  In other words, any part of the gospel
provides an entrée into the whole of the Evangelist's theology, or, to put it negatively,
there is no "undigested tradition" in the gospel.
Any material in the gospel has a definite role
and function within the total work.[4]  Finally,
redaction criticism attempts to say something
about the historical, sociological, and theological contours of the community to which the
gospel was addressed.  The kinds of groups within
the community and the theologies which they
advanced are legitimate concerns of the redaction
critic.[5]

In summary, composition criticism is
redaction criticism in its broadest sense because

---

[1]Ibid., pp. 1-2, 32, 40 cf. pp. 87, 92-102.

[2]Ibid., p. 2.

[3]We will also refer to Matthew as the
"First Gospel." This designation is not used in
a chronological sense, but it refers to the
position of the gospel in the canon.

[4]Ibid., pp. 5, 11.

[5]Ibid., pp. 47-48.

it includes all three ways of doing redaction criticism: it distinguishes between tradition and redaction, concentrates upon literary devices and compositional techniques of the Evangelist, and it includes the study of themes and motifs within the gospel.[1]

The utilization of this method, then, limits the scope of our investigation. We will investigate the eschatological discourse in Matthew as it stands within its immediate context, and then we will attempt to ascertain the function of it within the whole gospel. We are not taking this approach just to be consistent with a method. We feel that it is necessary because of the apparent impasse encountered by other approaches which have attempted to elucidate Matthew's purpose in this discourse.[2] We want to show that Matthew has redacted his sources, has possibly composed new material, and has placed the discourse within its present context in order to accomplish definite theological objectives. Put negatively, our interest is not with Matthew's sources. We are assuming the Two Source Theory, that is, that Matthew and Luke used Mark, Q, and traditions which were unique to their communities, but our primary interest is in Matthew's compositional use of his sources.[3] Our task is complete when the eschatological discourse has been analyzed within its immediate context and thematically related to the whole gospel.

---

[1]Ibid., pp. 36-48.  [2]See chapter one below.

[3]In spite of the current revival which supports Matthean priority, we still feel that the cumulative effect of all the evidence tends to support the Two Source Theory. Cf. W. R. Farmer, The Synoptic Problem: A Critical Analysis (New York: Macmillan, 1964).

# CHAPTER I

# THE ESCHATOLOGICAL DISCOURSE

# IN MATTHEW

## Introduction

The purpose of this chapter is to provide a
general introduction to the detailed exegesis
which follows, particularly in chapters two and
three. This chapter, then, will be a general
history of research. The reason is that one
would almost find it impossible to write a detailed "history of research on Matt. 24:1-31" in
isolation from so many other areas. For example,
in order to write a comprehensive history of research on Matthew 24 one would also need to cover
the history of research on Mark 13. In fact, the
field becomes so broad that a whole dissertation
could deal with a critique of the research on the
eschatological discourse in the Synoptic tradition. Therefore, in this chapter we have chosen
to analyze the general tendencies of research on
the eschatological discourse in Matthew, and to
summarize the exegetical issues which have
emerged from that discussion. In subsequent
chapters we will deal with the history of research on particular questions which are essential for the topic of that chapter.[1] This
procedure hopefully will keep us from discussing
what are actually irrelevant issues for our
thesis. A general survey of the exegetical
issues, though, is needed in order to gain a
perspective on the detailed issues, and it is to
that general framework that attention must now
be turned.

------

[1]E.g., Wisdom christology in Matthew is
discussed below in chapter two.

7

## Interpretative Key (1): Data
## outside of Matthew

Previous research into the eschatological discourse in Matthew has concentrated upon the discovery of the key by which to interpret it. This concern has been dominated by two obvious hypotheses: that the key is to be found within data outside of the gospel itself, or, that the key is within the gospel itself. We will begin with a survey of the former, and we will survey the three exegetical keys most often used to interpret Matthew's discourse: the fall of Jerusalem in C.E. 70, the parallel discourse in Mark 13, and the "Little Apocalypse" Theory.

### The Destruction of Jerusalem

The main key outside of the gospel by which many have tried to unlock Matthew's theological vault has been the destruction of Jerusalem in C.E. 70. A. Feuillet, for example, interprets Matthew 24 by saying that the whole chapter refers to the destruction of Jerusalem as a historical judgment wrought by the Son of Man (by means of the Roman armies) on an unbelieving Israel. Feuillet then argues that the references to the Parousia in Matthew 24 (vv. 3, 27, 37, 39) refer to the fall of Jerusalem, as does the phrase συντελείας τοῦ αἰῶνος (24:3). In other words, Feuillet interprets Matthean eschatology by the destruction of Jerusalem so that even the Parousia of the Son of Man is reduced to that event.[1] It is not our purpose here to re-

---

[1] A. Feuillet, "Le Sens Du Mot Parousie dans L'Évangile de Matthieu. Comparison entre Matth. xxiv et Jac. V,i-ii," in The Background of the New Testament and Its Eschatology, ed. W. D. Davies (Cambridge: University Press, 1956): 268-9.

view Feuillet since a critique will issue naturally as our exegesis unfolds.[1]  Feuillet's work
is an ostensible example of how data outside of
the gospel is used as the key to interpret Matthew
24.

The precarious nature of Feuillet's argument
becomes clear when his conclusions are contrasted
with those of interpreters who have proceeded
from literary analysis to historical data.  Willi
Marxsen, for example, is diametrically opposed to
Feuillet's conclusion.  Marxsen argues that the
whole discourse in Matthew is a "true Parousia
discourse" which refers to the time after Jerusalem's destruction.[2]  In a similar fashion,
D. R. A. Hare claims that Matthew ignores the
question of the destruction of Jerusalem altogether and is concerned only with the question
about "what is the sign of your coming and the

------

[1]Feuillet has been severely criticized at
two points.  First, he interprets the discourse
from the premise of his opening question, namely,
could one who writes after C.E. 70, as Matthew is
doing, report a prediction of Jesus--that the destruction of Jerusalem would usher in the End of
the Age--which proved untrue?  Therefore, Feuillet
feels that to interpret the discourse correctly
the combination of the destruction of Jerusalem/
End of the Age must be separated and the latter
eliminated entirely.  See Willi Marxsen, Der
Evangelist Markus (Göttingen, 1956; ET Mark the
Evangelist, trans. Geoffrey Buswell [Philadel-
phia: Fortress Press, 1969], esp. pp. 199-206).
Secondly, Feuillet's conclusions are joined
with his view of the priority of an Aramaic
gospel of Matthew.  See Blair, Jesus in the
Gospel of Matthew, p. 80.

[2]Marxsen, Mark the Evangelist, p. 203.

consummation of history?"[1]

It is not only the ambiguity of Matthew's historical allusions in the discourse which lead to such diverse literary conclusions, but it is also the nature of Matthean theology itself. Matthean theology, like Pauline theology, cannot be broken down into several components and studied in isolation from one another. Matthew's view of history cannot be studied apart from his view of eschatology, ecclesiology, or christology. In order to understand one area of Matthean theology, one must seek to understand the theology of the entire gospel. In other words, specific passages in Matthew should be approached with the whole gospel in view. Marxsen and Hare have sought to draw historical conclusions from a literary analysis of the gospel, but to begin with historical data outside of the gospel itself, as Feuillet has done, dooms to failure one's search for Matthew's theology as it is reflected in his literary activity.[2]

---

[1]Douglas R. A. Hare, The Theme of Jewish Persecution of Christians in the Gospel According to St. Matthew (Cambridge: University Press, 1967), p. 179.

[2]S. G. F. Brandon is another salient example at this point. His theory is that the fall of Jerusalem in C.E. 70 raised the question of theodicy so poignantly for Jews and Christians alike that the destruction became the theological question to be answered. He contends that the whole gospel of Matthew was written as a philosophy of history to deal with the challenge of C.E. 70. (See S. G. F. Brandon, The Fall of Jerusalem and the Christian Church [London: SPCK, 1951], p. 227.)

# Mark 13

The vast majority of commentators have not begun their interpretation of Matthew 24 with historical data outside of the gospel itself. Instead, they have begun with literary data and have approached Matthew with conclusions derived from Mark 13. What should be two distinct rays of theological light have been focused into one beam by this approach. To put it succinctly, Matthew 24 has been subordinated to an interest in Mark 13. Mark 13 is usually presumed to be earlier than Matthew, as well as his main source, and thus the more "authentic" of the two. The hope has been to recover Jesus' own view of the future, that is, of his Parousia, from a comparison of Matthew 24 with Mark 13.

## The "Little Apocalypse" Theory

The approach to Matthew 24 via Mark 13 has focused primarily in the "Little Apocalypse Theory," that is, that a Christian apocalypse existed before Mark which had been assembled out of fragments of an even earlier Jewish apocalypse.[1] As far as Matthew's gospel is concerned, A. H. M'Neile's commentary serves as a representative work. After discussing the probable contents of the "Little Apocalypse," M'Neile says: "The compiler of it gave some doubtless genuine sayings of Jesus. . . . Mt. and Lk., on the basis of Mk., compiled their discourses each

---

[1]One is referred to the excellent summary on the history of the "Little Apocalypse" in G. R. Beasley-Murray, Jesus and the Future (London: Macmillan and Co., Ltd., 1954), pp. 1-80.

11

in his own way."[1]  Although he mentions the
literary activity of Matthew and Luke, M'Neile's
concern throughout his exegesis of Matthew 24 is
clearly with the question of what verses might
have been in the original apocalypse.  He is not
concerned with the way in which Matthew composed
his own discourse.  Matthew's purpose is discussed in one sentence: "Mt., who wrote after 70,
could use the same discourse to encourage readers
who were disappointed that although the city had
fallen the Parousia was still delayed."[2]

The Little Apocalypse Theory today has been
largely abandoned, primarily because every verse
at one time or another has been considered part
of the little apocalypse.[3]  The salient point we
need to make is that while attention was focused
for so long (circa 1864-present) upon the little
apocalypse, the question of the raison d'être
for the composition of Matthew 24 was neglected.

However, while most scholars seem to be
abandoning the theory of a little apocalypse, the
legitimate concern to answer the question "what
did Jesus expect?" continues.  A recent example

---

[1]Alan Hugh M'Neile, The Gospel According to
St. Matthew (New York: St. Martin's Press, 1915),
p. 343.

[2]Ibid., p. 344.

[3]Lloyd Gaston, No Stone on Another, Supple-
ments to Novum Testamentum, no. 23 (Leiden:
E. J. Brill, 1970), p. 47.  For a succinct and
penetrating critique of the Little Apocalypse
Theory see Joachim Jeremias, New Testament
Theology, trans. John Bowden (New York: Charles
Scribner's Sons, 1971), pp. 126-127.

of one who seeks to answer the question about
what Jesus expected is Joachim Jeremias. He sees
only two synoptic apocalypses which are of any
importance for his purposes (Mark 13:1-37; Luke
17:20-37). Consequently, he does not deal with
Matthew 24 at all since he feels that it is simply
a combination of the other two apocalypses.[1]
S. E. Johnson, in an excellent commentary on
Matthew, begins his investigation of the eschatological discourse by acknowledging that it is a
Matthean rewrite of Mark 13, but, instead of
pursuing this line of thought, he quickly returns
to the form-critical concern to study "Jesus'
eschatological teaching."[2] Although this is a
legitimate and important concern, it has been the
predominant one. The result is that Matthean
theology in the eschatological discourse has
suffered exegetical malnutrition; it has been
studied largely with an interest only in re-
covering an earlier apocalypse behind Mark 13, or
in seeking to ascertain Jesus' view of the future.

## Conclusions

The common denominator in these ap-
proaches--utilizing the fall of Jerusalem, or
conclusions about Mark 13, or the Little Apocalypse Theory--is the assumption that the key to

---

[1]Ibid., p. 123.

[2]This critique of Johnson should not be
carried to the extreme because his commentary is
quite consciously a form-critical one. See
Sherman E. Johnson, The Gospel According to St.
Matthew, The Interpreter's Bible, vol. 7, ed.
George A. Buttrick (New York: Abingdon Press,
1951), pp. 541-542 cf. p. 239.

the interpretation of Matthew's eschatological
discourse is something outside of the gospel
rather than the gospel itself. The deeper exegetical issue raised here is really a methodological one: should one proceed from literary
analysis to theological concerns, historical backgrounds, and sociological settings of the text, or
vice versa? We contend that the weakness of prior
approaches to Matthew 24 is that they have not
proceeded from the concerns, whether theological
or historical, which are discernible in the
literary activity of the evangelist. This weakness is evident in the fact that, even after the
scrupulous application of these approaches, the
theological concerns and historical allusions of
Matthew 24 are still an enigma. Most interpreters
of Matthew 24 have sought to understand <u>Matthew's</u>
purpose by some referent outside of the Matthean
text itself. This is one of the methodological
concerns to which redaction criticism speaks,
namely, that exegesis should proceed from literary
analysis to theological concerns and historical-
sociological settings. Therefore, in the following chapters we will not be directly pursuing the
goals of defining Matthew's theological or historical relation to C.E. 70, delineating the parameters of a pre-synoptic apocalypse, or un-
folding the eschatology of Mark 13. We conclude
that our primary exegetical task is to unfold a
literary analysis of Matthew 24 before any
attempt, however minimal, is made to depict the
historical-sociological setting of this gospel.

### Interpretative Key (2): Data
### within the Gospel

The second basic approach to the eschatological discourse in Matthew has utilized
conclusions about the characteristics and themes
of the gospel itself. The most important conclusion in this respect has been about Matthew's

apocalyptic nature. The gospel has salient
apocalyptic characteristics. For example, it is
often pointed out that Jesus is the Son of Man in
Matthew, the word παρουσία for the advent of
Jesus is explicitly mentioned only in Matthew of
all the gospels (24:3, 27, 37, 39), and Matthew
is the only gospel which depicts the judgment
scene (25:31-46). It would seem obvious that one
should conclude with B. W. Bacon that Matthew is
"the most apocalyptic of our Gospels."[1]  Whether
or not they have directly built upon Bacon's
conclusion, interpreters have usually approached
Matthew 24 in strictly apocalyptic terms: Jesus
is the apocalyptic Son of Man who will come at
the End of the Age as Judge. Thus, Matthean
theology says that if one hopes to gain salvation, then one must be obedient to the words of
the earthly Jesus since it is he who will come as
the Son of Man.[2]

This view of Matthean theology implies that
the discourse, and perhaps the whole gospel, is
dominated by an apocalyptic, Son of Man christology. For example, E. P. Blair has concluded:

> Cullmann's conclusion that the
> Christology of the Synoptic evangelists is
> not a Son of Man but rather a Messiah
> Christology is surely erroneous as far as
> Matthew is concerned. . . . The dominant
> category in the Gospel of Matthew is

---

[1]B. W. Bacon, Studies in Matthew (New York:
Henry Holt and Co., 1930), p. 412.

[2]Wayne G. Rollins, The Gospels: Portraits
of Christ (Philadelphia: The Westminster Press,
1963), p. 54.

unquestionably that of the Son of Man. The sheer bulk of the Son of Man references and material abundantly testifies to the weight of this category in the writer's mind.[1]

The conclusion, or rather assumption, that the eschatological discourse in Matthew is dominated by an apocalyptic, Son of Man christology has far-reaching implications not only for interpreting the discourse itself but for all facets of Matthean theology. For example, ethics in Matthew are seen in typical apocalyptic terms of reward and punishment, and Matthew's church is seen as a group whose main purpose is to live righteously while they await the imminent advent of Jesus as the Son of Man. Matthew's gospel, then, becomes comparable to any other apocalyptic literature:

> Like all apocalyptic literature, Matthew is born out of insecurity. Though Matthew shares with us some of the most moving literature in the New Testament, we cannot avoid the impression that he writes for the specific purpose of supplying theological and psychological security to an island of anxious Jewish-Christian apocalyptics rather than for the purpose of creating an eternally classic document for a continuing Christianity.[2]

This conclusion about Matthew's apocalyptic ethics leads interpreters to conclude that the

---

[1]Blair, _Jesus in the Gospel of Matthew_, pp. 82-83.

[2]Rollins, _The Gospels: Portraits of Christ_, pp. 70-71.

function of the eschatological discourse is parenetical. Readers are warned to prepare for the
judgment of Jesus as the Son of Man. The immediate context of the eschatological discourse,
which closes the whole discourse with the theme
of judgment executed by the apocalyptic Son of
Man (25:31-46), seems to support that conclusion.
The upshot is that Matthew 25 becomes the interpretative key for Matthew 24.[1] Although we do
agree that the function of the discourse is parenetical, we are not certain that the interpretative key by which this conclusion is reached
is the correct one, namely, reading the discourse
in light of chapter 25 and an apocalyptic, Son of
Man christology.

The crucial issue which is raised by this
approach to the eschatological discourse in
Matthew is: what is the context of the discourse?
The usual conclusion which follows from "the
apocalyptic approach" is that the discourse
covers only chapters 24-25. If that is the case,
then one is forced to interpret Matthew 24 in
light of the subsequent parables and judgment
scene in chapter 25. But, what if the entire
discourse covers chapters 23-25? Obviously, one
could then interpret chapter 24 quite differently.
The question of the context of chapter 24 also
raises the larger issue of the overall structure
of Matthew. The debate over the structure of

---

[1]Günther Bornkamm, "End-Expectation and
Church in Matthew," in Tradition and Interpre-
tation in Matthew, trans. Percy Scott (London:
SCM Press, 1963), pp. 15-24; Béda Rigaux, The
Testimony of St. Matthew (Chicago: Franciscan
Herald Press, 1967), p. 173; and, David Hill, The
Gospel of Matthew (London: Oliphants, 1972),
p. 318.

Matthew is important for determining the context of Matthew 24, and we need to survey it before we can adequately review "the apocalyptic approach" to Matthew 24.  Since the debate is so voluminous, we will only highlight those issues which are pertinent to our discussion.

## The Context of the Discourse

B. W. Bacon's analysis of Matthew high-lighted the five formulae which occur at 7:28, 11:1, 13:43, 19:1, and 26:1.  Bacon contended that these formulae clearly distinguished five "books" in Matthew.  Matthew's gospel, he concluded, was modeled after the Torah.  Bacon believed that the Torah had five books of Moses' commandments each of which was introduced by a lengthly narrative. In a similar fashion, Matthew began each discourse of Jesus with an introductory narrative, and linked the discourse to the next narrative section by his stereotyped closing formula.[1]

Bacon has been severely criticized for restricting the narrative sections of the gospel to simply preparatory material.  Many commentators prefer to see the narrative framework as a continuous one in which the discourses are linked not only to the preceding material but to the subsequent material as well.[2]  In spite of this

---

[1]Bacon, Studies in Matthew, p. 81.

[2]Donald Senior, Matthew: A Gospel for the Church (Chicago: Franciscan Herald Press, 1973), p. 33.  For summaries of critiques of Bacon see W. D. Davies, The Setting of the Sermon on the Mount (Cambridge: The University Press, 1964), pp. 14-25, 61, 92-93, 107; Blair, Jesus in the Gospel of Matthew, pp. 132-133; and Rigaux, Testimony of St. Matthew, pp. 30-37.

valid critique, the majority of interpreters have
accepted Bacon's proposal that the formulary
summaries are <u>Matthean</u> summaries.  There is also a
consensus among commentators that Matthew's
summaries are probably intended to mark the end of
discourse material while simultaneously introducing the subsequent narrative material.  There
is agreement on these two points, though there are
many different interpretations of Matthew's
structure deduced from the formulae.[1]

---

[1]Cf. Ellis, <u>Matthew: His Mind and His
Message</u>, p. 14, and Senior, <u>Matthew: A Gospel for
the Church</u>, pp. 30-38.  It is extremely difficult
to accept Bultmann's view that the five formulary
summaries are no different than the connectives
καί and ίδού.  This seems to make the summaries
theologically sterile.  It does not seem feasible
either that their only function in Matthew is to
provide a transition from Q to the Markan material.  (See Rudolf Bultmann, <u>The History of the
Synoptic Tradition</u>, 2nd ed., trans. John Marsh
[New York: Harper and Row, 1968], p. 351 cf.
p. 334).  The formula at 11:1, for example,
"occurs in the midst of Q material" (Davies,
<u>Setting of the Sermon on the Mount</u>, p. 20).  The
main point, though, is that Bultmann never
questions the fact that the formulae are due to
Matthew's editorial work.  While accepting the
formulae as Matthean editorial activity, G. D.
Kilpatrick contends that the formulae are merely
liturgical devices which would make the material
more appropriate for reading in public.  (See
G. D. Kilpatrick, <u>The Origins of the Gospel
According to St. Matthew</u> [Oxford: Clarendon
Press, 1946], pp. 75-100.)  Kilpatrick's thesis,
though, has been seriously questioned.  (See
Davies, <u>Setting of the Sermon on the Mount</u>, p. 21
and the literature cited there.)

A summary formula occurs at 26:1, and it is very clear that this formula marks the end of the discourse at chapter 25 as well as the transition to the passion narrative.[1]  The debated question is where Matthew begins the discourse.  In other words, is chapter 23 part of the discourse in chapters 24-25, or is it a separate discourse?

## The relation of chapter 23 to chapter 24

There seems to be little doubt among commentators today, especially when the parallels in Mark and Luke are studied, that Matthew is responsible for the structure of chapter 23.[2]  It is important, then, that Matthew does not end the discourse against the Jews in chapter 23 with his characteristic formula.  The omission of the formula has suggested to many commentators that chapters 23, 24, and 25 constitute one unit of

---

[1]N. A. Dahl, "The Passion Narrative in Matthew," in Jesus in the Memory of the Early Church (Minneapolis, Minnesota: Augsburg Publishing House, 1976), p. 50; Hill, The Gospel of Matthew, p. 332; Senior, Matthew: A Gospel for the Church, p. 30; and Ellis, Matthew: His Mind and Message, pp. 94-98.

[2]This conclusion seems to be inescapable in view of the excellent article by Ernst Haenchen, "Matthäus 23," ZThK 47 (1951): 38-63.  Haenchen points out that there are discernible pre-Matthean units in this material, but the arrangement and structure of the material as a whole is certainly Matthew's.

discourse material in Matthew.[1]  Other commentators, though, conclude that chapter 23 is a
self-contained, independent discourse, and that
chapter 24 begins a new block of discourse material.  The usual argument brought against reading chapter 23 as part of the discourse in
chapters 24 and 25 is that Matthew changes the
audience.  In chapter 23 the audience is τοῖς
ὄχλοις καὶ τοῖς μαθηταῖς αὐτοῦ (23:1), but it
changes to οἱ μαθηταὶ αὐτοῦ in 24:1.[2]  Perhaps it
will provide some clarity if we proleptically
summarize our position, which is implicit in the
exegesis below, on the relation of chapter 23 to
chapters 24 and 25.

First, it does seem that Matthew intends
chapter 23 to be read as a separate discourse,
but it also seems that the Evangelist intends for
chapter 23 to provide the transition to the discourse in chapter 24.  Jesus' discourse ends in
23:39.  However, Matthean redaction--such as deleting the pericope on the "Widow's Gift" (cf.
Mark 12:41-44; Luke 21:1-4)--clearly shows that
24:1-2 is related contextually to the discourse
in chapter 23.[3]

--------------------------------

[1]E.g., Krister Stendahl, The School of St.
Matthew and Its Use of the Old Testament (Philadelphia: Fortress Press, 1968), pp. 24-29 (hereafter cited as Stendahl, School); and Davies,
Setting of the Sermon on the Mount, pp. 22-25.

[2]Rigaux, Testimony of St. Matthew, pp. 11,
86-90; and Ellis, Matthew: His Mind and His
Message, pp. 77-78.

[3]For a detailed discussion of this point
see below pp. 112-116.

Secondly, Matthew's shift from a public audience ("crowds and disciples") in 23:1 to a private one ("his disciples") in 24:1 is a stylistic device of the evangelist. It is a device by which Jesus reveals in private instruction to his "disciples" (i.e., Matthew's Church) the meaning inherent in his public discourse. Matthew has employed the same technique in 13:10 when Jesus' disciples ask him privately about the meaning of his public teaching in parables (cf. 13:1, 36).[1]

Thirdly, commentators have recognized for some time that Matthew provides a continuous narrative framework and that the themes of the framework culminate in the subsequent discourses.[2] The narrative material which precedes the discourse in chapter 23 begins at 19:3 (cf. 19:1-2). The narrative is unified by Jesus' journey to Jerusalem (cf. 19:1; 20:17, 29; 21:1, 12) where he enters the temple (21:23) and completes his teaching there (cf. 24:1). Most commentators agree that the main theme of this narrative section is the coming judgment. As the narrative progresses, the judgment focuses increasingly upon Israel (cf. 21:23, 31, 43) until it issues in the discourse of Woes in chapter 23.[3] The main point for our discussion is that 24:1-2 culminates the theme of Jesus' judgment upon Israel

---

[1]See the discussion below on pp. 106-108; and 217-218.

[2]E.g., Ellis, Matthew: His Mind and His Message, pp. 10-19, 63-67.

[3]Ibid., pp. 72-77.

which was foreshadowed in the narrative material (19:3-22:46) and highlighted in the Woes of chapter 23. In this context Matthew does not have to use his formula "Now when Jesus had finished these sayings." Jesus' action of permanently abandoning the temple in 24:1 shows as clearly as a formula would that this discourse (chapter 23) has ended.[1]

Finally, Matthew has created a caesura between 24:2 and 24:3. He does this, as we will show below, by the following structure: (1) Jesus explicitly announces judgment in 23:38 ("Behold, your house is forsaken"); (2) Jesus fulfills 23:38 when he definitively leaves the temple ("your house") in 24:1; and, (3) Jesus consummates the judgment when he prophetically announces the temple's physical destruction in 24:2. Matthew 24:2 ends the theme of judgment against Israel, and 24:3 begins a new theme, namely, the Parousia of Jesus. Matthew has structured a new introduction, then, for the eschatological discourse which begins in 24:4.[2]

In summary, the context of the discourse in chapter 24 should not be interpreted too quickly in light of the apocalyptic judgment scene and the christology of chapter 25. At any rate, one should certainly not move from the interpretation of these chapters to a general set of conclusions about Matthew's christology and ecclesiology.

---

[1]See the discussion below, pp. 116-119.

[2]See the discussion below, pp. 152-165; and 198-215. The problem of the extent and the ending of the eschatological discourse is discussed below on pp. 193-198.

Our aim in outlining what we have found to be the context of the eschatological discourse is a modest one. We do not intend to generalize from this particular section and outline Matthew's master plan for his gospel.[1] However, we are saying that although chapter 23 is a separate discourse from the one in 24:4-31 in terms of motifs (the fulfilled judgment of Israel/the Parousia and future judgment), it is also intricately related to the discourse in 24:4-31 in terms of Matthew's redactional pattern of public teaching/private revelation by Jesus. The christological and ecclesiological implications which follow from this will be evident as our exegesis unfolds.

## Conclusions

We have seen how the apocalyptic approach to Matthew 24 leads to conclusions about its contextual relation to chapter 25, and we discussed the implications which this approach has for understanding the structure of the whole gospel. We have just evaluated the conclusion that Matthew 24 should be interpreted only in view of chapter 25, but this approach to the eschatological discourse needs to be reviewed in two further respects. The first point is that the gospel is not approached as a whole. The second point concerns the presuppositions this approach holds about the nature of apocalyptic.

First, this approach to Matthew 24 does not suffer from the critique of other approaches offered earlier because it does seek to understand the discourse in light of Matthean themes.

---

[1] Note the caveat advanced by Senior, Matthew: A Gospel for the Church, p. 37.

However, Matthew 24 has usually been studied in isolation from Matthew as a whole. As we have seen, when Matthean themes were taken into account, they were usually taken from Matt. 25:31-46 rather than from the gospel as a whole. This predetermined Matthew 24 to function as eschatological parenesis in light of the coming judgment. In order to avoid such a narrow interpretation of this chapter, a holistic approach is needed which seeks to understand the overall function of the discourse in the gospel. A holistic approach is crucial given the interrelated nature of Matthean theology, but even more pertinent is the conclusion of recent gospel research that such an approach to any evangelist's work is necessary. In fact, this has almost become an axiom of gospel criticism. As Peter Ellis summarizes it: "Our understanding is that the true key to the interpretation of a gospel is . . . an analysis of his work as a whole rather than by comparison with other gospels utilizing the same or similar source material."[1] The present work attempts to fill that lacuna in our understanding of Matthew 24 by interpreting it within the context of the whole gospel.

The second point at which the apocalyptic approach to Matthew 24 needs to be reviewed is in its understanding of apocalyptic itself. Jesus is seen as the apocalyptic Son of Man who is to return as Judge, but what does this mean for Matthew? It has been assumed too quickly that apocalyptic eschatology is a homogeneous, monolithic structure to which scholars can refer as a readily accessible constant. One area of consensus in the present debate on apocalyptic, though, is that it is not at all such a constant.

---

[1]Ellis, Matthew: His Mind and His Message, p. vi.

Apocalyptic is now seen as a fluid and syncretistic phenomenon within late Judaism. For example, the eschatological texts from Qumran have alone destroyed the attempts to juxtapose the old stereotypes of a "Nationalistic-Davidic-Kingly Eschatology" with an "Apocalyptic-Son of Man-Other-Worldly Eschatology." Neither eschatology can be found in pure form in any text.[1]

The question becomes: what does it mean to say that Matthew 24 is "apocalyptical"? Or, to ask it another way: what kind of apocalyptic tradition informs Matthew's gospel? It has been assumed that apocalyptic is more heavily influenced by the prophetic than by the Wisdom tradition in Israel.[2] This assumption has led to the neglect of this, and of other, possible influences upon Matthean apocalypticism. In light of this observation, the question of just what kind of apocalypticism informs Matthean theology must be clarified. It will be suggested below that Matthew's apocalypticism is informed by that stream of the Jewish Wisdom tradition which contained the notions of Sophia's rejection, withdrawal to heaven, and appearance again from there as (or somehow associated with) the figure of the Son of Man.[3]

---

[1]Wayne Meeks, "New Testament Christology Evolving," Interpretation 21 (1967): 192.

[2]Cf. Gerhard von Rad, Old Testament Theology, vol. 2, trans. D. M. G. Stalker (New York: Harper and Row, 1965), pp. 303-307.

[3]See the detailed discussion below in chapter two.

26

The question of the kind of apocalyptic tradition which influences Matthew 24 raises another
question. If Matthew's apocalypticism is influenced by other traditions, as it surely is, then
in what sense does Matthew present Jesus as the
Son of Man? Does he present Jesus in chapter 24
only as the Son of Man, or does Jesus appear there
as a more complex figure? We will contend below
that Matthew's Son of Man concept in the eschatological discourse includes both the notion of
Jesus as apocalyptic judge and of Jesus as Wisdom
of God incarnate.[1]

The complexity of apocalyptic as a phenomenon raises one last question for those who would
approach Matthew 24 with apocalyptic stereotypes.
Matthew 24 is constantly referred to as an example of the "synoptic apocalypse." The question
is: what is an "apocalypse"? This is not an
innocuous question because in the current debate
on apocalyptic one problem has become that of
defining an "apocalypse" at all. Is an "apocalypse," for example, to be defined according to
certain characteristics like pseudonymity and
visions?[2] If so, then Matthew 24 would not meet

---

[1]This is the major thesis of chapter two
below.

[2]Cf. Martin Rist, "Apocalypticism," IDB 1:
157. On the apocalyptic debate see: J. Barr,
"Jewish Apocalyptic in Recent Scholarly Study,"
BJRL 58 (1975): 9-35; Klaus Koch, The Rediscovery
of Apocalyptic, SBT, no. 22 (Naperville, Illinois:
Alec R. Allenson, Inc., 1970); F. F. Bruce, "A
Reappraisal of Jewish Apocalyptic Literature,"
RevExp 72 (1975): 305-315; Robert W. Funk, ed.,
Apocalypticism, JThC, vol. 6 (New York: Herder &
Herder, 1969); and John J. Collins, Apocalypse:
the Morphology of a Genre, Semeia, vol. 14, 1979.

27

these criteria.  Or, if an apocalypse is defined
according to literary form, then which text is
the prototype?  The "Apocalypse" of John begins
with the letter or epistle form while The Testaments of the Twelve Patriarchs are in the form of
a last will and testament.  The question is complicated further by the fact that Mark 13, which
seems to be Matthew's main source for the eschatological discourse, might itself partake more of
the genre of a farewell discourse than of an
apocalypse.[1]

The question for our discussion, then, is:
what is the genre of Matthew 24?  We will contend
below that Matthew 24 has affinities with both
the genres of the farewell discourse and the apocalypse, but that in terms of its function within
the whole gospel Matthew 24 is a testament of
Jesus as Sophia.

## Conclusions on History
## of Research

We have seen that there are a number of un-
resolved issues orbiting the study of Matthew 24.
What is the immediate context of the discourse?
How is it related to chapters 23 and 25?  How is
it related structurally and thematically to the
gospel as a whole?  What is the genre of the discourse?  Is it an apocalypse, a farewell discourse, or some combination of both?  What are the
literary and theological functions of the dis-

---

[1]Gaston, No Stone On Another, pp. 42-60;
Béda Rigaux, The Testimony of St. Mark, trans.
Malachy Carroll (Chicago: Franciscan Herald Press,
1966); and F. Busch, whose view is summarized in
W. G. Kümmel, Promise and Fulfillment, SBT, no.
23, trans. Dorothea M. Barton (London: SCM Press,
Ltd., 1957), pp. 95-100.

course within its immediate context and within the whole gospel? Who is Jesus in the discourse for Matthew? Does Jesus speak only as the Son of Man or as some other figure? Does this discourse yield any insights into the larger historical and sociological settings of the gospel? We have already alluded proleptically to the answers which this study gives to some of these questions, but let us succinctly state our basic conclusions in the form of a thesis.

## Thesis

In our attempt to deal with these isssues we will seek to show that the "apocalyptic discourse" in Matthew (24:3-31) functions as a "testament" of Jesus, the Wisdom of God. We will contend that the interpretative keys for the discourse are within the gospel itself. In chapter two we will attempt to show that the keys to the interpretation of the discourse are the transitional verses (23:32-36, 37-39; 24:1-2) and the new introduction provided by Matthew in 24:3. We will show that Matthew begins his transition to the discourse at 23:32. In effect, 23:32-24:2 as a whole constitutes Matthew's transition to his new discourse at 24:3-31. Within these verses Matthew has Jesus speak as the Wisdom of God (cf. 23:34 par. Luke 11:49), pronounce judgment upon Israel (23:38), and fulfill that judgment by leaving the temple forever (24:1). However, as we will show in chapter three, the Jesus who speaks in 24:4 is still Jesus as Sophia. The function of his discourse in its immediate context is parenetical. It is an exhortation to "endure until the end" (24:13). The function of the discourse in terms of the whole gospel, which is the primary focus of chapter four, is that of a farewell speech of Jesus as Wisdom and as the (soon to be exalted) Son of Man.

29

# CHAPTER II
# THE CHRISTOLOGY OF THE
# DISCOURSE IN
# MATTHEW 24

## Introduction

As our brief survey of research showed,
many commentators conclude that the only christology of the discourse in Matthew 24 is an
apocalyptic, Son of Man christology.  This conclusion is based upon several obvious facts in
the discourse itself.  The apocalyptic character
of the discourse is evident because the key
question in it concerns the Parousia and the
cataclysmic "consummation of the Age" (24:3).
The discourse is also filled with characteristic
apocalyptic items: tribulation (24:9, 21) and
apostasy (vv. 4, 10), the appearance of deceivers
(vv. 11, 23, 24), and the breakup of the social
and natural orders (vv. 7, 29).[1]  The Son of Man
christology becomes explicit when his coming is
described in verse 30.  Further, there is no
serious question about the fact that in Matthew
the coming Son of Man is _Jesus_.  This is clearly
stated when the disciples ask Jesus in 24:3 about
the sign of _his_ coming (τῆς σῆς παρουσίας).  No
commentator really questions the fact that the
discourse in Matthew concerns the Parousia of
Jesus as the Son of Man.

However, the recognition that Matthew does
refer to Jesus as the Son of Man sheds little
light upon how the evangelist intends this dis-

---

[1]Cf. Joel 3-4; Dan. 7-12; Assumption of
Moses 10; Zech. 9-14; Ezek. 38-39.

course to be read.  For example, Jesus is the
speaker in the discourse, but is Jesus speaking
as the Son of Man or is he speaking as some other
figure?  If Jesus is speaking as a figure other
than the Son of Man, how does that alter one's
understanding of the discourse both in its immediate context and in terms of its function in the
entire gospel?  Does Matthew give any redactional
clues concerning the identity of Jesus as the
speaker?  Does the evangelist indicate how he intends the reader to understand Jesus' words?
These are the questions with which this chapter
will deal.

Our thesis in this chapter is that Matthew
identifies the speaker in chapter 24 as the
Wisdom of God.  We will attempt to show that
Matthean redaction has identified Jesus with the
Wisdom of God in the transitional verses which
precede chapter 24 (23:32-36, 37-39).  We will
argue that the primary way the evangelist achieves
the identification of Jesus with Wisdom is by his
redaction of the Q material in 23:34 (cf. Luke
11:49).  Matthew redacts what we argue is the Q
reading of ἡ σοφία τοῦ θεοῦ εἶπεν (Luke 11:49) to
read ἰδοὺ ἐγὼ ἀποστέλλω (23:34).  This change not
only attributes a saying of Wisdom to Jesus, but
it identifies him with Wisdom.

In the second part of this chapter we hope
to demonstrate that the Wisdom christology in
23:34 is not an isolated phenomenon in Matthew,
but that it is an important christological theme
in his gospel.  We will show that in the immediate
context of 23:34 Matthew has identified Jesus-
Sophia with Shekinah, a kindred figure to Wisdom.
Next, we will investigate Matt. 11:2-19 where the
evangelist has redacted the introduction (11:2:
"the deeds of the Christ") to correspond with the
concluding remark "Yet wisdom is justified by her
deeds" (11:19c).  In this passage the deeds of

31

Wisdom become the deeds of Jesus, and the upshot
of Matthean redaction here, as in 23:34, is that
Jesus is Wisdom.  Thirdly, we will try to demonstrate the importance of Wisdom christology for
the whole gospel by investigating how the evangelist has combined strategically his identification of Jesus with Wisdom with a major motif of
his gospel, namely, the rejection of Jesus by
Israel.  The importance of the rejection motif in
the First Gospel is that it seems to draw upon a
pre-Matthean theme of Israel's rejection of Wisdom
in such a way that the traditional rejection of
Sophia by Israel has become the rejection of
Jesus.  He is incarnate Wisdom (23:34) whose
messengers Israel has rejected throughout its
history (23:32-36).  Finally, we will suggest how
Matthew intends Jesus' discourse in 24:3-31 to be
read in terms of its immediate context.  We will
argue in part four below that Matthew has placed
his identification of Jesus with Wisdom (23:34) in
a position which culminates part of Matthew's rejection theme.  Israel's dual rejection of Jesus'
envoys (23:34) and of Jesus as Wisdom incarnate
(23:37) culminates in Jesus-Sophia's rejection of
Israel.  By his redaction Matthew shows that
Jesus' departure from the temple in 24:1 is the
definitive withdrawal of Wisdom's presence from
Israel.  Jesus' departure from Israel, though, was
simultaneously a turning toward his disciples to
reveal eschatological secrets to them (24:3).  We
will discuss the revelation of Jesus to the disciples in part five below.  Jesus' revelation
deals with their question of when Jesus-Sophia
will return as Son of Man.  The historical disciples who receive Jesus' revelation are presented redactionally as representative followers
of Jesus so that they coalesce in this gospel
with Matthew's own community.  Consequently, the
revelation about his Parousia which Jesus' historical disciples received has also become the
revelation transmitted to the disciples of

Matthew's community.  The revelation of eschatological secrets, that is, of Jesus-Sophia's return
as Son of Man, has become a "testament" for
Matthew's community.  The knowledge of those
secrets will help the disciples in Matthew's day
"endure until the end" (24:13).

## History of Research

The main question we want to address in
this chapter, then, is who is the speaker in the
eschatological discourse in Matthew 24?  Our
thesis is that the speaker is Jesus, the Wisdom
of God, and that Matthew has made that identification in 23:34-39, the transitional verses to
his eschatological discourse.  The most thorough
examination of Wisdom christology in the First
Gospel to date has been done by M. Jack Suggs.[1]
Any work which maintains that Matthew has a Wisdom
christology must take Suggs' work into account.
For our thesis it is also crucial that we review
Suggs' work because he bases his argument for a
Wisdom christology in Matthew upon what we argue
are the transitional verses to the eschatological
discourse, namely, Matthew 23:34-39.  Therefore,
a review of Suggs' arguments, as well as those of
his critics, will allow us to focus the questions
which need to be dealt with in our discussion.
The questions which have occupied Suggs and his
critics are: does Matthew have a Wisdom christology?  If so, how important is the christology
in his gospel?  Does a compositional analysis of
the gospel support the thesis that a Wisdom
christology is important in the First Gospel?

---

[1]M. Jack Suggs, Wisdom, Christology, and
Law in Matthew's Gospel (Cambridge, Massachusetts:
Harvard University Press, 1970).  This work will
hereafter be cited as Suggs, Wisdom.

33

What is the pre-Matthean background for such a christology? How does Matthew's Wisdom christology relate to his other christologies, particularly to his presentation of Jesus as the Son of Man? In an attempt to answer these questions, let us begin with a review of Suggs' argument and then proceed to a critique of it.

## M. Jack Suggs

We can begin a review of Suggs with a quotation which indicates how he understands Matthew's connection of 23:34-36 with 23:37-39. Speaking of Matt. 23:39 Suggs says:

> Matthew's most significant alteration in the passage occurs in this verse. The lament's connection with the doom oracle shows that Matthew regards it as a Wisdom word as well. For Matthew, Jesus is incarnate Wisdom, and the evangelist therefore both historicizes the final verse and gives it a specific reference to the Parousia by writing: "For I tell you that from this time on you will not see me until you say, 'Blessed is he who comes in the name of the Lord.'" That is, Matthew successfully transfers a Wisdom saying to Jesus because for him Jesus is identified with Sophia. It is in Wisdom's person that Jesus can speak of "how often" in relation to Jerusalem, for the call of Wisdom has been heard again and again in "the prophets and those sent"; the "how often" has nothing to do with the number of trips made to Jerusalem by the historical Jesus, but with how Wisdom in every generation has appealed to men through her prophets and has not been heeded. As this figure, Jesus can say--as no merely historical individual might--"I would have gathered your children

under my wings."  Jesus is Wisdom
incarnate.[1]

Suggs then attempts to show that this identification of Jesus with Wisdom is not an isolated
phenomenon in Matthew because it occurs again in
the saying of the easy yoke (11:28-30).  He notes
that 11:28-30 in Matthew is appended to a Q saying
(11:25-27) which has long been recognized to have
affinities with Wisdom traditions.  In Q, Suggs
argues, the saying in 11:25-27 tends toward a
gnosticizing Wisdom tradition in which "Wisdom"
(ταῦτα) has been hidden from the wise of the
world and revealed (ἀπεκάλυψας, 11:25) to
"Babes."[2]  Suggs argues from this that:

> The prayer shows every sign of
> having been derived from a type of Jewish
> wisdom thought which has passed through an
> apocalyptic medium.  It is sometimes
> assumed that a "revelation to babes rather
> than to the wise" runs directly against the
> current of Jewish thought.  And, if 4 Ezra
> were taken as the model, then such would
> appear to be the case. . . . But this
> overlooks the fact that in Jewish usage
> the "wise man" is also the good, the
> pious, the man who trusts in God.  The
> "wise" of 4 Ezra and the "babes" of the Q
> saying are, in fact, the "elect" under
> different titles.  The denial of wisdom to
> the "wise of the world" and its revelation
> to the "humble" is not something new in the
> Wisdom stream; indeed, it is almost a dogma
> of late Jewish wisdom, as Hahn correctly
> sees.[3]

---

[1]Ibid., pp. 70-71.    [2]Ibid., pp. 71-76.

[3]Ibid., pp. 83-84.

From this point Suggs then concludes:

> Matthew has once again moved beyond Q, for
> which Jesus as the Son is the mediator of
> revelation, the idealized σοφός; now the
> Son is identified with Wisdom.  Once again
> we have to observe that this fateful step
> of identifying Jesus with Sophia made by
> Paul at Corinth and by Matthew (in Syria?)
> is a development which was required before
> the gnosticising tendencies of their
> opponents could issue in the developed
> Gnosticism of the second century.  To
> quote Grant in relation to Matt. 11:28-30
> again, "There is a Wisdom-Christology in
> this passage which points toward the
> Gnostic speculations about Wisdom."[1]

In other words, Suggs is arguing that
Matthew has corrected a gnosticizing tendency in
Q by: (1) adding 11:28-30 to 11:25-27 and
(2) identifying the <u>content</u> of the revelation
(ταῦτα, 11:25) with the "deeds of Wisdom."  The
"deeds of Wisdom" are the deeds of Jesus (11:2,
19), and they include the "mighty works" of
11:20-24.[2]  Therefore, whereas in Q Jesus (and
John the Baptist) was only the representative of
Wisdom, Matthew has moved beyond Q and has identified Jesus with Wisdom.

One further point to be noted about
Matthew's addition of 11:28-30 to 11:25-27 is
that by this redactional move Matthew also identifies Jesus with Torah.  "Yoke," says Suggs,
means "the yoke of Torah."[3]  It is commonly

---

[1]Ibid., p. 96.    [2]Ibid., pp. 95-97.

[3]Ibid., pp. 100-108.

known that Wisdom and Torah were identified in
the development of the Wisdom tradition, especially in Sirach (cf. 24:3-23).[1]  From this pre-
Matthean development in the Wisdom tradition
Suggs concludes that:

> It is only against this background that
> Matt. 11:28-30 can be interpreted.  The
> invitation which Jesus offers is the old
> invitation of Wisdom, and the yoke which
> is offered is the yoke of Wisdom, the
> yoke of the Torah. . . . We should be
> very clear that in the Matthean setting
> what is offered by Jesus is not an alter-
> native to the yoke of the Torah.  Jesus
> speaks as Sophia, and in such a saying
> as 11:28-30 that means as Torah as well.[2]

## Critique of Suggs' Thesis

In general Suggs' thesis that Matthew has
identified Jesus with Wisdom and with Torah has
been accepted.[3]  However, he has been criticized

--------

[1]Ibid.  Cf. Rudolf Bultmann, The Gospel of
John.  A Commentary, trans. G. R. Beasley-Murray
(Philadelphia: The Westminster Press, 1971), p.
23; and Hans Conzelmann, "The Mother of Wisdom,"
in The Future of Our Religious Past, ed. James M.
Robinson, trans. Charles E. Carlston (New York:
Harper and Row, Publishers, 1971), p. 234.

[2]Suggs, Wisdom, p. 106.

[3]Lambrecht, "The Parousia Discourse," p.
316; R. G. Hamerton-Kelly, Pre-Existence, Wisdom,
and the Son of Man.  A Study of the Idea of Pre-
Existence in the New Testament (Cambridge:
University Press, 1973), pp. 31-37 (hereafter
cited as Hamerton-Kelly, Pre-Existence); and

basically at three points: (1) that he has built
hypothesis upon hypothesis in order to establish
his thesis; (2) that the Sophia motif is not as
prominent in Q as Suggs thinks; and, (3) that the
picture which Suggs draws of Sophia sending
envoys ("prophets") is too general to be
supported by the evidence.

First, has Suggs "dropped the critical
hammer on the wings of a moth" by asserting that
Jesus in Matthew is the Wisdom of God? W. G.
Thompson, for example, says: "I cannot help
wondering whether piling one hypothesis (the lost
wisdom-apocalypse) upon another hypothesis (Q) is
the most convincing way to begin a study of
Wisdom speculation in Matthew."[1]  We would agree
with Thompson that the first hypothesis--which
assumes a highly articulated Jewish Wisdom
myth--is questionable as a starting point.
Thompson's second point, though, seems a bit
innocuous.

First, every thesis builds hypothesis upon
hypothesis.  Certainly Q is a hypothetical
source, but to criticize Suggs for operating with
the Q hypothesis is like criticizing a physicist

---

Eduard Schweizer, The Good News According to
Matthew, trans. David E. Green (Atlanta: John
Knox Press, 1975), pp. 446-447 (hereafter cited
as Schweizer, Matthew).

[1]W. G. Thompson, review of Wisdom, Christology, and Law in Matthew's Gospel, by M. Jack
Suggs, in CBQ 33 (1971): 146.  See also M. D.
Goulder, review of Wisdom, Christology, and Law
in Matthew's Gospel, by M. Jack Suggs, in JThS
22 (1971): 568-569.

for using the model of an atom (which is also
hypothetical) to explain certain natural
phenomena.[1] The more appropriate criticism of
Suggs would be to review his <u>use</u> of Q--especially
his view of Q's relation to a gnosticizing Wisdom
tradition.

Secondly, it is a more serious criticism
to say that Suggs uses the hypothesis of a "lost
Wisdom Apocalypse."[2] Although Suggs does not
explicitly say this, it seems that he is following Bultmann's reconstruction of a pre-
Christian Jewish Wisdom myth.[3] Bultmann argues
for a "lost Wisdom Apocalypse" behind Q, and the
question of its existence is still debated.[4]
However, from the point of view of composition

---

[1]This was the reaction of most reviewers to
Suggs' use of the Q hypothesis. E.g., see
William J. Brogan, review of <u>Wisdom, Christology,
and Law in Matthew's Gospel</u>, by M. Jack Suggs, in
<u>ThS</u> 32 (1971): 305.

[2]Cf. Suggs, <u>Wisdom</u>, pp. 16, 19.

[3]Ibid., pp. 19, 41.

[4]See Schweizer, <u>Matthew</u>, p. 445; M'Neile,
<u>Gospel According to St. Matthew</u>, p. 342; H. van
der Kwaak, "Die Klage über Jerusalem (Matth.
XXIII 37-39," <u>NovTest</u> 8 (1966): 163-164; Haenchen,
"Matthäus 23," p. 56; B. J. Hubbard, <u>The Matthean
Redaction of a Primitive Apostolic Commissioning:
An Exegesis of Matthew 28:16-20</u>, SBL Dissertation
Series, no. 19 (Missoula, Montana: Scholars'
Press, 1974), p. 97 (hereafter cited as Hubbard,
<u>Matthew 28:16-20</u>).

criticism, the argument should not be whether there was a fully developed pre-Christian, Jewish Wisdom myth, or whether that myth had assumed a literary form before Q, but the argument should center upon what <u>Matthew</u> has done redactionally with the Wisdom sayings and allusions which <u>are in Q</u>.[1]

This is precisely the point on which the second major criticism of Suggs' thesis concentrates. The argument is that the Wisdom motif is not as prominent in Q as Suggs thinks. Consequently, Matthew has not corrected a gnosticizing Wisdom tendency in Q. M. D. Johnson is a major critic at this point. He says:

> First, it would seem that Matthew deliberately <u>avoids</u> an identification of Jesus with Wisdom. Matthew's readers would in all probability not have the occasion to check his source, and would therefore not derive from this passage any association of Jesus with Wisdom. If it is Matthew's conscious intention to point to Jesus in terms of Wisdom, why should he remove a logion from the mouth of Wisdom and attribute it to Jesus? Of course if the Lucan ascription of the saying to Sophia was also that of Q, it could be argued that Matthew assumes that

---

[1]No one, to my knowledge, has really addressed Suggs as to what difference it would make in his argument if there were no lost wisdom apocalypse. On this point he quite frankly acknowledges that "It might be possible to add another alternative, namely, that the oracle was a piece of oral tradition which had no literary history prior to its incorporation in Q." (See Suggs, <u>Wisdom</u>, p. 19 n. 28.)

Q identified Jesus with Wisdom.  Yet the removal of the attribution to Wisdom points toward a lessening of Matthean interest in Wisdom speculation.  By the same token it is difficult to believe that the Q source would incorporate a Wisdom logion without at the same time considering it a word of Jesus.  It is also questionable whether the Matthean passage can be read merely as an oracle of doom; there is also a "commissioning," fully in line with Matthew's concept of Jesus as the sender of prophets (5:12) and scribes (13:52).  The Matthean passage can best be read as a reflection of the universal primitive Christian conviction that Jesus "sent" or commissioned his disciples who must be prepared to face persecution.[1]

First, it is not at all clear what Johnson means when he says that Matthew's readers would not associate Jesus with Wisdom because they would not be able to check the sources of the evangelist.  This comment seems to presuppose a certain view of Matthean authorship and of Matthew's community, neither of which can be assumed a priori, not to mention the fact that it is not known what form of Q was used by Matthew's community.[2]  For example, if Matthew is the

---

[1]Marshall D. Johnson, "Reflections on a Wisdom Approach to Matthew's Christology," CBQ 36 (1974): 55.

[2]J. P. Brown, "The Form of Q Known to Matthew," NTS 8 (1961): 27-42 cf. P. Vassiliadis, "The Nature and Extent of the Q-document," NovTest 20 (1978): 49-73.

product of a <u>school</u> rather than of an individual, as Stendahl believes, then it is very probable that the community knew the sources used in the gospel. Stendahl, in a section entitled "Quotations related to Wisdom," concludes: "This type of literature [i.e., Wisdom literature] seems to have been studied in the school of Matthew and related to Jesus, equating him with Wisdom, as does Luke in 11:49."[1]

Secondly, to contend as Johnson does that the Q source would not utilize a Wisdom saying without considering it a word of Jesus seems to presuppose a certain view of Q as an "orthodox" Christian document (?). However, in a crucial article, J. M. Robinson has argued that although there are few explicit <u>passages</u> in Q which deal with Wisdom, the whole <u>Gattung</u> has a gnostic-wisdom tendency to it. On the one hand, Robinson points out that Matthew took the Wisdom trajectory in a more "orthodox" direction by his "correction" of Wisdom speculation in Q. On the other hand, the tendency of the Q <u>Gattung</u> itself ended in fully developed Gnosticism.[2]

---

[1]Stendahl, <u>School</u>, p. 142. Stendahl seems to believe that <u>for Luke</u> (not Q) "the Wisdom of God" is another name for Jesus. He adds, though, that the striking thing in a comparison of Matt. 23:34 and Luke 11:49 is that in Matthew Jesus is the acting subject, as the ἰδοὺ ἐγὼ ἀποστέλλω clearly shows (see Ibid., p. 92 n. 3).

[2]James M. Robinson, "<u>LOGOI SOPHON</u>: On the <u>Gattung</u> of Q," in <u>Trajectories through Early Christianity</u>, ed., Helmut Koester and James M. Robinson (Philadelphia: Fortress Press, 1971), pp. 71-74, 86-87, 90-91, 94-99, 103-113. Cf. R. M. Grant, <u>Gnosticism and Early Christianity</u> (New York: Columbia University Press, 1959),

Thirdly, the "prophets and wise men and scribes" of Matt. 23:34 refer to the long line of envoys sent to Israel over many generations. The reference is not just to the post-Easter disciples. Regardless of whether or not one wants to argue that Jesus is Wisdom in this verse, Matthew clearly has Jesus as the sender of these envoys ("Therefore I send you prophets . . . "). The time span covered in this verse is much larger than just the persecution faced by post-Easter disciples who were first sent out by the historical Jesus. The question is: who is this trans-historical Sender of the envoys?

The third major criticism against Suggs' thesis is that the picture which he draws of Wisdom sending envoys to each generation is a generalization based upon little extant textual evidence. The greater part of Johnson's article is devoted to a critique of Suggs' conclusion that "history" for this Wisdom tradition (and in Matthew) is the account of Wisdom's rejection. Johnson acknowledges that many elements in the Wisdom myth assumed by Suggs—the personification and pre-existence of Wisdom, her desire to reveal

---

p. 153.
    Suggs is clearly following Robinson's basic argument concerning the gnosticizing tendency in Q, an argument which Robinson explicated in a previous article. (See James M. Robinson, "Basic Shifts in German Theology," Interpretation 16 (1962): 76-97. Cf. Suggs, Wisdom, pp. 11-13.) For a discussion of Wisdom influence in Q, see Richard A. Edwards, A Theology of Q: Eschatology, Prophecy, and Wisdom (Philadelphia: Fortress Press, 1976), chapter five; and William A. Beardslee, "The Wisdom Tradition and the Synoptic Gospels," JAAR 35 (1967): 236-238.

herself to humanity, the identification of Wisdom
with Torah--"cannot be easily disputed."  "But,"
Johnson says, "the crucial point for Suggs'
thesis, . . . is that in every generation Wisdom
sends forth her personal representatives to speak
her message."[1]  Johnson carefully examines each
Wisdom passage used by Suggs (and Bultmann) to
support his thesis (Wisdom of Solomon 7-10; Prov.
1-9; Sirach 24; Baruch 3:37, 38).  His conclusion
is that there was no pre-Christian motif in the
Jewish tradition about Wisdom sending her envoys
to humanity.  He does allow, in agreement with
Suggs, that "foreign elements" were part of the
picture of personified Wisdom even in the Jewish
tradition.[2]  It is precisely the question of
"foreign elements" which leaves any conclusion
concerning the exact parameters of a pre-
Christian Wisdom myth an open question.  The
elements which Suggs utilizes are present in the
Wisdom tradition.  The only question is whether
or not these elements were combined into a highly
articulated, pre-Christian, Jewish Wisdom myth.
Johnson says "no," and Suggs echoes Bultmann's
"yes."  For our purposes it is relevant to note
that if there were no highly articulated Wisdom
myth, then it is quite possible that Matthew put
the elements of the Wisdom tradition together in
order to say that Jesus as Wisdom sent envoys to
each generation.  This would have to be supported
by a compositional analysis of Matthew, which we
intend to do, but it is important to point out
that Johnson, commenting on Wisdom 7:27 (" . . .
in every generation she passes into holy souls
and makes them friends of God, . . . "), concedes:

---

[1]Johnson, "Reflections on a Wisdom Approach
to Matthew's Christology," p. 46.

[2]Ibid., p. 53.

"Although we can be certain that the author did not view this as do Bultmann and Suggs, yet we must leave open the possibility that later Wisdom writers could have read into this the idea of Sophia inspiring her envoys to speak revelation."[1] Johnson does not attempt to answer the redactional question of why Matthew places passages with acknowledged Wisdom overtones in the contexts which he does.[2] Suggs, however, does attempt an answer, namely, that for Matthew Jesus is Wisdom incarnate.

## Summary of History of Research

It seems that many interpreters agree with Suggs that there is a Wisdom christology in the

---

[1]Ibid., p. 52. For a brief discussion of the Wisdom myth see U. Wilckens, "σοφία," TDNT 8: 507-515; Bultmann, Gospel of John, pp. 22-25; and Werner Georg Kümmel, The New Testament: The History of the Investigation of Its Problems, trans. S. McLean Gilmour and Howard Clark Kee (New York: Abingdon Press, 1970), pp. 350-355. For an authoritative statement of the pre-Christian Heilsgeschichte of Wisdom sending emissaries to each generation see James M. Robinson, "Jesus as Sophos and Sophia: Wisdom Tradition and the Gospels," Aspects of Wisdom in Judaism and Early Christianity, ed., Robert L. Wilken (South Bend, Indiana: Notre Dame Press, 1975), pp. 2-15; and Gerhard Friedrich, "προφήτης," TDNT 6: 821-822.

[2]Cf. Johnson, "Reflections on a Wisdom Approach to Matthew's Christology," p. 64.

First Gospel.[1]  The central question now is not
if Matthew has a Wisdom christology, but the
question is: how important is the christology in
his gospel?  The parameters of the debate have
been set.  On the one hand, Suggs says:

> For too long, the traces of Wisdom
> speculation present in Matthew have been
> treated as tangential or eccentric
> traditions foreign to the purpose and
> theology of the evangelist.  They
> constitute, in my opinion, certain proof
> that one aspect of Matthew's thought
> has been unfortunately neglected.  The
> description, "A Footnote to Matthean-
> Christology," cannot be used, because it
> is the express aim of this report to lift
> the Wisdom motif out of the footnotes of
> scholarly discussion, where it can be too
> quickly written off as an unexplained
> outburst of Johannine ideology.[2]

----

[1]See Hare, The Theme of Jewish Persecution
of Christians, p. 156; Hamerton-Kelly, Pre-
Existence, p. 67; Schweizer, Matthew, pp. 446-447;
Felix Christ, Jesus Sophia. Die Sophia-
Christologie bei den Synoptikern, ATANT, vol. 57
(Zürich: Zwingli-Verlag, 1970); and James M.
Robinson, "Jesus as Sophos and Sophia: Wisdom
Tradition and the Gospels," pp. 1-16.

[2]Suggs, Wisdom, p. 2.  Cf. W. G. Thompson's
conclusion after his review of Suggs: " . . . I
must say that Suggs has succeeded in proving that
Wisdom speculation is not a tangential or ec-
centric tradition foreign to the purpose and
theology of Matthew . . . " (W. G. Thompson,
review of Wisdom, by M. Jack Suggs, in CBQ 33
[1971]: 146).

On the other hand, M. D. Johnson concludes that
" . . . in spite of the brillance of Suggs' argument, perhaps it is best that the wisdom motif
remain in the scholarly footnotes where he found
it."[1]

The debate is yet an acorn.  When it does
become an oak, it will revolve around two issues
with which a composition-critical point of view
must deal.  First, the Wisdom myth and Heilsgeschichte outlined by Suggs is that: (1) Sophia
sought a dwelling place in Israel, and, finding
none, returned to heaven; (2) in each generation
Sophia issues her call to humanity, but (3) primarily through her prophets who (4) are Sophia's
representatives.  However, they (5) suffer the
same fate of rejection as did Sophia herself.
Such a view of salvation-history posits that:
"History is the story of the rejection and
persecution of Wisdom's envoys. . . . From before
creation, Wisdom knows the destiny of her
prophets whose blood will be required of this
γενεά."[2]

The question is: can such a Wisdom Heilsgeschichte be supported by a compositional analysis of the gospel itself?  This is a question
which Suggs does not (intentionally) broach.
Secondly, while Suggs does not say that the
Sophia christology is the central christology for
Matthew, he approaches this position when he
writes: " . . . it would not greatly overstate
the case to say that for Matthew Wisdom has

---

[1]Johnson, "Reflections on a Wisdom Approach
to Matthew's Christology," p. 64.

[2]Suggs, Wisdom, p. 21 cf. pp. 104-105.

'become flesh and dwelled among us' (John 1:14)."[1]
Suggs does have a section in his book on "the Son
of Man and Sophia in Q," but he does not discuss
the relation of Jesus as the Son of Man to Jesus
as Wisdom in Matthew.  He seems to subordinate
Matthew's Son of Man christology to his Sophia
christology.  We will argue below that the two
christologies are complementary in the First
Gospel.  On the one hand, the evangelist presents
the humiliation of Jesus' earthly life as the
rejection of Wisdom (cf. 23:34-39).  On the other
hand, he presents the exaltation of Jesus as the
enthronement of the glorious Son of Man who will
return as judge of all the nations (24:30-31 cf.
25:31-46).  Suggs does not see a clarification of
the relation between the two christologies in the
First Gospel as part of the scope of his work,
yet it is essential for us in view of the explicit Son of Man christology in the eschatological discourse.

     In summary, Suggs' work can be carried
further in two ways.  First, a compositional
analysis of the First Gospel is needed to see if
the centrality of a Wisdom christology in Matthew
can be supported.  Suggs has based his thesis
only upon particular and isolated passages
(11:25-30; 23:34-39).  Secondly, an analysis of
the relation of Matthew's view of Jesus as Son of
Man and as Sophia is needed to see if they are
complementary or in conflict with one another.
In this chapter we will be concerned only with
the first task--the centrality of a Wisdom christology in Matthew.[2]  We will begin with a brief

---

[1]Ibid., p. 57.

[2]Matthew's Son of Man and Sophia christologies are discussed below in chapter four.

review of the exegetical work already done on Matt. 23:34-39. We will then proceed to relate those conclusions to the Matthean compositional theme of Israel's rejection of Jesus.

## Part 1: Matthew 23:34: Jesus Is Identified with Wisdom

Matthew 23:34-36 is the departure point not only for Suggs but for anyone who wishes to explore the possibility of a Sophia christology in Matthew. The logion is preserved in Q, and there is no question that it is a saying from the Wisdom tradition.[1] There is also a consensus among commentators that Luke 11:49-51 preserves an older form of the oracle than does Matt. 23:34-36. The primary reason for this consensus is that the oracle in Luke begins with διὰ τοῦτο καὶ ἡ σοφία τοῦ θεοῦ εἶπεν. This phrase suggests either a quotation from an apocryphal writing which is no longer extant, or, at a minimum, εἶπεν suggests an older form than the present tense of Matthew's version.[2] In addition, if Luke's version is not

---

[1]The question of whether Q took the logion from a Jewish Vorlage, as Suggs contends, or whether it was a piece of oral tradition prior to its incorporation into Q can be bracketed for the moment. See Suggs' reconstruction of the pre-Christian form of the saying in Wisdom, pp. 13-24. See also Friedrich, "προφήτης," p. 835. For a discussion of 23:32, which we argue begins Matthew's transition to the discourse in 24:4, see part 2 of this chapter.

[2]Bultmann, History of the Synoptic Tradition, p. 114; Suggs, Wisdom, pp. 13-20, 58-61; Hare, The Theme of Jewish Persecution of Christians, p. 86; and Siegfried Schulz, Q: Die Spruchquelle der Evangelisten (Zürich: Theo-

an older form of the saying in Q, then it is
surely difficult to explain why Luke would change
a dominical saying into a Wisdom one, especially
since Luke seems to have little interest in Wisdom
speculation concerning Jesus (cf. Luke 7:28-29,
35).[1] If it is also the case, as we argue in the
section below, that Wisdom speculation in Q did
not fully identify Jesus with the transcendent,
pre-existent Sophia, then the ἐγὼ ἀποστέλλω
(present tense), which seems to place Matt. 23:34
in Jesus' ministry in Jerusalem, presents difficulties because the speaker in this oracle is
surely a supra-historical one. The difficulty
can be explained, however, if pre-existent Wisdom
is speaking before this tragic history begins and
uses the future tense as in Luke 11:49
(ἀποστελῶ).[2] Thus, if Luke's version preserves
an earlier Q version of the saying than does Matthew, then insight into the Matthean version can
be gained by comparing it with Luke's.

---

logischer Verlag, 1972), p. 336. Cf. T. W. Manson, The Sayings of Jesus (London: SCM Press,
1957), pp. 101-102 (hereafter cited as Manson,
Sayings). The question of whether or not the
oracle is a genuine saying of Jesus need not be
pursued here. If the saying were a genuine saying
of Jesus, certainly εἶπεν would suggest that he
was quoting Wisdom rather than identifying himself
with that figure. (See Suggs, Wisdom, p. 18; and,
Schultz, Q, p. 336.)

[1]Hans Conzelmann, The Theology of St. Luke,
p. 110 n. 1.

[2]See Suggs, Wisdom, pp. 13-29. We cannot
speak of the Q version as though both evangelists
had the same one, but only of an earlier version.
Cf. M. Eugene Boring, "Christian Prophecy and
Matthew 23:34-36: A Test Exegesis," SBL Seminar
Papers (1977): 117-126.

Matthew 23:34: Jesus Speaks
as Wisdom

The most important Matthean redactional
move for our purposes is the fact that ἡ σοφία
τοῦ θεοῦ εἶπεν with the future ἀποστελῶ in Luke
becomes ἰδοὺ ἐγὼ ἀποστέλλω (present tense) in
Matthew. Suggs builds his case upon this change.
He says that by means of this change the evangelist has identified Jesus with the Sophia of
God. However, several questions have surfaced in
the exegetical discussion.

First, could it be that Q, rather than
Matthew, has identified Jesus with Sophia? As we
have seen, M. D. Johnson points out that Q would
not likely incorporate a Wisdom saying without
considering it to be a word of Jesus.[1] If this is
the case, then Matthew's removal of the phrase
"the Wisdom of God said" and the substitution of
ἐγὼ ἀποστέλλω could actually be interpreted as a
lessening of Matthean interest in a Sophia christology.[2] There are several reasons, though, why
this does not seem to be the case.

As Suggs points out, the form of the saying
in Q (ἡ σοφία τοῦ θεοῦ εἶπεν) lends itself to the
conclusion that the oracle is a quotation by
Jesus rather than a saying of Jesus. Matthew does
give the oracle as a saying of Jesus (ἐγώ), and,
consequently, he changes the verbs to the present
tense.[3] Furthermore, it is one thing to say that
there are a few Wisdom sayings in Q which exhibit

---

[1]Johnson, "Reflections on a Wisdom Approach
to Matthew's Christology," p. 55. Cf. Wilckens,
"σοφία," p. 515.

[2]Ibid. [3]Suggs, Wisdom, p. 19.

51

Wisdom influence and which indicate that Jesus'
sayings are the source or reflection of God's
Wisdom, but it is quite another thing to imply
that there is a Sophia mythology or christology
in Q which identifies Jesus as the transcendent
Sophia of God.[1]  Suggs reflects the consensus of
most commentators that any Wisdom references in Q
are too few and too brief to reflect any kind of
identification or explication of Jesus as transcendent Sophia.[2]  On the one hand, it seems that
one can say as a minimum that Q: (1) became the
depository for what is now classified as the
Wisdom thread in the Synoptic sayings, and
(2) thinks of Jesus as the last, perhaps the most
authoritative, envoy of Wisdom rather than incarnate Wisdom itself.  In Q Jesus simply brings
Sophia's truth to humanity.[3]  On the other hand,
as a maximum one can say that Q is moving in the
direction of a Sophia christology, and that at the
last stage in the development of the Q tradition
one might conclude that there is a de facto identification of Sophia with Jesus--at least in terms
of Sophia's function as the sole mediator of
God's revelation.[4]  Thus, it is probably more

_____

[1]Edwards, A Theology of Q, p. 58.

[2]Ibid., p. 59.  Cf. Suggs, Wisdom, p. 58.

[3]Ibid., pp. 19, 28.  Cf. Beardslee, "The
Wisdom Tradition and the Synoptic Gospels," p.
237; and Hamerton-Kelly, Pre-Existence, pp. 35-36.

[4]Schultz, Q: Die Spruchquelle der Evan-
gelisten, pp. 224-230 cf. pp. 351-352; and S.
Kloppenborg, "Wisdom Christology in Q,"
LavThéolPhil 34 (1978): 129-147.

accurate to suggest that Matthew was not the first
to take the step of fully identifying Jesus with
Sophia, but that he developed the tendency already
present in Q. The trajectory seems to be that the
earliest tradition identified Jesus as the last
and most authoritative envoy of Sophia.[1] The
last development in the Q tradition makes a de
facto identification of Jesus with Sophia, at
least in terms of function. Finally, Matthew
makes a full identification of Jesus with Sophia
in terms of function and of "nature."[2] Matthew
"historicizes" the Sophia tendency in Q by identifying heavenly Sophia with the earthly Jesus
while the Q trajectory continued to develop the
Sophia christology which issued in second century
Gnosticism.[3]

---

[1]Suggs, Wisdom, pp. 19, 28. Cf. Dieter
Lührmann, Die Redaktion der Logienquelle, WMANT,
no. 33 (Neukirchen, 1969), p. 99.

[2]Cf. the discussion in Robinson, "Jesus as
Sophos and Sophia: Wisdom Tradition and the
Gospels," p. 11.

[3]This is not to deny that Matthew's Sophia
christology has a transcendent dimension to it;
for him Jesus is Sophia who has come to earth
seeking a "home." However, no one would deny
either that this gospel is not of the same stamp
as the Gnostic writings with a Sophia christology.
There is a world of difference between saying that
Jesus of Nazareth is preexistent Sophia who has
come to earth, and, as the Gospel of the Hebrews
says, that Sophia found a resting place in Jesus.
(Cf. Philipp Vielhauer, "The Gospel of the
Hebrews," New Testament Apocrypha, vol. 2, ed.
Wilhelm Schneemelcher, trans. R. McL. Wilson
[Philadelphia: The Westminster Press, 1964]: 161.)
It appears, though, that Matthew's Sophia chris-

In view of the present state of exegesis concerning Wisdom influence in Q, it seems that one must conclude that Matthew has not simply eliminated Q's reference to Sophia in order to de-emphasize Sophia speculation, but that he has enhanced and carried to fruition the Sophia christology latent at the end of the development of the Q tradition.[1]

A second major exegetical question is whether Matthew's ἐγὼ ἀποστέλλω refers to Jesus at all. If ἡ σοφία τοῦ θεοῦ in Luke 11:49 is simply a periphrasis for God, then this would mean that God, instead of Jesus, is being equated with Sophia.[2]  It is possible that Luke did understand the phrase that way, especially in light of Luke 7:35: "Yet wisdom is justified by all her children."  In Luke the phrase could mean: "God sends you his messengers."[3]  However, Matthew

---

tology also played an important role in this development toward the Gnostic Sophia christologies. (See Robinson, "Jesus as Sophos and Sophia: Wisdom Tradition and the Gospels," pp. 11-15.)

[1]Ibid., p. 10.

[2]M. D. Goulder, review of Wisdom, by M. Jack Suggs, in JThS 22 (1971): 569.  Cf. T. W. Manson, Sayings, p. 102.

[3]Joachim Jeremias, The Parables of Jesus, 2nd ed., trans. S. H. Hooke (New York: Charles Scribner's Sons, 1972), p. 162 (italics mine). Jeremias thinks that the phrase is part of the original parable.  Suggs, however, gives a cogent argument that the phrase is Lukan redaction. (See Suggs, Wisdom, pp. 33-36.)

does not follow the Lukan version. In 11:19c
Matthew has: "Yet wisdom is justified by her
deeds" (ἀπὸ τῶν ἔργων αὐτῆς). It is significant
that the evangelist opens this section with "Now
when John heard in prison about the deeds of the
Christ" (τὰ ἔργα τοῦ Χριστοῦ, 11:2 cf. Luke 7:18).
Suggs makes the crucial point that

> . . . the unusual form τὰ ἔργα τοῦ
> Χριστοῦ is matched exactly by the Matthean
> form of the Wisdom saying, which speaks of
> τὰ ἔργα (τῆς σοφίας). The two phrases
> serve as brackets for the sequence Matt.
> 11:2-19.[1]

Here, then, is a case where Matthew takes Luke's
circumlocution for "God," if indeed it is such,
and redacts it to equate the "deeds of the Christ"
with the "deeds of Wisdom." In effect, Matthew
has altered this Q material in order to identify
Jesus with Wisdom just as he does with the circumlocution in 23:34 (cf. Luke 11:49).[2]

Secondly, it is true, as T. W. Manson says,
that Jewish thought tended to personify God's
attributes such as mercy and justice, but the
precise phrase in Luke 11:49 ("the Wisdom of God
said") seems to occur nowhere else in Jewish
literature as a circumlocution for God.[3]

Thirdly, when Jesus uses ἐγώ in the First
Gospel, it is definitely an important christological term. Stauffer, for example, draws this
conclusion from his discussion of ἐγώ in Matthew

---

[1]Ibid., p. 37.    [2]Ibid., p. 57.

[3]Manson, Sayings, p. 102.  Cf. Suggs,
Wisdom, p. 18.

5:22 (ἐγὼ δὲ λέγω ὑμῖν) and the δεῦτε πρός με of Matthew 11:28:

> The Christ of the New Testament replaces not only sophia but all the intermediaries of Jewish theology, uniting their offices in one. All historical and cosmic lines intersect in His ἐγώ. . . . In this sense the christological ἐγώ of the Synoptists expresses in nuce the claim of Jesus to absoluteness.[1]

In summary, Matthew's ἐγὼ ἀποστέλλω in 23:34 leads us to declare with Robinson that:

> It is not enough to say Matthew simply eliminates the reference to Sophia. Rather one must recognize that he identifies Sophia with Jesus, by attributing to Jesus not only a saying previously attributed to Sophia, but by attributing to Jesus the content of the saying, namely, Sophia's role as the heavenly personage who throughout history has sent the prophets and other spokesmen. It is to himself as preexistent Sophia that he refers in saying a few verses later (Matt. 23:37): "How often I would have gathered your children together as a hen gathers her brood under her wings."[2]

---

[1]Ethelbert Stauffer, "ἐγώ," TDNT 2: 348-349. Cf. Suggs, Wisdom, p. 59; and Hare, The Theme of Jewish Persecution of Christians, p. 140.

[2]Robinson, "Jesus as Sophos and Sophia: Wisdom Tradition and the Gospels," p. 11.

## The Meaning of 23:34-36
## in Matthew

Form-critically, Matt. 23:34-36 is Wisdom's oracle of doom.[1] In Q (cf. Luke 11:49-51) the oracle refers to Sophia's prophets who are sent (which includes Jesus) and rejected. Matthew turns Q's Wisdom oracle into a dominical saying by writing, "Therefore, I [Jesus] send you prophets." The meaning of the evangelist's use of ἐγὼ ἀποστέλλω for ἡ σοφία τοῦ θεοῦ is clear. By this change the evangelist not only identifies Jesus with Sophia, but he also assigns to Jesus Sophia's function of sending prophets.[2] Thus, the primary meaning of the oracle in Matthew is the rejection of the envoys sent to Israel by Jesus as Sophia. This meaning is not only supported by the evangelist's change of ἐγὼ ἀποστέλλω, but it is supported by his other redactional activity in verses 34-36 as well.[3] For our purposes the most important redactional consideration at this point is the context of the oracle in our gospel.

---

[1]Christ, Jesus Sophia, pp. 120-132.

[2]Suggs, Wisdom, pp. 59-60. Cf. Robinson, "Jesus as Sophos and Sophia: Wisdom Tradition and the Gospels," p. 11; and Hare, The Theme of Jewish Persecution of Christians, pp. 88-96.

[3]For the possible redactional material in Matt. 23:34-36 see Suggs, Wisdom, pp. 14-29; and Christ, Jesus Sophia, pp. 120-135.

## Part 2.  Wisdom Christology
### as an Important Theme
### in Matthew

### The Matthean Context of Wisdom's Oracle

The Matthean context of verses 34-36
actually begins with verse 32: "Fill up, then,
the measure of your fathers."[1]  Verse 32 seems to
be an editorial connective which Matthew provided
in order to effect a smooth transition from the
last Woe (23:29-31) to the announced persecution
of Jesus' envoys (23:34-36), and to the consequent judgment to fall upon the persecutors
(23:37-39).[2]  Verse 32 is important for the evangelist's purpose, as we shall see, because it
provides the transition not only to the lament
over Jerusalem (23:37-39), but it also begins his
transition to the whole discourse in 24:3-31.[3]

---

[1]We will only give here the results of our
exegesis of Matt. 23:32-36 which directly relate
to our discussion of the context of the oracle.
The themes of these verses are dealt with in
detail below.  For the definition of "this generation" (23:36) and for the judgment which is to
befall them, see below pages 60-62; and 78-119.
For the theme of Israel's rejection of the
prophets (23:30, 31, 34-35), see below pages
70-81; and 94-112.

[2]Haenchen, "Matthäus 23," p. 52.

[3]Krister Stendahl, "Matthew," Peake's
Commentary on the Bible, ed. Matthew Black
(London: Thomas Nelson and Sons Ltd., 1962), col.
691i (page 793).  Cited hereafter as Stendahl,
"Matthew."

Matthew retains διὰ τοῦτο as the connective in verse 34. However, whereas διὰ τοῦτο in Luke serves to explain a statement made by Sophia in the past (διὰ τοῦτο . . . εἶπεν), in Matthew the διὰ τοῦτο has a causal force and describes an act being performed by Jesus in the present (ἰδοὺ ἐγὼ ἀποστέλλω). The meaning in our gospel then becomes: "Because of this situation just described, I, Jesus, am sending to you, etc."[1] Matthew clearly sees a causal connection between 23:32-33 and 23:34-36. If πληρώσατε in verse 32 can be read as an imperative, then the meaning of verses 34-36 becomes: "bring the sin of your fathers to fruition by doing what they left undone," namely, rejecting Jesus himself and his messengers who have come after him (i.e., Christian prophets).[2] Schweizer thinks it

---

[1]Hare, The Theme of Jewish Persecution of Christians, p. 87.

[2]Schweizer, Matthew, p. 443. Ἀποστέλλω in 23:34 does not necessarily imply that Matthew's community still has an organized missionary effort directed at the Jews. It simply suggests that his community is still being persecuted and rejected by the Jews as were the historical Twelve and Jesus himself. Matthew 23:34, especially with the evangelist's characteristic "your synagogues" (cf. 4:23; 9:35; 10:17; 12:9; 13:54), only suggests that Matthew's community is separate from the Synagogenverband and characterizes the relationship with it as continuous with that of Jesus and the Twelve (cf. 5:10-12; 10:17, 23). The envoys from Matthew's community, like the Twelve and the prophets, are still sent out by Jesus-Sophia, but theirs is a world-wide mission (24:14; 28:19), the rejection of which puts them in a direct line with the prophets of old (cf. Jubilees 1:12), with Jesus himself, and

probable that Matthew is writing with 27:25 in mind,[1] and it is very probable that the evangelist has "christianized" 23:34 by connecting the killing of the prophets with the allusion to the crucifixion of Jesus (cf. Acts 7:52).[2] The rejection of Jesus and his envoys, as πληρώσατε τὸ μέτρον τῶν πατέρων ὑμῶν implies, will allow God's judgment to fall upon apostate Israel when their apostasy has reached full measure (cf. Gen. 15:16).[3] The deliberative subjunctive of 23:33 (πῶς φύγητε) with the explicit use of γεέννης, the place of future punishment (cf. 5:22; 25:41), clearly implies that the final judicial sentence has not yet been pronounced against the Jews.[4] However, as 23:36 states, all these acts of bloodshed (ταῦτα πάντα cf. 23:30, 31, 34-35) will reach full measure (ἥξει cf. Luke 11:51, ἐκζητηθήσεται) during "this generation" (τὴν γενεὰν ταύτην). "This generation" means the generation of Jews then living (cf. 11:16) who reject

---

with the Twelve (cf. 24:9).

[1]Ibid., p. 444. Cf. John R. Donahue, "Passion Narrative," IDB supplementary volume, ed. Keith Crim (Nashville: Abingdon Press, 1976), p. 644.

[2]Haenchen, "Matthäus 23," pp. 53-63. Cf. Hare, The Theme of Jewish Persecution, pp. 89-91.

[3]Gerhard Delling, "πληρόω," TDNT 6: 294; and Hill, Matthew, p. 314.

[4]Joachim Jeremias, "γέεννα," TDNT 1: 658; M'Neile, The Gospel According to St. Matthew, p. 339.

Jesus himself (cf. 27:25), and their descendants who reject Jesus' disciples until the coming of Jesus as the Son of Man (cf. 24:14, 30-31; 25:31-46).[1] The relation between the future judgment implied in 23:33 and the present judgment implied in 23:36 is that those who deny Jesus as Wisdom in this world will be denied by him as Son of Man at the final judgment. This idea of judgment is similar to that reflected in the commission given to the messengers who preach to the Jews (cf. 10:5-7): "So everyone who acknowledges me before men, I also will acknowledge before my Father who is in heaven; but whoever denies me before men, I also will deny before my Father who is in heaven" (10:32-33).[2] It is for this reason (διὰ τοῦτο, v. 34), that the apostasy of the Jews might reach full measure, that Jesus has continued to send messengers to Israel. Both present and future aspects are coalesced in this context: "Behold, your house is forsaken and desolate. For I tell you, you will not see me again, until you say, 'Blessed be he who comes in the name of the Lord'" (23:38-39).[3] The rejection

---

[1] Hare, The Theme of Jewish Persecution, p. 96. This conclusion is bound up with our conclusion below that in Matthew's view of salvation history the "time of Jesus," and thus "his generation," extends from the beginning of his preaching (4:17) until his Parousia. The "time of Jesus," then, of necessity includes the time of all his disciples and their preaching mission. See the detailed discussion of this matter below on pp. 283-300.

[2] Cf. Hamerton-Kelly, Pre-Existence, p. 26. Notice that Matthew has "I" instead of "Son of Man" as in the Lukan parallel (cf. 12:8-9).

[3] Cf. Robinson, "Jesus as Sophos and Sophia:

of Jesus and his prophets will have the effect
(ὅπως, 23:35) of bringing all of God's accu-
mulated wrath to bear on this last generation for
all of the "righteous blood" which has been shed
(πᾶν αἷμα δίκαιον, 23:35 cf. Luke 11:50).[1]  The
messengers have been sent to preach repentance,
but Israel has persecuted both Jesus and his
messengers.  Thus, judgment is pronounced (v. 36)
upon all Israel for their rejection of Jesus.[2]

In summary, the pre-Matthean meaning of the
oracle in 23:34-36, namely, the persecution and
rejection of Wisdom's envoys, has been enhanced
by Matthean redaction.  The evangelist links
verses 32 and 34 with διὰ τοῦτο and emphasizes
thereby that the persecution and rejection of
Christian prophets is still the story of the rejection of Wisdom's envoys.  The rejection of
Jesus' disciples is a continuation of the same
Heilsgeschichte.  Matthew's redaction has made
two modifications in this view of history: Jesus
himself is identified with Sophia, and Wisdom's
"prophets" now include Jesus' disciples.[3]  This

---

Wisdom Tradition and the Gospels," p. 13.

[1]Hare, The Theme of Jewish Persecution of
Christians, p. 88.

[2]The judgment for Matthew is not only
against Jerusalem Jews who were living at the
time of Jesus' passion.  Τὴν γενεὰν ταύτην, as we
hope to show below, means all Israel.

[3]Suggs, Wisdom, p. 60.  Cf. Schweizer,
Matthew, pp. 443-444.

becomes even clearer when the other part of the context of Wisdom's oracle in 23:34-36 is investigated, namely, 23:37-39.

Matt. 23:37-39: the Lament
over Jerusalem

Bracketing the context of Matt. 23:34-36 on the other side is 23:37-39. This pericope has been identified as a traditional lament of Wisdom.[1] In the context of our gospel, as our discussion of 23:34 has shown, it is a lament of <u>Jesus</u> as Sophia over Jerusalem. We want to show that Matthew has verses 37-39 in the same context as verses 32-36 for two reasons. One reason is that verses 37-39 enhance the primary meaning of the oracle in 23:34-36, namely, the rejection of the envoys sent by Jesus-Sophia to Israel. The other reason is that verses 37-39 continue the transition to the pronouncement of judgment over Israel in 24:1-2.

It would be very helpful in discovering his redactional purpose if we could say with assurance that Matthew has brought the oracle (vv. 34-36) together with the lament (vv. 37-39). However, it is unclear whether or not the evangelist preserves the order of Q. If he does, then Matthew is <u>continuing</u> the quotation from Q and Luke has separated the lament from its Q context (cf. Luke 13:34-35).[2] The other possi-

---

[1]Form-critically speaking, these verses contain several different forms. See the detailed discussion in Edwards, <u>Theology of Q</u>, pp. 132-133.

[2]Bultmann, <u>History of the Synoptic Tradition</u>, pp. 114-115; Wilckens, "σοφία," p. 515; and Suggs, <u>Wisdom</u>, pp. 63-66.

bility is that verses 37-39 could be an independent oracle which Matthew has combined with
verses 34-36.[1] For our purposes we can say that
it is significant that the evangelist has either
allowed 37-39 to remain in the same context with
32-36, or that he has combined two separate
oracles to achieve his purpose. The latter seems
more likely, but the important thing is that
Matthew has these units in the same context while
they are in completely different contexts in
Luke.[2] This is a significant point for discovering the evangelist's redactional purpose,
and we need to probe it further. Why has Matthew
combined the units into this context, or, if they
were united in Q, why has he simply allowed them
to remain together?

Matthew 23:37-39, like 23:34-36, has tradi-
tionally been identified as an oracle of Sophia.[3]
The speaker in Q is definitely some figure other
than Jesus. The metaphor in which the speaker

---

[1]Hill, Matthew, p. 315; and Hare, The
Theme of Jewish Persecution of Christians, p. 140.

[2]See the reasons advanced by Manson,
Sayings, p. 102; Kümmel, Promise and Fulfillment,
pp. 80-81; Sjef van Tilborg, The Jewish Leaders
in Matthew (Leiden: E. J. Brill, 1972), pp. 69-70;
and Christ, Jesus Sophia, pp. 136-137.

[3]See Bultmann, History of the Synoptic
Tradition, pp. 114-115; Wilckens, "σοφία,"
p. 516; Suggs, Wisdom, p. 63; and Christ, Jesus
Sophia, p. 138 and the literature cited there.

laments over Jerusalem ("How often would I have
gathered your children together as a hen gathers
her brood under her wings") implies a speaker who
lived in a much wider timespan than the life of
the historical Jesus.[1] The metaphor requires a
divine, heavenly figure, and the subject of "would
I have gathered" (ἠθέλησα ἐπισυναγαγεῖν) is either
God, the Shekinah,[2] Sophia,[3] or some combination
of the three. Klostermann points out that the
Hebrew Bible uses the metaphor of a bird to indicate God Himself.[4] The word "wings" in the
Hebrew Bible (πτέρυγας) is used quite often to
depict the "wings of YHWH" under which Israel can
hide for His sustaining care and protection.[5]
Further, in their desire to circumlocute the
Tetragrammaton, the Rabbis would speak of the
"wings of God's presence (Shekinah)." It is often
pointed out in relation to Matt. 23:37 that a
proselyte to Judaism was "brought under the wings
of the Shekinah."[6] The relation between Sophia

---

[1]Christ, Jesus Sophia, p. 138.    [2]Ibid.

[3]Bultmann, History of the Synoptic
Tradition, p. 114.

[4]Erich Klostermann, Das Matthäusevangelium,
Handbuch zum Neuen Testament, no. 4 (Tübingen:
J. C. B. Mohr [Paul Siebeck], 1938), p. 190.

[5]Exod. 19:4; Deut. 32:11; Ruth 2:12; Pss.
17:8; 36:7; 57:1; 61:4; 63:7. Cf. 2 Esd. 1:30.
For a detailed discussion of this subject see
J. A. Wharton, "Wing," IDB 4:852; and Str-Bill.,
p. 943.

[6]Ibid. The Shekinah was the presence of
God, but it was also distinct from God Himself.
Cf. C. G. Montefiore and H. Loewe, A Rabbinic
Anthology (New York: World, 1963), p. 67.

and Shekinah in diverse contexts of Jewish thought is commonly known.[1] Thus, in view of the fact that the logion in Matt. 23:37-39 accords so well with the commonly accepted view of Sophia and Shekinah, most commentators are not hesitant to say that the speaker in Q is heavenly Wisdom depicted as the Shekinah who seeks to gather Jerusalem under its wings.[2]

However, this does not mean that an identification of Jesus with heavenly Sophia has been effected in Q.[3] The importance of the Matthean context of 23:37-39 comes to the fore here since, as we discussed above, it is his redaction in 23:34 (ἐγὼ ἀποστέλλω) which takes an oracle of

---

[1]E.g., Sirach 24:10; Prov. 8; 11QPs[a] 18:20. For a detailed discussion see T. Preiss, Le Fils de l'Homme (Montpellier: n.p., 1951-1953), pp. 73-76; Tomas Arvedson, Das Mysterium Christi: Eine Studie zu Mt 11.25-30 (Leipzig: Alfred Lorentz, 1937), pp. 158-168; and Suggs, Wisdom, p. 66.

[2]Schultz, Q: Die Spruchquelle der Evangelisten, pp. 351-355; Suggs, Wisdom, p. 67; Bultmann, History of the Synoptic Tradition, pp. 114-115; Christ, Jesus Sophia, p. 143; Schweizer, Matthew, p. 436; Arvedson, Das Mysterium Christi, p. 161; and O. H. Steck, Israel und das gewaltsame Geschick der Propheten: Untersuchungen zur Überlieferung des deuteronomistichen Geschichtsbildes im Alten Testament, Spätjudentum und Urchristentum, WMANT, no. 23 (Neukirchen, 1967), p. 232.

[3]See the discussion on pp. 51-53 above.

heavenly Sophia from Q and identifies that figure with Jesus. Matthew 23:37-39, which in Q demands another subject than Jesus as the speaker, implies that as a saying of Jesus he is identified with the speaker. Suggs summarizes this point when he says:

> It [Matt. 23:37-39] can be properly attributed to Jesus only when the step is taken which Matthew takes in the preceding pericope, that is, when Wisdom and Jesus are identified. Matthew intends the saying to be understood as a word of incarnate Wisdom whom he sees in Jesus.[1]

If Jesus does speak as Wisdom in this context, then there is another implication which needs to be explored. If Jesus for Matthew is Sophia incarnate, then can one say, because of the almost inseparable relation between Sophia and Shekinah, that for the evangelist Jesus as Sophia also embodies the Shekinah?[2] Matthew 23:38 seems to suggest that Jesus as Sophia and as the Shekinah are identical. Before attention is turned to 23:38 itself, let us briefly sketch the development of the concept of the Shekinah.

---

[1]Suggs, Wisdom, p. 67. This clearly implies, especially in the use of ποσάκις (23:37 par. Luke 13:34), that for Matthew Jesus is pre-existent Wisdom as well as Wisdom incarnate. However, it is certainly not clear what "pre-existence" would mean to Matthew and to his community. See the discussion of this matter in excursus 1 below.

[2]Cf. J. Abelson, The Immanence of God in Rabbinical Literature (New York: Harmon Press, 1969), pp. 58-65, 78-85.

## The Shekinah in Jewish Tradition

The word "Shekinah," or "that which dwells,"
is a derivative of shākan ("to dwell").  The word
"Shekinah" does not occur in the Hebrew Bible, but
the roots behind the concept are the many allusions in the Tanak to God's presence on earth,
particularly to God's presence in the Ark (cf.
Num. 10:33-36) and in the pillar of cloud which
guided them through the wilderness (e.g., Exod.
13:24-25).

In the earlier stages of its development
God's presence was conceived of in concrete terms.
For example, the cloud was a concrete sign of
God's presence and was, therefore, in some sense
differentiated from God Himself/Herself (cf.
Exod. 33:9, 10).  It seems that this gave impetus
to the later notion that the medium of God's
presence had the nature of personality.  This
development, in turn, led to several different
conceptions in post-biblical literature.[1]

In the Targums the presence of God came to
be associated with God's "glory" (yekara cf.
Ezek. 1:28) and God's "word" (memra).  When God's
presence is expressed in the Targums, the tendency is to say that the memra speaks, the yekara
appears, and the Shekinah (Shekinta) dwells.[2]

---

[1]W. O. E. Oesterley and G. H. Box, The
Religion and Worship of the Synagogue.  An Intro-
duction to the Study of Judaism from the New
Testament Period, 2nd ed. (London: Sir Isaac
Pitman and Sons, Ltd., 1911), pp. 217-230.  Cf.
Abelson, The Immanence of God in Rabbinical
Literature, pp. 78-85.

[2]Cf. T. Jonathan Lev. 26:11; Jerusalem T.
Lev. 9:6; T. of Onkelos Gen. 16:13.  See D. Moody,

The Shekinah in the Targums, as a sign of God's presence, seems to be impersonal in character, that is, the concept is a circumlocution for the omnipresence of God.[1] The same is true to some extent in the Talmud. In the Talmud, however, the Shekinah is seen by some Rabbis as an intermediary which is distinct from God. It belongs to God, yet it is capable of taking independent action.[2] In the Mishna there are only two references to the Shekinah (cf. Sanh. 6:5). The most important for our discussion is: "If two sit together and words of the Torah [are spoken] between them, the Shekinah is present with them" (Aboth 3:2 cf. Matt. 18:20). In general it can be said that in the development of the notion of God's presence in the Targums, the Mishna, and the Talmud, the Shekinah never became a personal, divine being who takes the place of God Himself/Herself. The term Shekinah is generally a reverent way of speaking about God.[3]

---

"Shekinah," IDB 4:317; and G. B. Caird, The Revelation of St. John the Divine, Harper's New Testament Commentaries (New York: Harper and Row, Publishers, 1966), p. 263.

[1]Oesterley and Box, Religion and Worship of the Synagogue, p. 218; and A. M. Ramsey, The Glory of God and the Transfiguration of Christ (London: Longmans, Green and Co., 1949), pp. 19-20.

[2]See Oesterley and Box, Religion and Worship of the Synagogue, pp. 218-220 for references.

[3]George Foot Moore, Judaism in the First Centuries of the Christian Era. The Age of the Tannaim, 3 vols. (Cambridge, Massachusetts: Harvard University Press, 1954), 1:420, 436.

It is difficult to say exactly when Sophia
and Shekinah first became related concepts.  In
the Wisdom literature the concept of the Shekinah
clearly appears in Sirach.  The relation of Sophia
and Shekinah can be seen in the notion of Sophia's
dwelling in the midst of God's people as the
pillar of cloud (24:4), as Torah (24:23), and as
God's presence in the temple (24:10-11).[1]  It is
this last idea which is important for understanding the saying in Matt. 23:38.

## Matt. 23:38: a traditional
## Jewish saying

Matt. 23:38, as a traditional Jewish saying,
seems to mean that "Gott verlässt mit dem Tempel
gleichzeitig Israel überhaupt."[2]  The warning
"God will forsake your house" is a traditional
prophecy in Judaism, and it usually alludes to
the destruction of Jerusalem.[3]  The prophecy was
developed both in the apocalyptic and Wisdom
traditions.[4]  The prophecy of Jerusalem's

---

[1]Cf. Sirach 24:1-4, 7, 8.  See Christ, Jesus
Sophia, p. 36 and the literature cited there.

[2]Ibid., p. 140.

[3]Steck, Israel und das gewaltsame Geschick
der Propheten, pp. 237-239.

[4]Wolfgang Trilling, Das Wahre Israel.
Studien zur Theologie des Matthäus-Evangeliums,
3rd rev. ed., SANT (München: Kösel-Verlag, 1964),
p. 86 (hereafter cited as Trilling, Wahre); Georg
Strecker, Der Weg der Gerechtigkeit, FRLANT, vol.
82, 3rd ed. (Göttingen: Vandenhoeck and Ruprecht,
1971), p. 113 (hereafter cited as Strecker, Weg).

destruction and of the temple's destruction is
given in the Hebrew Bible itself. For example,
Micah 3:12 says: "Therefore because of you Zion
shall be plowed as a field; Jerusalem shall become
a heap of ruins" (cf. Jer. 26:18). In apocalyptic
the destruction of Jerusalem and of the temple is
referred to in terms very similar to Matt. 23:38.
For example, 2 Baruch 8:2: "Enter, ye enemies,
And come, ye adversaries; For he who kept the
house has forsaken (it)" (cf. 2 Baruch 4:1). In
1 Enoch 89:56 it reads: "And I saw that He forsook
that their house and their tower and gave them
all into the hand of the lions." A saying in
2 Esd. 1:33 is very similar to Matt. 23:38: "Thus
says the Lord Almighty: Your house is desolate."
In the Wisdom tradition Wisdom is said to dwell
in Israel, particularly in the temple (cf. Sirach
24:1-12, 23). The implication here is that Wisdom
dwells in the temple as the Shekinah.[1]

All of these traditions (the Hebrew Bible
itself, the apocalyptic and Wisdom traditions)
put forth the idea that at the destruction of
Jerusalem God will forsake the city, and, by
implication, will leave the city desolate. If
God's presence (Shekinah) left the temple, then
God's protection would be withdrawn, and not only
Jerusalem but the whole nation would be doomed.
It was believed that the Shekinah, which dwelt in
the temple, would abandon the city at the time of

---

[1]John G. Snaith, Ecclesiasticus, The
Cambridge Bible Commentary (London: Cambridge
University Press, 1974), p. 121; and Otto Michel,
"οἶκος," TDNT 5:120. This tradition, however, is
in marked opposition to other Wisdom writers in
which Sophia seeks a home on earth and, finding
none (even in Israel), returns to heaven (cf.
1 Enoch 42:1-3).

its destruction.[1] If the Shekinah abandoned the city, the people could not keep the Law.[2] Consequently, they would be considered an unholy people.[3] It is clear, then, that behind the warning ἰδοὺ ἀφίεται ὑμῖν ὁ οἶκος ὑμῶν in 23:38 is the concept that the very presence of God will leave Israel.

## Jesus as Shekinah in Matt. 23:38

The concept of the Shekinah's abandonment of the temple is strongly implied in Matt. 23:37-39. In Matt. 23:21 it is emphasized that anyone who swears by the temple swears by God Himself/Herself because God dwells in the temple.[4]

---

[1] See Josephus, De Bello Judaico 6.5.3 (290-295); Montefiore, Rabbinic Anthology, p. 67; and Adolf Schlatter, Der Evangelist Matthäus: seine Sprache, seine Ziel, seine Selbständigkeit, 6th (Stuttgart: Calwer Verlag, 1963), pp. 16-19.

[2] Cf. Montefiore, Rabbinic Anthology, pp. 405-406.

[3] Klostermann, Matthäusevangelium, p. 191. It should be noted that there were conflicting rabbinical notions about the fate of the Shekinah after the temple's destruction in C.E. 70. One belief was that the Shekinah completely left the universe (e.g., Exod. Rabba 2:2). Another belief was that the Shekinah hovered around the western wall (e.g., Yalḳut on I Kings 8). A third basic belief was that the Shekinah disseminated itself to the whole world after the destruction (cf. Abelson, The Immanence of God, pp. 120-130 and the literature cited there).

[4] See M'Neile, St. Matthew, p. 334; Schweizer, Matthew, p. 441.

Matthew 23:16-22 extends the concept even further; it extends " . . . the concept of holiness to the temple in such a way that the temple, as the locus of the shekinah of God [italics mine] sanctifies (ἁγιάσας) everything in it, even the gold decorations."[1] There seems to be very little doubt that the concept of the Shekinah's presence in the temple is implied in Matthew 23 and that it is an important motif for the evangelist.

Matthew's redaction of 23:38 bears out the implied concept of the Shekinah's threat to abandon the city. Most commentators have noted that the evangelist has γάρ instead of δέ in Jesus' words (23:39 cf. Luke 13:35b). Matthew's use of γάρ causally links ἀφίεται with Jesus' departure from the temple: "Behold your house is left to you because I tell you, you will not see me until . . ."[2] This redactional move virtually equates Jesus with the Shekinah of God.[3] E. Schweizer had already concluded in his study of 23:37 that "Jesus [as Shekinah] . . . comes to occupy the place of God himself. The point of the passage is that God becomes concretely real on earth and that this takes place in Jesus."[4] He

---

[1]Gottlob Schrenk, "ἱερόν," TDNT 3:243.

[2]See J. Lambrecht, "The Parousia Discourse. Composition and Content in Mt., XXIV-XXV." L'Évangile selon Matthieu. Rédaction et théologie, ed. M. Didier (Gembloux: J. Duculot, 1972), p. 316 (hereafter cited as Lambrecht, "The Parousia Discourse"); cf. Trilling, Wahre, p. 86.

[3]Strecker, Weg, p. 113.

[4]Schweizer, Matthew, p. 444.

concludes further on Matthew's γάρ in 23:39:

> The use of the conjunction "for" in the
> Greek text shows that Matthew's purpose
> is to say: with the departure of Jesus,
> God has departed from his house, fulfilling
> the divine judgment announced by the
> prophets (Jer. 12:7; cf. Ezek. 8:6; 11:21;
> Eth. Enoch 89:56; Syr. Bar. 8:2; 2 Esdras
> 16:37). Not until Jesus returns will the
> period of God's absence come to an end.[1]

Matthew emphasizes very strongly that the presence
of Jesus is somehow "God with us."[2] The equation
of Jesus with the Shekinah seems to be a variation
of Matthew's "God with us" theme.[3]

---

[1]Ibid., p. 445. Arens also contends that
23:39 when "Addressed to the Jews . . . was equivalent to saying that the Lord would be absent with
his Shekinah (ὁ οἶκος ὑμῶν! cf. Jer. 22,5; I Kgs.
9,7ff.)." (Eduardo Arens, The ELTHON-Sayings in
the Synoptic Tradition. A Historico-Critical
Investigation, Orbis Biblicus et Orientalis, vol.
10 [Göttingen: Vandenhoeck and Ruprecht, 1976],
p. 294 [hereafter cited as Arens, ELTHON].) Cf.
M'Neile, St. Matthew, p. 342; Haenchen, "Matthäus
23," p. 56; and van der Kwaak, "Die Klage über
Jerusalem," pp. 163-164.

[2]Matt. 1:23 cf. 18:20; 28:20. See
Schweizer, Matthew, pp. 444-445; and Hubbard,
Matthew 28:16-20, p. 97.

[3]Strecker, Weg, p. 113. We will discuss
exactly how Matthew conceived of Jesus' presence
on pages 241-247 below.

But, even more than this, the threat in 23:38 is within the Matthean context where Jesus has just been identified as Sophia incarnate (23:34). The traditional threat issued against Israel in 23:38 is a prophetic word of judgment. The judgment is the loss of God's presence, and the cause of the judgment is Israel's rejection of God's envoys (cf. 23:32-37).[1] Matthew has taken two Sophia logia (23:34-36, 37-39) and has made them sayings of Jesus. This means that Jesus explicitly appears as incarnate Sophia and as the Shekinah whom Israel has rejected. They have also rejected all of the envoys Jesus-Sophia has sent to them.[2]

Thus, Matthew has Jesus speak in 23:37-39 as Wisdom. The "how often I would have gathered your children together" refers to the prophets and other envoys Jesus-Sophia has sent to Israel over the generations (23:37 cf. 23:34). "How often" also alludes to the fact that Sophia's envoys have not been heeded. Israel's "house is forsaken" because they have rejected both Jesus-Sophia and his envoys. Because of their rejection, Israel has forfeited any claim to the presence of God in Jesus.[3]

### Matt. 23:39: Jesus as Sophia-Son of Man

We have seen that Jesus is Sophia incarnate

---

[1] Steck, Israel und das gewaltsame Geschick der Propheten, p. 231.

[2] Christ, Jesus Sophia, p. 150.

[3] Suggs, Wisdom, p. 71 cf. pp. 66-67.

for Matthew in 23:34-36, and that he appears in 23:37-39 as the Shekinah. Verse 38 threatened that the judgment upon Israel for rejecting God's envoys, who were sent by Jesus-Sophia, would be the departure of God's presence from the temple and the city. The prophecy of God's departure ("your house is forsaken") actually represents a prophecy of the destruction of Jerusalem.[1] The departure of the Shekinah would mean the end of the temple, of the city, and of the nation. The departure of God's presence goes hand in hand with the withdrawal of Wisdom. Felix Christ is correct when he says:

> Die Weisheit erscheint hier als <u>Schekina</u>, vgl. Sir 24,10; 11QPs[a]XVIII,20: Die Weisheit wohnt im Tempel. Die Weisheit verlässt den Tempel zusammen mit Gott. Es liegt eine "Schekina-Sophiologie" vor.[2]

Matthew has explicitly identified Jesus as Sophia-Shekinah, and Israel is confronted with the threatened loss of <u>his</u> presence. The loss of Jesus' presence is the loss of God's presence as far as the evangelist is concerned.[3] His use of γάρ in verse 39 links the loss of God's presence with the loss of Jesus' presence. The point of verse 39 for Matthew, then, is that the period of God's absence will not end until Jesus returns.[4]

---

[1]Steck, <u>Israel und das gewaltsame Geschick der Propheten</u>, pp. 237-239; Trilling, <u>Wahre</u>, p. 86; and Strecker, <u>Weg</u>, p. 113.

[2]Christ, <u>Jesus Sophia</u>, p. 141.

[3]Schweizer, <u>Matthew</u>, pp. 444-445.

[4]Ibid.

This is the meaning of "you will not see me again, until you say, 'Blessed is he who comes in the name of the Lord.'" Matthean redaction in verse 39 bears this out in one place other than just his use of γάρ.

The original reading in Q seems to have been ἕως ἥξει ὅτε εἴπητε (Luke 13:35). This reading best explains all other variant readings.[1] If ἕως ἥξει ὅτε εἴπητε is the Q reading, then this would imply that ὁ ἐρχόμενος is a different person than the speaker.[2] We have already discussed on other grounds why the speaker in Q is Sophia. Sophia in Q is speaking eschatologically of "the coming one."[3]

Matthew, however, has already identified Jesus with Sophia (23:34, 37). The evangelist thus redacts ἕως ἥξει ὅτε εἴπητε to read ἀπ' ἄρτι ἕως ἄν εἴπητε. 'Απ' ἄρτι has been isolated by

---

[1] "Οτε with the subjunctive is rare in Koine (see F. Blass and A. Debrunner, A Greek Grammar of the New Testament, trans. Robert W. Funk [Chicago: University of Chicago Press, 1961], § 382[2].) Because of this many copyists most likely omitted ἥξει ὅτε (see Bruce Metzger, A Textual Commentary on the Greek New Testament [London: United Bible Societies, 1971], p. 163.)

[2] Barnabas Lindars, New Testament Apologetic. The Doctrinal Significance of Old Testament Quotations (Philadelphia: The Westminster Press, 1961), p. 173.

[3] Suggs, Wisdom, p. 70 n. 22. Cf. Edwards, Theology of Q, pp. 78-79.

several commentators as characteristic of the
evangelist's redaction.[1]  The expression appears
two other times in the First Gospel (never in
Luke or in Mark), and in each case it points to
Jesus' Parousia (cf. 26:29, 64).  The quotation
"Blessed is he who comes in the name of the Lord"
is from Ps. 118:26.  In Luke 13:35 the same quotation refers to Jesus' entry into Jerusalem.  In
contrast, Matthew has the Jerusalem saying (23:39)
after Jesus' entry into Jerusalem (cf. 21:9).  In
Matthew the quotation and ἀπ' ἄρτι ("again") do
not refer to Jesus' entrance into Jerusalem, but
they refer to the fact that Israel will see his
future advent as the Son of Man.[2]

In other words, the beginning of the judgment to befall Israel in 23:37-39 for Matthew
will be the loss of Jesus-Sophia's presence, and,
consequently, the loss of God's presence.  It
will be argued below that the evangelist understands this judgment to have been fulfilled in
Jesus' time when he leaves the temple for the
last time (cf. 24:1).  Matthew understands the
judgment to fall upon Israel because they have
continually rejected God's messengers, which for
Matthew have been sent by Jesus himself (23:34).[3]

---

[1]Trilling, Wahre, p. 68; Hare, The Theme of
Jewish Persecution of Christians, p. 154; Suggs,
Wisdom, p. 70 n. 2; and Hill, Gospel of Matthew,
p. 316.

[2]Arens, ELTHON, p. 294; Stendahl, School,
p. 93; and Hill, Gospel of Matthew, p. 316.

[3]This definitely implies that the historical
disciples are included in the rejection of the
messengers sent by Jesus.  The rejection of
Jesus' historical disciples by the Jews takes
place in Matthew 10.  Matthew "de-eschatologizes"

The judgment comes to Israel also because they

---

Mark 13:9-13 by placing this material in Matt. 10:17-21. He ostensibly does this because the mission of the Twelve and of their rejection in the life-situation of Jesus is past (see below, ch. 3 part 4). In chapter 10 Matthew is concerned only with the Jewish rejection of the Twelve's message. His interest in their rejection is seen in the fact that Jesus gives them few instructions about preaching, no instructions about what to teach converts, and Matthew does not even report the mission itself of the return of the missionaries (cf. Mark 6:12, 30; Luke 9:6, 10; see Hare, Jewish Persecution, pp. 97-98).
     One further implication of the messengers' rejection in 23:34 is that for the evangelist the rejection which his church experiences in the post-resurrection period is continuous with the history of all the messengers (including the Twelve) sent by Jesus. (Hare, Jewish Persecution, pp. 80-114 has an excellent discussion of the redactional changes which Matthew has made in 23:34 to effect this continuity of rejection between his church and all the messengers sent by Jesus. See also Haenchen, "Matthäus 23," pp. 53-63.) Jesus' promise to both the Twelve and to Matthew's community is "Blessed are you when men . . . persecute you . . . on my account. . . . for so men persecuted the prophets who were before you" (5:11-12). "The disciples," says Friedrich, "when persecuted by the Jews, are in this respect descendants of the prophets, Mt. 5:12." (See Gerhard Friedrich, "προφήτης," TDNT 6:835 cf. Schweizer, Matthew, p. 97.)

have rejected Jesus, the Sophia-Shekinah of God. Consequently, Israel will not have the presence of Jesus-Sophia again until he returns as Son of Man.[1] As Felix Christ summarizes it: "Jesus Sophia wird nicht mehr zu sehen sein, bis er bei der Parusie als der Menschensohn zum Gericht wiederkommen wird."[2] The relation of Jesus as Sophia to Jesus as Son of Man in the First Gospel will be discussed below, but 23:37-39 (together with 23:32-36) suggests that in Matthean Christology Jesus as Son of Man will bring to completion what is revealed by Jesus as incarnate Sophia.[3] Our exegesis of 23:37-39 (and of 23:32-36) clearly leads us to believe that Matthew's eschatology, particularly his view of Jesus as the coming Son of Man, has been heavily influenced by Wisdom speculation.

The main point under discussion at present, however, must be whether or not any Matthean

---

[1] Ὁ ἐρχόμενος in 23:39 clearly seems to mean the Son of Man. See J. D. Kingsbury, Matthew: Structure, Christology, Kingdom (Philadelphia: Fortress Press, 1975), p. 86 (hereafter cited as Kingsbury, Structure); and Christ, Jesus Sophia, pp. 147-148.

[2] Ibid., pp. 149-150; cf. Wilckens, "σοφία," p. 515.

[3] Cf. the discussion of Windisch about the eschatological emphases in the Wisdom tradition and the implications of those emphases for interpreting the Sermon on the Mount. (See Hans Windisch, The Meaning of the Sermon on the Mount, trans. S. MacLean Gilmour [Philadelphia: Westminster Press, 1951], pp. 42-43.)

compositional theme (as opposed to two pericopae) supports the conclusion that for him Israel has continually rejected Jesus-Sophia and his envoys. One important passage in this regard is Matt. 11:2-19.

## Wisdom's Children:
## Matt. 11:16-19

Matthew 11:19b is the most important logion for our purposes. Wisdom is personified in this logion: "Yet wisdom is justified by her deeds." The parallel verse in Luke 7:35 probably gives the Q reading: "Yet wisdom is justified by all her children."[1] There is no question that the Sitz im Leben of this unit (11:16-19) is earlier than Q. On the one hand, a strong case could be built for placing this pericope in the life-situation of Jesus. The tradition is strongly Semitic and the language readily translates back into Aramaic, which locates it at least as early as the Palestinian tradition. The children at play is a vivid description of a Palestinian street-scene. Vividness of detail has been found to be more characteristic of the earliest development of the tradition than it has of its later augmentation. The application of the parable (11:19) reflects a high estimate of the Baptist because it tends to put his ministry on a level with that of Jesus. This is more characteristic of Jesus than it is of the early Church. If the Aramaic bar nash stands behind it, the reference to the Son of Man in 11:19 could easily be used in the context as a first person reference to Jesus himself. The phrase which designates Jesus as "a glutton and a drunkard, a friend of tax collectors and sinners" (11:19) seems to belong

---

[1]See the detailed discussion of Matt. 11:19c immediately below.

to the controversies during Jesus' ministry rather
than to the later polemical situation between the
early Church and Judaism.  Finally, the parable
and its application fit so well together that
they could have belonged together from the beginning.[1]  On the other hand, unless one is prepared to argue that Matt. 11:19b is an exception
to the rule that parables from the life-situation
of Jesus did not have applications appended to
them, it seems to have been an independent
logion.[2]  Whether or not 11:19b was originally
part of the similitude, however, does not alter
the fact that in its context in the First Gospel
(and in Q, cf. Luke 7:33-35) it must be interpreted in connection with 11:16-19a.

## The point of the
## parable in Matthew

The point of the similitude in Matt.
11:16-19a is surprisingly clear.  Virtually all
researchers agree that the simile is built around
children playing in the market place.  They are
"piping and dancing," as at weddings, and "wailing
and mourning," as at funerals, but it all is to no
avail.  Their other playmates will not play; they
are "spoilsports" because they will not respond
to any appeal.  There does not seem to be a dispute between the children concerning what game

---

[1]For a detailed discussion see Jeremias,
Parables of Jesus, pp. 160-165; and Norman Perrin,
Rediscovering the Teaching of Jesus (New York:
Harper and Row, 1967), pp. 86, 119-121 (hereafter
cited as Perrin, Rediscovering).

[2]Suggs, Wisdom, pp. 33-48; cf. Perrin,
Rediscovering, pp. 86-87.

they should play. Rather, the emphasis is upon the children who sit by the side of the street and blame the other children for not "dancing" as they "piped."[1]

If the introduction to the parable is taken literally, then "this generation" is like the children sitting in the market place (11:16 cf. Luke 7:31) who were looking for playmates. This would mean that they stood as passive observers and expected John to dance and Jesus to lament. Another possible interpretation would be to say that Jesus and John are like the children who "piped" and that the Jews represent those who "did not dance." Either meaning is possible in the life-situation of Jesus, particularly since the introductions to parables are often provided by the tradition as it develops.[2] However, in the Matthean introduction "this generation" is clearly likened to the children who are sitting in the market place (11:16). They prefer the less demanding role of flute-players and dirge-singers, but these children expect the "others" (τοῖς ἑτέροις, only in Matthew), namely, John and Jesus, to do the strenuous part of dancing and lamenting to their music. These children complain to John and Jesus that "We piped to you, and you did not dance; we wailed, and you did not mourn" (11:17).[3] Jesus' reply is that John offered them an ascetic

---

[1]See Jeremias, Parables of Jesus, pp. 160-165; and Hill, Matthew, pp. 201-202 for excellent summaries of the parable.

[2]Schweizer, Matthew, p. 264; cf. Hill, Matthew, p. 202.

[3]Ibid. Cf. Jeremias, Parables of Jesus, pp. 161-162.

way (he "came neither eating nor drinking"), but
they rejected him by saying "He has a demon"
(11:18).  "'I' came eating and drinking," Jesus
says, "but you rejected the way I offered by
reproaching me" ("Behold, a glutton and a drunkard, a friend of tax collectors and sinners,"
11:19a).[1]  The point of Jesus' remark is that
"God sends you his messengers, the last messengers, to the last generation before the catastrophe.  But all you do is to give orders and
criticize."[2]

Matthew 11:19c

The parable is thus completely intelligible
without 11:19c.  This generation has rejected
both John and Jesus.[3]  However, if Matt. 11:19c
is an original part of the parable, then Jesus
ends with: "Yet Wisdom[4] is justified [in every

---

[1]"Son of Man" here would most likely mean
"I."  Cf. Ibid., p. 162; Perrin, Rediscovering,
p. 120; and Johnson, St. Matthew, p. 385.

[2]Jeremias, Parables of Jesus, p. 162.

[3]Wilckens, "σοφία," p. 516.

[4]Here "Wisdom" is equivalent to God
(cf. Ibid) or to "godly Wisdom" (cf. Christ,
Jesus Sophia, p. 65).

generation][1] by[2] her deeds."  Whether or not
verse 19c is a secondary interpretation attached
to the original parable, it is an interpretation
retained in Q.[3]

Matthew 11:19c in Q poses the question: is
the logion in Q intended to interpret only the
parable, or does it interpret a larger block of
material?  T. W. Manson, for example, sees
11:2-19 as the conclusion to the first main
section of Q.  It is perhaps the longest contin-

---

[1]If ἐδικαιώθη is a gnomic aorist, as
Jeremias contends, then this translation is justified (see Jeremias, Parables of Jesus, p. 162
n. 42; and Blass-Debrunner, A Greek Grammar § 333,
1).  Ἐδικαιώθη does not mean "condemned" as
Schlatter contends (Schlatter, Matthäus, pp.
374-375; cf. Wilckens, "σοφία," p. 516 n. 351;
and Christ, Jesus Sophia, p. 64).  Ἐδικαιώθη can
also have eschatological connotations which would
imply that Wisdom will be justified at the judgment of the Son of Man (see Wilckens, "σοφία," p.
516; and Christ, Jesus Sophia, p. 64 and the
literature cited there).

[2]The meaning could be quite different if
ἀπό (=min) were read exclusively, i.e., as "apart
from" (see Wilckens, "σοφία," p. 516 n. 353).
The meaning would then be that Wisdom is justified in spite of the rejection of Jesus and John
by the Jews.  The causal or instrumental use of
ἀπό, however, is quite natural.  (See Nigel
Turner, A Grammar of New Testament Greek, vol. 3
[Edinburgh: T. and T. Clark, 1963], p. 258; and
Stendahl, "Matthew," p. 684.)

[3]See Suggs, Wisdom, pp. 34-36; and Edwards,
Theology of Q, pp. 98-99.

uous block of Q material, and both Matthew and
Luke seem to deal with it as a unit.[1]  We are not
particularly interested at this point in how Luke
treats this section as a unit.[2]  However, there
is a consensus among interpreters that verse 19c
in Luke (=Luke 7:35: "Yet wisdom is justified by
all her children") means that Wisdom is justified
by all those who accept John and Jesus, though
there is no mention of such a group in the parable
itself.[3]  Nor does our discussion absolutely
depend upon whether or not Matt. 11:2-19 was a
continuous unit in Q, though we are inclined to
think that it was a unit.  Our only point is that
the very fact that both Matthew and Luke develop
this Q material as a unit suggests that they
understood verse 19c as an allusion to a larger
block of material than just the parable itself.

---

[1]Manson, Sayings, p. 71.  See also Bacon,
Studies in Matthew, pp. 205-211, and Johnson,
St. Matthew, p. 384.

[2]See the excellent summary by Suggs,
Wisdom, pp. 36-37.

[3]Ibid.  Cf. Schweizer, Matthew, pp. 259-260.
It is generally conceded that πάντων is a Lukan
addition (see Adolf von Harnack, Sprüche und
Reden Jesu [Leipig: n.p., 1907], p. 18; Schlatter,
Matthäus, p. 376; A. Loisy, L'Évangile selon Luc.,
[Paris: n.p., 1924], p. 228; and M.-J. Lagrange,
Évangile selon Saint-Luc.,[Paris: Librairie
Victor Lecoffre, 1948], p. 226).  Leivestad
suggests that the addition was made by Luke so
that "all Wisdom's children" would correspond to
"all the people" (πᾶς ὁ λαός) of Luke 7:29 (see
R. Leivestad, "An Interpretation of Mt 11,19,"
JBL 71 [1952]: 180).

If this is the case, then for Q the meaning of the entire unit is summarized in: "Wisdom is justified by [all] her deeds/children."

It is not clear, though, whether the Q reading should be ἔργων as in Matthew or τέκνων as in Luke.[1] In the Q material John sends disciples to ask if Jesus is the one "who is to come" (ὁ ἐρχόμενος, Matt. 11:3; Luke 7:19). Jesus does not explicitly answer the question, but he reminds them of his deeds, which are all a fulfillment of prophecy (Matt. 11:4-6 cf. Isa. 29:18-19; 35:5-6; 61:1). After John's disciples depart, Jesus characterizes John as a prophet who ranks above the other prophets (Matt. 11:7-9; Luke 7:24-26). John is the greatest among "those born of women" (Matt. 11:10-11; Luke 7:27-28). In Q this is followed by the parable of the children in the market place (Matt. 11:16-19; Luke 7:31-35) which culminates in the logion "wisdom is justified by her deeds/children."

From this sequence it is clear that in Q John and Jesus are obedient messengers of Wisdom. They are the "children of Wisdom" who are rejected by this generation. Or, if "deeds" is the Q reading, then the deeds of Jesus and John, as

---

[1]Some commentators conclude that ἔργων is a Matthean alteration (Strecker, Weg, p. 102; and Suggs, Wisdom, p. 33). Others, though, conclude that ἔργων is the original reading (e.g.; Jeremias, Parables of Jesus, p. 162; and Hill, Matthew, p. 202). Still others contend that the differences between Matthew and Luke rest on a translation problem in the tradition before them. See the discussions in Jeremias, Parables of Jesus, p. 162 n. 44; and Manson, Sayings, p. 71.

deeds of Wisdom's messengers, are rejected.
Although the first option seems more probable
(that Jesus and John are Wisdom's children), in
either case the meaning is clear: Jesus and John
are envoys of Wisdom and their special status is
due to the fact that they are the heralds of the
Eschaton. Jesus' ministry is the fulfillment of
prophecy (Matt. 11:4-6; Luke 7:22-23), and in Q
he is the Son of Man (Matt. 7:19; Luke 7:34)
while John is Elijah (Matt. 11:10; Luke 7:27).
Thus, even if it is only dependent upon the
parable (Matt. 11:16-19) and not upon the larger
context (11:2-19), in Q the logion in Matt. 19c
clearly means that Jesus and John are both
Wisdom's children because they both do the work
of God.[1]

The meaning of 11:19c in Matthew

It is important to notice that Jesus is not
identified with Sophia in this Q logion. Jesus
is only the "one who does God's work, which is
being a child (or deed) of God."[2] But it does
appear that Matthean redaction identifies Jesus
with Sophia in this unit.

As we have seen, both Matthew and Luke deal
with 11:2-19 as a unit presumably because it was
already a continuous unit in Q. It is generally
agreed by commentators that Matthew himself has
provided the introduction to this unit in his

---

[1]Edwards, Theology of Q, p. 99; Suggs,
Wisdom, p. 55; Wilckens, "σοφία," p. 516; and
Schweizer, Matthew, p. 447.

[2]Edwards, Theology of Q, p. 99; Schweizer,
Matthew, p. 447; and Hill, Matthew, p. 202.

gospel: "Now when John heard in prison about the deeds of the Christ" (τὰ ἔργα τοῦ Χριστοῦ cf. Luke 7:18).[1] The unusual phrase "the deeds of the Christ" is considered by virtually every commentator to be redactional material of the evangelist. Several reasons are advanced for this conclusion. First, Χριστός never appears in Q as a designation of Jesus.[2] Χριστός in Matt. 11:2 is almost used as a technical term. "The language here," says Hill, "seems to be that of later Christianity." Perhaps, as he suggests, the evangelist is expressing his own knowledge of what John only hoped for and expected.[3] Secondly, virtually every interpreter agrees that the phrase must mean something similar to "the Messianic deeds."[4] One would expect to read "the deeds of Jesus" instead of the "deeds of the Christ," and many manuscripts have Ἰησοῦ inserted in order to

---

[1]Ibid., p. 197; Suggs, Wisdom, p. 56; and Schweizer, Matthew, p. 254.

[2]Suggs, Wisdom, p. 56.

[3]Hill, Matthew, p. 97; cf. Schweizer, Matthew, p. 256.

[4]Suggs, Wisdom, p. 37; Strecker, Weg, pp. 102, 177; M.-J. Lagrange, Évangile selon Saint Matthieu [Paris: Librairie Victor Lecoffre, 1948], p. 223; Klostermann, Matthäus, p. 100; Arvedson, Mysterium Christi, pp. 209-215; Pierre Bonnard, L'Évangile selon Saint Matthieu, Commentaire du Nouveau Testament, vol. 1 (Neuchâtel: Delachaux et Niestlé, 1963), p. 164; George Bertram, "ἔργον," TDNT 2:642; and Stendahl, "Matthew," p. 684.

make a sharper contrast with Matt. 11:3.[1] The
cumulative effect of these points seems to be
that the phrase τὰ ἔργα τοῦ Χριστοῦ is due to
the redaction of the evangelist.

When the larger context in Matthew is
studied, there is no doubt that the deeds of the
Messiah are crucial to the whole context of
11:2-24. The transition which Matthew provides
to the woes against the cities of Galilee reads:
"then he began to upbraid the cities where most
of his mighty works (δυνάμεις) had been done,
because they did not repent" (11:20 cf. Luke
10:13). The fact that Matthew uses δυνάμεις
instead of ἔργα in 11:20 does not detract from
his point. The δυνάμεις are part of the ἔργα.[2]
The evangelist's point is that the ἔργα of 11:2
include the δυνάμεις which have been performed as
far back as chapters 8-9. John's question in
11:3 summarizes the christological deeds of the
preceding chapters, and it only enhances the
christological thrust of the whole account up to
this point.[3]

---

[1]Metzger, Textual Commentary on the New
Testament, p. 29.

[2]Suggs, Wisdom, p. 56.

[3]H. J. Held, "Matthew as Interpreter of the
Miracle Stories," TI, pp. 251-252. Cf.
Schweizer's remark: "The obvious reason for
placing the episode [11:2-6] here is that it
interprets what is happening in Jesus' own person
(chapters 5-7 and 8-9)." (Schweizer, Matthew,
p. 255.) See also the discussions in Christ,
Jesus Sophia, p. 76, and Hill, Matthew, p. 197.

In summary, τὰ ἔργα τοῦ Χριστοῦ in 11:2 is
due to Matthean redaction.  Matthew 11:2 and
11:19c, then, become the "brackets" of the unit
in 11:2-19.  The two phrases "the deeds of the
Christ" and the "deeds of Wisdom" frame the entire
section.[1]  When the evangelist is speaking of τὰ
ἔργα τοῦ Χριστοῦ (=Jesus' deeds), he is also
speaking about the "deeds of Wisdom" (ἐδικαιώθη
ἡ σοφία ἀπὸ τῶν ἔργων αὐτῆς).  Matthew speaks of
the ἔργα (or "results") of Wisdom and interprets
this from the perspective of 11:2.  As Schweizer
says, "He [Matthew] thus equates the works of
God's wisdom with the works of Jesus."[2]  The
evangelist has consciously modified a saying
about the "deeds of Wisdom," and a saying
about the "children of Wisdom," if τέκνων were
the Q reading, into a saying about Jesus' deeds.
He has done this "in order to identify Jesus with
Wisdom."[3]  Jesus is no longer just an official
voice of Wisdom, but he is Wisdom itself.[4]  For
Matthew Wisdom has made an "absolute and unqualified appearance in Jesus Christ."[5]  The deeds of

---

[1]Suggs, Wisdom, p. 37; and Schweizer,
Matthew, pp. 254, 260.

[2]Ibid., p. 265 cf. Strecker, Weg, p. 102.

[3]Suggs, Wisdom, p. 57.

[4]Christ, Jesus Sophia, p. 77 says: "Auch bei
Mt. erschient also Jesus nicht nur als Organ der
Weisheit, sondern als Weisheit selbst."

[5]Suggs, Wisdom, p. 57.

Wisdom in 11:19c refer back to the beginning of chapter 11 and the works of Jesus (i.e., 11:2=11:5), but they also refer to the whole sweep of Jesus' mighty works (δυνάμεις) in chapters 8-10 and in the pericope immediately following 11:19 (vv. 20-24). This, in turn, means that the deeds of Jesus justify Jesus as Sophia, that is, for Matthew Wisdom justifies itself.[1]

## Summary of Wisdom Christology in Matthew

If one compares the redaction of the evangelist here (11:2-19) with his redaction in 23:32-39, then several conclusions emerge. First, Matthew has identified Jesus with Wisdom (23:34). Secondly, this means that Matthew has assigned to Jesus Wisdom's role of sending envoys to Israel (ἐγὼ ἀποστέλλω), all of whom Israel has rejected (23:34-35, 37). Finally, Jesus came to Israel as Sophia itself and performed the deeds of Sophia, but he himself was rejected by Israel (11:16-19). Israel will be judged both for their rejection of Sophia's envoys and of Jesus-Sophia himself. Israel will lose the very presence of God, the Shekinah (23:38), when Jesus-Sophia withdraws his presence from them. They will not have God's presence again until Jesus-Sophia returns as the Son of Man (23:39).

Given this understanding of Matthean redaction and christology, one can easily understand why several commentators argue that Matthew reflects a view of history in which Sophia's

---

[1]Cf. the remark of Felix Christ: "Durch die Gleichsetzung der Werke der Weisheit mit den Werken Jesu hat Mt auch ἐδικαιώθη genauer bestimmt und historisiert: die Rechtfertigung ist bereits geschehen" (Jesus Sophia, p. 76).

spokespersons and Sophia itself are constantly
rejected. One can also see why they argue that
the evangelist understands Sophia, in the person
of Jesus, as one who seeks a dwelling in Israel,
is rejected, and withdraws to heaven until the
final consummation.[1] All commentators who hold
this understanding of Matthean christology agree
that certain texts from the Wisdom and apocalyptic
traditions form the background for Matthew's
Sophia christology and view of history.

There is a dispute among them on the point
of whether or not the background of Matthean
christology is a highly developed, cohesive myth
of Sophia's rejection and return to heaven. I
do not believe that there is enough extant textual
evidence to support the hypothesis of a highly
developed, pre-Matthean Sophia myth. However, I
do feel--and this is where most commentators
agree--that there is enough textual evidence to
support the hypothesis that a pre-Matthean
generalized picture of Sophia's rejection and
withdrawal existed, and that it constituted the
raw material out of which Matthew redacted his
Sophia christology. We will first review the
textual evidence which is agreed upon as the raw
material for a generalized picture of Wisdom's
rejection. Finally, we will summarize the
rejection motif in Matthew, which we believe

---

[1]Suggs, Wisdom, pp. 31-62; Christ, Jesus
Sophia, pp. 61-154; and Schweizer, Matthew, pp.
264-265, 446-447. James M. Robinson seems to
be concluding the same thing with each subsequent
article (cf. "Basic Shifts in German Theology,"
pp. 76-97; "LOGOI SOPHON: On the Gattung of Q,"
pp. 71-113; and "Jesus as Sophos and Sophia:
Wisdom Tradition and the Gospels," pp. 1-16).

supports the hypothesis of a Sophia christology
and Heilsgeschichte of rejection in the First
Gospel, and attempt to show that it culminates
at Matt. 23:32-24:2.

### Part 3.  Matthew's Motif of the
### Rejection of Jesus as Wisdom

#### The Pre-Matthean Picture of the
#### Rejection of Wisdom

The question we would like to address here
is: are there elements in the Wisdom tradition
from which Matthew could draw his redactional
picture of Israel's rejection of Jesus-Sophia and
his envoys?  As we have seen, it is unclear
whether or not there was a highly developed,
cohesive Wisdom myth to this effect.  Even Suggs
is more cautious at this point than most reviewers
seem to realize.[1]  We feel that there are enough
elements in pre-Matthean Wisdom texts to support
the hypothesis that a generalized picture of
Wisdom's rejection and withdrawal existed and
could have been used by Matthew in his portrait
of Jesus.[2]

A summary of this tradition would be that:
Wisdom seeks Israel through the Law and through
her messengers, but she is rejected and withdraws
her presence from them.  One text, for example,
says:

Wisdom cries aloud in the street; . . .

---

[1]Suggs, Wisdom, p. 44.

[2]For a comprehensive list of Wisdom texts
which deal with these mythical elements see the
chart in Christ, Jesus Sophia, pp. 158-163.

Because I have called and you refused to
listen, . . . I also will laugh at your
calamity; . . . Then they will call upon
me, but I will not answer; they will
seek me diligently but will not find
me (Prov. 1:20, 24, 26, 28).

Baruch 3:14 says that Wisdom was given to Israel
through the Law (cf. 3:37; 4:1), but she became
like a widow and "was left desolate because of
the sins of my children, because they turned away
from the law of God" (4:12 cf. 4:19). In 1 Enoch
93:8 the divided kingdom is depicted as the upshot
of those who have forsaken Wisdom. Unrighteousness follows in the wake of Wisdom's rejection
(cf. 1 Enoch 42:3). One of the signs of the end
of the age will be that "wisdom shall withdraw
into its chamber, and it shall be sought by many
but shall not be found, and unrighteousness and
unrestraint shall increase on earth" (2 Esd.
5:9b-10 cf. Prov. 1:28). According to Sirach
24:4 Wisdom declares: "I dwelt in high places,
and my throne was in a pillar of cloud." Here
Wisdom appears as the Shekinah, symbolized by the
"pillar of cloud" (cf. Exod. 33:9), and as the
Shekinah comes to dwell in the Jerusalem temple
(Sirach 24:8, 10, 11). In this tradition Wisdom
too seeks a home (24:7), but does not return to
heaven as other Wisdom writers suggest.[1] In
1 Enoch Wisdom is said to withdraw until her
return as the Son of Man (cf. 42:1-2). The
"spirit of Wisdom" dwells in the Son of Man (49:3
cf. 51:3), and 1 Enoch suggests that Wisdom as
the Son of Man shall return as judge (cf. 42:1-2;
51:3; 84:3; 92:1; Wisdom of Sol. 9:4). The locus
classicus for the withdrawal of Wisdom is

---

[1]Snaith, Ecclesiasticus, pp. 120-121.

1 Enoch 42:1-2:

> Wisdom found no place where she might dwell;
> Then a dwelling-place was assigned her in
> the heavens.  Wisdom returned to her place,
> And took her seat among the angels" (cf.
> 2 Baruch 48:24, 33, 36).

An important passage which depicts Wisdom as seeking Israel in every generation through messengers is Wisdom of Solomon 7:27: "in every generation she [Wisdom] passes into holy souls and makes them friends of God and prophets." This is the same transcendent Wisdom which is depicted in other passages as being inaccessible to men and women (cf. Job 28; Baruch 3:15; Sirach 24:4; Prov. 1:28).  Yet here Wisdom "goes about seeking those worthy of her" (Wisd. of Sol. 6:16) and "hastens to make herself known to those who desire her" (Wisd. of Sol. 6:13).  The Wisdom of Solomon 10-11 depicts how Wisdom works in each generation to choose her envoys.  Jacob and Joseph are given as examples of Wisdom's representatives (10:9-14), and it is claimed that through Moses Wisdom delivered the Israelites from Egypt (10:15-19 cf. Sirach 24:30-34; 11QPs[a] 1-4; Prov. 8:22-32).[1]

It is easy to see from this brief survey why many commentators (Bultmann, Suggs, Wilckens, F. Christ, et. al.) believe that these traces about Wisdom were developed into a coherent myth in which Wisdom sought a dwelling-place on earth, sent messengers to Israel in each generation,

---

[1]See Suggs, Wisdom, pp. 40-48.  See Robinson, "Jesus as Sophos and Sophia," pp. 1-15 for a history of the tradition concerning Wisdom's emissaries.

dwelt in Israel in the temple (as the Shekinah) until she was rejected, and finally withdrew to heaven until her return as the Son of Man.[1]

There is certainly a similarity between these elements in the Wisdom/apocalyptic traditions and the oracles in Matt. 23:34-36 and 23:37-39. Suggs is correct when he contends that:

> It is only a short step from the Wisdom of Solomon [7:27; 10-11] to the apocalyptic and fully deterministic view of history which is implied in our oracle. In the oracle of doom under consideration here [Matt. 23:34-36], the "prophetic generations" are represented as reckoned in advance by Sophia--from Abel to Zechariah; the meaning obviously is "from the first rejected 'friend of God' to the latest." Between these termini, we are expected to be able to interpolate the intervening generations. History is the story of the rejection and persecution of Wisdom's envoys. . . . From before creation,

---

[1]Wilckens, "σοφία," pp. 508-509. Part of the argument here is based upon the material found in the Similitudes (1 Enoch 37-71). The absence of the Similitudes from the Qumran materials has led to a debate as to whether or not they are pre-Synoptic. I cannot see that their date makes a great deal of difference for our discussion here since we are only trying to illustrate the kind of tradition which seems to appear, from whatever sources, in the First Gospel. Cf. J. C. Hindley, "Towards a Date for the Similitudes of Enoch: An Historical Approach," NTS 14 (1968): 551-565; and Suggs, Wisdom, p. 49.

> Wisdom knows the destiny of her prophets
> whose blood will be required of this γενεά.[1]

Our purpose is not to recapitulate the voluminous
literature on the debate about a Wisdom myth in
Judaism. Our only point is that many, if not all,
of these elements become focused in the oracles
of Matt. 23:34-36, 37-39. But, most importantly,
if Matthew has identified Jesus as Sophia-Shekinah
in 23:34-39, then for the evangelist Israel's
rejection is the rejection of <u>Jesus</u> as Sophia,
and of the envoys Jesus has sent, and of those he
continues to send (ἐγὼ ἀποστέλλω, 23:34). Suggs
and F. Christ have carefully analyzed the tradition history of the oracle in connection with the
Wisdom tradition, but the question which remains
is: does <u>Matthew</u> have a compositional theme of
rejection which would lend support to the contention that he views Israel's rejection of Jesus
as the rejection of Sophia? Succinctly, is there
any basis in the First Gospel, other than his
redactional activity in 11:2-19 and 23:32-39, to
indicate that he viewed the continued rejection
of Jesus' messengers as the rejection of Sophia's
messengers?[2]

## The Rejection Motif in Matthew

Virtually every Matthean commentator has
recognized that the evangelist engages in a

---

[1]Ibid., p. 21. See also Christ, <u>Jesus
Sophia</u>, p. 142; and Ernest G. Clarke, <u>The Wisdom
of Solomon</u>, The Cambridge Bible Commentary
(Cambridge: University Press, 1973), p. 66.

[2]Cf. Suggs, <u>Wisdom</u>, pp. 21, 60-61.

polemic. Although the target of Matthew's polemic has been variously identified, there is a consensus among researchers that his polemic involves the idea that "Israel" (however it is defined) has rejected Jesus and that Jesus has, in turn, rejected Israel.[1] Israel's rejection of

---

[1]See Ellis, Matthew: His Mind and His Message, pp. 114-125. Various suggestions have been offered as the background of Matthew's polemic: (1) against the Synagogenverband (see Blair, Jesus in the Gospel of Matthew, pp. 99-102, 141, 161; Senior, Matthew: A Gospel for the Church, pp. 72-77; Georg Strecker, "The Concept of History in Matthew," JAAR 35 [1967]: 225; Ellis, Matthew: His Mind and His Message, pp. 4-8, 32-37, 47-59; Stendahl, School, pp. xi-xii; and Reinhart Hummel, Die Auseinandersetzung zwischen Kirche und Judentum im Matthäusevangelium, Beiträge zur evangelischen Theologie, vol. 33 [München: Chr. Kaiser Verlag, 1963], pp. 28-33 [hereafter cited as Hummel, Auseinandersetzung]); (2) against "false prophets" (see Eduard Schweizer, "Observance of the Law and Charismatic Activity in Matthew," NTS 15 [1970]: 213-230; Davies, Sermon on the Mount, pp. 199-208; and Gerhard Barth, "Matthew's Understanding of the Law," TI, pp. 159-164); (3) against Gnostics (cf. Davies, Sermon on the Mount, pp. 193-208); (4) against Jamnia (cf. Ibid., pp. 272-315; Ellis, Matthew: His Mind and His Message, pp. 5-6, 36 n. 27; Kilpatrick, Gospel According to St. Matthew, pp. 109-123; Stendahl, School, p. xii n. 1; and Hare, Theme of Jewish Persecution, p. 168); and (5) against Paulinists (cf. Davies, Sermon on the Mount, pp. 316-341; and Barth, "Matthew's Understanding of the Law," TI, pp. 159-164).

Jesus is, of course, a traditional motif in the Synoptic tradition. What is distinctive about Matthew's redaction of this motif, as we hope to show below, is that he not only has the traditional feature of Israel's rejection of Jesus culminate in the passion story (cf. 27:25), but he also emphasizes Jesus' rejection of Israel. This latter theme, as we argue below, culminates in the same context in which the evangelist has identified Jesus with Wisdom (23:34-24:2). The redaction of the evangelist makes it clear that for him Jesus' rejection of Israel means the withdrawal of Wisdom from them. In the same context, though, it becomes clear that for Matthew Israel has rejected <u>Wisdom</u> and the emissaries sent by Wisdom (cf. 23:34-39). In other words, Matthew has redacted the traditional Christian motif of Israel's rejection of Jesus so that it adheres to the pre-Matthean tradition of Wisdom's rejection. The rejection motif, then, moves in two directions in the First Gospel: Israel's rejection of Jesus and his rejection of Israel. Let us briefly summarize the motif in Matthew.

## Israel's rejection of Jesus

Israel's rejection of Jesus is foreshadowed at the beginning of the gospel. When the Magi come to Herod and inquire about the birth of the "king of the Jews," the news not only troubles Herod but "all Jerusalem" as well (2:2-3), and an attempt is made to kill Jesus (2:16). The rejection of Jesus which is foreshadowed in 2:3 and 16, however, is not clarified for the reader until the parable of the children in the market place. Israel, as "this generation" (11:16), is condemned for their rejection of the deeds of John and

Jesus (11:16-19).[1]  However, Israel's rejection of
Jesus, as the last of God's messengers and as the
<u>sender</u> of the messengers (ἐγὼ ἀποστέλλω, 23:34),
is certainly implied in Israel's rejection of
God's messengers who precede him.  Israel rejected
John's message and said that "he has a demon."
They later reject Jesus' message and make the same
accusation against him (9:34 cf. 12:24).[2]

The first explicit reference to Israel's
rejection of Jesus appears in 9:3 where the
scribes accuse Jesus of blasphemy because he has
forgiven the sins of the paralytic.  The rejection
theme appears in 9:34 when the Pharisees conclude:
"He casts out demons by the prince of demons."  In
the sabbath controversy (12:1-14), when Jesus
proclaims that "the Son of Man is lord of the
sabbath" (12:8) and that his disciples can break
the sabbath law (v. 2), the rejection theme is
enhanced as Matthew concludes with the first
reference to the Pharisees' plot to kill Jesus
(12:14 cf. Mark 3:6).  Jesus' declaration that
"something greater than the temple is here" (12:6)
should be noted.  Now an anti-temple polemic seems
to intertwine with the rejection motif.  The
claims that the Son of Man (Jesus) is Lord of the
sabbath, that his disciples were free from the
Jewish regulations concerning the sabbath, and the
implication that Jesus himself is greater than the
temple, arouse the ultimate hostility--murder--
from the Pharisees.  Israel's rejection of Jesus
culminates in the evangelist's rendering of the

---

[1]See the discussion above on pp. 88-92.
See also Ellis, <u>Matthew: His Mind and His
Message</u>, p. 117.

[2]Ibid., p. 116.

passion (26:47-27:66).  Jesus is condemned to
death on the charge of blasphemy because he has
accepted the titles "Christ" and "Son of God"
(26:63-65), and "all the people" accept the
responsibility for his death sentence with the
cry: "His blood be on us and on our children"
(27:25).[1]  The Jewish rejection of Jesus is

---

[1]See Hare, Theme of Jewish Persecution, pp.
134-141.  Several points which highlight the
evangelist's redaction in the passion narrative
are worthy of notice.  The Jews come together
twice to plot Jesus' death (26:3-4; 27:1), and
once they try to make certain that he "stayed
dead" (27:62-66).  The money used to pay Judas to
betray Jesus is called "blood money" by the Jews
(27:4).  The Jews left the choice up to Judas by
saying: "See to it yourself" (27:4), but notice
that the priests do accept the money (27:6a), thus
implicitly assuming the responsibility for Jesus'
death.  The Jews are again given a choice concerning Jesus in the trial before Pilate.  Pilate,
in almost identical words as the Jewish leaders
themselves, says "I am innocent of this man's
blood; see to it yourselves [italics mine]"
(27:24).  The Jewish leaders had decided already
in their own trial that Jesus deserved to die
(26:66), and now "all the people" accept the
responsibility for Jesus' death with a cry which
corresponds to an admission of guilt (cf. Jer.
26:15).  (See J. A. Fitzmyer, "Anti-Semitism and
the Cry of 'All the People' [Mt 27:25]," ThS 26
[1965]: 677-681; Senior, Matthew: A Gospel for the
Church, pp. 75-76; and Ellis, Matthew: His Mind
and His Message, pp. 116-117).  To put it
succinctly, I do not believe that the theme of
Israel's rejection of Jesus in Matthew can be reduced to mean only the Jewish leaders, but it
applies to Israel as a whole (see appendix 1).

complete when "all the people" accept the responsibility for his death.[1]

## Jesus' rejection of Israel

The consequence of Israel's rejection of Jesus is that Israel is, in turn, rejected by him and loses her privileged place in salvation-history. The theme of Jesus' rejection of Israel becomes explicit in chapter 11, but it too is implicit at least as early as chapter 3. In the evangelist's presentation of John's preaching to the Pharisees and Sadducees (3:7 cf. Luke 3:7), John concludes with the warning that "Even now the axe is laid to the root of the trees; every tree therefore that does not bear good fruit is cut down and thrown into the fire" (3:10). In the story of the healing of the Centurion's servant (8:5-13), Jesus marvels at the faith of this Roman, and he contrasts it with faith in Israel by saying "not even in Israel have I found such faith" (8:10). Jesus then foretells that "the sons of the kingdom will be thrown into outer darkness" (8:12 cf. 21:43).

As mentioned, Jesus' rejection of Israel becomes explicit in chapter 11. Israel is "this generation" which would accept neither John nor Jesus (11:16-19), and it is clear that Israel will be judged for their rejection of these messengers (11:20-24). In 12:38-42 Israel ("this generation," 12:42) is condemned again because they

---

[1]See John R. Donahue, "Passion Narrative," IDB, supplementary volume, ed. Keith Crim (Nashville: Abingdon Press, 1976), p. 644; and, Nils A. Dahl, "The Passion Narrative in Matthew," Jesus in the Memory of the Early Church (Minneapolis: Augsburg Publishing House, 1976), pp. 47-48.

refuse to recognize Jesus who is "greater than Jonah" and "greater than Solomon." Indeed, as Ellis contends: "The whole of the narrative in chs 11-12 has as its redactional purpose to draw the lines between the true and the pseudo-Israel."[1]

Some commentators see the definitive line now drawn between "Israel" and the true followers of Jesus, his disciples (cf. 12:48-50), as a theme which continues until the end of the gospel. The distinction Matthew has drawn seems to be very clear in his contrast between the "crowds" and the "disciples."[2] Ellis, for example, claims that:

> In the parable discourse (ch 13), the lines already drawn are now taken for granted. Pseudo-Israel is presented as "those outside the house" (13:1) to whom Jesus speaks in parables because, as he tells his disciples, "the mysteries of the kingdom are revealed to you, but they are not revealed to them" (13:11) and because "they (pseudo-Israel) look without seeing and listen without hearing or understanding" (13:13). The true Israel is presented as those "inside the house" (13:36), who have revealed to them "the mysteries of the kingdom" (13:11), and to whom it can be said: "Happy are

_____

[1]Ellis, Matthew: His Mind and His Message, pp. 117-118; cf. Rigaux, Testimony of St. Matthew, pp. 139-140.

[2]See the discussion on ὄχλος in Matthew in appendix 1 below.

104

your eyes because they see, your ears
because they hear" (13:16).[1]

Although the definition of "Israel" at this point
is not clear,[2] it is clear that from chapter 14 on
Jesus directs his teaching primarily to his
disciples and away from the Jews.[3]  A closer
examination of 13:10-17 supports this distinction.
At this point (chap. 13) in the First Gospel
Israel only loses the benefit of Jesus' teaching.
Later, as we shall see, Israel totally loses the
presence of Jesus (cf. 24:1).

---

[1]Ellis, Matthew: His Mind and His Message,
p. 118.

[2]It is difficult to define what "Israel"
means in Matthew's gospel until one defines the
relation which Matthew's church has to the Judaism
of its day.  This is an extremely complex question
on which no consensus of opinion has been reached.
Sjef van Tilborg has argued that "Israel" means
only the religious leaders who led the people
astray in Jesus' day (see van Tilborg, Jewish
Leaders, pp. 46-67).  Hare contends that Matthew
does not separate the leaders from the people and
that "Israel" thus means all the people of Israel
(Hare, Theme of Jewish Persecution, pp. 151-152
cf. p. 94).  J. D. Kingsbury argues that "Israel"
denotes "the Jews" and that Matthew does not limit
them geographically to Palestine (Kingsbury, The
Parables of Jesus in Matthew 13 [Atlanta: John
Knox Press, 1969], p. 67).  It will become evident
in what follows that our research tends to
support Kingsbury's thesis.

[3]Ellis, Matthew: His Mind and His Message,
p. 118.

Jesus withdraws his teaching
from Israel: Matt. 13:10-17

Matthew 13:10-17, constructed in antithetic
parallelism, serves to distinguish between the
disciples (ὑμῖν, v. 11b), to whom the "secrets of
the kingdom" have been given, and the Jews
(ἐκείνοις), from whom the secrets are withheld
(v. 11c). Jesus privately tells his disciples
about both their privileged standing and the
judgment which has befallen the Jews.[1] Because
the Jews do not have "the secrets of the kingdom,"
this means that they have lost their prerogatives
as God's chosen people. As Kingsbury puts it,
" . . . their loss is, ultimately, nothing less
than that of the kingdom itself and of eternal
fellowship with God (25:29f; cf. 8:12)."[2]

The rejection of Israel in this passage is
further enhanced by the reason Jesus gives for
speaking in parables: "This is why I speak to them
in parables, because seeing they do not see, and
hearing they do not hear, nor do they understand"
(13:13). First, Matthew has changed Mark's ἵνα
(4:12) to ὅτι. Mark's implication is that Jesus
speaks in parables in order that the people might
not understand, but Matthew's implication is that
their inability to understand is a condition which
has existed for many generations because of their
obduracy. This is certainly the point of the
quotation from Isaiah 6:9-10 (vv. 14-15) which

---

[1]Kingsbury, Parables of Jesus in Matthew
13, p. 47.

[2]Ibid., p. 48.

Matthew has inserted at this point.[1]  Furthermore,
since Matt. 13:13 directly answers the question
of 13:10 ("Why do you speak to them in parables?"), which refers back to ὄχλοι πολλοί
(v. 2), it is clear that Israel as a whole is
condemned here.[2]  Jesus' rejection of Israel in
13:10-17 has an eschatological note of finality
in it.  As the End approaches, the crisis becomes
more acute and the rejection of Israel becomes
more complete.[3]

---

[1]Hare, Theme of Jewish Persecution, p. 149.
When Isa. 6:9-10 is cited outside of the Synoptic
tradition, it is used explicitly to refer to the
Jewish rejection of Jesus himself (cf. John
12:37-40) or of their rejection of the Gospel
(cf. Acts 28:23-28).  In the Johannine context
the implication is that Israel's obduracy is part
of God's plan (12:40).  In Acts the implication
is that the Gospel is preached to the Gentiles
because the Jews rejected it (28:28).  Both of
these themes could be present in Matthew (see
appendix 4).  The importance of the theme of
Israel's obduracy for Matthew might be seen in the
fact that this is the only fulfillment quotation
in his gospel which is placed on the lips of
Jesus himself (see Schweizer, Matthew, p. 299;
and Peter von der Osten-Sacken, "Leistung und
Grenze der johaneischen Kreuzestheologie," EvTh
36 [1976]: 154-176).

[2]Trilling, Wahre, p. 78; and Kingsbury,
Parables of Jesus in Matthew 13, p. 49.

[3]Rigaux, Testimony of St. Matthew, p. 140.

The theme of Israel's rejection is sounded again and again (15:7-9, 12-14; 16:12), but the next salient place is the "Parable of the Wicked Tenants" (21:33-46 par. Mark 12:1-12). The evangelist adds this conclusion to the parable: "Therefore I tell you, the kingdom of God will be taken away from you and given to a nation (ἔθνει) producing the fruits of it" (21:43). Jesus is teaching in the temple (cf. 23:12, 23), and he is addressing the Pharisees and the chief priests (21:23 cf. 21:45). The vineyard (vv. 33, 39-41) was a traditional symbol for Israel whose owner was God (cf. Isa. 5:1-7).[1] The tenants rejected every servant the owner sent to them (vv. 34-36), and they finally killed the owner's son (v. 38). The servants are symbolic of the prophets whom God has sent to Israel over the generations, and the son, of course, for Matthew is Jesus himself.[2] Because Israel will reject the son, Jesus concludes that the kingdom of God will be taken from them (21:43 cf. v. 45). God's judgment is thus pronounced over the Jewish nation and the kingdom, whether eschatological or a present relationship,[3]

---

[1]Jeremias, Parables of Jesus, pp. 70-71; cf. Hare, Theme of Jewish Persecution, p. 151.

[2]Senior, Matthew: A Gospel for the Church, p. 74; cf. Jeremias' remark: "This 'parable', if from Jesus, is unique because it is 'pure allegory.'" (See Jeremias, Parables of Jesus, p. 70.)

[3]Hare, Theme of Jewish Persecution, p. 153.

will be taken from them[1] and given to the ἔϑνος.[2]

The theme of Jesus' rejection of Israel is continued in the "woes" against the Pharisees and scribes (23:1-36). The evangelist ends this section with the lament over Jerusalem (23:37-39), a Q saying (cf. Luke 13:34-35), so that the position in which Matthew has placed this saying sheds light upon his theme of the rejection of Israel. It does not mean simply the rejection of the Jewish leaders,[3] but it means that Israel <u>as a whole</u> is rejected.[4]  These are Jesus' last words

---

[1]Barth, "Matthew's Understanding of the Law," pp. 111-112. Barth suggests that this means that Matthew's church is in a situation in which "the fronts against Judaism are not completely hardened" (Ibid., p. 112).

[2]Hare, <u>Theme of Jewish Persecution</u>, p. 153 takes ἔϑνος to mean the Church. Others, however, connect this verse with Matt. 28:19 and refer it to the "Gentiles" in general (e.g., Schweizer, <u>Matthew</u>, p. 414). See the discussion of Matt. 24:14 below for our conclusion concerning ἔϑνος in that context.

[3]Contrast Sjef van Tilborg, <u>Jewish Leaders in Matthew</u>, pp. 67-70.

[4]Hare, <u>Theme of Jewish Persecution</u>, p. 152. This seems to be the case whether or not ὁ οἶκος ὑμῶν can be restricted to mean "the temple" (see Davies, <u>Sermon on the Mount</u>, pp. 298-300; and Hare, <u>Theme of Jewish Persecution</u>, p. 154).

to the crowds (cf. 23:1) which, of course, include
the Jewish leaders.[1]  "House" (οἶκος) in Matt.
23:38 could mean the temple or the city, but,
however it is interpreted, Matthew's use of γάρ
in 23:39 clearly shows that for him the departure
of God's presence from His/Her house, in the
person of Jesus, is the fulfillment of God's
judgment heralded long ago by the prophets.
Matthew 23:39, which addresses all Jerusalem (cf.
v. 37), affirms that God's presence will withdraw
from the city until the Parousia of Jesus.[2]
Jesus' lament over the city also means that the
commonwealth will be deserted.  This is ultimately
borne out in the trial scene when "all the people"
(πᾶς ὁ λαός) cry out: "His blood be on us and on
our children" (27:25).[3]

---

[1]J. C. Fenton, The Gospel of St. Matthew,
The Pelican New Testament Commentaries
(Baltimore: Penguin Books, 1963), p. 355.

[2]Schweizer, Matthew, pp. 444-445.  Schweizer
assumes that Israel is not definitively rejected.
As we discuss below, we do not see any future
mission to or a conversion of Israel by Matthew's
church.

[3]Hare, Theme of Jewish Persecution, p. 150;
Donahue, "Passion Narrative," p. 644.  Matthew
uses ὁ λαός in 27:25 with an ethnic connotation
so that it includes the whole people of Israel
(Fitzmyer, "Mt 27:25," pp. 677-681).

## Summary of Matthew's
## Rejection Motif

In Matthew Jesus rejects Israel because they rejected him. Our argument is that the evangelist's rejection motif should be interpreted in light of his Sophia christology. Jesus as Sophia has come to dwell in Israel for their salvation (cf. 1:21). The presence of Jesus in Israel is the very presence of God (cf. 1:23). Israel, however, rejects Jesus and his presence is withdrawn from them (cf. 23:32-39). Our contention is that these themes culminate in the same context in Matthew, namely, 23:32-24:1-2. We have already investigated most of this context, but let us briefly summarize our conclusions.

In the time of Jesus ("this generation," 23:36) Israel consummates its perpetual rejection of God's messengers (23:32, 34-35, 37a). For Matthew it is Jesus who has sent all of the messengers to the previous generations of Israel (23:34). This was Jesus' function as the Wisdom of God (cf. 23:34; Luke 11:49). The difference for "this generation" is that now Jesus himself has come as Sophia, but he too is rejected. Israel's rejection of Jesus as Sophia evokes his pronouncement of judgment: "your house is forsaken" (23:38). Jesus as Sophia will withdraw his presence from Israel, and they will not have the presence of God again until he returns as the Son of Man (23:39). What we would like to show now is that the motif of Jesus' rejection and withdrawal from Israel culminates in Matthew when Jesus (as Sophia) leaves the temple in 24:1 (the theme of Israel's rejection of Jesus culminates in the passion narrative). In Matthew's gospel Jesus never enters the temple again after 24:1. After he leaves the temple in 24:1, Israel has lost both the teaching and the presence of Jesus-Sophia. In other words, Matthew has the motif of Jesus' rejection of Israel culminate in

111

the same context in which he identifies Jesus as
Sophia (23:34), in which judgment is pronounced
upon Israel for their rejection of Sophia's envoys
(23:32-36, 37-39), and in which Jesus as Sophia
withdraws from them (23:39; 24:1). The culmination of this motif here is not accidental. For
the evangelist Israel's rejection of Jesus is the
story of their rejection of Wisdom and its messengers. We feel that Matthew's rejection motif
gives compositional support to the thesis that the
evangelist views salvation history in terms of
Israel's rejection of Wisdom and Wisdom's
consequent withdrawal from them.

### Part 4. Jesus-Sophia's Definitive Withdrawal from Israel (24:1-2)

The point we would like to make in our
exegesis of Matt. 24:1-2 is this: that for Matthew
Jesus' departure from the temple in 24:1 constitutes  Sophia's permanent abandonment of Israel,
an abandonment which fulfills the judgment pronounced in 23:38. We will argue that ἐξελθών
(24:1) denotes the termination of Jesus' teaching
activity among the Jews, and that ἱερόν in 24:1
is synonymous in its Matthean context with οἶκος
in 23:38. This means, then, that when Jesus
definitively terminates his preaching in the
temple (ἐξελθών, 24:1), he is fulfilling the
judgment which he pronounced upon Israel's house
in 23:38. Israel loses the presence of Jesus
until his Parousia as the Son of Man (cf. 23:39).
At that time he will render eschatologically final
the judgment (the loss of Jesus' presence) which
had taken place in his lifetime.

### The Context of 24:1-2

We have already discussed how the evangelist's redaction required us to read 23:32-36

112

with 23:37-39. In that context Jesus speaks as Sophia (23:34) and pronounces judgment upon Israel (23:38). We also discussed how 23:32 changed the style into an apocalyptic oracle and effected a smooth transition to the prediction of Jerusalem's destruction.[1] Now we would like to discuss more fully how Matthean redaction has placed 23:32-39 and 24:1-2 in the same context. The point would be, of course, that the Jesus of 23:32-39, who is Jesus as Sophia, is the same Jesus who leaves the temple in 24:1.

First, the evangelist has omitted the story of the "Widow's Mite" which comes immediately after the Jerusalem saying in both Mark and Luke (cf. Mark 12:41-44; Luke 21:1-4). There is a consensus among interpreters that Matthew has omitted this pericope in order to link directly καὶ ἐξελθὼν ὁ Ἰησοῦς ἀπὸ τοῦ ἱεροῦ ἐπορεύετο with ἰδοὺ ἀφίεται ὑμῖν ὁ οἶκος ὑμῶν (23:38). Lambrecht expresses the opinion of many commentators:

> The fact that Matthew has omitted the section about the widow's penny (Mk., XII,41-44) deserves more attention. Because of that, in Matthew the intro- duction to the eschatological discourse follows immediately the Woes (ch. XXIII). It seems that this omission is not without purpose: Matthew obviously wants to connect the announcement of XXIV,2 with that of XXIII,38.[2]

Obviously, Matthew has connected 23:38 with 24:1

---

[1]See the discussion above on pp. 58-63.

[2]Lambrecht, "The Parousia Discourse," p. 314.

113

also, and we would argue that this is just as important as its relation with 24:2.[1]  But, however one might interpret Matthew's omission of the pericope, surely the <u>general</u> point is that it directly links 23:37-39 (which is also linked to 23:32-36) with 24:1-2.[2]

Secondly, Psa. 118:26 is quoted in Matt. 23:39.  In Luke 13:35 the same quotation refers to the entry of Jesus into Jerusalem.  Matthew has placed the Jerusalem saying (23:37-39) <u>after</u> Jesus' entry into Jerusalem (cf. 21:9).  It <u>is</u> clear that the quotation does not refer to Jesus' entry into the city, but, as the context shows, to the <u>future</u> coming of Jesus as the Son of Man. E. Arens' conclusion is pertinent here: "The Triumphant Entry already having taken place, the phrase οὐ μή με ἴδητε ἀπ' ἄρτι ἕως ἂν εἴπητε Εὐλογημένος etc. can only have an eschatological meaning and very probably refers to his Second Coming."[3]  Both of the expressions λέγω γάρ and ἀπ' ἄρτι, the latter of which is a phrase peculiar to Matthean eschatology (cf. 26:29, 64), point to Jesus' Parousia.  The Parousia is then

---

[1]E.g., Schweizer says: " . . . Matthew has left out the story of the widow's offering . . . in order to connect 24:1-2 closely with chapter 23.  Thus Jesus' departure from the temple [24:1] is appended directly to 23:38-39."  (Schweizer, <u>Matthew</u>, p. 448.)

[2]M'Neile, <u>St. Matthew</u>, p. 342; cf. Hill, <u>Matthew</u>, p. 318.

[3]Arens, <u>ELTHON</u>, p. 294.  We agree with Arens' main point although we would not refer to Jesus' advent as the "Second Coming."

discussed immediately in the subsequent discourse (chap. 24).[1] Matthew's redaction of Psa. 118:26--placing it after the entry into Jerusalem and before the eschatological discourse, and his additions of λέγω γάρ and άπ' άρτι--strongly links it with 24:1-2.

Thirdly, there is thematic unity between 23:37-39 and 24:1-2. Jesus enters the temple at 21:23, in 23:38 he announces it desolation, and in 24:1 he leaves it for the last time.[2] The words of Jesus in 23:39 (ού μή με ίδητε άπ' άρτι) are concretely fulfilled in 24:1 when Jesus leaves the temple. Jesus does not enter the temple again, and from this point on in the First Gospel he teaches only his disciples. For example, he refuses to answer directly the question of the High Priest even though he is <u>adjured</u> to do so (26:63). Jesus only reiterates the basic thought of 23:39 and says that "from this time on" (άπ' άρτι) he will only be seen as the triumphant Son of Man.[3] Furthermore, Jesus will not be "recognized" by Israel again from 23:39 on in the First Gospel (cf. 27:39-44, 45-56). At Jesus' death the temple veil is rent (27:50-51) as proof that God (and Jesus) has left Israel's "house" to them (23:38). It is only at the End, at his Parousia, that Israel will recognize Jesus.[4]

---

[1]Stendahl, <u>School</u>, p. 93; see also Hill, <u>Matthew</u>, p. 316.

[2]Ibid., p. 319.   [3]Schweizer, <u>Matthew</u>, 499.

[4]Joachim Lange, <u>Das Erscheinen des Auferstandenen im Evangelium nach Mattäus. Eine traditions-und redaktions-geschichliche Untersuchung zu Mt 28,16-20</u>, Forschung zur Bibel, vol. 11 (Würzburg: Echter Verlag, 1973), pp. 335-338 (hereafter cited as Lange, <u>Erscheinen</u>).

Finally, if οἶκος ("house") in 23:38 is synonymous with ἱεροῦ ("temple") in 24:1, as we hope to show, then the argument is even stronger for reading 23:37-39 and 24:1 in the same context.

In summary, Matthew has clearly structured the context of 24:1-2. The evangelist's omission of the story of the Widow's Mite, his use of Psa. 118:26 to allude to Jesus' Parousia rather than to his entrance into Jerusalem, the thematic unity (Jesus in the temple--Jesus' departure from the temple), and the synonymy of οἶκος (23:38) and ἱεροῦ (24:1), clearly show that Matthew intends 23:37-39 (and consequently 23:32-36) to be read with 24:1-2. Jesus does not magically turn into the apocalyptic Son of Man in 24:1. He is still the Jesus-Sophia of 23:32-39, and when his presence leaves the temple in 24:1, the judgment of 23:38 is fulfilled.

### Jesus Leaves the Temple (24:1a)

Matthew describes Jesus' departure from the temple in these terms: καὶ ἐξελθὼν ὁ Ἰησοῦς ἀπὸ τοῦ ἱεροῦ ἐπορεύετο. Mark has the much smoother καὶ ἐκπορευομένου αὐτοῦ ἐκ τοῦ ἱεροῦ (13:1). In this section we would like to show that Matt. 24:1 is the culmination of the motif of Jesus' rejection of Israel. This is expressed in characteristic Matthean style, namely, his use of ἐξέρχομαι, through his presentation of Jesus' departure from the temple. In 24:1 the evangelist is not simply describing Jesus' walk out of the temple, but his permanent abandonment of it in judgment.

First, the use of ἐξέρχομαι is character-istic of Matthean style. The evangelist consis-tently uses the aorist participle as an intro-ductory participle in order to link pericopae

with the preceding material.[1]  Matthew usually has
the aorist participle followed by an aorist indicative.[2]  Whenever the evangelist wants two actions
to belong to the same event, he consistently puts
the preparatory aorist participle and follows it
with the aorist of the main verb.[3]  In 24:1,
however, Matthew has the aorist participle
(ἐξελθών) followed by an imperfect (ἐπορεύετο).
Most commentators agree that the evangelist has
the aorist participle and the imperfect, in contrast to Mark's imperfect, in order to suggest
that Jesus has left the temple in a definitive way
(ἐξελθών) and is now beginning a new activity
(ἐπορεύετο).  The emphasis in Matthew, in other
words, is on Jesus' going away. Lambrecht
summarizes it this way: "Jesus has left the
temple.  It is while he is going away (ἐπορεύετο:
imperf. and used absolutely) that the disciples
approach him and point out the temple buildings
to him.  Not so in Mark."[4]  When Mark has a
compound verb followed by the same preposition, as
in 13:1 (ἐκπορευομένου--ἐκ), it is also characteristic for Matthew to omit the compounded

---

[1]Klostermann, Matthäus, p. 10.  E.g.,
εἰσελθών (9:25; 22:11; 26:58); προσελθών (4:23;
8:2, 19; 9:18; 18:21; 21:28, 30; 25:20, 22, 24;
26:39, 49; 27:58; 28:2, 18).

[2]See the discussion in Schlatter, Matthäus,
p. 23; and Lambrecht, "Parousia Discourse,"
p. 34 n. 5.

[3]See the literature cited in Barth,
"Matthew's Understanding of the Law," p. 59 n. 9.

[4]Lambrecht, "Parousia Discourse," p. 34 n.
5.

preposition and substitute another verb or another preposition for it (ἐξελθών--ἀπό).[1]  Both ἐξελθών and ἐπορεύετο clearly show that it is Matthean redaction at work in 24:1.

If the context determines the meaning of a word, then Matthew's use of ἐξέρχομαι in 24:1 is basically clear.  Jesus' departure from the temple in 24:1 culminates the theme of Jesus' rejection of Israel.  Ἐξελθών in 24:1 does not mean that Jesus simply left the temple on this occasion as on other occasions.  Ἐξελθών denotes that Jesus terminated his activity in the temple and left it in judgment.  Ἐξελθών in 24:1 denotes a turning point in Jesus' work in accordance with the divine plan.  Judgment is now fulfilled against an un-believing Israel.

Furthermore, 23:37-39, which immediately precedes 24:1, should be read in the same context. Jesus pronounces the judgment in 23:38 that "your house is forsaken."  This verse in Matthew occurs between the promise against "this generation" (23:36) and the prediction of the temple's destruction (24:1-2).  The general meaning of Jesus' departure from the temple is clear: "The abandonment of Israel by God is then symbolized by the departure of the Messiah and his disciples from the Temple and the city to the Mount of

---

[1]When it is used of Jesus, the general function of ἐξέρχομαι in Matthew is to denote the beginning or termination of some divine activity. The theological use of ἐξέρχομαι in Matthew might be more important than we have emphasized (see appendix 5).

Olives (24:1, 3). The abandonment is permanent."[1]

The full significance, though, of Jesus' departure from the temple can be seen only when it is clear who Jesus is for the evangelist in this passage. From our exegetical discussion above, it is clear that the Jesus who leaves the temple in 24:1 is also for Matthew the Wisdom of God. Jesus' departure from the temple is the culmination of the theme of his rejection of Israel. Now Jesus, who is Wisdom-Shekinah, leaves the temple. When Jesus leaves the temple in 24:1, God Himself/Herself departs from Israel.[2]

Matthew uses ἐξέρχομαι in his character-istic fashion (as an aorist participle) to express a great turning point in Jesus' ministry and in salvation history: Israel has lost the presence of God because of the departure of Jesus-Sophia from the temple. The kingdom has now been taken away from them (cf. Matt. 21:43) and their house stands forsaken and desolate (cf. Matt. 23:38).

## The Relation of Ἱεροῦ (24:1) to Οἶκος (23:38)

### Introduction

We have already shown that Matt. 23:38 is to be read in the same context as 24:1.[3] We have

---

[1]Hare, _Jewish Persecution_, p. 154. See also Ellis, _Matthew_, p. 119; and Steck, _Israel und das gewaltsame Geschick der Propheten_, p. 293 n. 4.

[2]Schweizer, _Matthew_, p. 408.

[3]See the discussion above, pp. 112-116.

also suggested that Jesus' departure from the
temple fulfills the judgment which he pronounced
in 23:38: "Behold, your house (οἶκος) is forsaken." If Jesus' departure from the temple
(ἱεροῦ) in 24:1 fulfills the judgment which was
pronounced in 23:38, as we are contending, then
the question is: what is the relation between
οἶκος and ἱεροῦ for the evangelist in this context? In other words, if Jesus' departure from
the temple in 24:1 does culminate the rejection
theme in the First Gospel and fulfills the judgment of 23:38, then upon whom does this judgment
fall? Is the judgment only upon the temple (as
anti-temple polemic), or only upon the Jewish
leaders, or upon just the city of Jerusalem, or
is it upon <u>all</u> of the Jewish people? This is not
an insignificant question because the answer to it
will determine how one reads the subsequent discourse (24:3-31). We contend that Matthew intends
οἶκος and ἱεροῦ to signify all of Israel from the
time of Jesus until the End of the Age. When
Jesus-Sophia leaves the temple in 24:1, the very
presence of God leaves all Israel forever. Jesus
seals this indictment by his pronouncement concerning the temple's destruction (24:2), and, as
we will show, the redaction of the evangelist has
a caesura between 24:2 and 24:3. Jesus-Sophia has
definitively turned his back in judgment upon
Israel (24:1-2), but in 24:3 he turns to those
who have accepted him (the disciples) and leaves
them his testament before he goes to his death
(cf. 26:1-2).

ʾΙεροῦ and οἶκος

As we begin to investigate the relation
between οἶκος and ἱεροῦ in the Matthean context,
we have to allow for the possibility that the
evangelist's use of ἱερόν might be significant

120

even though it is not redactional (cf. Mark 13:1).[1] It is often not possible to make any distinction between ἱερόν and ναός even though, generally speaking, ἱερόν is a much more comprehensive term.[2] Ναός can mean only the sacred sanctuary, but ἱερόν usually includes almost all of the temple precincts and, at times, even the temple hill.[3] The disciples' question in 24:1

---

[1]Ναός is used nine times in Matthew (cf. 23:16[2], 17, 21, 35; 26:61; 27:5, 40, 51).

[2]There is often no real distinction between ναός and ἱερόν in either meaning or in range (Otto Michel, "ναός," TDNT 4:882 cf. p. 884 n. 19). The uses of ναός in Matt. 23 seem to refer specifically to the sanctuary, and seem to be sayings from before C.E. 70 which the evangelist incorporated into his gospel (Schweizer, Matthew, p. 433. This is not to suggest that Matthew was written before 70).
On the other hand, ναός has a broader meaning than just the sanctuary for Matthew. Matthew 27:5 says that Judas cast 30 shekels εἰς τὸν ναόν, but "If ναός is taken to mean the temple in the narrower sense, one may ask how Judas could bring the money into it, since only priests were allowed access. We may thus assume that it is used in a broader sense, as in Jn" (Michel, "ναός," p. 884; see also Allen, St. Matthew, p. 287; and Schrenk, "ἱερόν," p. 235).

[3]Ibid., pp. 232-233; W. F. Stinespring, "Temple, Jerusalem," IDB 4:551; Ezra P. Gould, A Critical and Exegetical Commentary on the Gospel According to St. Mark (New York: Scribner's, 1905), p. 241; and Vincent Taylor, The Gospel According to St. Mark (London: Macmillan, 1955), p. 457.

makes it clear that ἱερόν alludes to the whole
temple complex. The disciples point out to Jesus
"the buildings of the temple" (τὰς οἰκοδομὰς τοῦ
ἱεροῦ).[1] Thus, it seems that congruent with the
general meaning of the word, ἱερόν in 24:1 refers
to the whole temple complex. But, since it is to
be read in the same context with οἶκος (23:38),
the question becomes: how does οἶκος modify the
meaning of ἱερόν?

In the exegesis above we saw that the
meaning of the pronouncement in 23:38 was that if
God's presence abandoned the temple, then the
whole nation was doomed. Matthew's redaction of
23:38-39 utilizes the implied concept of the
Shekinah's departure from the temple, and consequently all of Israel.[2] In other words, even
though ἱερόν means the temple complex in 24:1, the
relation of ἱερόν to οἶκος in 23:38 makes Jesus'
act of leaving the temple equivalent to his
departure from the whole nation.

This is quite in keeping with the way οἶκος
is used not only in the First Gospel but in
Judaism as well. Οἶκος is used in Judaism to
indicate (1) the temple proper, (2) Jerusalem
itself, (3) the temple complex and the city of
Jerusalem (=the people), and (4) the temple, the
city, and the whole commonwealth of Israel.[3] The
overwhelming consensus is that οἶκος in Matthew

_____

[1]Schrenk, "ἱερόν," p. 235.

[2]See Michel, "οἶκος," pp. 119-158 for the
possible meanings of οἶκος and its relation to
ἱερόν.

[3]Str-Bill., 1:943-944.

23:38 includes the temple, the city, and all of Israel. The reason is that the whole commonwealth stands together under the protection of God's presence.

Billerbeck, for example, has cogently argued that οἶκος, when it means only "temple," never has a plural suffix like ὑμῶν in Matt. 23:38. The suffix is always singular, and, as Billerbeck says, "Wo byt in der Bedeutung 'Tempel' ein Suffix bei sich hat, bezeiht sich dieses immer auf Gott."[1] His conclusion, then, is: "Danach ist 'euer Haus' Mt 23,38 nicht der Tempel, sondern 'euer Gemeinwesen.'"[2] Virtually every commentator agrees with him. Strecker concludes: "Demnach steht auch οἶκος als Teil für das Ganze. Dass 'euer Haus' verlassen wird, bedeutet nichts anderes, als dass die Juden selbst allein gelassen werden."[3] M'Neile also concludes: "Οἶκος is not the temple only, but the city with the temple at its centre, which is virtually the nation."[4] Michel brings out the broader implication of οἶκος in the context of the whole saying in 23:38:

> At a first glance it might appear that the "house" (ὁ οἶκος ὑμῶν) refers to the temple at Jerusalem, but it is not impossible that in accordance with prophetic and apocalyptic usage (En. 89:50ff.; Test. L. 10) the city and the people themselves are rushing onward to destruction.[5]

---

[1]Ibid., p. 944.   [2]Ibid.

[3]Strecker, Weg, p. 113.

[4]M'Neile, St. Matthew, p. 342.

[5]Michel, "οἶκος," p. 125.

T. W. Manson wants to argue that "your house" is bitter irony which means that it is their house more than it is God's, but even he concludes that "In any case, the Temple and the Jewish commonwealth stand and fall together."[1]

Even if one wanted to argue that οἶκος means only the temple in Matthew, it is still clear that the evangelist would understand the loss of God's presence from the temple to mean judgment upon the whole commonwealth. Even a casual reading of Matthew, though, shows that οἶκος cannot be restricted in every case to mean only the temple (cf. 10:6; 15:24). Furthermore, when there is such wide agreement among commentators that οἶκος includes the whole commonwealth, then the conclusion seems inescapable.[2] The Matthean context almost demands that interpreters read οἶκος as all of Israel: Ἰερουσαλήμ (v. 37), τὴν γενεὰν ταύτην (v. 36), and the use of the plural pronoun (ὑμῶν) with οἶκος (v. 38). Because of the context, we feel safe in concluding that whether the evangelist used ἱερόν or ναός, it is clear that his purpose is to say that God's departure from Israel, announced by the prophets, is fulfilled when Jesus departs from the temple.[3] Jesus' departure from the temple means judgment for the entire nation.

---

[1]Manson, Sayings, p. 127.

[2]See Steck, Israel und das gewaltsame Geschick der Propheten, p. 228; Trilling, Wahre, p. 86; Bonnard, Matthieu, p. 344; Hill, Matthew, p. 316; Allen, St. Matthew, p. 251; Haenchen, "Matthäus 23," p. 55; and Klostermann, Matthäusevangelium, p. 191.

[3]Schweizer, Matthew, pp. 444-445.

Thus ἀφίεται (23:38) is fulfilled in Jesus'
departure from the temple in 24:1.[1]  The conclusion to be drawn from this is that when Jesus
leaves the temple (24:1), the presence of God
leaves Israel.[2]  This clearly implies that
23:38-39, when read in conjunction with 24:1 as
the evangelist seems to have intended, means that:

> Das "Verlassenwerden" vollzieht sich im
> Scheiden Jesu.  Nicht züfallig nimmt also
> Jesus in diesem Spruch den Platz der
> Schechina ein: . . . Durch das Scheiden
> Jesu wird Israel seiner eigentlichen
> Bestimmung beraubt.[3]

For Matthew the judgment in Jesus' time is
the loss of His presence.  With the loss of Jesus'
presence, Israel loses God's presence (Shekinah)
and Wisdom itself.  The judgment falls upon all
Israel not only because they have continuously
rejected the prophets, but now they have rejected
the Sender of the prophets.

### Summary of Ἱερόν and Οἶκος

Several conclusions can be drawn concerning
ἱερόν in 24:1.  (1) Ἱερόν is to be read in the
same context as οἶκος of 23:38.  (2) Ἱερόν in
24:1 refers to the whole temple complex, but

---

[1] Eduard Schweizer, "Matthäus 21-25,"
Orientierung an Jesus zur Theologie der Synop-
tiker, ed. Paul Hoffmann (Freiburg: Herder,
1973), p. 368.

[2] M'Neile, St. Matthew, p. 342.

[3] Strecker, Weg, pp. 113-114.

(3) in relation to οἶκος and the threat in 23:38, which seems to entail all of Israel, ἱερόν is synonymous with οἶκος and (4) alludes to the judgment of 23:38 in which God's presence has left His people. (5) The upshot of the Shekinah's departure from the temple is that the city is left defenseless and open to destruction. (6) The Matthean context virtually equates Jesus' departure from the temple with the departure of the presence of God in the Jewish tradition (γάρ, 23:39), and (7) 23:38 is fulfilled when Jesus leaves the temple in 24:1.

The warning in Matt. 23:38 seems to entail all three aspects of judgment--past, present, and future,[1] but the most important fact for the evangelist, perhaps, is that it is <u>Jesus</u> (ἐγώ, 23:34) who has sent the prophets whom Israel has murdered. All of the deeds necessary for judgment (ταῦτα πάντα, 23:36) have been fulfilled in "this generation" (=Jesus' time).[2] Jesus pronounces

---

[1]᾿Αφίεται looks back to past events, namely, the persecution of the prophets (υἱοί ἐστε τῶν φονευσάντων τούς προφήτης, v. 31). ᾿Αφίεται also refers to the same deeds by Israel in the time of Jesus (v. 32) because they are rejecting messengers <u>he</u> is sending to them (ἐγώ ἀποστέλλω, v. 34). ᾿Αφίεται also refers to Matthew's time since Israel has rejected messengers from his community who have been sent out in the name of Jesus (cf. chap. 10).

[2]The judgment which Matthew has in mind in verses 37-39 could be somewhat different than that of verses 32-36. In verses 32-36 Israel has only rejected the prophets, but in 37-39 they have rejected Jesus himself (ἠθέλησα ἐπισυναγαγεῖν, v. 37. Cf. Lambrecht, "Parousia

judgment upon all of Israel (οἶκος ὑμῶν, 23:38)
and with his departure from the temple (24:1) the
very presence of God leaves Israel--this <u>is</u> the
judgment (γάρ, 23:39).  In accordance with Jewish
tradition Matthew sees the departure of the
Shekinah as the prelude to the temple's physical
destruction.  For him the judgment of God is still
effective in Israel because their house (=the
commonwealth) is still "forsaken" in his time,
that is, it is devoid of Jesus' presence.  Israel

---

Discourse," p. 316).  However, the murder of the
prophets (23:31), of Zechariah (23:35), of Jesus
(27:20 cf. 27:25), and the persecution of those
whom Jesus is sending to the Jews in Matthew's
time (23:34) are not unrelated events for Matthew.
The present generation of Jews directly partici-
pates in the evil of the former generations (cf.
Sjef van Tilborg, <u>Jewish Leaders</u>, p. 168).  Thus,
in Jesus' departure from their "house" Israel is
abandoned by God in the present, that is, in
Jesus' time.  His departure from the temple is
Israel's present judgment.  The measure of their
fathers is "filled up" (πληρώσατε, v. 32) and the
judgment "will (has) come upon this generation"
(ἥξει ταῦτα πάντα ἐπὶ τὴν γενεὰν ταύτην, v. 36).
   It must be noted, though, that if ταῦτα
πάντα (v. 36) refers to the acts of bloodshed
committed by the Jews and not to the punishment
they will receive, then the meaning of verses
32-36 is altered.  Jesus' departure in 24:1 is
then not the punishment of Israel, it only refers
to his impending death.  According to this interpretation, the judgment forewarned in 23:38
refers to the destruction of the temple and the
οὐ μή με ἴδετε of v. 39 refers to the literal
seeing of Jesus rather than to the discernment of
his significance (cf. Lambrecht, "Parousia
Discourse," pp. 316-317).

127

will see Jesus again only in the future, and they
will see him then as judge. Thus, for the evangelist the judgment of God against Israel would
seem to be permanent: it is the culmination of
the rejection of Jesus by Israel.[1]

From our perspective, therefore, it appears
that Matthew sees the judgment of God beginning
in Jesus' departure from the temple, continuing
in the (future?) physical destruction of the
temple, and culminating in the eschatological
judgment of Jesus as the Son of Man. Although it
is open to debate whether Matthew sees an eventual
conversion of Israel or whether the judgment is a
permanent condition, there is little evidence in
Matthew of future salvation for the Jews.[2] It is
preferable, then, to see Jesus' departure from the
temple in 24:1 as the beginning of the culmination
of the whole rejection theme in Matthew. The
theme is capped off when "all the people" accept
the responsibility for Jesus' death (27:25).
Perhaps D. R. A. Hare summarizes it best:

> While Matthew takes the Jerusalem-saying
> (23:37-9) from Q and makes no major
> alteration in it, the position he gives
> it illuminates his doctrine of the
> rejection of Israel. It is made the
> final word in Jesus' valedictory to the

---

[1]See H. Wansbrough, "St. Matthew," A New
Catholic Commentary on Holy Scripture, ed.
Reginald Fuller (New York: Nelson, 1969), p. 735.

[2]Hare, Theme of Jewish Persecution, pp.
148-149. Contrast W. G. Kümmel, Introduction to
the New Testament, trans. Howard Clark Kee
(New York: Abingdon Press, 1975), p. 116.

Jewish nation.  Placed between the promise
of judgment upon "this generation" and the
subsequent prediction of the destruction
of the Temple (24:1f.), the Jerusalem-saying
declares that Israel's "house" has been
abandoned.  Not the Temple but the
commonwealth of Israel is meant by ὁ οἶκος
ὑμῶν.  Not the desolation of the city but
the rejection of the rejecting nation is
here predicted.  The abandonment of Israel
by God is then symbolized by the departure
of the Messiah and his disciples from the
Temple and the city to the Mount of Olives
(24:1, 3).  The abandonment is permanent.
Henceforward, the Messiah will no longer
show tender concern for Israel; ἀπ' ἄρτι
Israel will know him only as Judge.[1]

After commenting on the physical destruction of
the temple, which is implied in Jesus' departure
(Hare believes that Matthew alludes to C.E. 70),
Hare comments on the future ramifications of
Jesus' action for Matthew:

It cannot be maintained, however, that for
Matthew the destruction of Jerusalem was
the decisive punishment of Israel's guilt.
This temporal punishment was merely the
visible sign of the truly severe punishment
which was visited upon Israel when God
deprived her of possession of the Kingdom.
This crucial punishment, symbolized by
the destruction of the city will be
consummated at the final judgment, when
the erstwhile sons of the Kingdom will
be cast out into outer darkness (8:11f.).
It is none the less a present reality.

---

[1]Hare, Theme of Jewish Persecution, p. 154.

## Israel is no longer the People of God.[1]

For Matthew the loss of Jesus' presence was
Israel's judgment. The Parousia of Jesus and the
final judgment will only make it clear to Israel
that they forfeited God's rule and presence when
Jesus departed from the temple.

We are now in a position to summarize the
Matthean meaning of the phrase καὶ ἐξελθὼν ὁ
Ἰησοῦς ἀπὸ τοῦ ἱεροῦ ἐπορεύετο. Jesus leaves
the temple, which he entered in 21:23, for the
last time. His departure (ἐξελθών) suggests the
termination of his mission to Israel. Israel has
soundly rejected Jesus and, in turn, he rejects

---

[1]Ibid., p. 156 (italics mine). Israel has
brought the measure of their Fathers' sins to
completion (cf. 23:32) by rejecting Jesus himself.
Thus, they have incurred God's judgment. Israel
is no longer God's people--that is the meaning of
the judgment (cf. 23:36, 38). One should not
conclude, however, that this rules out the participation of "this generation" (23:36) in the final
judgment. The loss of Jesus' presence means the
loss of Israel's status as God's people. Israel
("this generation") does not realize that their
rejection of Jesus is the rejection of Sophia-
Shekinah and the loss of their special status.
They do not realize either that Jesus is also the
Son of Man whose coming (23:39) will confirm
explicitly the loss of their status. At the
Parousia of Jesus Israel will not only see that
Jesus is the Son of Man, but they will understand
also that Jesus-Son of Man will bring to completion the judgment which was begun by Jesus as
incarnate Sophia (see appendix 4 for a discussion
of ἔθνος and its relation to Israel in Matthew).

them by leaving their "house," which is virtually
the nation, forsaken and desolate (23:38). When
Jesus goes from the temple in 24:1, the very
presence of God itself leaves the people. Israel
will not see Jesus again until he comes either as
their King or as their judge (23:39), and it is
most likely as the latter. Jesus now continues
on his mission (ἐπορεύετο) which leads immediately
to death (cf. 26:1-2), and ultimately to exaltation (28:16-20), with his true disciples obediently following him.[1] From this point on Jesus
will turn his attention solely to teaching his
disciples. In 24:1, then, Matthew takes over
Mark's introduction, but he alters it in some
very important ways. The opening phrase ("Jesus
left the temple and was going away") emphasizes
the judgment pronounced in 23:38: "your house is
forsaken." The unemphatic, circumstantial clause
in Mark (ἐκπορευομένου αὐτοῦ ἐκ τοῦ ἱεροῦ) is
given more emphasis by Matthew in the principal
clause ἐξελθὼν ὁ ᾿Ιησοῦς ἀπὸ τοῦ ἱεροῦ ἐπορεύετο.
F. W. Beare summarizes what we feel is the correct
thrust of Matt. 24:1:

> The departure from the temple is given a
> deliberate emphasizing, even the aorist
> of the participle adds to the impression
> of finality. Jesus is not merely going

---

[1]See the discussion in appendix 2 on
πορεύομαι in Matthew. Πορεύομαι is used to
indicate one going on one's way in order to
complete a mission. In Matthew Jesus' immediate
mission is his Passion, but his Passion leads to
his exaltation as Risen Lord. In this context,
then, πορεύομαι could be understood as a "farewell
term" which indicates the departure of Jesus
from this phase of his ministry.

out of the temple on this occasion as on others; he has left it forever and is going on his way to complete his mission.[1]

### Part 5.  Jesus' Disciples as Representative of Matthew's Community

As soon as Jesus leaves the temple in judgment, Matthew has his disciples approach him. The importance of the evangelist's emphasis upon his "disciples" here and in 24:3 cannot be over-estimated.  In asking the questions of who his disciples are and how they approach him (in contrast to those who reject Jesus), we are really asking the question about the audience whom the evangelist has Jesus address in 24:1-2 and in 24:3.  Obviously, any insight into Matthew's understanding of the auditors (or readers) of Jesus' words will give an understanding of how Matthew intends this material to be read.

Our thesis is that "his disciples" (ὁ μαθηταὶ αὐτοῦ), or the phrase οἱ μαθηταί, is a phrase by which Matthew indicates not only the Twelve but his own church community.  We will contend further that προσέρχομαι, which is part of the stereotyped phrase, indicates that Matthew's community should approach Jesus as a figure worthy of worship just as the Twelve did in their day.  In other words, the phrase προσῆλθον οἱ μαθηταὶ αὐτοῦ has cultic overtones and depicts the Matthean community at worship before their Lord.  We will first investigate the evangelist's use of the phrase "his disciples,"

---

[1]F. W. Beare, "The Synoptic Apocalypse: Matthean Version," Understanding the Sacred Text, ed. John Reumann (Valley Forge, Pa.: The Judson Press, 1972), p. 124 (hereafter cited as Beare, "Apocalypse").

and then we will proceed to his redactional use of προσέρχομαι with that phrase.

## The Phrase "His Disciples" in Matthew

In the parallel verses to Matt. 24:1, it is important to notice that Mark has only one disciple address Jesus (εἷς τῶν μαθητῶν αὐτοῦ, 13:1) and Luke has simply the circumstantial τινων (21:5). Matthew, however, has "his disciples" (οἱ μαθηταὶ αὐτοῦ). Οἱ μαθηταὶ αὐτοῦ seems to be a characteristic Matthean formula for the disciples. The phrase repeatedly occurs throughout the gospel along with simply οἱ μαθηταί.[1] The phrases can sometimes be combined as in Matt. 10:1: τοὺς δώδεκα μαθητὰς αὐτοῦ.[2] The phrase "his disciples" seems to be synonymous with the Twelve (οἱ μαθηταί) who are Jesus' most intimate followers. When "disciples" is used impersonally, or when it denotes a group other than the intimate associates of Jesus, Matthew distinguishes this quite clearly (9:14; 10:24-25, 42; 11:2; 22:15-16).[3] On one level, then, Matthew uses

---

[1]See 5:1; 8:23; 9:19, 37; 10:42; 12:49; 13:36; 15:12, 23, 32; 16:21; 17:6, 10, 13; 18:1; 19:10; 21:6, 20; 23:1; 24:1, 3; 26:1, 8, 26, 35, 45, 56; 27:64; 28:8, 13, 16; cf. 9:10, 11, 14; 10:24, 25; 11:2; 12:1, 2; 14:12, 15, 19, 22, 26; 15:33, 36; 16:5, 13, 20, 24; 17:16, 19; 19:13, 23, 25; 26:17, 18, 19, 20, 40; 28:7.

[2]Cf. Matt. 11:1 and 20:17. Note that the critical apparatus for 20:17 adds μαθητάς.

[3]Only 8:21 is ambiguous. See Kingsbury, Parables of Jesus in Matthew 13, p. 41.

133

"disciples" to indicate the Twelve.

On another level, though, the "disciples"
are not simply figures of the past for Matthew.
Οἱ μαθηταί or οἱ μαθηταὶ αὐτοῦ in the First Gospel
cannot be reduced to mean only the Twelve or just
the general followers of Jesus in his day.[1] The
"disciples" in the First Gospel do not become
simply "ideal Christians" of the past.  In this
gospel they are quite often persons of "little
faith" who "stumble" in their relationship with
their Lord (cf. 6:30; 14:31; 16:8; etc.).  They
are not ideal Christians who never experience
fear, anxiety, and failure, but they are the ones
who cry out: Κύριε, σῶσον, ἀπολλύμεθα (8:25 cf.
14:30).

However, an acknowledged theme in the
evangelist's presentation of the disciples is
that they have, in spite of their failures, a
post-Easter understanding of who Jesus is and of
how they are to relate to him.  Matthew's presentation of the disciples as enlightened, post-
Easter followers of Jesus clearly reflects the
interests of a post-resurrection community.  A
brief look at the evangelist's redaction of Mark's
presentation of the disciples will allow
Matthew's portrait to stand out more clearly.

---

[1]Ernest R. Martinez has advanced this
argument.  His thesis is that the οἱ μαθηταί
αὐτοῦ and οἱ μαθηταί can be differentiated in
Matthew so that the former means an indefinite
group of Jesus' followers and the latter means
only the Twelve (cf. Martinez, "The Interpretation
of ʽOI MATHĒTAI in Matthew 18," CBQ 23 (1961):
281-292).

## Matthew's redaction of Mark's
## portrait of the disciples

The main feature of Matthew's portrait of the disciples is that he constantly edits Mark's theme of the disciples' misunderstanding out of the text. The upshot of Matthew's redactional activity is that the disciples in his gospel become enlightened, though not perfect, followers of Jesus. This fact is so well documented by Matthean redaction critics that we will only give a few examples of the evangelist's editorial process here.

Markan commentators have noted for some time that Mark has an identifiable redactional structure in his portrait of the disciples. He utilizes the passion predictions to paint his portrait. The structure consists of Jesus' prediction (cf. 8:31; 9:31; 10:33-34), the subsequent misunderstanding of the disciples (cf. 8:32-33; 9:33-34; 10:35-37), and Jesus' teaching about the meaning of discipleship (cf. 8:34-38; 9:35-37; 10:38-45).[1]

The second passion prediction is perhaps the clearest example of how Matthew redacts the Markan portrait. After Jesus predicts his suffering and death (cf. Mark 9:31), Mark has: "but they did not understand the saying" (9:32). Matthew deletes the disciples' misunderstanding and simply has: "And they were greatly distressed"

---

[1]For a full discussion of this structure in Mark see Ernest Best, "Discipleship in Mark: Mark 8:22-10:52," SJTh 23 (1970): 323-337; Georg Strecker, "The Passion Predictions in Mark," Interpretation 22 (1968): 421-442; and Perrin, What is Redaction Criticism?, pp. 40-60.

(17:23).  Matthew's version obviously implies that
the disciples fully understood Jesus' prediction
about his death.[1]  Another example is the pericope
in which Jesus reveals himself to his disciples
while he is walking on the water.  Mark closes the
episode with "they did not understand about the
loaves, but their hearts were hardened" (6:52).
Our evangelist, however, has: "And those in the
boat worshiped him, saying, 'Truly you are the
Son of God'" (14:33).  The point is that Matthew
consistently edits out Mark's emphasis that the
disciples are not enlightened followers of Jesus
until after the resurrection.[2]

The evangelist, then, has not "historicized"
the disciples, that is, they are not simply
figures of the past in Matthew's gospel (=the
Twelve), nor has he "idealized" them so that they
are only model Christians.  The upshot of
Matthew's redactional presentation of the disciples is that they are enlightened, post-Easter
followers of Jesus who are capable of understanding him and carrying forth his mission (cf.
28:16-20).  Matthew's consistent revision of the
disciples' misunderstanding " . . . testifies to
Matthew's abiding concern to show that the
Apostles, who will later be sent to teach (28:19),

---

[1]Ellis, Matthew: His Mind and His Message,
pp. 64-65.

[2]Cf. Mark 4:13 par. Matt. 13:18; Mark
6:51-52 par. Matt. 14:33; Mark 9:6 par. Matt.
17:4; Mark 9:10 par. Matt. 17:9; Mark 10:32 par.
Matt. 20:17.  See Senior, Matthew: A Gospel for
the Church, pp. 58-67; Ellis, Matthew: His Mind
and His Message, pp. 64-67; Blair, Jesus in the
Gospel of Matthew, pp. 102-109; and Kingsbury,
Parables of Jesus in Matthew 13, pp. 41-47.

136

truly understood the message they were to preach."[1]  Their understanding meant that they also knew that carrying forth Jesus' mission might mean sharing his fate (cf. 10:17-25; 24:9, 13).  To put it succinctly, the "disciples" represent not only the true followers of Jesus in his time, but they also represent the post-Easter community of Matthew's day.  The disciples become <u>representative</u> Christians.  The primary means by which the evangelist expresses their paradigmatic character is through the expression "persons of little faith."

## The disciples as "persons of little faith"

The disciples in the First Gospel have understanding, but "understanding" in Matthew does not necessarily mean that they have a strong faith.  In other words, the evangelist does not do away entirely with the Markan notion of the disciples' misunderstanding,[2] but he does reinterpret the misunderstanding in Mark with the concept of "little faith."  In Mark misunderstanding and lack of faith seem to be intimately connected.  Matthew, however, has rejected the idea that understanding automatically leads to

---

[1]Ellis, <u>Matthew: His Mind and His Message</u>, p. 65.  Matthew's portrait of the disciples might be a more positive one than Mark's, but a better way to understand it would be, as we argue below, that Matthew is simply reflecting the consciousness of his community that they are to carry on the mission and message of Jesus-Sophia (see chapter 4 below).

[2]Cf. Matt. 15:16 par. Mark 7:18; Matt. 16:9 par. Mark 8:17.

faith. The disciples in Matthew have understanding, but they lack faith in the sense of
complete trust in God and faithful obedience to
God's will.[1]

Matthew has the disciples reach understanding after they are instructed by Jesus (cf.
13:51; 16:12; 17:13). They do not remain devoid
of understanding, as in Mark. It is simply that
in Matthew's reinterpretation of discipleship,
understanding does not necessarily lead to faith,
trust, and obedience. For Matthew discipleship
consists of more than a proper understanding of
who Jesus is; it also entails trust and action.
"The true disciple for Matthew," as Ellis says,
" . . . not only understands and accepts Jesus'
teaching. He believes Jesus, trusts Jesus, relies
on Jesus, and commits himself to the love of
Jesus."[2] Thus, Matthew does not completely remove
Mark's emphasis on the misunderstanding of the
disciples. Rather, he interprets it with the
notion that although the disciples have a post-
resurrection understanding of who Jesus is, they
are still "men and women of little faith."[3]

---

[1]Barth, "Matthew's Understanding of the
Law," TI, pp. 113-114. For the relation of
συνιέναι and πίστις in Matthew see Ibid., pp.
105-116. On πίστις as trust and obedience in
Matthew see Bornkamm, "End-Expectation and Church
in Matthew," TI, pp. 27-32; and Ellis, Matthew:
His Mind and His Message, pp. 149-150.

[2]Ibid.

[3]H. J. Held, "Matthew as Interpreter of the
Miracle Stories," TI, p. 292.

The notion of "little faith," though, does not mean that the Matthean disciples are <u>devoid of</u> faith (cf. Mark 4:40); it means that they are persons of <u>little</u> faith (Matt. 8:26). In Matthew the disciples[1] address Jesus with the divine predicate κύριε in the form of a prayer: "Save, Lord; we are perishing" (8:25 cf. Mark 4:38). As Bornkamm has shown, this prayer in itself is a confession of discipleship. Thus, in the First Gospel Jesus does not reproach the disciples for their lack of faith but for their little faith (ὀλιγοπιστία). In Matthew, as Bornkamm says, little faith " . . . always denotes a faith that is too weak, that is paralyzed in the storm (8.26; 14.31) and in anxiety (6.30; 16.8), and thus is . . . not sufficiently mature to withstand the pressure of demonic powers."[2]

The same concept is brought out again at Jesus' epiphany on the water. The disciples recognize Jesus as the Lord and Son of God (14:28, 33), but he calls their fear and lack of trust "little faith." In fact, Matthew's understanding of discipleship is beautifully expressed in Jesus' rebuke of Peter: "O man of little faith, why did you doubt?" (14:31).[3] Peter has faith,

---

[1]Οἱ μαθηταὶ αὐτοῦ, 8:23 cf. Mark 4:36.

[2]Bornkamm, "The Stilling of the Storm in Matthew," <u>TI</u>, p. 56. For a discussion of the phrase "persons of little faith" in contrast to "persons of trust" in rabbinical sayings see Held, "Matthew as Interpreter of the Miracle Stories," <u>TI</u>, pp. 293-296.

[3]See Ellis, <u>Matthew: His Mind and His Message</u>, p. 149.

but it has not yet become the kind of trust which will sustain him in a crisis. The same concept of faith is implied in the story about the feeding miracle. The disciples understand, in contrast to Mark's presentation of the disciples, but Jesus calls their attitude "little faith" (Matt. 16:8 cf. Mark 8:17, 18).[1]

It is true that the notion of "little faith" was already in Matthew's tradition (cf. Matt. 6:30; Luke 12:28). However, the notion of little faith in all subsequent passages in Matthew is used only in dialogues between Jesus and his disciples (8:26; 14:31; 16:8; 17:20), and it always appears in a situation which "tests" their faith. The situation might be anxiety over what to eat (6:30; 16:18), or a crisis in which they face immediate death (8:26; 14:31), or a difficult situation which they cannot control (17:20).[2] The "disciples of little faith" become paradigmatic of the kind of faith which all disciples of Jesus possess.[3] Matthew's use of the expression "little faith" (ὀλιγοπιστία or ὀλιγόπιστος) thus "becomes a typical situation of discipleship as a whole."[4]

Therefore, in his redaction of Mark's

---

[1]See Held, "Matthew as Interpreter of the Miracle Stories," _TI_, pp. 292-293.

[2]Ibid.

[3]Ellis, _Matthew: His Mind and His Message_, p. 149.

[4]Bornkamm, "The Stilling of the Storm in Matthew," _TI_, p. 56.

portrait of the disciples, Matthew uses the notion of "little faith." The disciples in Jesus' own lifetime clearly have a post-Easter understanding of Jesus, but they do not have corresponding faith, the essence of which is complete trust in Jesus. The evangelist's portrait of the disciples in Jesus' lifetime enables their struggles to become representative of all disciples. They are not simply model Christians. Even a disciple of Peter's stature is rebuked for his "little faith" (14:31 cf. 16:23). The disciples of Jesus' life-time operate on the historical level as figures of the past who have struggles with their faith, but those struggles are the essence of disciple-ship for Matthew. Their struggles become representative of the struggles of all Christians. Consequently, Matthew's portrait of the disciples draws his own community into the picture because they too, if they are concerned with being true followers of Jesus, are struggling with the essence of discipleship: a proper understanding of Jesus which leads to complete trust in him.[1]

"Persons of little faith" does not designate those who have fundamentally rejected Jesus, as did Israel. It merely means those who have faith in Jesus, but who are struggling to overcome the difficulties involved in that relationship. The address of Jesus in 24:1 and in 24:3 will be to a community for whom the "disciples" are representatives of just such a struggle. The disciples, then, if one can assume de facto that Matthew is addressing a Christian community, include the community of Matthew's time. J. D. Kingsbury, from his work on Matt. 13, summarizes Matthew's portrait of the disciples very well:

---

[1]See Senior, Matthew: A Gospel for the Church, pp. 58-67.

141

The net effect of Matthew's editorial
activity as regards the capacity of the
disciples for understanding is clearly to
project on to them the image of being the
enlightened followers of Jesus. With
respect to chapter 13, this means that the
disciples of Jesus are fully capable of
comprehending his parables. With respect
to the whole of the Gospel, it means that
Matthew endows the disciples before Easter
with insight that, according to Mark,
Luke, and John, they do not attain until
after Easter. The result is that the
correlation in the first Gospel between
the disciples of Jesus and the Christians
of Matthew's day is so close that the
disciples of the text simply become
the representatives of the Christians, or
Church, of this later age [italics mine].[1]

The importance of this conclusion is obvious. Matthew 24:1-2, as well as the following
eschatological discourse (24:3-31), is directed
primarily at the members of Matthew's church
community--they are "the disciples" who share
Jesus' mission and fate.[2] This conclusion becomes

---

[1]Kingsbury, Parables of Jesus in Matthew 13,
p. 42; cf. Senior, Matthew: A Gospel for the
Church, p. 54.

[2]Contrast Ellis, for example, who sees
24:1-2 as addressed to the "crowds and the disciples in the temple area" and 24:3-31 as addressed "to the disciples alone on Mount Olivet."
He clarifies his understanding in these terms:
"As in the Sermon on the Mount, the discourse has
the disciples (or more properly Matthew's community) as its primary audience and as its secondary audience those readers, particularly Jews

even more apparent when Matthew's redactional use
of προσέρχομαι with "his disciples" is investigated.

## Προσέρχομαι in Matthew

Προσέρχομαι occurs fifty-two times in
Matthew.[1] In forty-nine of its occurences προσέρχομαι is used of others who approach Jesus (cf.
17:7; 26:39; 28:18). J. Schneider has shown that
προσέρχομαι has definite cultic overtones.[2] In
Hellenistic literature προσέρχομαι is often used
in the cultic sense of "to come before the deity."
In the Septuagint προσέρχομαι is also used
cultically in the sense of "to come before God,"
"to come to sacrifice," or "to worship" (cf. Num.

---

tending toward Christianity, who could not make up
their minds about leaving Judaism and the leader-
ship of the Jamnian Pharisees. . . . The apocalyptic discourse in ch 24 is for both audiences
but especially for the primary audience" (Ellis,
Matthew: His Mind and His Message, p. 79).
    Perhaps part of the confusion, if it is
such, arises from Ellis' interpretation of οἱ
μαθηταί in 18:1 (cf. Ibid., pp. 68-70). In 24:3,
however, we have to agree with Beare that: "As is
usual in Matthew, οἱ μαθηταί are not merely the
twelve or even some broader group of immediate
followers, but the representatives of the Christian believers of the evangelist's time" (Beare,
"Apocalypse," p. 124).

[1]See Allen, St. Matthew, p. 31.

[2]Schneider, "ἔρχομαι," p. 683.

18:14; Jer. 7:16).[1] Προσέρχομαι is also used as an invitation by Wisdom to approach her respectfully and to obey her.[2]

J. D. Kingsbury, following Schneider, has shown how Matthew uses προσέρχομαι with cultic overtones. Three times in Matthew those who approach Jesus address him as κύριος (8:25; 17:14-15; 18:21), which is an important christological term in the First Gospel.[3] Hummel has pointed out that καὶ προσῆλθον (αὐτῷ) οἱ μαθηταὶ αὐτοῦ seems to be a stereotyped Matthean formula by which the disciples approach Jesus privately for additional instruction about his public message.[4] The same formula is found in 13:36 where Jesus sends the crowds away (ἀφεὶς τοὺς ὄχλους cf. 13:1-10), and then his disciples come to him and

---

[1] Ibid.

[2] Sirach 24:19: προσέλθετε πρός με, οἱ ἐπιθυμοῦτές μου cf. 4:15; Prov. 8:32-36; 9:1-6. See Ibid., and Christ, Jesus Sophia, p. 36.

[3] Kingsbury, Parables of Jesus in Matthew 13, p. 40. Cf. Bornkamm's remark: " . . . the title and address of Jesus as κύριος in Matthew have throughout the character of a divine Name of Majesty" ("End-Expectation and Church in Matthew," TI, pp. 42-43). See also Schweizer, Matthew, pp. 210-211.

[4] Hummel, Auseinandersetzung, pp. 85-86. Kingsbury reaches virtually the same conclusion in his discussion of Matt. 13:36 (see Parables of Jesus in Matthew 13, pp. 38-47). Contrast, though, Lambrecht, "Parousia Discourse," p. 317 n. 18.

ask him the meaning of his parable.[1]  Our investigation of οἱ μαθηταὶ αὐτοῦ in the First Gospel seems to support Hummel's argument.

We have seen how the phrase "his disciples" in Matthew is synonymous with Jesus' most intimate followers, that is, those who even in his lifetime seem to have a post-Easter understanding of him. The disciples understand who Jesus is and thus approach him (προσέρχομαι) with veneration. Again, Kingsbury succinctly states the conclusion:

> Matthew's use of προσέρχομαι suggests that for him, too, it has acquired a cultic connotation.  Indirectly it ascribes a lordly dignity to Jesus, for people approach him with the same reverence that would be due to a king or deity.  Accordingly, when Matthew states in v. 10a [chap. 13] that "the disciples came . . . to him," he provides us with a thumbnail sketch of Jesus by portraying him as a person of royal dignity whom the disciples approach in full awareness of his majestic status.[2]

In 24:1 the disciples reverently approach Jesus because they understand that he is the Wisdom of God whose presence is about to leave Israel.  If, as his true followers, they are to share Jesus' mission, then they must understand it and particularly his relationship to Israel.  They reverently approach him (24:1), and Jesus teaches them concerning his drastic action (24:2).

---

[1]Kingsbury, Parables of Jesus in Matthew 13, pp. 38-47.

[2]Ibid., pp. 40-41.

Jesus' Answer to His Disciples about
His Withdrawal from the Temple

## The disciples point out the temple
## buildings to Jesus (24:1b)

The disciples reverently approach Jesus for
the purpose of "pointing out" (ἐπιδεῖξαι) to him
the buildings of the temple.[1] The evangelist's
use of ἐπιδείκνυμι does not imply that Jesus had
not visited the temple before or that the disciples were more familiar with it than he.[2] Jesus
in the Gospel of Matthew is obviously familiar
not only with the physical appearance of the
temple (4:5) but with its cultic procedures as
well (cf. 12:1-7; 21:12-13). Rather, it is
enigmatic to the disciples how Jesus could, first
of all, pronounce judgment upon such a magnificent structure, and then "turn his back" in judgment upon it (ἐξελθών). This was the very
structure in which the presence of God had dwelt.
The temple represented the whole commonwealth of
Israel, and the disciples, according to Matthew,
simply could not understand that Jesus had
rejected it all. Here we have Matthew's redactional structure in which the disciples misunderstand Jesus' public teaching and/or action and
have to be taught by Jesus concerning its meaning
(cf. 24:2).

It is noteworthy that Mark simply has

---

[1]'Επιδεῖξαι is an aorist infinitive of
purpose.

[2]Against C. G. Montefiore, The Synoptic
Gospels, vol. 2 (New York: KTAV Publishing House,
Inc., 1968), p. 310.

διδάσκαλε ἴδε (13:1b). Matthew's change to
ἐπιδείκνυμι seems to indicate a stronger attempt
on the disciples part to explain, perhaps to try
and demonstrate, to Jesus the heilsgeschichlich
significance of the temple.[1] Ἐπιδείκνυμι (nor
δείκνυμι) does not occur with any frequency in the
First Gospel, but Luke uses it only once and Mark
does not use it at all.[2] In those places which
are peculiar to Matthew (or which are due to his
redactional acitivity), and where persons try to
"point out" something to Jesus, both words (ἐπιδείκνυμι, δείκνυμι) have the significance of
trying to explain, to demonstrate, or even to
convince Jesus about something. In each instance
Jesus gives an unqualified negative response to
the attempt.[3]
    The same thing is true in 24:1. The

---

[1]Heinrich Schlier, "δείκνυμι," TDNT 2:26-27.

[2]Both words occur a total of three times in
Matthew and in Luke together (i.e., only counting
places which are peculiar to Matthew).

[3]In 4:8 the devil takes Jesus to "a very
high mountain" (cf. Luke 4:5) and "showed"
(δείκνυσιν cf. ἔδειξεν in Luke 4:5) him "all the
kingdoms of the world" in order to try and convince Jesus to worship him (v. 9). Jesus responds
with an unqualified rejection of the attempt (v.
10). In 16:1 the Pharisees and the Sadducees
approach (προσελθόντες) Jesus to "test"
(πειράζοντες cf. Mark 8:11; Luke 11:29) him by
asking him to show (ἐπιδεῖξαι) them a sign.
Jesus condemns them for their attempt (16:4 cf.
16:21 in which Jesus shows [δεικνύειν cf.
διδάσκειν in Mark 9:31] his disciples that he must
go to Jerusalem [only in Matthew] to suffer and
die there).

147

disciples, in view of Jesus' threat against the temple (23:38), indeed against the people of God, approach him with the purpose of trying to understand his rejection of the most glorious symbol of God's elected people.[1] Jesus' answer is an unqualified negative one given with great solemnity (cf. v. 2b, ἀμὴν λέγω ὑμῖν): the whole magnificent structure will be destroyed. His statement only reiterates what he had already declared to the Pharisees in 12:6: λέγω δὲ ὑμῖν ὅτι τοῦ ἱεροῦ μεῖζόν ἐστιν ὧδε.

It is certainly not impossible that this pericope, which is addressed to Matthew's community, is directed toward those who are not yet fully convinced that God has indeed pronounced judgment upon the house of Israel (23:38), that He/She has left it (24:1), and that He/She has chosen instead to dwell among those who follow Jesus (viz., Matthew's church). The physical evidence of the judgment of Israel for Matthew would be the destruction of the temple buildings themselves. This evidence, in turn, is based upon Israel's rejection of Jesus and Jesus' reciprocal rejection of them. Note that the emphasis in Mark seems to be upon the magnificence of the temple structure itself.[2] Matthew's interest, however, is in the religious significance of the temple.

---

[1]We are not arguing that one can draw a psychological profile of the Twelve from Matthew's presentation, but we are suggesting that this is his literary portrait of the disciples as representative Christians.

[2]Cf. ποταποὶ λίθοι καὶ ποταπαὶ οἰκοδομαί, 13:1; ταύτας τὰς μεγάλας οἰκοδομάς, 13:2a. See Taylor, St. Mark, p. 500; and Rudolph Pesch, Naherwartungen. Tradition und Redaktion in Mark 13 (Düsseldorf: Patmos-Verlag, 1968), p. 85.

It had always been the place of God's presence and the religious center of the commonwealth. Thus, the consternation of the disciples in Matthew is over the fact that now God seems to have rejected His/Her own people. On the one hand, their consternation stands between Jesus' pronouncement of judgment upon the temple (23:38) and his definitive departure from it (24:1), but, on the other hand, it precedes his explicit, solemn prediction of its destruction (24:2). In Mark, as in Luke, the pronouncement of the temple's destruction is not preceded by a warning of judgment, as in Matt. 23:38, but by the story of the Widow's Offering (Mark 12:41-44; Luke 21:1-4). Luke goes on to have an indefinite group (τινων λεγόντων, 21:5) emphasize the flagrant <u>adornment</u> (κεκόσμηται) of the temple in contrast to the widow's poverty. Luke's presentation seems to enhance the contrast between poverty and opulence.[1] Although he has the same story preceding this section, Mark does not continue the contrast of poverty versus adornment. He simply has one disciple (13:1) emphasize the magnificence of the structure itself. Matthew's redactional activity, then, quite plainly shows that the lack of understanding on the part of Jesus' disciples, or Matthew's church, is over the <u>religious significance</u> of God's (and Jesus') rejection of Israel. The concern in the First Gospel is clearly not over the <u>physical</u> destruction of the magnificent buildings alone.

---

[1]Luke seems to have abandoned the eschatological interest in the temple's destruction. He seems much more concerned about the interpretation of the Law in the temple. This concern is indicated by the statement just before the widow's offering (20:47) which is immediately followed by the prediction of the temple's destruction (21:5-6). See Conzelmann, <u>Theology of St. Luke</u>, p. 79.

If Matthew wrote after C.E. 70, then his redactional emphasis upon the religious significance would be quite in keeping with the fact that he was writing after the building itself was gone. This was a time when the religious question of "why has God allowed the destruction?" was still a poignant one.[1]

It seems that Matthew's use of οἰκοδομή here means that the disciples had pinned their religious hopes too much upon the temple building as the visible evidence of God's election and presence with Israel (cf. 1 Esd. 5:56-73, esp. v. 70).[2] Οἰκοδομή also has a figurative meaning which Matthew possibly uses. The term refers to God's "building" in the sense of the community of God.[3] If the evangelist's meaning is more

---

[1]Matthew's redactional activity includes his omission of Mark's references to the grandeur of the structure (ποταποὶ λίθοι . . . ποταπαὶ οἰκοδομαί . . . μεγάλας οἰκοδομάς), his placement of the incident after the warning of judgment (23:38) instead of after the widow's offering (Mark 12:41-44), and his presentation of all the disciples (=Matthew's church), instead of just one disciple (Mark 13:1), who come to Jesus with the purpose of pointing out (ἐπιδεῖξαι) to him the religious significance of the temple.

[2]Barnabas 16:1, for example, speaks of "the error of the Jews who set their hope on the temple building, εἰς τὴν οἰκοδομὴν ἤλπισαν." (See Michel, "οἶκος," p. 145.)

[3]The Christian community is called an οἰκοδομή (I Cor. 3:9; Eph. 2:21). In Eph. 2:21 "this οἰκοδομή becomes the holy temple in which Jesus Christ is the corner-stone and which is built on the foundation of the apostles" (Ibid).

figurative than literal, then he is implying that
the community of God is no longer connected with
the temple (the οἶκος of Israel, 23:38 cf. 10:6),
but with the Christian community where Jesus
himself is present (cf. 18:20; 28:20).[1] The theme
of Jesus' presence in Matthew's church will be

---

[1]Matthew only uses οἰκοδομή once (24:1) and
a case should not be built upon this one occur-
ence. He does, though, use οἰκοδομέω eight times,
at least five of which are figurative (cf. 7:24,
26; 16:18; 21:33, 42; cf. 23:29; 26:61; 27:40).

Two very interesting passages in this
connection are Matt. 16:18 and 21:42. Matt. 16:18
occurs after Jesus blesses Peter (16:17) for his
recognition that Jesus is "the Christ, the Son of
the Living God" (16:16). Only Matthew then has
Jesus promise Peter that "on this rock I will
build my church" (οἰκοδομήσω μου τὴν ἐκκλησίαν,
16:18). Peter's religious insight here is in
direct contrast to that of the disciples in 24:1
who still are attracted, at the very least
impressed, by the οἰκοδομή (=Israel, the Judaism
of Matthew's day; cf. ὁ οἶκος ὑμῶν in 23:38)
which Jesus, who is "greater than the temple"
(12:6), has rejected.

The other verse (21:42) occurs in the
parable of the "wicked tenants" (21:33-46). In
Matthew the parable quite clearly refers to
Israel's rejection of Jesus. The rejection of
Jesus as the "stone which the builders (οἱ
οἰκοδομοῦντες) rejected" (21:42) leads to the
message of the parable itself which only Matthew
states explicitly: "the kingdom of God will be
taken away from you and given to a nation (ἔθνει)
producing the fruits of it" (21:43). See
Schweizer, Matthew, p. 414.

discussed later.[1]  For the task at hand, a closer
examination of Jesus' answer (v. 2) seems to
support the conclusion that the temple, the place
of God's presence, had been permanently
abandoned by Jesus.

## Jesus predicts the temple's destruction (Matt. 24:2)

Matthew begins Jesus' answer to his disciples in 24:2 with ἀποκριθεὶς εἶπεν.  The evangelist's redactional use of ἀποκριθεὶς εἶπεν,
especially in conjunction with προσέρχομαι, shows
that he uses the construction in key places where
Jesus (or others) is about to teach, condemn,
accept, reveal, or pronounce judgment.  Ἀποκριθεὶς εἶπεν is not simply an empty stylistic
formula in Matthew, but the form, which occurs
forty-two times in his gospel, is one which most
often conveys a solemn teaching of Jesus.

The disciples have approached Jesus for the
purpose of trying to understand the meaning of
his departure from the temple.  The temple had
always been the place where the true people of God
focused their hopes for salvation.  Surely Jesus'
departure does not mean that he has forsaken the
temple!  As mentioned above, here is the Matthean
pattern where the disciples misunderstand Jesus,
and then implicitly ask him to teach them the
meaning of his action.  Jesus' answer is not only
teaching about the future of the temple, but it
is also a solemn reaffirmation of the judgment
which he pronounced in 23:38 and fulfilled in
24:1.  The formula ἀποκριθεὶς εἶπεν enhances the
fact that the presence of God, in Jesus-Sophia,

---

[1]See the discussion of Matt. 24:3 in
chapter 3 below.

has left the temple and does not plan to return. Jesus continues on his way from the temple (ἐπορεύετο, 24:1), the former place of the Shekinah, to the Mount of Olives (24:3), which becomes a new place of revelation, and reiterates the judgment upon the temple as he goes. A brief look at both parts of Jesus' answer reveals what Matthew intends the "disciples" (his church) to understand.

## Οὐ βλέπετε ταῦτα πάντα (Matt. 24:2)

The first part of Jesus' answer is a rhetorical question: "You see all these, do you not?" Certainly the disciples had literally seen "all these things" because they had just shown the temple buildings to Jesus.[1] Βλέπω here obviously refers to more than literal sense perception. The context leads us to believe that βλέπω alludes to religious understanding and insight given by revelation from Jesus.

First, Matthew has replaced Mark's Βλέπεις with οὐ βλέπετε. This change ostensibly corresponds with the number of disciples who accompany Jesus.[2] The οὐ, however, functions not only to express the expectation of an affirmative answer, but it also has the effect of an α-privative. Οὐ used with βλέπω implies that the disciples are being asked about what is inaccessible to empirical perception, not about the literal buildings.[3]

---

[1]Rudolf Pesch, "Eschatologie und Ethik. Auslegung von Mt 24,1-36," BL 11 (1970): 226.

[2]Klostermann, Matthäusevangelium, p. 191.

[3]Wilhelm Michaelis, "ὁράω," TDNT 5:350 n. 174 cf. pp. 343-345; and Bl-D §426.

The action of the disciples, in trying to show
Jesus the buildings of the temple, indicates that
they really have not perceived what has taken
place in his departure from the temple, namely,
the total rejection of Israel.

The primary reason why Jesus rejected Israel
is that they have been a people devoid of divine
insight (cf. 13:11-13). From Matthew's viewpoint,
Israel has been totally unable to perceive God's
true messengers and has rejected them in every
generation (23:32-39). Jesus' pronouncement of
judgment in 23:38 obviously makes the corresponding οὐ μή με ἴδητε of 23:39 allude to
Israel's failure to discern Jesus' significance,
not just to their literal view of him at the
Parousia.[1]

Israel's inability to perceive God's revelation is surely the point of Matthean redaction
in 13:13-15. As Kingsbury has shown, the evangelist has redacted Jesus' answer in 13:13a
("This is why I speak to them in parables") to
correspond to the introduction in 13:10b ("Then
the disciples came and said to him, 'Why do you
speak to them in parables?'" cf. Mark 4:10, 12).[2]
The second part of Jesus' answer in Matt. 13:13
is even clearer. In Mark Jesus speaks to them in
parables "so that (ἵνα) they may indeed see
(βλέποντες βλέπωσιν) but not perceive (μή
ἴδωσιν)" (4:12a). In Matthew, however, Jesus
explains that he speaks to the crowds in parables

---

[1]See the discussion on pp. 75-92 above.
Contrast Lambrecht, "Parousia Discourse," pp.
316-317.

[2]We are essentially following the discussion of Kingsbury, Parables of Jesus in Matthew
13, pp. 48-51.

because (ὅτι) they are in a state of imperception (ὅτι βλέποντες οὐ βλέπουσιν, 13:13).[1]  In his redaction of Mark's quotation of Isaiah 6:9, Matthew has a parallel structure in which βλέπω is synonymous with "perceive" (ἴδητε).  The evangelist does not have Jesus speak to the crowds in parables in order to make them spiritually blind, but he speaks to them in this way because they are spiritually blind and incapable of perceiving his revelation.  As Kingsbury concludes: "For Matthew, the fact that Jesus speaks to the crowds in parables substantiates the circumstance that they have already proved themselves towards the Word of revelation."[2]

The use of βλέπω in 24:2, particularly if οὐ is the equivalent of an α-privative, is similar to Matthew's use of it in 13:13.[3]  The disciples really do not perceive the significance of Jesus' departure from the temple.  Jesus must teach them that his departure from the temple means that he has rejected Israel.  Matthew's emphasis, then, is decidedly upon Jesus' departure from the temple rather than upon the buildings themselves.  He makes this clear when he deletes "these great buildings" (cf. Mark 13:2) and makes "all these things" (ταῦτα πάντα) the object of βλέπω.

---

[1]M'Neile, St. Matthew, p. 190.

[2]Kingsbury, Parables of Jesus in Matthew 13, p. 49.  One way Matthew depicts the acceptance of the message and revelation of Jesus is by the act of seeing (βλέπειν) or hearing (ἀκούειν; e.g., 11:4; 13:13-16; cf. Gerhard Kittel, "λέγω," TDNT 4: 121).

[3]It is possible that οὐ is a later insertion.

Ταῦτα πάντα (Matt. 24:2)

The question is: to what does ταῦτα πάντα refer? There are at least two possibilities. First, the phrase could refer to the literal buildings. In this case Matthew has simply substituted the shorter ταῦτα πάντα phrase for Mark's longer one. Βλέπω would then mean literal sight rather than "religious" perception. A second possibility, if we continue to follow our line of interpretation, is that ταῦτα πάντα refers to "all these things," that is, the judgment which is about to befall the unbelieving and disobedient Israel because of its rejection of Jesus. In this case ταῦτα πάντα would refer back to: (1) 23:38, or (2) 23:36, or perhaps as far back as (3) 23:34.

Ταῦτα πάντα is definitely a Matthean summary phrase which seems to occur in a stereotyped pattern.[1] Hummel has argued this point most convincingly. The pattern in 24:1-2 is identical to other places in Matthew: Jesus turns away from public teaching to teach his disciples in private. This is accomplished in 24:1 by Jesus' departure from the temple and by the formula προσῆλθον οἱ μαθηταὶ αὐτοῦ.[2] The pattern is evident most prominently in 13:36 where the same formula occurs in a similar situation: the disciples ask Jesus a question, and he teaches them privately.[3] There

---

[1]Sjef van Tilborg, Jewish Leaders, p. 67 n. 2 lists all of the occurences of ταῦτα πάντα in Matthew. Cf. Schweizer, Matthew, p. 448.

[2]See pp. 112-132 above.

[3]Hummel, Auseinandersetzung, p. 86; cf. Kingsbury, Parables of Jesus in Matthew 13, p. 92.

is no question asked by the disciples in 24:1,
but, when they point out the temple buildings to
Jesus, their actions have the same result as a
question. Their attempt shows that they did not
understand the wider instruction just given in
chapter 23 about the divine judgment upon Israel.
As Hummel says:

> In 24,1 stellen die Jünger freilich keine
> Fragen, sondern zeigen Jesus die
> Tempelgebäude. Das hat aber dieselbe
> Folge wie sonst die Frage, nämlich die
> weitere Belehrung über das in Kap. 23
> bereits angeklungene Thema des göttlichen
> Strafgerichtes über das Judentum. Matthäus
> verbindet also die Pharisäerrede mit dem
> Wort über die Tempelzerstörung (24,2) durch
> das Schema: öffentliche Verkündigung--
> geheime Belehrung. Den noch verborgenen
> Sinn von Mt 23 sieht er in der
> Tempelzerstörung enthüllt. Die geheime
> Belehrung wird mit der Frage eingeleitet:
> "οὐ βλέπετε ταῦτα πάντα;"[1]

The phrase ταῦτα πάντα is a Matthean summary
phrase by which, in this instance, Jesus teaches
his disciples privately about the judgment he has
pronounced against Israel. The phrase here is an
apocalyptic formula of judgment, particularly in
combination with the solemn pronouncement (not in
Mark or in Luke): ἀμὴν λέγω ὑμῖν. This formula,
followed by the announcement of the temple's

---

[1]Hummel, Auseinandersetzung, p. 86. For
a more traditional view see Lambrecht, "Parousia
Discourse," p. 317 n. 19.

destruction, makes it clear that Matthew wants
ταῦτα πάντα to signify the culmination of the
judgment pronounced on Israel.[1] Ἀμὴν λέγω ὑμῖν,
which is clearly redactional,[2] also occurs (along
with ταῦτα πάντα) in the judgment pronounced in
23:36: ἀμὴν λέγω ὑμῖν, ἥξει ταῦτα πάντα ἐπὶ τὴν
γενεὰν ταύτην. Ταῦτα πάντα in this verse seems to
mean "all these deeds," that is, all of the acts
of bloodshed mentioned in verses 34-35.[3] The same
theme of judgment continues into 23:38 when Jesus
announces that "your house is forsaken,"[4] into
23:39 when Jesus solemnly pronounces "For I tell
you (λέγω γὰρ ὑμῖν), you will not see me
again, . . .," and into 24:1 when Jesus abandons
(ἐξελθών) the temple.[5] Throughout this context,

---

[1]Pesch, "Eschatologie und Ethik," p. 226.

[2]Lange, Erscheinen, p. 131; cf. Trilling,
Wahre, pp. 171-172; and Strecker, Weg, p. 124
n. 13.

[3]M'Neile, St. Matthew, p. 340; Sjef van
Tilborg, Jewish Leaders, p. 67; and Lambrecht,
"Parousia Discourse," p. 315.

[4]It is true, as Lambrecht contends, that
Matt. 23:36 and 23:38 come from different contexts, but the difference applies to Q, not to
the Matthean context. Cf. Hare's conclusion
(Theme of Jewish Persecution, pp. 95-96).

[5]As a formula, λέγω γὰρ υμῖν is virtually
equivalent to ἀμήν in its solemnity (see
Lambrecht, "Parousia Discourse," p. 318; Davies,
Sermon on the Mount, p. 102; Suggs, Wisdom,
pp. 111-115; and Strecker, Weg, p. 124).

then, "Truly I say to you" is used in conjunction with ταῦτα πάντα as an apocalyptic formula which reveals the judgment of God against unbelieving Israel.[1] When the disciples show that they do not understand (by attempting to point out the temple buildings to Jesus), Jesus explicitly teaches them the meaning of the judgment: in the destruction of the temple the judgment upon Israel is completely fulfilled. The Matthean phrase ταῦτα πάντα in 24:2 is, then, unambiguous in this regard.[2] All of these verses (23:34-38) cluster around the same theme--the judgment of Israel culminates in the destruction of the temple.[3]

Thus, 24:2 is an "I saying" of Jesus which is heavily redacted by the evangelist in order to

---

[1]Ταῦτα πάντα could be the revelation of secret eschatological knowledge (cf. Suggs, Wisdom, pp. 88-95). It is clear in Matthew that, in connection with some form of λέγω υμῖν, the formula is typical of one bearing a revelation (cf. Strecker, Weg, p. 124 n. 13).
On ἀμήν see Jeremias, New Testament Theology, vol. 1: 35-36; and Schlier, "ἀμήν," pp. 335-338. On ἐγώ as carrying a similar kind of authority as ἀμήν see Albert Schweitzer, The Quest of the Historical Jesus, trans. W. Montgomery (New York: Macmillan Publishing Co., 1968), pp. 372-375; and Stauffer, "ἐγώ," pp. 348-349.

[2]Pesch, "Eschatologie und Ethik," p. 226; Strecker, Weg, p. 240; Schweizer, Matthew, p. 448; and Hummel, Auseinandersetzung, pp. 86-87.

[3]Although I believe that Matthew is written after C.E. 70, this literary argument need not imply the destruction of 70.

climax the teaching of Jesus about the judgment against Israel. In private instruction to the disciples, Matt. 24:2 solemnly conveys that the judgment pronounced on Israel in 23:36-38 issues in the destruction of the temple. "All these things" are explicitly revealed to the disciples when Jesus says that "there will not be left here one stone upon another, that will not be thrown down."

Matthew 24:2b

Matthew has used the saying from Mark 13:2b with hardly any changes.[1] We have seen how Matthew has heavily redacted his introduction to this apophthegm (24:1-2a) so that this specific

---

[1]Οὐ μὴ ἀφεθῇ, just as in Mark, is an emphatic negative for the future (Ernest DeWitt Burton, Syntax of the Moods and Tenses in New Testament Greek [Edinburgh: T. and T. Clark, 1973], p. 78). As Taylor says, ὧδε "adds vividness to the saying, almost suggesting a gesture" (Taylor, Mark, p. 501). However, we cannot be certain that ὧδε is a Matthean addition because of its good textual attestation in Mark. Matthew's version deletes the harsh οὐ μή of Mark (cf. Allen, St. Matthew, p. 253) and has the future passive καταλυθήσεται instead of the futuristic subjunctive καταλυθῇ. The Lukan parallel has the same future passive reading (except with the dative λίθῳ). Καταλυθήσεται could be a "divine passive" in Matthew which suggests that God Himself/Herself will act to "throw down" the stones of the temple. This is a characteristically apocalyptic style of speech, and it could come from the so-called "little apocalypse" or even from Jesus himself (Jeremias, New Testament Theology, pp. 13, 126; and Bultmann, History of The Synoptic Tradition, p. 120).

160

prophecy of Jesus culminates the theme of judgment
upon Israel.  Jesus' pronouncement of judgment is
explicit in 24:2b, but symbolically the judgment
is performed by his departure from the temple in
24:1.[1]  As we have seen, when Jesus leaves the

---

[1]Our concern is with the meaning of this
prophecy in its Matthean context, that is, how it
relates to the interpretation of the eschatological discourse (24:3-31), not with its possible
Sitz im Leben Jesu.
The literature on this saying is voluminous
and the different opinions almost overwhelm any
interpreter.  We simply cannot entertain questions
at this point such as: "Is this a genuine saying
of Jesus, did he really predict the destruction
of the temple, and, if so, was his prediction
accurate (since the temple was destroyed by
fire)?"  Although there is considerable debate
over its precise form, the majority of commentators believe that the saying is a genuine saying
of Jesus.
The confusion arises from the fact that this
tradition is found in the gospels, as well as
elsewhere in the New Testament, in several forms.
The relevant passages are divided into two groups.
The first group, Mark 13:2 par. and Luke 19:44,
speaks only of Jerusalem's destruction.  A second
group of sayings (e.g., Mark 14:58 par.; 15:29
par.; John 2:19 cf. Acts 6:14; 2 Cor. 5:1) states
the destruction of Jerusalem, but these sayings
also mention or imply the building of a new
temple.  In effect, the latter would be not only
prophecies of judgment but possibly of salvation
as well (see F. Flückiger, "Die Redaktion der
Zukunftsrede in Mark 13," ThZ 26 [1970]: 404-409).
The original form, if there was only one form,
and the original context in which the statement(s)
was spoken become the crucial points for interpretation.  The relevant literature includes:

temple, it means for Matthew that God's presence
has abandoned it.  When God's presence abandons
the temple, the city and the whole nation are left
defenseless.  In other words, the loss of God's
presence <u>is</u> the judgment.  The physical destruction which follows (at whatever time) is only
evidence of the fact that God's judgment began
when the word of judgment was spoken (23:38), and
was executed when God's presence (in the person of
Jesus-Sophia) abandoned the temple (24:1).

Matthean redaction here indicates that the
evangelist wants to differentiate clearly between
the prophesied destruction of the temple and the
"consummation of the Age" (24:3).  The physical
destruction of the temple is part of the <u>past</u>
judgment upon Israel.  The destruction of the
temple does not initiate the end-time events, nor
is it the End itself.  It refers, rather, to the
loss of Israel's prerogatives in relation to
the kingdom.  The loss of God's presence, and the

---

Bultmann, <u>History of the Synoptic Tradition</u>, pp.
120-121; Taylor, <u>St. Mark</u>, p. 501; G. R. Beasley-
Murray, <u>A Commentary on Mark Thirteen</u>, pp. 22-24;
Eduard Schweizer, <u>The Good News According to Mark</u>,
trans. Donald H. Madvig (Atlanta: John Knox Press,
1970), pp. 261-268; Jan Lambrecht, <u>Die Redaktion
des Markus-Apocalypse: Literarische Analyse und
Strukturuntersuchung</u>, Analecta Biblica, no. 28
(Rome: Päpstliches Bibelinstitut, 1967), pp. 73-
80; Pesch, <u>Naherwartungen</u>, pp. 84-87; Gaston, <u>No
Stone on Another</u>, pp. 65-69 (p. 65 n. 1 has ex-
bibliography); and Lars Hartman, <u>Prophecy Interpreted: The Formation of Some Jewish Apocalyptic
Texts and of the Eschatological Discourse Mark 13
par.</u>, Coniectanea Biblica, New Testament Series
(Lund: CWK Gleerup, 1966), pp. 219-222.

corresponding privileges, constitutes the whole point of the judgment against Israel.[1]

The question for our purposes is: does Matthew see any relation between the physical destruction of the temple (24:2) and the "consummation of the Age" (24:3)? In other words, how does verse 2 relate to verse 3? Whether or not the evangelist is writing before or after C.E. 70, on purely literary grounds we conclude that when Jesus makes the pronouncement in 24:2, the judgment against Israel is completely executed. Once Jesus has prophetically announced judgment (23:38) and actually departed from the temple (24:1), its physical destruction is a surety.[2]  The announce-

---

[1]It is simply not enough, then, to ask whether καταλύω refers to: (1) the results of military action (whether C.E. 70 or not), or (2) some cosmic, apocalyptic (as opposed to a natural) catastrophe.  Καταλύω is a theologically important word in these kinds of contexts.  Καταλύω is used this way, for example, in Matt. 5:17 where Jesus says that he has not come to "destroy," that is, to "set aside," or to "invalidate," the Law (cf. Friedrich Büchsel, "λύω," TDNT 4:336 cf. p. 338 for meanings of καταλύω).  Once again the meaning of a word, as in the case of βλέπω, oscillates between the literal and the figurative.  The figurative seems to coincide with Matthew's overall point--that the judgment against Israel would culminate in the temple's destruction, and that Israel would lose its prerogatives (be "set aside") as God's people (cf. Ibid.; Trilling, Wahre, pp. 175-180; and Allen, St. Matthew, p. 46).

[2]In the prophetic concept of the "word of God," the historical fulfillment of God's judgment begins at the point the words are spoken, or

ment of the temple's physical destruction only reiterates the fact that Jesus-Sophia has permanently left the temple. Jesus leaves the temple (ἐξελθών), continues on his way from it (ἐπορεύετο), and reiterates the fact of judgment to the disciples as he goes (24:2). As soon as Jesus leaves the temple and pronounces its destruction, Israel is no longer God's people.[1]

This means that Jesus-Sophia's rejection of Israel is complete and that Matthew begins a new thought with verse 3. The evangelist constructs a new setting (the disciples come to Jesus on the Mount of Olives), and takes up the new question about Jesus' Parousia. In other words, Matthew has de-eschatologized Mark's reference to the temple's destruction.[2] His redaction has created a caesura between verses 2 and 3, and it has provided a new setting for a "parousia discourse." As Marxsen says: "Verse 3 actually introduces a new discourse which treats entirely of the Parousia still to come, but whose date is completely open and no longer connected with historical utterances."[3] We will discuss this point,

---

when the symbolic actions are performed, by the prophet (see Gerhard von Rad, Old Testament Theology, vol. 2, trans. D. M. G. Stalker [New York: Harper and Row, 1965], p. 95 cf. pp. 80-95).

[1]Hare, Theme of Jewish Persecution, p. 156.

[2]Ibid., p. 163.

[3]Marxsen, Mark the Evangelist, p. 199; cf. Pesch, "Eschatologie und Ethik," p. 227; Strecker, Weg, p. 240 n. 2; Beare, "Apocalypse," pp. 121-22; Schweizer, Matthew, pp. 448-449; and Schweizer, "Matthäus 21-25," p. 369. Contrast S. Brown, "The Matthean Apocalypse," JSNT 4 (1979): 3.

and its implications for interpreting the eschatological discourse, in detail in the next chapter.[1]  In closing this chapter, let us summarize Matthew's redaction which portrays Jesus as the Wisdom of God who has departed from Israel.

## Summary of Conclusions

The purpose of this chapter was to show that, on the basis of Matthean redaction of Q material in 23:34 (cf. Luke 11:49), Jesus is identified with the Wisdom of God.  The primary way the evangelist achieved his portrait of Jesus as Wisdom was to put a saying of Wisdom into Jesus' mouth.  Matthew redacts Q's ἡ σοφία τοῦ θεοῦ εἶπεν (Luke 11:49) to read ἰδοὺ ἐγὼ ἀποστέλλω (23:34).

This change not only identified Jesus with Sophia, but it also transferred to Jesus Wisdom's function of sending messengers to Israel.  In Q Jesus is one, or perhaps even the last, of Wisdom's ambassadors, but in Matthew Jesus is more than the last messenger before the Eschaton.  He is the personage who sent all of the messengers.

The Matthean context of Jesus' oracle as Wisdom shows that Matthew's point is that every generation in Israel has rejected God's messengers.  He is concerned to show, though, that the

---

[1]It does not follow from this that Matthew 24:15-22 must refer only to the past event of Jerusalem's destruction (cf. Hare, Jewish Persecution, p. 177; and Beare, "Apocalypse," pp. 124-133).  The caesura exists whether Matthew is writing before or after C.E. 70.  For the view that 24:2 and 24:3 cannot be so sharply separated, see Lambrecht, "Parousia Discourse," p. 318, especially n. 22.

envoys whom Israel continually rejected were sent by Jesus, the Wisdom of God.

Matthew's further point is that Israel has not only rejected the messengers sent by Jesus, but they have rejected Jesus himself. Jesus' deeds are deeds of Wisdom incarnate, as well as Messianic deeds. However, Israel has rejected Jesus' deeds just as they rejected the deeds of those sent by him to each generation. Israel has rejected Wisdom's messengers, which is serious enough, but when they rejected Jesus, they rejected Wisdom itself.

Judgment is pronounced over Israel because of their continual rejection of Wisdom and its envoys. The judgment is that "your house is [and will continue to be] forsaken" (23:38). The judgment means that Israel will lose the presence of God (the Shekinah) which is embodied in Jesus-Sophia. Therefore, for Matthew the departure of Jesus from the temple means that Israel has lost God's presence.

In Israel's rejection of Jesus Matthew sees the perennial rejection of Wisdom. Matthew is evidently working with a generalized, traditional concept in which Wisdom seeks a dwelling-place in Israel, but is rejected and withdraws from them. He has skillfully placed his identification of Jesus with Wisdom in a context which culminates a rejection motif in his gospel. Israel's continual rejection of Jesus' messengers, and now the rejection of Jesus-Sophia himself, culminates in Sophia's rejection of Israel. Jesus-Sophia withdraws his presence from them. The evangelist's redaction indicates that he intends for Jesus' departure from the temple (24:1) to be read in the same context as Jesus' pronouncement of judgment (23:38). Israel's house is forsaken because of their continual rejection of Jesus' envoys

166

and, finally, of Jesus himself (23:32-36, 37-39).

Thus, for Matthew the departure of Jesus
from the temple is the definitive withdrawal of
Wisdom's presence from Israel. Jesus' departure
is the permanent loss of God's presence for
Israel. When he leaves the temple in 24:1, Jesus
has fulfilled his pronouncement of judgment in
23:38.

The loss of God's presence from the temple
also means the withdrawal of His/Her protection
and guidance. To put it succinctly, the loss of
God's presence from the temple means the doom of
the whole nation. When Jesus permanently abandons
the temple in 24:1, it means that all Israel is
rejected.

Matthew has Jesus teach his disciples the
significance of his action. The loss of his
presence from the temple is the prophetic fulfillment of the judgment pronounced in 23:38.
Furthermore, the loss of God's presence in Israel
is the judgment, and it will ultimately issue in
the temple's destruction. The significance of
Jesus' action, then, is: the loss of Jesus'
presence is the judgment of God upon Israel,
even though only the disciples can perceive it
(βλέπω). The pronouncement of the temple's
physical destruction (24:2) is simply a re-
iteration of the judgment for the disciples' sake
so that they will understand the significance of
his departure from the temple.

It is obvious that neither Israel nor
Jesus' followers would perceive the significance
of Jesus' action if he did not reveal it to them.
Matthew, though, only has Jesus' "disciples"
approach him for the revelation. The concept of
the "disciples" operates on two levels for
Matthew. On the one hand, the disciples represent

the intimate followers of Jesus in his time to
whom he teaches the "secrets of the kingdom of
heaven" (cf. 13:11). In contrast to the crowd,
they are taught by Jesus (cf. 13:11, 16-17).
Jesus deliberately withholds his teaching from the
crowd because their obduracy impedes their ability
to understand him (cf. 13:10, 13, 14-15, 34). The
"disciples," however, do perceive who Jesus is and
have faith in him. Their faith is not yet complete trust. It is "little faith," but it is
faith, and they approach Jesus (προσέρχομαι) with
due veneration.

On the other hand, the "disciples" operate
as representative followers of Jesus. For Matthew
the disciples have post-Easter faith. He does not
historicize them and encapsulate them into Jesus'
own time. The evangelist does not idealize the
disciples either. They are persons of "little
faith" who follow Jesus with fear and have to cry
out for him to save them. By means of this
portrait of the disciples, Matthew is able to
include in his gospel the problems of any post-
Easter follower of Jesus. Of course, his target
is his own church community. Thus, the "disciples" of Jesus' time are coalesced with
Matthew's own community and its problems so that
the phrase includes both groups.

Consequently, Jesus' teaching to the disciples about his departure from the temple does
not just apply to Jesus' time. It also tells
Jesus' followers of Matthew's day that the judgment against Israel was the loss of Jesus'
presence. For Matthew the judgment was completed
and sealed in the past (Jesus' time) when Jesus
permanently left the temple. The judgment against
Israel belongs to the past, not to the Eschaton.
Even if the temple is (or has been) physically
destroyed, that is only the empirical aftershock
of the judgment which took place in Jesus'

abandonment of it.  Matthew's community must understand that Jesus' abandonment of Israel was permanent.  His presence now dwells with the "disciples," Matthew's community, and not with Israel
(cf. 18:20; 28:20).

By relegating the judgment of Israel to the
past (including the temple's destruction), and by
constructing an entirely new scene in 24:3,
Matthew creates a caesura between 24:2 and 24:3.
After 24:2 Jesus-Sophia turns his attention solely
to the disciples.  He reveals eschatological
secrets to them in private upon the Mount of
Olives.  The revelation concerns the question of
when Jesus-Sophia will return as Son of Man.
Matthew's church has inherited this revelation
from the disciples who received it in Jesus' time.
The revelation has become a "testament" which
should help the disciples of Matthew's time
"endure until the end" (24:13).  It is upon the
testament of Jesus-Sophia that we must now focus
our attention.

## Excursus I: The Pre-Existence
## of Jesus in Matthew

There is general agreement that Matthew
identifies Jesus with pre-existent Wisdom, but it
is extremely difficult to say exactly what that
entails for his christology.  The concept of
"pre-existence" itself has many connotations in
the various streams of Jewish traditions which
influence the Synoptic tradition.[1]

---

[1]On the possible understandings of pre-
existence used for Christ in the New Testament
see Fred B. Craddock, The Pre-Existence of Christ
in the New Testament (New York: Abingdon Press,
1968), pp. 18-19.  See also the major study by

It is commonly known that Wisdom was a personified, preexistent principle used by God when He/She began creation (cf. Job 28). Personified Wisdom takes an active part in the creative act in Prov. 8:22-30. In the development of this tradition preexistent Wisdom is commanded by God to dwell in Israel (cf. Sirach 24:7, 9, 10-12). Wisdom is also identified with Torah in this tradition (Sirach 24:22, 23). A variant form of this tradition is found in 1 Enoch 42:1-3 where Wisdom seeks a dwelling place, is rejected, and returns to heaven. It was preexistent Wisdom also who dwelt in holy souls and made them prophets for each generation.[1]

It seems that Matthew draws primarily from this complex of ideas about preexistent Sophia for his presentation of Jesus. In the context of Matthew 23:34-39 the identification of Jesus with preexistent Wisdom allows Jesus to assume Wisdom's function as the Sender of prophets to each

---

Hamerton-Kelly, Pre-Existence, p. 21. Much fruitful research is being done with the christological hymns and their relationship to Wisdom and the category of preexistence (see Elisabeth S. Fiorenza, "Wisdom Mythology and the Christological Hymns of the New Testament," in Robert L. Wilken, ed., Aspects of Wisdom in Judaism and Early Christianity [Notre Dame, Indiana: University of Notre Dame Press, 1975], pp. 17-42).

[1]The identification of Wisdom with Torah was developed further by the Rabbis (e.g., Aboth 3:14) while Hellenistic Judaism, particularly Philo, identified Sophia with the Logos. See Hamerton-Kelly, Pre-Existence, pp. 19-20.

generation. The problem, of course, for our understanding of Matthew's christology is that he, like most of the New Testament writers, does not explicitly state the myth(s) of pre-existence which he assumes, nor does he elaborate upon the "nature" of the pre-existent Christ. Matthew's main interest seems to be in the incarnation of Christ and the soteriological function which he performs in the history of salvation.[1] Even in the infancy narratives, a place where he could explicitly depict a clear understanding of Christ's pre-existence, Matthew only seems to imply that Jesus was pre-existent in the mind of God when God planned the soteriological function of Christ as the fulfillment of the scriptures (cf. 1:8-25).[2]

We must be careful not to conclude, though, that the pre-existence of Jesus was unimportant for Matthew or his community simply because the direct assertion "Jesus is Wisdom" does not appear. For Matthew, Jesus is a trans-historical figure who has sent Israel prophets in each generation. Jesus is the one who would have gathered his children often if only they would have let him (ποσάκις, 23:37). The notion of Jesus' pre-existence must be deduced from the structure of Matthew's redaction, except perhaps in his explicit use of symbols like Son of Man, but the use of traditional images and language implies that pre-existence is a more important category for Matthew than is usually assumed.

---

[1]The New Testament writers as a whole seem to be interested primarily in the pre-existence of Christ as it relates to his soteriological function within salvation history (cf. Craddock, Pre-Existence of Christ, pp. 83-84).

[2]Cf. Hamerton-Kelly, Pre-Existence, 77-79.

<u>Excursus II: Prophets, Wise Men,</u>
<u>and Scribes in Matt. 23:34</u>

There is a consensus among those who accept
the argument that Matthew has identified Jesus
with Sophia that the "prophets, wise men, and
scribes" in 23:34 include Matthew's community.[1]
As we have seen, the net effect of Matthew's
redaction makes the statement an act which Jesus-
Sophia performs <u>in every generation</u>: "Because of
this (διὰ τοῦτο), I (ἐγώ), Jesus, am sending
(ἀποστέλλω) to you prophets and wise men and
scribes."[2] However, there is neither a consensus
about what these terms imply functionally for such
figures within Matthew's community, nor about the
implications the terms have for its organization.
It is possible that the terms imply little or
nothing about distinct offices or functionaries
within Matthew's community. Many researchers,
though, believe the terms to be important to the
evangelist's church.

The majority of commentators contend that
Matthew has preserved the older reading concerning
the messengers since Luke's version, in which he
couples "apostles" with "prophets" (11:49), is a

---

[1]Bornkamm, "End-Expectation and Church in
Matthew," <u>TI</u>, p. 39; Johnson, <u>Matthew</u>, p. 539;
Hill, <u>Matthew</u>, pp. 314-315; Stendahl, <u>School</u>,
p. 34; cf. Jack Dean Kingsbury, <u>Matthew</u>, Proclamation Commentaries (Philadelphia: Fortress Press,
1977), pp. 74-76, 90, 97, 101.

[2]Hare, <u>Theme of Jewish Persecution</u>, p. 87;
cf. Schweizer, <u>Matthew</u>, pp. 178, 443.

distinctively Hellenistic-Christian one (cf.
1 Cor. 12:28; Eph. 2:20; 4:11).[1]

The Matthean version of "prophets, wise men,
and scribes" is a traditional Jewish one, and it
implies that Matthew characterizes Christian
missionaries in terms which were used in contemporary Jewish institutions.[2] The terms γραμματεῖς
and σοφούς imply that there were those in the
community who were adept in the interpretation and

---

[1]M'Neile, St. Matthew, p. 339; Friedrich,
"προφήτης," TDNT 6: 835; Haenchen, Matthäus 23,"
p. 53; Johnson, Matthew, p. 539; and Allen,
Matthew, p. 250. ᾿Απόστολος occurs frequently in
the New Testament, but infrequently in Hellenistic
Judaism. It is not an exclusively "Christian"
term, but an adapted one. It occurs in the LXX
only once (I Kings 14:6). It appears that
ἀπόστολος became the early Christian designation
for one who is sent with full authority after the
fashion of the institution of the šlîaḥ in later
rabbinical Judaism (cf. Karl Rengstorf,
"ἀπόστολος," TDNT 1: 421 cf. pp. 407-408).

[2]Allen, Matthew, p. 250. Bornkamm argues
that this phrase is evidence that Matthew's church
had not yet separated from the Synagogue
(Bornkamm, "End-Expectation and Church in
Matthew," TI, p. 39). This conclusion, however,
does not necessarily follow from the traditional
Jewish language of Matt. 23:34. In the same
verse Matthew uses the redactional "your synagogues," which implies separation from that
institution (cf. 4:23; 9:35; 10:17; 12:9; 13:54).

teaching of the Scriptures.[1] Stendahl has contended that a school of Christian scribes who were adept in their use of the _pesher_ method produced the First Gospel.[2] Matthew 13:52 does imply that there were teachers of the Law (πᾶς γραμματεύς) who were disciples of Jesus (μαθητευθεὶς τῇ βασιλείᾳ) and who were, consequently, "wise persons" (cf. 7:24). In the context of chapter 13 the disciples (13:36) are those who have understood the parables about the kingdom (13:51). They are especially qualified then to teach the "gospel of the kingdom" (4:23; 9:35; 24:14) which, as we will discuss below, is directly related to Jesus' Word-Deed redefinition of the Law in terms of the love command.[3] The explicit mission of the disciples is to "make disciples" (μαθητεύσατε, 28:19), and this primarily means teaching them to

---

[1]See Joachim Jeremias, "γραμματεύς," TDNT 1: 740-742; Bornkamm, "End-Expectation and Church in Matthew," TI, p. 25; and Wilckens, "σοφία," TDNT 7: 505.

[2]Stendahl, School, pp. 35, 190-206. Stendahl perhaps goes too far when he suggests that the _form_ of the First Gospel is a manual for church administration and teaching (Ibid., p. 35). See the critiques of his position by Bornkamm, "End-Expectation and Church in Matthew," pp. 50-51; and Bertil Gärtner, "The Habbakkuk Commentary (DSH) and the Gospel of Matthew," STh 8 (1955): 1-24. For a succinct presentation of the _pesher_ method as employed at Qumran see Daniel Patte, Early Jewish Hermeneutic in Palestine, SBL Dissertation Series, no. 22 (Missoula, Montana: Scholars Press, 1975), pp. 299-308.

[3]See the discussion of Matt. 24:14 in chapter 3 below.

live according to Jesus' redefinition of God's will.[1]

The "prophets" in Matthew's community also proclaim the "gospel of the kingdom."[2]   In Matthew this means that they not only proclaim the Law as redefined by Jesus, but they continue his charismatic deeds as well.[3]   Matthew has strong warnings against false prophets who cause "lawlessness" (ἀνομία) to multiply.[4]   Matthew's warnings imply that there are true prophets in the community whose function is to proclaim God's Law as interpreted by Jesus and to warn of the judgment to fall upon those who practice ἀνομία.[5]   It is not clear whether the community prophets are itinerant ones who wander from church to church (cf. 10:41), or whether their activity is confined exclusively to the community.[6]

---

[1]Διδάσκοντες αὐτοὺς τηρεῖν πάντα ὅσα ἐνετειλάμην ὑμῖν (28:20), namely, the love command (cf. Matt. 22:34-40).

[2]Cf. 10:41 with 10:7.

[3]Cf. 10:1 with 9:8; 10:20, 24-25; 24:11, 24.

[4]Cf. 7:15-23; 24:11-12.

[5]Cf. 5:12; 7:19, 21-23; 10:41; 23:34.   See Schweizer, Matthew, p. 179; and Kingsbury, Matthew, p. 102.   The false prophets seem to be enthusiasts who disregard the commands of Jesus (see the discussion of 24:5 in chapter 3 below).

[6]Schweizer believes that they are itinerant prophets ("Observance of the Law and Charismatic Activity in Matthew," pp. 218-224; contrast É. Cothenet, "Les prophètes chrétiens dans l'Évangile selon saint Matthieu," L'Évangile

It seems, then, that Matt. 23:34 suggests that there could be at least two groups with similar, though distinct, functions within the Matthean community. First, there are the scribes and wise persons who interpret the redefined Law of Jesus in <u>pesher</u> fashion. The second group consists of the charismatic prophets. They too proclaim the words of Jesus, but they validate their message by special claims to Jesus' presence and ἐξουσία.[1]

Although there were probably groups with specific functions in the community, there seem to be no hierarchical offices as in contemporary Judaism. Matthew's community, in contrast to the "scribes and Pharisees," seems to forbid the acceptance of titles (cf. 23:8-12).[2] Even the

---

<u>selon Matthieu</u>, ed. M. Didier (Gembloux: J. Duculot, 1972), pp. 291-293; and Jack Dean Kingsbury, "The Verb <u>Akolouthein</u> ("To Follow") as an Index of Matthew's View of His Community," <u>JBL</u> 97 (1978): 63-67.

[1]Contrast Ibid., pp. 68-70. Other possible groups include the "Righteous" (cf. 10:41), and the "little ones" (e.g., 10:42). The "Righteous Ones" most likely are seen in the general eschatological perspective of anyone who will be pronounced thus at the final judgment (cf. 13:43, 49; 25:37, 46. See Schweizer, <u>Matthew</u>, p. 181; and Cothenet, "Les Prophètes chrétiens," pp. 297-298). If they are a distinct group within the community, then they too are probably teachers (cf. David Hill, "<u>Dikaioi</u> as a Quasi-Technical Term," <u>NTS</u> 11 [1965]: 296-302). The μικροί simply is another designation in Matthew for "the disciples" (see Cothenet, "Les prophètes chrétiens," pp. 296-297).

[2]Matthew never speaks of ἐπίσκοποι, and

authority which Jesus gives to Peter (16:19) is
given to the entire community (18:18).[1]  In
Matthew Peter is simply representative of the
disciples as a whole.[2]  Matthew's community is

---

when πρεσβύτεροι is used it always denotes leaders
of the Jews (15:2; 16:21; 21:23; 26:3, 47, 57, 59;
27:1, 3, 12, 20, 41; 28:12).

[1]Schweizer, Matthew, p. 180; Davies, Sermon
on the Mount, p. 228; and Paul Hoffmann, "Der
Petrus-Primat in Matthäusevangelium," Neues
Testament und Kirche, ed. J. Gnilka (Freiburg:
Herder, 1974), pp. 94-114.

   Paul Minear contends that Matthew's community is composed of the ὄχλοι and the μαθηταί.
The ὄχλοι are the general followers of Jesus and
the μαθηταί are προφηται who have received special
gifts of vision and knowledge which set them apart
from the ὄχλοι.  His thesis rests upon his assumption that Matthew's "Gospel was designed as a
manual for Church leaders," namely, the
"disciples" as "prophets," and that "his Gospel
concentrated upon the training of prophet-
teachers" (Minear, "False Prophecy and Hypocrisy
in the Gospel of Matthew," Neues Testament und
Kirche, ed. J. Gnilka [Freiburg: Herder, 1974],
p. 79 cf. pp. 76-77).  For a general critique of
this view of ὄχλοι in Matthew see appendix 1.

   Although Matthew's community has function-
aries, it is not as hierarchically developed as
the Qumran community (cf. Davies, Sermon on the
Mount, pp. 208-256; and Joachim Gnilka, "Der
Kirche des Matthäus und die Gemeinde von Qumrân,"
BibZeit, Neue Folge 7 [1963]: 43-63).

   [2]See Günther Bornkamm, "The Authority to
'Bind' and 'Loose' in the Church in St. Matthew's
Gospel," Jesus and Man's Hope, ed. D. G. Buttrick,
vol. 1 (Pittsburgh: Pittsburgh Theological

organized by Jesus' interpretation of the Law in terms of the love command. This means that they are all brothers and sisters (23:8), and they are not to exalt one member of the community over another in hierarchical fashion (23:11-12).[1] Thus, while the "prophets, wise men, and scribes" in 23:34 imply distinct functionaries, the terms refer also to all disciples with no hierarchical restrictions.[2]

Although there is some agreement concerning the sociological structure of Matthew's community (its egalitarian nature, and at least the two functionaries of teachers and prophets), there is little agreement concerning the socio-economic status of the community. There is general agreement about the community's general location (Syria), and perhaps further data about Christians and Jews in this area will enhance our understanding of the socio-economic status of the Matthean community.[3]

---

Seminary, 1970): 37-50.

[1]Gnilka, "Der Kirche des Matthäus und die Gemeinde von Qumrân," pp. 51-57; Edgar Krentz, "The Egalitarian Church of Matthew," Currents in Theology and Missions 4 (1977): 333-341; Rengstorf, "ἀπόστολος," pp. 424-425; and Kingsbury, Matthew, p. 103.

[2]Schweizer, Matthew, pp. 179, 181; cf. Bornkamm, "End-Expectation and Church in Matthew," pp. 18, 39; and Strecker, Weg, p. 40 cf. p. 38.

[3]Cf. Wayne A. Meeks and Robert L. Wilken, Jews and Christians in Antioch in the First Four Centuries of the Common Era (Missoula, Montana: Scholars Press, 1978).

Commentators have long posited a Syrian
location for the Matthean community.  B. H.
Streeter located it in Antioch, and B. W. Bacon
suggested the general area of eastern Syria.[1]  A
great deal can be said for a Syrian location.  The
Didache, a Syrian document (ca. 100), is heavily
dependent upon the First Gospel and reflects many
of the same concerns.  The problem of false
prophets reflected in the Didache is most noteworthy.  They, just as in Matthew, preach ἀνομία
(cf. Didache 11:8-11; 16:3).  As we will see, the
problem of false prophets within the community who
cause ἀνομία is an important concern of Matthew's
(24:10-12).[2]  Syria also had an apocalyptic outlook, again reflected in the Didache (chap. 16),
similar to that of Matthew.[3]  Apocalyptic enthusiasm in Syria was enhanced until at least the
late second century, perhaps because of the
"Nero redividus myth," and the Didache's interpretation of the "desolating sacrilege" of Matt.
24:15 in terms of the "World-Deceiver" reflects
these concerns.[4]

---

[1]B. H. Streeter, The Four Gospels.  A
Study of Origins (London: Macmillan and Co., Ltd.,
1930), pp. 486-487; and Bacon, Studies in Matthew,
pp. 35-36.  Cf. H. D. Slingerland, "The Trans-
jordanian Origin of St. Matthew's Gospel," JSNT 3
(1979): 18-28.

[2]See the discussion of 24:10-12 in chapter
3 below.

[3]See the discussion in Schweizer, Matthew,
pp. 182-184.

[4]See the discussion in Streeter, The Four
Gospels, p. 487.

In general, then, commentators have accepted
a Syrian location for the community which produced
Matthew's gospel.[1]  There are, though, two widely
divergent views of the sociological mobility and
economic status of the community.  On the one
hand, E. Schweizer has argued that Matthew's
community is a community of itinerant, homeless,
charismatic prophets who ascetically renounce
conjugal relations, wealth, and dependence upon
anything except the Spirit.  Schweizer bases his
argument upon the literary evidence of the
Didache, the Gospel of Thomas, the Pseudo-
Clementines, and the Apocalypse of Peter.  He
argues that this literary evidence reflects the
situation of a strain of Syrian Christianity
which persisted until well into the fourth
century.  This group of Syrian Christians, as the
poor and the homeless, lived in fervent expectation of the Parousia.  Their type of discipleship,
contends Schweizer, is imitation of the poor, un-
married, and homeless Jesus who is presented in
Matthew's gospel as the model of this lifestyle.[2]
On the other hand, J. D. Kingsbury argues that
Matthew's community is a prosperous city church
whose ethic is primarily one of the "higher
righteousness" (5:20) rather than one of radical
asceticism.[3]

---

[1]Eduard Schweizer, Church Order in the New
Testament, SBT, trans. Frank Clarke (Naperville,
Illinois: Alec R. Allenson, Inc., 1959), p. 51;
and Kilpatrick, Origins of the Gospel According to
St. Matthew, pp. 124-134.

[2]Schweizer, Matthew, pp. 182-184; and
Schweizer, "Observance of the Law and Charismatic
Activity in Matthew," pp. 213-230.

[3]Kingsbury, "The Verb Akolouthein ("To
Follow") as an Index to Matthew's View of His

Our analysis of the eschatological discourse suggests that Matthew's community is an open one which will admit Jew or Gentile and treat all as brothers and sisters (cf. 24:11-12 to 23:8). The community is conscious of its participation in the world-wide mission (24:14 cf. 28:20), which could suggest a cosmopolitan constituency and outlook. The community, though, seems to be in a socially hostile situation with Gentiles (cf. 24:9 to 10:18, 22) and completely alienated religiously, if not socially, from the institutions of Judaism (cf. 10:5-6, 17; 21:43; 23:34-24:2). We may speculate that Matthew's community is a sociologically and economically marginal group which interprets their rejection and lower economic rank as the necessary upshot of following the humiliated Jesus. Although the community is open to all, it is somewhat sectarian in character because of its interpretation of the Law by Jesus' life. "Hypocrisy" is defined as "lawlessness," that is, not giving one's full allegiance to their sectarian understanding of the Jewish Law. Consequently, the correct interpretation of the Law occurs only "in the name" of Jesus (cf. 18:20; 28:20). God, in Jesus, has left the temple (cf. 23:38; 24:1-2) and the institutions of Judaism in order to dwell in Matthew's community. If, as we argue below, the Matthean community is conscious

---

Community," pp. 64-73; cf. Kilpatrick, <u>Origins of the Gospel according to St. Matthew</u>, pp. 124-134.

of itself as one organized and commissioned by Jesus-Sophia, then it would appear that a fruitful path for research would be to examine what it would mean socially and economically in a Wisdom oriented community to take upon oneself the "yoke" of Jesus-Sophia (11:28-30).[1]

---

[1]See, e.g., William R. Schoedel, "Jewish Wisdom and the Formation of the Christian Ascetic," Aspects of Wisdom in Judaism and Early Christianity, ed. Robert L. Wilken (Notre Dame, Indiana: University of Notre Dame Press, 1975), pp. 169-197.

# CHAPTER III

# THE TESTAMENT OF JESUS

## Introduction

Our thesis has been that Matthew intends
24:3-31 to be read as a testament of Jesus-Sophia.
If the thesis is subdivided, it would have three
parts. (1) The speaker in the discourse is
Jesus-Sophia. (2) Matthean redaction has created
a caesura between 24:2 and 24:3. He has done
this (a) by depicting the judgment of Jesus-Sophia
against Israel as fulfilled with his permanent
departure from the temple (24:1) and his announcement of its destruction (24:2), and (b) by constructing a completely new introduction in 24:3
for the subsequent discourse. (3) The redaction
of the introduction in verse 3 shows that Matthew
intends the subsequent discourse to be read as a
Parousia discourse, that is, the discourse is a
revelation of what will happen from the time of
Jesus' departure (his death) until his Parousia
as the Son of Man. It does not deal with the
predicted destruction of the temple (24:2). The
destruction of Jerusalem could be either past or
future for Matthew, depending upon the date one
assigns to the gospel.

In the previous chapter we argued that
Matthean redaction presented Jesus-Sophia as the
speaker in the discourse and created a caesura
between 24:2 and 24:3. This leaves unanswered
the question of what the discourse actually says,
that is, its function and extent in the gospel as
well as its meaning. In order to answer this
question, our presentation will proceed in three
general stages. In the first stage we will
attempt to answer the question of the genre and
the extent of the discourse in Matthew. Does
this discourse have more affinity with the genre

183

of an apocalypse or a farewell discourse? Does
determining the genre help us interpret the function of the discourse? Where does the discourse
actually end? We will attempt to show that the
discourse shares characteristics with both the
apocalypse and the farewell discourse. This means
that the function of the discourse, like that of
an apocalypse, is a recitation of events to precede the End in order to encourage a community in
a distressful situation. It also means that the
discourse, like a testament, imparts instructions
about the task and fate of the hearers which will
befall them after Jesus-Sophia's departure. We
will attempt to show that the testament per se
ends at 24:31, and that Matthew has seven parables
following it (24:32-25:46) in order to reenforce
parenetically the instructions and injunctions
given in verses 3-31. Interpreters agree,
however, that these conclusions are dependent upon
one's interpretation of 24:3. Therefore, the
second stage of our argument will consist of a
detailed analysis of Matthean redaction in the
introduction to the discourse (24:3). The primary
questions are: to whom is the discourse addressed,
and what is the subject of the discourse? We will
see that several Matthean redactional themes are
focused in 24:3 and give the portrait of Jesus
as he addresses only one question from his disciples, namely, that of the appearance of the sign
of his Parousia which will, in turn, initiate the
End. The content of the whole discourse attempts
to answer the disciples' question about Jesus'
Parousia. The third stage of our discussion,
then, will analyze Jesus' answer to that question.
We will see that Matthew uses traditional material
but that he rearranges it, and perhaps composes
new material (e.g., 24:10-12), in order to provide
a new context for the traditional material. The
new context indicates what is of special importance to him and to his community. On the one
hand, his special concerns will appear as threats

184

posed to his community by false prophets and the "abomination of desolation" which threatens all Christians.  On the other hand, the evangelist's concerns are reflected in the world-wide mission which his community and the Church-at-large must attempt in spite of those threats.  For Matthew the consolation which Jesus' discourse gives is that the knowledge imparted in it will help Christians endure in their mission until the End (cf. 24:13, 14).

## Part 1.  The Genre and Extent of the Discourse

### Farewell or Apocalyptic Discourse?

As we discussed in chapter 1, most interpreters view Matthew 24 as an apocalyptic discourse.  This emphasis undoubtedly grew out of research into the so-called "Little Apocalypse," and from the undeniable apocalyptic characteristics within the discourse itself.[1]  It is untenable to conclude, in view of the debate concerning apocalyptic, that a discourse is an "apocalypse" because it has apocalyptic characteristics.  As we noted earlier, the nature of the particular apocalyptic tradition of any text has to be considered.[2]  Many of the characteristics one would usually expect to find in an apocalyptic text do not occur in Matthew 24.  For example, to cite only a few, there are no visions, the text is not pseudonymous, and numerology does not occur.  A simplistic categorization of Matthew's

---

[1]See the discussion on pp. 14-18 above.

[2]Cf. John J. Collins, ed., Apocalypse: The Morphology of a Genre, Semeia, vol. 14 (Missoula, Montana: Scholars Press, 1979).

discourse as "apocalyptic" is meaningless because his apocalypticism seems to be influenced by Wisdom speculation.

In recent years it has been suggested that the apocalyptic discourse in Mark 13 takes the form of a farewell discourse.[1] Several commentators have proposed also that Matthew's apocalyptic discourse should be read as a farewell discourse. Peter Ellis, for example, notes that the farewell discourse of the Fourth Gospel is located at the Last Supper. Comparing the Fourth Gospel with the Synoptics, he says:

> The synoptic authors, on the other hand, for reasons that go back to the author of the Markan apocalyptic discourse, retained the last sayings of Jesus in their account of the supper and the agony in the garden, and chose to situate the farewell discourse one day before the last supper and on the Mount Olivet instead of in the supper room.[2]

---

[1]E.g., Rigaux, Testimony of St. Mark, pp. 16-23; Gaston, No Stone on Another, pp. 42-65; F. Busch, Zum Verständnis der synoptischen Eschatologie: Markus 13 neu untersucht (Gütersloh: Gerd Mohn, 1938), pp. 44-56; and W. Michaelis, Der Herr verzieht nicht der Verheissung (Bern: n.p., 1942), pp. 22-26.

[2]Ellis, Matthew: His Mind and His Message, p. 84; cf. L. Cope, "Matthew XXV: 31-46 'The Sheep and the Goats' Reinterpreted," NovTest 11 (1969): 33. Stendahl sees Jesus' farewell discourse primarily as the parable in Matt. 25:31-46 (see Stendahl, School, p. 26 n. 5). But it is not possible to reduce Jesus' farewell discourse to the parable of judgment only since that para-

The genre has been analyzed in great detail.[1] Briefly, a farewell discourse is " . . . an address which often has the character of a testament, in which the leader, facing the prospect of approaching death, or handing over his office for some other reason, says farewell to his

---

ble hinges upon the central concern of the chapter depicted in 24:3, namely, Jesus' Parousia and the end of the age. To put it succinctly, it might be possible to expand Jesus' farewell discourse to include 25:31-46, but it is not possible to reduce the whole farewell discourse to that similitude (cf. L. Cope "Matthew XXV: 31-46 'The Sheep and the Goats' Reinterpreted," p. 33).

[1]For detailed descriptions of farewell discourses see Otto Eissfeldt, The Old Testament: An Introduction, trans. Peter R. Ackroyd (New York: Harper and Row, Publishers, 1965), pp. 12-16; E. Stauffer, "Abschiedsreden," Reallexikon für Antike und Christentum, vol. 1, ed. by Theodor Klauser (Stuttgart: Hiersemann, 1950), cols. 29-35; Johannes Munck, "Discours d'adieu dans le Nouveau Testament et dans la littérature biblique," in the Festschrift for M. Goguel, Au Sources de la tradition chrétienne (Paris: n.p., 1950), pp. 155-170; and Hans-Joachim Michel, Die Abschiedsrede des Paulus an Die Kirche Apg 20,17-38. Motivgeschichte und theologische Bedeutung (München: Kösel-Verlag, 1973). Raymond Brown has a detailed analysis of the genre as it applies to the Fourth Gospel, and a few remarks as it applies to the Synoptic apocalypse(s). See Raymond Brown, The Gospel According to John (xiii-xxi), The Anchor Bible, vol. 29A (Garden City, New York: Doubleday, 1970), pp. 597-601.

people or to his followers."[1] There are numerous examples of farewell discourses in the biblical tradition.[2] The broad features of the form are: (1) a great person speaks just before his/her death; (2) instructions, commands, and commissions are given to his/her successors; (3) predictions about the fate of his/her followers are given along with (4) appeals for his/her followers to live in unity and/or love; (5) words of consolation, peace, and hope are expressed for his/her followers; (6) threats of judgment are usually made for those who either persecute the followers, or for the followers who do not remain faithful to the speaker's commands and appeals; (7) a suc-

---

[1]Eissfeldt, The Old Testament: An Introduction, p. 13.

[2]Some examples in the Tanak are: Gen. 47:29-50:14, Deuteronomy (the entire book), Josh. 23:1-24:32, 1 Sam. 12, and 1 Kings 2:1-9. Some New Testament examples of the genre are: John 13-17, Acts 20:17-38, and 2 Tim. 3:1-4:8. Some extra-biblical examples of the genre are: 1 Macc. 2:49-68, 2 Macc. 7, all of The Testaments of the Twelve Patriarchs, Tob. 14:3-11, and 2 Esd. 14:28-36.

We are not including a discussion of the Greek tradition on the farewell discourse since it is somewhat different than the Jewish tradition. In particular the Greek tradition seeks to embody an ideal in the speech of the departing figure, who is usually a θεῖος ἄνθρωπος, while the Jewish tradition presents the departing figure within the context of the community and salvation history. Cf. Stauffer, "Abschiedsreden," cols. 29-30; and Karl Holl, "Die schriftstellerische Form des griechischen Heiligenlebens," Gesammelte Aufsätze zur Kirchengeschichte, vol. 2 (Tübingen: J. C. B. Mohr, 1928).

cessor is sometimes chosen; and (8) usually the address is closed with a prayer for those who are left behind.[1] There is no prescribed order in which these characteristics must appear in any given discourse. If most of these elements do appear in a discourse, regardless of the order, then an interpreter may conclude that he/she is dealing with a farewell discourse. Furthermore, there is no prescribed length for a farewell discourse. The length of the discourse probably was determined by the needs (instructional, pareneti- cal, etc.) of the particular situation.[2] Thus, because of the flexibility of the genre, we are hesitant to call Matthew's eschatological dis- course a "farewell discourse." The designation, in fact, could be misleading if one assumes that a literary norm exists to which we could subject our analysis of Matthew's discourse.[3] We could superficially parallel characteristics of fare- well discourses with the discourse in Matthew and conclude that we have that genre, though we have

---

[1]Cf. Munck, "Discours d'adieu dans le Nouveau Testament et dans la littérature biblique," p. 159; Brown, The Gospel According to John (xiii-xxi), pp. 598-601; and Ethelbert Stauffer, New Testament Theology, trans. John Marsh (New York: The Macmillan Co., 1955), pp. 344-347.

[2]See Amos Wilder, Early Christian Rhetoric. The Language of the Gospel (London: SCM Press, Ltd., 1964), p. 29.

[3]See Wilder's caution, for example, about calling John 13-17 a farewell discourse (Ibid., p. 43).

to note that these elements can be omitted or re-arranged within the body of any farewell discourse.[1]

The problem, then, is that Matthew's discourse does not precisely fit the genre of the farewell discourse. One of the main ingredients of almost every farewell discourse is missing in Matt. 24, namely, Jesus never explicitly predicts his own death, or for that matter even the fact that he is going away, though this is implied in the disciples' question in 24:3.

The only point we are trying to make with this brief discussion is that Jesus' discourse in Matt. 24 does not fit neatly into either the apocalypse or the farewell discourse forms. The discourse shares characteristics with both forms, but it cannot be reduced to one or the other.[2]

The combination of the two forms, though, is not unusual and is well-attested in apocalyptic

---

[1]For example, in Matthew Jesus speaks just before his death (cf. 26:1), and 23:39 certainly implies his departure as well as a successor (the Son of Man). The setting for the speech is an intimate one ("privately") with his closest followers ("the disciples," 24:3). He foretells their fate (24:4-8, 9-12, 15-31), exhorts them to endure (24:13), commissions them to carry on his message (24:14 cf. 4:23;28:19-20), indirectly appeals for their unity and love (cf. 24:4-5, 10-12), and encourages them (24:22).

[2]Contrast Ellis, Matthew: His Mind and His Message, p. 86.

literature.[1]   Scholarship today seems to be moving
toward the consensus that Jesus' discourse in
Matt. 24 seems to combine the characteristics of
the apocalyptic and farewell discourses, and,
further, that these elements were already combined
in the pre-Matthean "Synoptic Apocalypse."[2]   The
discourse should be interpreted as an apocalyptic
one, that is, events which the speaker (Jesus)
predicts actually occurred prior to or are contemporary with the writer (Matthew).[3]   The discourse also functions parenetically, as do other
apocalyptic texts, and it basically encourages a
community in a distressful situation.[4]   The

---

[1]E.g., Enoch 91-105; 2 Esd. 14:28-36;
2 Baruch 77.   Cf. Rigaux, Testimony of St. Mark,
p. 17.

[2]Cf. Ibid., p. 83; Rigaux, Testimony of St.
Matthew, p. 89; Brown, Gospel According to John
(xiii-xxi), pp. 601-603; and Ellis, Matthew: His
Mind and His Message, p. 84.

[3]Ibid., p. 86.   This point will be evident
most forcefully in the exegesis of Matt. 24:15-22
below.

[4]On the parenetical function of apocalyptic
see Amos E. Wilder, Eschatology and Ethics in the
Teaching of Jesus (New York: Harper and Brothers,
Publishers, 1950); and D. S. Russell, The Method
and Message of Jewish Apocalyptic (Philadelphia:
Westminster Press, 1964).   Contrast Louis
Ginzberg, "Some Observations on the Attitude of
the Synagogue towards the Apocalyptic-Eschato-
logical Writings," JBL 41 (1922): 115-136; and
Martin Buber, "Prophecy, Apocalyptic, and the
Historical Hour," USQR 12 (1957): 9-21.

question which we will address is that of Matthew's redaction of this discourse. We are not addressing the question of genre as much as we are addressing the question of the discourse's <u>function in Matthew</u>.

Although Jesus' discourse in Matthew 24 lacks characteristics crucial for determining a precise genre, the <u>position</u> of the discourse in the First Gospel is crucial. The rift between Jesus and Israel climaxed with Jesus' theological review of history, his leaving the temple, and the pronouncement of its destruction (24:1-2). Now the time has come for the Master to combine predictions for the future with ethical injunctions for his faithful followers. The implication of their question about his Parousia clearly is that he is about to leave them (24:3). In 24:3 "Jesus is represented as looking beyond the imminent Passion and offering words of advice and comfort to the disciples about the time before his 'return.'"[1] Matthew positions this in his gospel as Jesus' last discourse with his disciples before he goes to meet his death (cf. 26:1). The setting of imparting necessary information just prior to the Master's death is essential for any farewell discourse. Our thesis is that Jesus' discourse in Matt. 24 is a farewell discourse in terms of function by virtue of its position in the gospel.[2] The discourse does not meet all of the formal criteria for the genre of a farewell discourse, but the primary characteristics of a farewell discourse can be verified. Jesus takes

---

[1]L. Cope, "Matthew XXV: 31-46 'The Sheep and the Goats' Reinterpreted," p. 33.

[2]Cf. Gaston, <u>No Stone on Another</u>, p. 42.

his faithful followers aside privately (κατ' ἰδίαν), reveals to them their task and what will occur after his death, encourages them to endure, and even speaks in the most general sense of a successor (the Son of Man).[1] The caesura by which Matthew sets 24:3-31 apart as a separate Parousia discourse intentionally renders this material as a private revelation in which the disciples learn what is to occur after Jesus' death.

In summary, Matthew has positioned the Parousia discourse in his gospel so that its over-all function is that of a testament from Jesus-Sophia. The testament, though, is mediated through apocalyptic language and imagery so that the discourse combines apocalyptic prediction and parenesis. Hare's statement that "Matthew's purpose in this last great discourse (chs. 24f.) is . . . to prepare Christians for enduring faithfulness during the indefinite period that remains" is quite accurate.[2] However, this is not true only in the sense of apocalyptic parenesis. Apocalyptic parenesis and prediction are combined with the setting and ingredients necessary for a farewell discourse. Matthew's community is encouraged not simply because of a series of predictions, but because the predictions were made by Jesus-Sophia and left as a continuous legacy to them.

## The Scope of the Discourse

The caesura which Matthew places between

---

[1]Ellis, Matthew: His Mind and His Message, p. 83; cf. Pesch, Naherwartungen, p. 100.

[2]Hare, Theme of Jewish Persecution, p. 178.

24:2 and 24:3 has already been discussed, and there is a general consensus that the evangelist's introduction to the apocalyptic discourse begins with 24:3.[1] The question is: where does the apocalyptic testament of Jesus end?

Matthew follows Mark's discourse for the most part (cf. Matt. 24:3-25; Mark 13:1-23) until Matthew inserts the Q pericope at 24:26-28. The evangelist returns to his Markan source at 24:29 (=Mark 13:24) and continues the Markan material until 24:36 where he breaks away from Mark completely (cf. Mark 13:32). Matthew then continues with Q material (24:37-41, 42-44, 45-51; 25:14-30) and material which was unique to his community (25:1-13, 31-46). On the surface, then, it appears that Matthew ends his apocalyptic testament at either 24:36 (where he ceases to follow Mark) or at 25:46 (where his summary formula follows in 26:1). We held any conclusions about the parameters of the discourse in abeyance until the detailed exegesis was done, and it is our conclusion that the evangelist ends Jesus' testament at 24:31. A proleptic summary of our exegetical reasons for this conclusion might be helpful.

First, the question about Jesus' Parousia which introduces the discourse (24:3) is definitively answered in 24:30-31.[2] Matthew is the only

---

[1]See Ellis, Matthew: His Mind and His Message, p. 83; and Hare, Theme of Jewish Persecution, p. 178.

[2]We do not feel that Matt. 25:31 directly answers the disciples' question in 24:3. The disciples clearly ask about when (πότε) the sign (σημεῖον) of Jesus' Parousia (τῆς σῆς παρουσίας) will appear. Matthew 24:30 answers their

evangelist to carry over explicitly the question about the "sign" of the Parousia (cf. 24:3, 30-31; Mark 13:4, 26-27; Luke 21:7, 27-28). Secondly, 24:29-31 is the transition pericope to seven Parousia parables in Matthew. Peter Ellis has shown that Matthew uses themes of pericopae which end a section as transitional material to the next section.[1] Mark's conclusion to the discourse seems to begin in 13:28 with the parable of the fig tree.[2] As we shall see, one major theme of

question with καὶ τότε φανήσεται τὸ σημεῖον that is, εὐθέως δὲ μετὰ τὴν θλῖψιν (24:29), and ὄψονται τὸν υἱὸν τοῦ ἀνθρώπου ἐρχόμενον ἐπὶ τῶν νεφελῶν (24:30). Matthew 25:31 is more general in its depiction: ὅταν δὲ ἔλθῃ ὁ υἱὸς τοῦ ἀνθρώπου. Matthew 25:31 seems to begin an answer to the implied question: "What will happen after the Son of Man comes?" The answer is τότε καθίσει ἐπὶ θρόνου δόξης αὐτοῦ and the ἔθνη will gather before him (25:32). Matthew 25:31 could be answering the implied question of 24:3: "What will happen at the consummation of the Age?" The problem, of course, is that the disciples do not ask what will happen after the consummation of the Age. They ask, rather, what (τί) is the sign (τὸ σημεῖον) of the consummation of the Age, that is, when will the consummation begin (πότε ταῦτα ἔσται)?

[1]Ellis, Matthew: His Mind and His Message, pp. 17-19, 87-94.

[2]There are several reasons for this conclusion. (1) The parable seems to separate quite easily from the preceding material of the apocalyptic discourse. Luke seems to feel that a transitional phrase is needed (cf. καὶ εἶπεν παραβολὴν αὐτοῖς, 21:29; see Jeremias, Parables of Jesus, pp. 93 n. 13, 119; C. H. Dodd, The

verses 29-31 in Matthew's discourse is the judgment which will ensue at the Parousia. Matthew
has expanded Mark's conclusion with six more parables, all of which emphasize the need to prepare
for the judgment.[1] The seven parables are: the
Fig Tree (24:32-36), the Days of Noah (24:37-41),
the Householder (24:42-44), the Wise Servant
(24:45-51), the Ten Maidens (25:1-13), the Talents
(25:14-30), and the Sheep and the Goats
(25:31-46). It has been noted for some time that
a characteristic of Matthean style is the propensity to organize material in blocks of seven.[2]

---

Parables of the Kingdom, rev. ed. [New York:
Charles Scribner's Sons, 1961], p. 107 n. 1; and
Bultmann, History of the Synoptic Tradition, p.
123). (2) The point of comparison in the parable
does not seem to be about the Parousia and what it
will bring, but about "the signs of the time of
salvation" (Jeremias, Parables of Jesus, pp. 119-
120 cf. Bultmann, History of the Synoptic Tradition, p. 123). (3) The application of the parable
does not seem to refer to the Parousia alluded to
in Mark 13:26-27. Ἐγγύς ἐστιν ἐπὶ θύραις (Mark
13:29) denotes "an event which will happen soon,"
and the original subject of ταῦτα γινόμενα . . .
ἐγγύς ἐστιν seems to be the "kingdom of God" as in
Luke 21:31 rather than the Son of Man as in Mark
and Matthew (Kümmel, Promise and Fulfillment, pp.
20-21; contrast Beasley-Murray, Commentary on Mark
Thirteen, pp. 95-98).

[1]Ellis, Matthew: His Mind and His Message,
p. 91; cf. Bornkamm, "End-Expectation and Church
in Matthew," TI, pp. 22-24.

[2]Allen, St. Matthew, p. lxv; and Ellis,
Matthew: His Mind and His Message, p. 13.

This expansion is not an isolated incident since Matthew has also expanded the Markan parable discourse to seven parables (Mark 4:1-34 cf. Matt. 13:23-37).[1] It seems, then, that Matthew intended the seven Parousia parables in 24:32-25:46 to be read as a unified section.[2]

A third reason we feel that Matthew ends the apocalyptic testament at 24:31 is that the "seeing" of the sign of the Son of Man balances off the prediction in 23:39, a transition verse to the discourse, that the Jews will not see Jesus until the Parousia.

Finally, verses 3-31 contain the necessary elements for a testament: the beloved Master privately assembles his faithful successors (v. 3), gives them warnings against those who oppose them (vv. 6-8, 9-12, 15-22), instructs them for carrying on his work (v. 14), offers them encouragement and hope (vv. 13, 22, 31), and alludes to the fate of oppressors (v. 30).[3]

---

[1]Ibid., pp. 59-67, 91; and Rigaux, Testimony of St. Matthew, p. 81.

[2]Ellis has suggested that Matthew has seven Parousia parables to balance the seven Woes of chapter 23 (Ellis, Matthew: His Mind and His Message, pp. 81-94). We call them "parables" only for convenience. It is not certain that all of them, particularly the judgment scene (25:31-46), formally qualify as "parables" (cf. Schweizer, Matthew, p. 475; and Hill, Matthew, p. 330).

[3]Cf. Ellis, Matthew: His Mind and His Message, p. 83.

It is quite possible, and even feasible, that one could extend the testament to include the seven parables because there is no change of setting or of speaker through 25:46.[1] The sheer diversity of opinion among commentators cautions against any dogmatism in this regard. Whether the discourse formally concludes at 25:46 or elsewhere, 24:3-31 definitely constitutes a significant independent block within it. However, since the question in verse 3 is definitively answered in verses 30-31, since verses 3-31 seem to form a unified section as opposed to the subsequent parables, and since all the necessary ingredients of a testament are found between verses 3 and 31, our conclusion is that Matthew has formally ended the testament at verse 31.

## Part 2.  The Introduction to the Discourse (24:3)

### The Relation of 24:1-2 to 24:3

The view one takes regarding the relation of 24:3-31 (the Parousia) to 24:1-2 (the prediction of the destruction) will determine how one interprets the eschatological discourse. The key question for interpreters has been: where does the evangelist locate his church community in the sequence of events and what significance does he attach to that position? The question involves a discussion of Matthew's eschatology, ecclesiology, and his view of salvation history. A discussion of each area would take us too far afield. However, at the risk of oversimplifying, all of these areas focus into three general views which are relevant for interpreting the eschatological discourse.

---

[1]Cf. Stendahl, "Matthew," p. 692.

## The disciples' question

The discussion focuses upon the disciples' question in 24:3c: εἰπὲ ἡμῖν, πότε ταῦτα ἔσται, καὶ τί τὸ σημεῖον τῆς σῆς παρουσίας καὶ συντελείας τοῦ αἰῶνος; The dilemma is not only whether there is more than one question, but it concerns more precisely how the question(s) relates to the destruction of the temple in verses 1 and 2. If the question is concerned with the destruction, then how does the following discourse (vv. 4-31) answer it? If it does not allude to the destruction, then why does Matthew retain Mark's first question (ταῦτα ἔσται)? Is the question only taken over pro forma by Matthew, or, if not, what is its referent? There have been three general answers to the problems of verse 3. Each answer, in turn, determines how the discourse is interpreted.

## A. Feuillet

The first answer is that given by A. Feuillet. Feuillet argues that Matthew envisions three stages before the End: (1) the signs preceding the End; (2) the destruction of Jerusalem; and (3) the Parousia of the Son of Man. Feuillet claims, though, that the Parousia, as well as "the consummation of the Age" (συντελείας τοῦ αἰῶνος), does not refer to the final coming of the Son of Man at the end of history, but to the historical judgment of the Jewish nation in the fall of Jerusalem in C.E. 70. The destruction of Jerusalem is the end of the old age, the age of Israel as God's people, and the judgment has been effected by the Son of Man through the armies of Rome. Therefore, verse 3 and the whole eschatological discourse refer to the destruction of Jerusalem in C.E. 70.[1]

---

[1]Feuillet, "Le Sens Du Mot Parousie dans

Although Feuillet's argument does have the virtue of consistency, it has largely been rejected because of his assumption that Jesus' "historical" prediction of the destruction was connected with the fall of Jerusalem and that Matthew, writing after C.E. 70, would not use a prediction of Jesus which had been proven incorrect. His argument has also been rejected because συντελείας τοῦ αἰῶνος would have to mean two different things in Matthew. In 24:3 the phrase would mean the fall of Jerusalem, but in chapter 13 (vv. 39, 40, 49) it seems to refer to the final judgment.[1]

## J. Lambrecht and P. Ellis

A second view maintains that Matthew's redactional activity is focused upon the predicted destruction of the temple as a punishment of the Jewish nation (23:36, 38; 24:1-2). However, this does not mean that Matthew has separated the destruction of the temple (24:1-2) from the Parousia of the Son of Man (24:3). It means, quite to the contrary, that Matthew has shown their connection more clearly than has Mark. Lambrecht clearly

---

L'Évangile de Matthieu," pp. 263-280; cf. W. F. Albright and C. S. Mann, Matthew, The Anchor Bible, vol. 26 (Garden City, New York: Doubleday and Company, 1971), pp. 290-299.

[1]Feuillet, "Le Sens Du Mot Parousie dans L'Évangile de Matthieu," pp. 270-275. See the critiques by Hare, Theme of Jewish Persecution, p. 178; Blair, Jesus in the Gospel of Matthew, p. 80 n. 105; and Kingsbury, Matthew: Structure, Christology, Kingdom, p. 29 n. 119.

states this view:

> This editorial emphasis on the
> destruction of the temple as a punishment
> did not prevent Matthew from distinguishing
> better than Mark between the destruction of
> the temple and the parousia--end of the
> world. In Mk., XIII,4 the two questions
> with ταῦτα and ταῦτα . . . πάντα are much
> intertwined. Mt., XXIV,3 runs as follows:
> "Tell us, when will this (=the destruction
> of the temple) be, and what will be the
> sign of your parousia and of the close
> of the age?" . . . We may expect that the
> Matthaean discourse will answer the double
> question of XXIV,3. What is the connection
> between the temple event and the end of
> the world?[1]

This means that verses 15-22 clearly refer
to the destruction of the temple in C.E. 70 while
the rest of the discourse concerns the Parousia.[2]
This view has the merit of being extremely logical, and it explains ταῦτα ἔσται, which Matthew
takes over unchanged from Mark. In this interpretation ταῦτα ἔσται refers to the destruction
of Jerusalem and is dealt with in verses 15-22.
If verses 15-22 do not deal with ταῦτα as the destruction of Jerusalem, then what is Matthew's
reason for including a question which is not

---

[1]Lambrecht, "Parousia Discourse," p. 318.

[2]Ibid., p. 318 n. 22; and Ellis, <u>Matthew:
His Mind and His Message</u>, pp. 88-89. We will set
aside for the moment the question of whether the
disciples ask two questions (Lambrecht) or three
questions (Ellis) in 24:3.

answered in the discourse?  Another merit of this
view is that "parousia" means "return at the End
(="the consummation of the Age") in this context
as opposed to "presence" or return before the End
as Feuillet has suggested.[1]

One problem with this view, however, is that
the disciples' first question ("When will these
things be?"), alluding to the fall of Jerusalem,
is not answered (=verses 15-22) until after their
second question (about the End) is answered
(=verses 4-14).  Why would Matthew answer the
second question first?  Ellis has succinctly
answered that:

> The purpose of the discourse, as D. R. A.
> Hare rightly says, is to "prepare Christians
> for enduring faithfulness in the indefinite
> period that remains."  It is for this
> reason that the discourse begins by dealing
> with the end time (synteleia tou aiōnos) in
> 24:4-14 instead of with the first question
> of 24:3 which concerns the fall of
> Jerusalem.[2]

However, if the purpose of the discourse is only
parenesis in face of the End, not in view of
C.E. 70, then one could logically assert that
Matthew's discourse does not allude to the fall
of Jerusalem at all--even in verses 15-22.  This
is precisely what Hare does assert:

> Matthew's purpose in this last great

---

[1]Lambrecht, "Parousia Discourse," p. 318.

[2]Ellis, Matthew: His Mind and His Message,
p. 90.

discourse (chs. 24f.) is not to show
Jesus' predictions have been fulfilled
in the events of A.D. 70 but to prepare
Christians for enduring faithfulness
during the indefinite period that
remains. <u>Matthew therefore totally
ignores the first question</u>, [italics
mine] which for his generation is no
longer vital, and makes the discourse
as a whole an answer to the second,
viz., "What is the sign of your final
coming and the consummation of history?"
In this way Matthew can retain the close
relationship between the eschatological
flight (vv. 15-28) and the final coming
of the Son of man (vv. 29-31) which is
found in Mark.[1]

This is precisely the point at which Ellis
is critical of Hare.[2] Quite clearly, though, if
one accepts Hare's conclusion on the purpose of
the discourse, and we are not arguing that his
conclusion is invalid, then one is pressed to
argue that ταῦτα ἔσται refers to the destruction
of Jerusalem and that Matthew answers this in
verses 15-22.

<u>D. R. A. Hare</u>

It is even more difficult to believe, and
this is a third interpretation of verse 3, that
Matthew has taken over πότε ταῦτα ἔσται from Mark

---

[1]Hare, <u>Theme of Jewish Persecution</u>,
pp. 178-179.

[2]Ellis, <u>Matthew: His Mind and His Message</u>,
p. 88.

and totally ignores it in the discourse.[1]  To say
that the evangelist uses the question from Mark
but totally ignores it in his discourse is tanta-
mount to saying that ταῦτα ἔσται is "undigested
tradition."  We simply cannot read ταῦτα ἔσται in
this manner--for methodological reasons if for no
other reason.[2]

---

[1]Hare, Theme of Jewish Persecution, p. 179;
cf. Pesch, "Eschatologie und Ethik.  Auslegung von
Mt 24,1-36," p. 228; and Strecker, Weg, p. 240
n. 2.

[2]Hare sees Matthew's ignoring the disciples'
first question as consistent with Matthew's style
(Hare, Theme of Jewish Persecution, p. 179).
However, this seems to imply that the evangelist
simply forgot to mention it again, or, as is the
case of the question in 24:3, that he ignores it
because the material is "no longer vital" for his
generation.  This answers the question of "why
then does Matthew include all of the mission
material" in chapter 10, which is the focus of
Hare's argument, with "it serves no real purpose,
it is simply undigested tradition."  Admittedly,
we are in the realm of methodological opinion
here, but it seems to me that we must assume a
purpose on Matthew's part for including this
material in chapter 24 (and in chapter 10).
Otherwise the question of Matthean redaction becomes meaningless; we cannot distinguish between
what is redactionally important and what is simply
sloppy structuring on the part of the evangelist.
We are trying to avoid the danger of over-inter-
pretation, which sees every Matthean alteration
of Mark as theologically important, but we are
also trying to see what specific understanding of
the eschatological discourse emerges from the
cumulative effect of Matthew's redaction.  His
redaction of 24:3 is a major component in the

In summary, if the first question (ταῦτα ἔσται) refers to the destruction of Jerusalem in C.E. 70, then the alternatives are clear. (1) The whole discourse can refer to C.E. 70. In that case "parousia" and "consummation of the Age" both refer to the destruction of 70 (Feuillet). Or, (2) the destruction of 70 can be seen as one of the signs preceding the coming of Jesus at the End and is discussed in verses 15-22 (Ellis, Lambrecht). Or, (3) the destruction of 70 is mentioned in verse 3 by the evangelist, but, since it is not important to the purpose of his discourse, Matthew does not elaborate on it again--even in verses 15-22 (Hare, Pesch). All of these commentators refer to C.E. 70, and that is valid after the literary-critical exegesis of the text is done. However, at this point in the discussion we are not asking the historical question of whether or not verse 3 refers to C.E. 70. We are asking the literary question of whether or not it refers to the predicted destruction of the temple in verses 1-2.

In light of our exegesis thus far, we have concluded (following Pesch, E. Schweizer, Marxsen, and Strecker) that Matthew has clearly delineated between the judgment pronounced on the temple (24:1-2) and the Parousia discourse (24:3-31). Matthew does this by presenting the predicted destruction and the actual loss of Jesus' presence as God's judgment upon Israel.[1] It would seem natural, then, to argue that ταῦτα ἔσται does not refer again to the destruction of the temple but that it refers to Jesus' Parousia. This is pre-

total redactional picture for this discourse.

[1]See the discussion above on pp. 119-132 and appendix 5.

cisely what R. Walker contends.

## Rolf Walker

Walker argues, like many others (Marxsen, Pesch, E. Schweizer, and Strecker), that Matthew brings 23:37-39 into a close relationship with 24:1. The evangelist does this by deleting the pericope of the "Widow's Gift" which both Mark and Luke retain before their eschatological discourses (cf. Mark 12:41-44; Luke 21:1-4). Walker contends that Matthew's reason for doing this is to give a concrete interpretation to "your house desolate" (23:38). The interpretation for Matthew of "your house desolate" is the destruction of the temple (24:2). Walker contends that the evangelist places a caesura between 24:2 and 24:3, as we have also argued, by deleting Mark's phrase "opposite the temple." Matthew's purpose in deleting this phrase is to concentrate upon describing the "last things." Consequently, Matthew redacts Mark's question in 13:4 to accord with his purpose of writing a proper Parousia discourse. Walker is worth quoting in detail. He says:

> Liest man Mk. 13,4 (=Lk. 21,7!): Sage uns, wann wird dies geschehen, und welches ist das Zeichen dafür (καί konjunktiv), wann dies alles vollendet werden soll (--die Zerstörung des Tempels und die letzten Dinge gehören in eine gemeinsame Zukunft--), so heisst es Mt. 24,3: Sage uns, wann dies geschehen wird und (καί explikativ: "und zwar", "d.h.") welches das Zeichen deiner Wiederkunft und der Vollendung der Welt ist. M.a.W., der Evangelist zieht das von Markus (oder Q?) überkommene πότε ταῦτα ἔσται durch seine Textgestaltung vom zuvor genannten Tempel weg ganz nach "vorne" und interpretiert es als Frage nach dem Welt-Ende, die nun nichts mehr mit der

Frage nach dem Schicksal des Tempels zu tun
hat. Matthäus will, aufs Ganze seiner
Arbeit an 24,3 gesehen, nur 24,1f. mit
23,37-39, nicht aber die ganzen Kapitel
23 und 24f. zu einer thematischen Einheit
verbinden.[1]

It is clear that the crux of Walker's argument is that καί in Mark 13:4 is conjunctive. It
connects the destruction of the temple (ταῦτα)
with the eschatological consummation and means
that the destruction is one sign which will precede the End. In this case "all these things"
(ταῦτα πάντα) to be accomplished at the End
include the destruction of the temple as a preceding "sign" for Mark.[2] If Matthew's καί is also
read conjunctively, then his meaning, even though
he deletes ταῦτα συντελεῖσθαι πάντα and specifically adds τῆς σῆς παρουσίας καί (conjunctive)
συντελείας τοῦ αἰῶνος, is the same as Mark's.
Matthew simply sharpens up the question, but the
meaning is the same.[3] However, if Matthew's καί
is read epexegetically, and we believe this to be
consonant with the whole scene created by Matthean
redaction, then the disciples' question reads as
Walker contends: "Tell us, when will this happen,
that is (καί), what will be the sign of your
Parousia and the consummation of the Age?"[4]

---

[1]Rolf Walker, Die Heilsgeschichte im ersten
Evangelium, p. 59.

[2]Taylor, St. Mark, p. 502.

[3]Ibid. Cf. Gould, St. Mark, p. 243.

[4]The argument that ταῦτα is plural and thus
could not refer only to the Parousia does not
hold because in Mark ταῦτα is seen to refer to
the destruction only. Pesch refers to this

Walker's argument means that the whole discourse is a Parousia discourse, as we have also argued, and that the whole discourse is <u>future</u> oriented. This would mean that verses 15-22 do not refer to the destruction of the temple (v. 2) nor to C.E. 70 if Matthew writes after that event. This is, then, the last alternative given to Matthew's meaning of ταῦτα ἔσται--it does not allude to the temple at all. Thus, Matthew has not mentioned the destruction (=ταῦτα ἔσται) in the question of verse 3, and he has not simply ignored it in his discourse. According to Walker, it was never the evangelist's intention for ταῦτα ἔσται to refer to the destruction of the temple.

We feel that Walker is essentially correct, and that verses 15-22 do not refer to the destruction of Jerusalem in C.E. 70. We will argue below that verses 15-22 allude to the desecration of Christian sanctuaries in the near future for Matthew.[1]

Let us now move with this survey in mind to a detailed analysis of Matthean redaction in verse 3.

--------

"absolute" use of ταῦτα several times in Mark and cautions: "Den Plural sollte man nicht auf 'series of events' deuten, die man in der Rede zu erkennen glaubt" (Pesch, <u>Naherwartungen</u>, p. 101 n. 147). This accords with the singular τὸ σημεῖον (Ibid., p. 103; cf. Beasley-Murray, <u>Commentary on Mark Thirteen</u>, p. 27).

[1]Walker, <u>Heilsgeschichte im ersten Evangelium</u>, p. 110 n. 139; cf. Lambrecht, "Parousia Discourse," p. 318 n. 22. See our discussion of 24:15-22 below.

## Matthew's Redaction in 24:3

### Jesus sits on the Mount of Olives (24:3a)

Matthew has painted a new scene in 24:3, and the first significant brushstroke in it is the phrase καθημένου δὲ αὐτοῦ ἐπὶ τοῦ ὄρους τῶν ἐλαιῶν.[1] In this scene Jesus moves to the mountain, and with this move the evangelist separates the discourse to follow from the events of verses 1-2. Mark has the same change of scene, but the scene in Mark seems to refer more clearly than the Matthean one does back to the prediction of the destruction of the temple.[2] Luke omits this change of scene altogether; he thus makes the question in 21:7 clearly refer to the prediction of the destruction.[3]

---

[1]Καθημένου is a genitive absolute used for a concordant participle. The use of the genitive absolute in this way seems to be characteristic of Matthean style (e.g., 1:20; 5:1; 8:1, 5, 28; 21:23; 24:3; 27:17 cf. 9:10, 18; 17:9; 18:24).

Δέ is substituted for Mark's καί approximately sixty times (cf. Allen, St. Matthew, p. xx); ἐπί for Mark's εἰς is also a typical Matthean change (Ibid., p. xxvii cf. 24:30). It appears that Mark has εἰς for ἐν (Pesch, Naherwartungen, p. 97) and that Matthew has interpreted it with ἐπί (cf. Matt. 27:19).

[2]See the discussion of πότε ταῦτα ἔσται below on pp. 218-220 cf. pp. 152-165.

[3]M'Neile, St. Matthew, p. 344. Luke seems to be dealing with the relation of the Parousia (perhaps of its delay) to the fall of Jerusalem (cf. Conzelmann, Theology of St. Luke, p. 121 n. 3).

The next significant thing to notice in
Matthew's setting is that Jesus is "seated"
(καθημένου).  Jesus is also sitting in Mark's
account, but κάθημαι (καθίζω) seems to have more
significance for Matthew in relation to Jesus'
teaching than it does for Mark.  Jesus consistently sits to teach in the First Gospel, and in
each case the emphasis is clearly redactional.[1]
Schneider has shown that κάθημαι (καθίζω) quite
often implies that the one seated is due reverence.[2]  J. D. Kingsbury has argued quite convincingly (with reference to Matt. 13) that Matthew
pictures Jesus as sitting in order to attribute
honor to him when he assumes the role of teacher
(5:1; 24:3), of judge (19:28; 25:31), and of ruler
(20:21, 23; 26:64).  But, even more than this, it
seems " . . . that Matthew's intention is to
fashion a setting that will in itself attribute
honour to Jesus and underline, not merely a
Rabbinic, but even a divine dignity."[3]  Although
Kingsbury is speaking primarily about Matt. 13:2,

---

[1]Cf. 5:1; 13:1, 2; 15:29; 24:3.  Fenton,
for example, says of Matthew: "Jesus sits to
teach; this was usual, but is emphasized in this
Gospel" (Fenton, Gospel of St. Matthew, p. 77).

[2]Divine figures in Egypt, in the Near East,
and in the Greek world assume a sitting posture
as a distinctive sign of their deity.  In Jewish
literature God is often pictured as seated upon
His throne (e.g., Isa. 6:1-4; Psa. 47:8), an
image which also occurs in Matthew (5:34; 23:22).
See Carl Schneider, "κάθημαι," TDNT 3: 441-442.

[3]Kingsbury, Parables of Jesus in Matthew 13,
p. 23.

and although the setting is not precisely the same as in 24:3, the overall emphasis is the same: Jesus, with the dignity of the teacher, is about to reveal eschatological secrets to his disciples.[1]  However, in this instance, he speaks not just as a teacher but as the Wisdom of God and as the soon coming Son of Man.[2]  In this apocalyptic context Jesus-Sophia must be paid due reverence.[3]

Secondly, Jesus is seated upon the "mount of Olives."  The majority of commentators see the "mount of Olives" as an allusion to Zech. 14:4 where the mount of Olives is the locus of redemption (and of apocalyptic judgment) in the last days.[4]  It seems that this line of interpretation has been followed because: (1) the context in Matt. 24 is also apocalyptic; (2) Matthew simply follows Mark in this instance where the allusion to Zech. 14:4 seems to be very clear; and,

---

[1]In 13:2 Jesus is sitting in a <u>boat</u> and addresses the <u>crowds</u> on the shore, whereas in 24:3 he sits on the mountain and addresses only his disciples.

[2]Notice that only Matthew has τῆς σῆς παρουσίας (24:3b).  In chapter 4 we will discuss the two sittings of Jesus in 24:3 and 25:31 as complementary parts of Matthew's humiliation-glorification christological structure.

[3]The concept of God sitting upon the throne is also a strong one in apocalyptic literature (e.g., Rev. 4:2-11; 5:7-14; etc.), and in the New Testament the Messianic King is enthroned along with God (Rev. 3:21; Matt. 26:64; Col. 3:1 cf. Schneider, "κάθημαι," p. 442).

[4]Fenton is representative in this case (<u>St. Matthew</u>, p. 382).

(3) the only other _explicit_ reference to the mount
of Olives in the Tanak is 2 Sam. 15:30, which is
not in an apocalyptic context.[1]

Although the allusion to Zech. 14:4 seems
to be present in Matthew, it should not be assumed
too quickly that this is the case and that Matthew
took over the mount of Olives _pro forma_ from Mark.
We think that the Matthean context suggests that
the mount of Olives is the place of the revelation
of eschatological secrets (by Jesus-Sophia-
Shekinah) instead of the actual locus of end-time
events. Several factors support this conclusion.

First, it is extremely well-known how
Matthew redactionally uses "mountain" as a _place
of revelation_.[2] It is never suggested in Matthew,

---

[1]Schweizer, _Good News According to Mark_, p.
267; and G. A. Barrois, "Olives, Mount of,"
_IDB_ 3: 598.

[2]5:1; 28:16 cf. 8:1; 14:23; 15:29; 17:1, 9;
26:30. See Blair, _Jesus in the Gospel of Matthew_,
p. 134; J. D. Kingsbury, "The Composition and
Christology of Matt. 28:16-20," _JBL_ 93 (1974):
575; Lange, _Erscheinen_, pp. 392-446; Hubbard,
_Matthew 28:16-20_, p. 73; and Günther Bornkamm,
"The Risen Lord and the Earthly Jesus: Matthew
28:16-20," _The Future of Our Religious Past_, ed.
James M. Robinson (New York: Harper and Row,
1971), p. 204.
However, Nepper-Christensen has argued
against the theological significance of "mountain"
in Matthew. This conclusion is a result of his
thesis that there is no typological thought of
any kind in Matthew (cf. Nepper-Christensen,
_Das Matthäusevangelium: Ein Judenchristliches
Evangelium?_, pp. 173-177).

even in the eschatological discourse, that any mountain will be the locus of the Parousia.

Secondly, Matthew has deleted Mark's reference to Jesus sitting upon the mount "opposite the temple" (κατέναντι τοῦ ἱεροῦ). G. Strecker sees this deletion of the reference to the temple as consistent with Matthew's effort to make a conscious division between the prediction of the temple's destruction (24:1-2) and his Parousia discourse (v. 3).[1] This is particularly true if Mark has used this phrase to set up an intentional allusion in his Parousia discourse back to the temple's destruction. In other words, for Mark "Die eschatologische Rede wird angesichts des Tempels gehalten, für den Evangelisten und seine Gemeinde angesichts des zerstörten Tempels!"[2] This means that even if κατέναντι has a symbolic meaning in Mark in 13:3, the break between the two scenes (vv. 2 and 3) should not be stressed.[3] By the same token, Matthew's redactional work is clear. Jesus does not give the eschatological discourse in view of the temple's predicted destruction because for Matthew that event is already the completed judgment upon Israel.[4]

---

[1]Strecker, Weg, p. 240.

[2]Pesch, Naherwartungen, p. 100.

[3]Ibid. Cf. Kümmel, Promise and Fulfillment, p. 99; and Marxsen, Mark the Evangelist, p. 168.

[4]Strecker, Weg, p. 240. Again, the prediction itself is the completed judgment for Matthew. However, if Matthew is writing after C.E. 70, then the physical destruction of the temple would be the historical counterpart of Jesus' pronouncement against and abandonment of the temple during his ministry.

Matthew, then, deletes the important Markan phrase "opposite the temple" because it is inconsistent with his attempt to separate the predicted destruction of the temple (vv. 1-2), which he sees as the past and fulfilled judgment upon Israel, from Jesus-Sophia's revelation of eschatological secrets (vv. 3-31). For Matthew the "kingdom," God's rule and presence, seems to be synonymous with the presence of Jesus-Sophia with his disciples (28:20b cf. 1:23; 18:20), or, in other words, with Matthew's church. The evangelist's deletion of "opposite the temple" in this light would then mean that the center of revelation, which is located in Jesus-Sophia-Shekinah, has moved from the temple (Judaism) to "the disciples" (=Matthew's church).[1]

In summary, the mount of Olives as a place of revelation by Jesus-Sophia-Shekinah seems to fit the Matthean context better than the interpretation which sees the mount of Olives as the locus of apocalyptic events (cf. Zech. 14:4).[2]

---

[1]This conclusion is important for our interpretation of "a holy place" in 24:15 as a veiled reference to the Church, that is, sanctuaries of Jesus-Sophia-Shekinah, rather than the temple at Jerusalem.

[2]Matthew's omission of Mark's "against the temple" takes on added significance if Werner Kelber is correct in his interpretation of the mount of Olives in Mark. Arguing in history of religion terms, Kelber points out that the "mountain" is important in religious (not geographical) terms as the locus of revelation. He contends that the destruction of the temple meant the loss of the religious Center for Mark's community (Mark is post-70). The new Center

The next Matthean phrase also bears out this conclusion: προσῆλθον αὐτῷ οἱ μαθηταὶ κατ' ἰδίαν
λέγοντες.

## The disciples approach
## Jesus (24:3b)

Προσῆλθον . . . οἱ μαθηταί is the same
Matthean formula which we examined in our discussion of Matt. 24:1b.[1] Προσέρχομαι, as we have
seen, has cultic overtones in the First Gospel.
The disciples "approach" Jesus in verse 1b, but
they do so "in order to point out the buildings
of the temple" to him. In other words, they are
incapable, for a short time, of understanding the
significance of Jesus' rejection of Israel. Jesus
asks them if they really do not "understand all
these things" (βλέπετε ταῦτα πάντα), and he makes
his point explicit by announcing the destruction
of the temple (v. 2). Οἱ μαθηταί, as we have
seen, clearly represent Matthew's community.
Thus, it seems that verses 1-2 are directed to

---

became Galilee rather than Jerusalem. The dia-
lectic of the revelation of Jesus on the mount of
Olives as opposed to the temple mount serves to
reveal Galilee as the new locus of the kingdom
(Werner Kelber, The Kingdom in Mark [Philadelphia:
Fortress Press, 1974], pp. 78, 104-107). Cf.
Mircea Eliade on the "symbolism of the Center,"
which is often the summit of a (cosmic) mountain
(see William G. Doty and Wendell C. Beane, eds.,
Myths, Rites, Symbols. A Mircea Eliade Reader,
vol. 2 [New York: Harper and Row, Publishers,
1975], pp. 372, 380-385).

[1]See the discussion above, pp. 143-146.

those within Matthew's church who still cling, if even partially, to the false hope that salvation lay in Israel, which is here symbolized by Jerusalem and the temple.

By way of contrast, the disciples approach Jesus himself (αὐτῷ) in verse 3, not to point out the buildings of the temple to him, but to question him on a completely different subject--his Parousia. Matthew, by his deletion of "opposite the temple," is sharply distinguishing the (former?) misunderstanding of some (or all?) in his community who still hoped that God's presence was with Israel. That view, which the disciples held even in Jesus' time, has proven erroneous because God's presence, in Jesus, has left the temple (ἐξελθών, 24:1 cf. Ezek. 11:23) and has moved to a new place of revelation--the mount of Olives. The disciples now approach <u>him</u> because it is in his presence alone, not in the institutions of Israel, that God reveals Himself/Herself.[1]

Note that Mark has only four disciples (Peter, James, John, and Andrew) "question" (ἐπηρώτα), rather than "come to" (προσέρχομαι) Jesus, whereas Matthew has οἱ μαθηταί. Matthew has clearly substituted οἱ μαθηταί here, just as he did in 24:1 for εἷς τῶν μαθητῶν αὐτοῦ (Mark 13:1), to indicate that the revelatory discourse which follows is addressed to Matthew's community.[2]

---

[1]This assumes a break of Matthew's church with the <u>Synagogenverband</u>.

[2]Bornkamm, "End-Expectation and Church in Matthew," <u>TI</u>, p. 21.

The phrase κατ' ἰδίαν points in the same direction. It clearly means "privately" and denotes private instruction or revelation in this context.[1] As M'Neile says, "The discourse is a secret revelation to a chosen few."[2] The phrase in Mark is more of a discourse to a chosen few--Peter, James, John, and Andrew--as opposed to a larger following of disciples (cf. εἰς τῶν μαθητῶν αὐτοῦ, Mark 13:1). In Matthew, however, the same phrase is retained and is to all of the "disciples," or to his church community in contrast to the crowds.[3] As Schweizer explains it:

> Verse 3 is characteristically transformed by Matthew. Once more it is all the disciples who "come to" Jesus; the expression "in private" no longer refers to the four distinguished by Mark from

---

[1]Kelber, Kingdom in Mark, pp. 33-34; Hill, Matthew, p. 319; cf. Ulrich W. Mauser, Christ in the Wilderness, SBT, vol. 39 (Naperville, Illinois: Alec R. Allenson, Inc., 1963), p. 119.

[2]M'Neile, St. Matthew, p. 344.

[3]Cf. Taylor, St. Mark, p. 502; Pesch, Naherwartungen, pp. 97-100; and Ernst Lohmeyer, Das Evangelium des Matthäus, Kritisch-exegetischer Kommentar über das Neue Testament, 2nd ed., Wilhelm Meyer, ed. (Göttingen: Vandenhoeck and Ruprecht, 1958), p. 192.
Matthew has done the same thing essentially in 13:36a where Jesus explains the parable of the tares to his disciples privately, i.e., "in the house" (Kingsbury, Parables of Jesus in Matthew 13, pp. 92-93 cf. pp. 40-47).

the rest, but to the entire band of
disciples, in other words, the whole
community of Jesus, separated from
the people of Israel.[1]

Matthew 24:3a and 24:3b, then, show heavy
Matthean redaction.  The scene he has painted
shows the disciples (Matthew's church) coming
reverently to Jesus, who is clearly a figure
worthy of such reverence.  He is seated upon the
mount of Olives and the scene is thus set by the
evangelist's redaction for Jesus to reveal secrets
of the End-time to his disciples in private.  The
revelation is "apocalyptic" in nature, as is
shown by the disciples' question (cf. τῆς σῆς
παρουσίας, and συντελείας τοῦ αἰῶνος), but the
discourse also has the character of a "testament,"
if not that of a farewell speech.  Jesus, obviously a great figure, one worthy of reverence, is
imparting information as well as encouragement to
his followers and successors which will help them
"endure until the end" (v. 13).  The information
imparted concerns Jesus' Parousia and what will
transpire until that event.  It is now necessary,
then, to analyze Matthew's redaction of the disciples' question in order to see exactly what the
Parousia of Jesus will mean in the subsequent
discourse.

## The Disciples' Question

### "Your Parousia" (τῆς σῆς παρουσίας)

We have already discussed how Matthew's
redaction of verse 3 shows his concern for the
future Parousia of Jesus as Son of Man, and for
the events which will precede it.  In verse 3

---

[1]Schweizer, _Matthew_, p. 448.

Matthew is no longer addressing the destruction of the temple. We feel, with R. Walker, that Matthew's additions of "your Parousia" and the "consummation of the Age," together with the καί explicative, make it clear that this discourse is a Parousia discourse in the fullest sense, and that it is an interpretation for a Christian community which knows itself to be moving toward the goal of all history--Jesus' Parousia.

The question now is: what does Matthew mean by "your Parousia?" The phrase could have several overtones.

It is generally known that Parousia literally means "arrival,"[1] and that the word in the New Testament designates Jesus' eschatological advent.[2] Parousia does not occur elsewhere in the Synoptics, but it is used four times in the First Gospel and it is only in the eschatological context of chapter 24 (vv. 3, 27, 37, 39). This use of παρουσία by Matthew would suggest that it is to be understood eschatologically, that is, as a future event.

Secondly, it is the Parousia of Jesus in Matthew (τῆς σῆς παρουσίας). This fact clearly interprets the "Parousia of the Son of Man" in 24:27, 37, 39. Jesus is the Son of Man whose future arrival Matthew's community awaits.[3]

---

[1]Albrecht Oepke, "παρουσία," TDNT 5: 859.

[2]Ibid., p. 865; cf. Schweizer, Matthew, p. 481; and Klostermann, Matthäusevangelium, p. 193.

[3]See Blair, Jesus in the Gospel of Matthew, pp. 77-78.

Thirdly, the evangelist introduces the word "Parousia" without any antecedent explanation.[1] However, Parousia is joined with "consummation of the Age," and this phrase has been mentioned previously in the gospel (13:39, 40, 49 cf. 28:20). This would suggest that for Matthew the Parousia of Jesus as Son of Man inaugurates the consummation.[2]

Fourthly, of the Synoptics it is only in Matthew that the Parousia of Jesus and the consummation of the Age are explicitly linked together. This link gives the disciples' question a precision that is not found in Mark.[3] The disciples in Mark 13:4 ask Jesus "what will be the sign when these things (=destruction of Jersalem) are all to be accomplished?" But, in Matthew the "sign" now refers to Jesus' advent and to the "consummation of the Age." Thus, once again the evangelist clearly distinguishes between the predicted destruction of the temple and the coming of the Son of Man which will inaugurate the consummation, but in the process he links Jesus' Parousia with the consummation of the Age.[4]

---

[1]Allen, St. Matthew, p. 254.

[2]Schweizer, Matthew, pp. 448-449.

[3]See Hill, Matthew, p. 319.

[4]Schweizer, Matthew, pp. 448-449; cf. Hill, Matthew, p. 319; and Kingsbury, Structure, pp. 29, 158.

"Consummation of the Age"
(συντέλεια τοῦ αἰῶνος)

These four points are clarified further when the phrase συντέλεια τοῦ αἰῶνος is reviewed. Συντέλεια τοῦ αἰῶνος occurs only in Matthew in the Synoptic tradition (13:39, 40; 24:3; 28:20), and it is generally taken to be Matthean composition.[1] The evangelist's phrase could have been evoked by συντελεῖσθαι in Mark 13:4, which Luke simply interprets with γίνεσθαι.[2] Most importantly, however, is the fact that the phrase is a stereotyped apocalyptic phrase. Συντέλεια seems to have been a technical term in apocalyptic, especially in Daniel (LXX), to denote the "end" (Dan. 11:35, 40; 12:4, 7). Several times in Daniel συντέλεια clearly refers to the eschatologically appointed "end" (8:19 cf. 11:27; 12:6, 13a).[3] The use of αἰῶνος with συντέλεια implies a distinct point of time in a salvation-historical sense as opposed to a general notion of "eternity." In other words, the expression συντέλεια τοῦ αἰῶνος ("the end of the aeon") seems clearly to mean the "end of the world" in Matthew, that is, " . . . the termination of the existing world order when present history has run its course."[4]

---

[1]Fenton, St. Matthew, p. 383; and Trilling, Wahre, p. 43.

[2]Gerhard Delling, "τέλος," TDNT 8: 66 n. 10.

[3]Ibid., pp. 65-66.

[4]Kingsbury, Parables of Jesus in Matthew 13, p. 107; cf. Hermann Sasse, "αἰών, αἰῶνος," TDNT 1: 203-208; Trilling, Wahre, p. 43; and Schweizer, Matthew, p. 309. This is especially true of Matt. 28:20.

Another use of the phrase in apocalyptic was in connection with the final judgment. The "consummation of the Age" would bring the judgment (cf. 1 Enoch 10:12; 16:1; 2 Baruch 69:4; 82:2; 83:7). A survey of the use of the phrase in the First Gospel will show that the concept of the final judgment is linked clearly with Matthew's use of the phrase "consummation of the Age."

The phrase first occurs in the interpretation of the parable of the tares (13:39, 40), which is "an expression of Matthaean thought and theology to the very core."[1] The central message of the parable's interpretation is focused upon "the 'harvest', defined as the 'End of the Age' (v. 39b), and what is to take place at this time," namely, that the Son of Man will send out his angels to inaugurate the final judgment.[2] In other words, the phrase συντέλεια τοῦ αἰῶνος is defined clearly in Matt. 13:39-40 as: (1) the end of present history, and (2) the judgment.

This should help define τῆς σῆς παρουσίας, which has not been mentioned explicitly before in the First Gospel, when it is brought into connection with συντέλεια τοῦ αἰῶνος in 24:3. The Parousia of Jesus as Son of Man (24:3, 27, 37, 39) inaugurates the "consummation of the Age," that is, the end of present history and the beginning of the final judgment. It would seem, then, that Matthew's view of the "end" envisions at least

---

[1]Kingsbury, Parables of Jesus in Matthew 13, p. 95.

[2]Ibid., pp. 106-107; cf. M'Neile, St. Matthew, pp. 200-201; Allen, St. Matthew, p. 153; and Hill, Matthew, pp. 236-237.

two acts--the Parousia of Jesus as the Son of Man, and the final judgment.[1]

Thus, when the disciples ask Jesus about "his Parousia" and "the close of the Age," Matthew has neatly structured the answer (the discourse) according to his view of the End--the Parousia (24:4-31), the necessity of being ready to face the End and the judgment (24:32-25:30), and the judgment itself (25:31-46). The very question of the disciples, therefore, places Matthew's community in an ethical-eschatological tension between the time of Jesus' ministry and his return.[2] The discourse in chapter 24 will, of necessity, contain strong ethical exhortations for Matthew's church.

In summary: (1) συντέλεια τοῦ αἰῶνος means the eschatological end of history for Matthew[3] which will (2) be inaugurated, not by the destruction of the temple, but by the Parousia of Jesus as Son of Man, and this is (3) a future

---

[1]Trilling, Wahre, p. 149; and Kingsbury, Parables of Jesus in Matthew 13, p. 107.

[2]Kingsbury, Structure, pp. 158-159.

[3]In addition to the sources already cited see: Hare, Theme of Jewish Persecution, p. 179 n. 1; Kingsbury, "The Structure of Matthew's Gospel and His Concept of Salvation-History," CBQ 35 (1973): 468-469; Davies, Sermon on the Mount, p. 181; Hartman, Prophecy Interpreted, p. 221; Allen, St. Matthew, p. 254; and Str-Bill. 1: 949.

event.[1]  Matthew's redaction here again clearly
distinguishes between the judgment against Israel
(24:1-2), which is past, and the Parousia of Jesus
as the Son of Man, which is a future event.
Jesus' Parousia will inaugurate the last judgment,
and it is between these two events that Matthew's
community (the disciples) exists.

### Summary: Matthew's Redaction of 24:3

Matthew has constructed a new scene in 24:3.
The scene he has painted shows the disciples
(Matthew's church) reverently coming to Jesus.
Jesus is clearly an authoritative figure (κάθημαι)
who is worthy of reverence (προσέρχομαι).  The
disciples ask Jesus about his Parousia which, in
the subsequent discourse, is clearly the coming
of the Son of Man (24:26-31).  Thus, part of the
christology which informs the discourse is Matthew's Son of Man christology.  In this immediate
context it is an apocalyptic Son of Man christology which emphasizes the future Parousia and
the end of the present world order (συντέλεια τοῦ
αἰῶνος).

The discourse itself answers the disciples'
question about Jesus' Parousia, not about his

---

[1]As we have seen, to say that συντέλεια τοῦ
αἰῶνος is an eschatological event does not mean
necessarily for some that the Parousia is still a
future event for Matthew (cf. Feuillet, "Parousie
dans L'Evangile de Matthieu," pp. 261-280; and P.
Benoit, L'Évangile selon Saint Matthieu, 2nd rev.
ed. [Paris: Éditions du Cerf, 1953], pp. 136-145).
However, contrast with this view the conclusions
of Oepke, "παρουσία," pp. 866-867; Allen, St.
Matthew, p. 254; Hill, Matthew, p. 266; Schweizer,
Matthew, p. 347; Kingsbury, Structure, p. 107 cf.
pp. 114-120; and Rigaux, St. Matthew, pp. 132-133.

pronouncement of judgment upon Israel (24:1-2).
The way in which Matthew has constructed the new
scene shows that the judgment Jesus pronounced
upon Israel (23:38; 24:2) was crystallized in
Jesus' final departure from the temple. Whether
or not the judgment of 24:2 alludes to C.E. 70 for
Matthew is unclear. If it does, then the evangelist clearly saw in that event the fulfillment of
Jesus' pronouncement. What is clear, however,
is that the eschatological discourse in verses
15-22 does not refer back to the judgment which
was pronounced in 23:38 and 24:2. The discourse
deals only with the Parousia and the consummation
of the age. This is clear--if not in the disciples' question--in Matthew's deletion of
"opposite the temple" in 24:3a (cf. Mark 13:3).

The apocalyptic character of the discourse,
then, is seen clearly in the Son of Man christology, and in the question about the Parousia and
the end of the age, but the <u>setting</u> of the discourse also shows its character as a "testament."
It is Jesus-Sophia who answers the disciples'
question. The setting has Jesus-Sophia, obviously
a figure worthy of worship (cf. 14:32-33), privately (κατ' ἰδίαν) imparting information and encouragement to his successors which will help them
"endure until the end" (24:13). This is also his
last discourse with them before his public ministry ends and he goes on his way to death (cf.
26:1-2). Thus, the eschatological discourse has
both an apocalyptic character and, if not the form
of a farewell discourse, the function of a
testament.

<u>Part 3. The Testament of
Jesus-Sophia: False
Prophets and Jesus'
Presence in
the Church</u>

We have seen that the redactional keys to

225

the eschatological discourse are: (1) that Jesus-
Sophia is delivering it (23:32-39), (2) that it is
a Parousia discourse (24:3), that is, it deals
apocalyptically with what is to occur between the
time of Jesus' death and his Parousia, and
(3) that it is addressed to Matthew's community
(the disciples). At this point, then, we want to
give a summary of what the discourse actually
says. If these redactional points are the interpretative keys to the discourse, then they will be
crucial to our reading of it. Therefore, we will
proceed by giving a literary analysis of each
section of the discourse while, at the same time,
we will seek to understand its implications as a
discourse of Jesus-Sophia to Matthew's community.
It was noted earlier that one aspect of redaction
criticism is to ask questions about the kind of
auditors for whom this discourse is relevant.[1]
While we will not take our analysis to the sociological and historical limits (what ethnic groups
composed the community, the geographical location,
etc.), we will attempt to suggest the kind of
theological community this was, and we will suggest what types of opponents are addressed by the
apologetic parts of the discourse. Succinctly,
literary criticism always will precede any discussion of the community setting, but the two will
be tightly bonded, though always distinguished, as
we proceed.

### Troubles before the End (24:4-8)

Matthew 24:4-8 follows Mark 13:5-8 very
closely. This fact, along with Matthew's radical
departure from Mark in Matt. 24:9-14, is the primary basis for delineating this as the first sub-
section of the discourse. A further reason for

---

[1]See Donahue, Are You the Christ?,
pp. 47-48, 209-212.

this delineation is that this section is held together by two basic thoughts: (1) see that you are not deceived (v. 4b), and (2) "the end is not yet" (v. 6c cf. v. 8: πάντα δὲ ταῦτα ἀρχὴ ὠδίνων). This section seems to describe the "beginning" of troubles (v. 8) rather than the time of crisis immediately before the Parousia itself (cf. 24:29).[1]

The disciples have just asked about the sign of Jesus' Parousia and about the end of the Age. He replies that first "many" (πολλοί) will be preaching either that (a) they themselves are the Messiah, or (b) that he (Jesus) has already returned (v. 5). The disciples should take care not to be led astray by this end-time confusion (v. 4b). He tells them, secondly, that the social order itself will seem to be breaking up. They will hear of "wars and rumors of wars" and of "kingdom against kingdom" (vv. 6-7a), but they are not to fear because it is part of God's plan (δεῖ γενέσθαι, v. 6). These things are only the preliminaries; they are not the End itself (the "consummation of the Age" cf. ἀλλ' οὔπω ἐστὶν τὸ τέλος, v. 6). Thirdly, he tells them that even when they hear that the natural order itself seems to be breaking up ("famines and earthquakes in various places," v. 7c), all (πάντα) of this--the deceivers, the wars, the natural catastrophes--is simply the prelude to the final consummation ("all this is but the beginning," v. 8). It is not the τέλος itself. Let us look at how Matthew works this answer out in detail even though he

---

[1]We have subdivided the discourse on the basis of its content and on the basis of what we feel are Matthean transitional phrases, especially when compared with Mark 13. Both of these criteria will be evident in the subsequent exegesis.

227

closely follows Mark.

The Matthean understanding of Jesus' answer is that the "disciples," that is, Matthew's community (cf. 24:3), are to take heed lest they be led astray. The implication is that others within the community have been led astray already (πλανήση, v. 4).[1] It seems that apostasy will increase as the End draws closer, and, consequently, the warning against deception is sounded several times in the discourse (vv. 4, 5, 11, 24).[2] The main point is that one of the purposes of the discourse, which is sounded right at the beginning (v. 4), is to prepare Christians for enduring faithfulness until the End does arrive (cf. vv. 8, 13).[3] Matthew's community will not

---

[1]See the detailed discussion in the section immediately below on Matthew's community situation with respect to false prophets.

Here πλανήση is the active voice with the causative sense of "to lead astray" and has the figurative meaning of to be "deceived" (see Bauer, A Greek-English Lexicon, p. 671 #1B). Πλανάω occurs eight times in Matthew (4 times in Mark, once in Luke), and four times in the eschatological discourse alone (24:4, 5, 11, 24). In Matthew πλανάω clearly refers to the threat of apostasy. See the discussions of the parable of the "Lost Sheep" in Matthew, and especially compare Matt. 18:12 with Luke 15:4 (see Hill, Matthew, pp. 273-274; Schweizer, Matthew, p. 365; and Herbert Braun, "πλανάω," TDNT 6: 242).

[2]The idea that apostasy will increase before the End is a well-established eschatological theme in Judaism and in early Christianity (see Ibid., pp. 241-245).

[3]Hare, Theme of Jewish Persecution, p. 318.

only face deception, though that is the main point of this section, but it will face persecution (24:9) and possible displacement (24:20). The strain upon the community ultimately will be so great that even the "elect" will come close to losing salvation (24:22).

The prediction of "wars and rumors of wars" (v. 6) is a common part of Jewish eschatological traditions,[1] and it seems that the predictions are quite general in nature.[2] The prophecy is of a general nature in Matthew too, but Matthew has made the prophecy more certain, and perhaps more immediate, than has Mark (μελλήσετε δὲ ἀκούειν cf. Mark's ὅταν δὲ ἀκούσητε).[3] Just as Matthew's

---

[1]See Taylor, St. Mark, p. 505; and M'Neile, St. Matthew, pp. 345-346 for exhaustive references to Jewish literature.

[2]Taylor, St. Mark, p. 505. This does not mean that it is impossible to conclude that a real war loomed on the horizon for Matthew's church.

[3]Pesch, "Eschatologie und Ethik," p. 229; Marxsen, Mark the Evangelist, p. 203; and Klostermann, Matthäusevangelium, p. 195. Cf. Bl-D §382(4); §356. In such predictions it is difficult to determine whether the wars are present and threatening (cf. Jer. 4:19), or far away (cf. Dan. 11:44; see Beasley-Murray, Commentary on Mark Thirteen, p. 35). In light of this ambiguity, any interpretations of these predictions as before or after C.E. 70 are tenuous. The predictions must be taken as general, yet with the possibility that Matthew believes their fulfillment to be imminent.
This use of μέλλω is characteristic of Matthean style (cf. 16:27; 17:12, 22; 20:22). See Allen, St. Matthew, pp. 182, 216.

community is not to be led astray by deceivers
(v. 4b), so here the community is to see that it
is also not to be afraid (ὁρᾶτε, μὴ θροεῖσθε).
Again, it is not clear whether Matthew understands
this imperative only as a prohibition of a present
attitude, or whether the prohibition extends into
the future as a general principle. The latter is
the more likely possibility.[1]

One is not to fear because these events
"must take place" (δεῖ γενέσθαι). These events
are not as contingent as they might appear;
indeed, they belong to the divine plan for history. Δεῖ expresses God's plan for the eschatological drama.[2] The implication is that although
these events are not the τέλος itself, they are
part of God's working toward the τέλος.[3] Matthew
makes this point explicit when he writes "but the
end (τὸ τέλος) is not yet." His point is that the
τέλος, that is, the End of the Age, is not to be
identified with these events. The τέλος, which is
here virtually synonymous with τῆς σῆς παρουσίας
and συντελείας τοῦ αἰῶνος (24:3), is of a different nature than these events (cf. 24:29-31).[4] The

---

[1]Cf. Bl-D §461(1) and Maximillian Zerwick,
Biblical Greek, trans. Joseph Smith (Rome: Scripta
Pontificii Instituti Biblici, 1963), §248.

[2]Most commentators point to Dan. 2:28 (LXX)
as the locus classicus (cf. Walter Grundmann,
"δεῖ," TDNT 2: 23; and Taylor, St. Mark, p. 505.
Cf. also Rev. 1:1; 4:1; 22:6).

[3]Beasley-Murray, Commentary on Mark
Thirteen, p. 34.

[4]Feuillet, "Le Sens Du Mot Parousie," p.
271; cf. Trilling, Wahre, p. 43; and Kingsbury,
"The Structure of Matthew's Gospel," p. 468. Τὸ

τέλος in Matthew's view is not to be identified with any particular war, though the τέλος could certainly be a time of war and horror.[1]  The evangelist is not denying that there will be such wars, or even sufferings as a result of them (v. 8).  His point, however, is that they should not be feared because they are part of God's plan. What should be feared is the judgment of the Son of Man which will occur after his Parousia, that is, at the τέλος (cf. 16:27).  The judgment in Matthew is clearly part of the τέλος, and it

---

τέλος here means the "end of this Age" and the beginning of the "Age to come."  It is the End of the eschatological drama (Bauer, Greek-English Lexicon, p. 819 #1B), and is the equivalent of the Hebrew Qēṣ (Str-Bill., 1: 949-950; cf. Francis Brown, S. R. Driver, and C. A. Briggs, Hebrew and English Lexicon of the Old Testament [Oxford: Clarendon Press, 1966], p. 893 #1).

In Matthew τέλος means the point at which present history has run its course (Kingsbury, Structure, p. 28).  Τέλος in Matthew cannot be reduced to mean only the fall of Jerusalem in 70 (Feuillet).  One cannot even say that in this context τέλος refers to the End which will begin (or has begun) with C.E. 70 and the consequent Parousia and συντελείας τοῦ αἰῶνος (cf. Allen, St. Matthew, p. 254).  The events mentioned here are of a general nature and are not specific indications that Jerusalem has been or is about to be destroyed (Manson, Sayings, p. 325 cf. Hill, Matthew, p. 317).

[1] See Beasley-Murray, Commentary on Mark Thirteen, p. 34; and Marxsen, Mark the Evangelist, pp. 172-173.

follows the Parousia of the Son of Man (cf. 25:31-46).[1]

However, not only will there be wars and clashes between nations (v. 7a) before the τέλος, there will be disturbances in nature as well (v. 7b). These disturbances are also part of the general apocalyptic expectations of what is to precede the τέλος.[2] These disturbances, just like the rumors of wars, are also under God's δεῖ (v. 6) and are not the τέλος itself.

All of these things (πάντα δὲ ταῦτα, v. 8) are the beginning of the sufferings (ὠδίνων) which are to precede the τέλος. The evangelist's addition of πάντα in verse 8 refers to the deceivers (v. 5), to the wars (vv. 6-7a), and to the natural

---

[1]It is true that neither Matthew nor Mark describe any judgment scene in their actual description of the Son of Man's coming (Mark 13:24-27 cf. Matt. 24:29-31). This leaves open the possibility that some of Mark's community might suppose that the τέλος has come in a raging war through which they are living (Marxsen, Mark the Evangelist, p. 173). But, in Matthew's case the Parousia and the "end of the Age" (τέλος) are specifically asked about (24:3) and described (24:29-31; 25:31-46). The Parousia in Matthew is clearly associated with the judgment of 25:31-46 (cf. 24:30b with 25:31) and distanced from "wars and rumors of wars" (οὔπω ἐστὶν τὸ τέλος, 24:6).

[2]Beasley-Murray, Commentary on Mark Thirteen, p. 37; and Taylor, St. Mark, p. 505.

disasters (v. 7b).[1] All of these things are the premonitory signs of the New Age; they themselves do not immediately lead up to the τέλος. The order of events seems to be: (1) the appearance of deceivers (perhaps both false christs and false prophets); (2) wars and disturbances (the break-up of the social order); and, (3) earthquakes, and famines (the break-up of the natural order).[2]

Matthew calls all of these things the beginning of ὠδίνων (v. 8). He could simply mean the "birth pangs of the New Age" which, perhaps, suggests a certain hopeful detachment for his readers. However, the term seems to suggest the difficulties that God's people must endure before their deliverance comes.[3] Some, if not all, of these things are being experienced by Matthew's community now--at least the deceivers (vv. 10-12 cf. 7:21-23) and possibly the sufferings of 24:9. The evangelist uses ὠδίνων as the lead-in to his addition of θλῖψιν in verse 9a. One gets the impression that verse 8 should not be paraphrased: "These things are only the beginning of birth pangs for the New Age." The more likely meaning should read: "These things already denote the beginning of the sufferings which you must endure

---

[1]Indeed the allusion seems to be back to the ταῦτα of verse 3 since ταῦτα there alluded to the Parousia and the consummation.

[2]Manson, Sayings, p. 325; cf. Marxsen, Mark the Evangelist, p. 204.

[3]Howard Clark Kee, "The Gospel According to Matthew," The Interpreter's One-Volume Commentary on the Bible (New York: Abingdon Press, 1971), p. 639.

until the End" (cf. 24:13).[1]

The keynote of this section, then, is the dual admonition to "see that no one leads you astray" (v. 4b) because "the end is not yet" (v. 6c). The admonition not to be deceived <u>in relation to the End</u> is a theme which is sounded repeatedly throughout the discourse (vv. 4-6 , 8, 10-13 , 14c cf. 23-26). At this point we would like to explicate this theme of the discourse, and to suggest its relevance for Matthew's community as parenesis from Jesus-Sophia. The greatest danger suggested by these verses is the threat of false prophets who seduce "the disciples" (Matthew's community) into apostasy. In other words, we will argue that to be "led astray" (πλανάω) equals apostasy, and that the threat comes from false prophets within the community who propound what Matthew considers to be a false understanding of Jesus' presence. A key verse with which to begin is Matt. 24:5, a verse in this section.

### False Prophets in Matthew

The threat of false prophets is addressed clearly in verse 5. The most important Matthean

---

[1]See Pesch, <u>Naherwartungen</u>, p. 124. There is only general agreement that ὠδίνων denotes events to precede the τέλος. Whether the background for Matthew's understanding is rabbinical or mythological is disputed, as well as whether the background suggests cheerfulness and hope, or suffering and chastisement (see Str-Bill. 1: 950; Hill, <u>Matthew</u>, p. 320; Fenton, <u>St. Matthew</u>, p. 383; Allen, <u>St. Matthew</u>, pp. 254-255; Johnson, <u>Matthew</u>, p. 544; Stendahl, "Matthew," p. 793; and Beasley-Murray, <u>Commentary on Mark Thirteen</u>, pp. 37-38).

change in this verse is undoubtedly the addition of "Christ" to Mark's "I am he" (13:6). Before this change, though, occurs the important phrase (also in Mark and in Luke 21:8) ἐπὶ τῷ ὀνόματί μου. We must first investigate the meaning of this phrase in Matthew.

Matthew, Mark, and Luke all have πολλοὶ . . . ἐλεύσονται ἐπὶ τῷ ὀνόματί μου. Ἔρχομαι in this context undoubtedly refers to the <u>eschatological</u> coming of deceivers to precede the Parousia of the Son of Man.[1] This is particularly true in Matthew's context.[2] His allusion is undoubtedly to eschatological deceivers.[3]

It is noteworthy that only in Matthew is the resurrection called by the Jewish leaders "the last fraud" (ἡ ἐσχάτη πλάνη, 27:64), and the story of the guard at the tomb (only in Matthew) is Christian polemic against this charge (27:62-66; 28:12-15).[4] The implication of Matt. 27:64 is

---

[1]Schneider, "ἔρχομαι," p. 670; and Braun, "πλανάω," pp. 245-247.

[2]See 23:39; 24:3, 30, 39, 42, 44; 25:10, 19, 31 cf. 3:11, 16; 7:15; 8:29; 11:3; 13:25; 16:27, 28; 21:5, 9.

[3]This does not preclude the possibility that the deceivers are already present for Matthew's church. His use of the future tense (ἐλεύσονται) does not exclude this possibility either (Bl-D §323[1]).

[4]Schweizer, <u>Matthew</u>, pp. 519-521.

that belief in Jesus' resurrection is the "last fraud" while belief in his Messiahship was the first fraud.[1] In 27:63 Jesus himself is called an "imposter," that is, one who leads people astray (cf. John 7:12, 47). In other words, it seems that Matthew's community was aware of a tradition which applied to Jesus (and to his disciples?) the later Jewish eschatological idea of the false Messiah.[2] If Matthew's community was aware of such a Jewish tradition, then this fact could shed light upon the evangelist's change to "I am the Christ." Perhaps those who would attempt to lead Matthew's church astray would be proclaiming that Jesus is the Christ, but their proclamation, from Matthew's viewpoint, was distorted. Perhaps they themselves claimed to be the Christ.

Ἐπὶ τῷ ὀνόματί μου

The difficult phrase ἐπὶ τῷ ὀνόματί μου is instructive in this regard. Interpreters of Mark 13 have investigated thoroughly the possible meanings of the phrase, and they have made numerous suggestions about its meaning.[3] The first

---

[1]Hill, Matthew, p. 358; and Fenton, St. Matthew, p. 448.

[2]Braun, "πλανάω," p. 251. It will become evident below that the real problem in Matthew's community was not that of messianic pretenders in general, although his community undoubtedly had heard of such figures, but that of Christian prophets who in an enthusiastic state claimed to be Jesus himself. As we shall see, Matthew was not opposed to their enthusiasm as such, but he was opposed to their erroneous understanding of Jesus' presence.

[3]First, the phrase could mean "claiming my

thing to notice is that the deceivers in Matthew
are <u>within</u> the Christian community.  Ἐπὶ τῷ
ὀνόματί μου is a technical phrase identifying one
who confesses that Jesus is the Christ.[1]  Secondly,

---

name," that is, "they will arrogate to themselves
both the powers and position which belong by right
to Jesus alone."  These are the messianic pretenders in the widest sense; they are not claiming
to be Jesus (Beasley-Murray, <u>Commentary on Mark
Thirteen</u>, p. 31).

Secondly, the phrase could mean "with an
appeal to me and to my words."  In this case, they
claimed either to be Jesus himself, who had re-
appeared, or a reincarnation of Jesus (Schweizer,
<u>Matthew</u>, p. 268; and Kelber, <u>Kingdom in Mark</u>, p.
115), or they claimed to be Jesus as the Son of
Man (Pesch, <u>Naherwartungen</u>, p. 111).

Thirdly, the phrase could mean "on my
authority," that is, the pretenders invoked Jesus'
name.  The problem here is that this seems to be a
<u>non sequitur</u> because those who claimed the author-
ity of Jesus' name simultaneously claimed that
name for themselves, that is, they claimed his
identity (cf. Beasley-Murray, <u>Commentary on Mark
Thirteen</u>, p. 31).  It could mean that they claimed
to be commissioned by Jesus (Klostermann, <u>Markus-
evangelium</u>, p. 133), that is, they are identifying
themselves as "Christians" (Julius Wellhausen, <u>Das
Evangelium Marci</u> [Berlin: Georg Reimer, 1909], p.
101).  The problem is obviously not solved with
regard to Mark, and Matthean interpreters use all
of these different nuances.

[1]Matt. 18:5; Acts 2:38; 4:17, 18; 5:28, 40;
Luke 24:47; cf. Mark 9:39 (see Hans Bietenhard,
"ὄνομα," <u>TDNT</u> 5:271).  Jeremias shows that πολλοί
can have <u>both</u> a restrictive and a comprehensive
meaning.  Πολλοί can refer to the Christian
community exclusively, or to those outside of

ἐπὶ τῷ ὀνόματί μου, when used christologically,
always is used positively in relation to its referent.  In other words, the phrase ἐπὶ τῷ ὀνόματί
μου in the New Testament is used always to depict
someone's positive relation to Christ.  It is
never used in the New Testament to refer to those
outside of the Christian community.[1]  The deceivers in Matt. 24:5, then, seem to be Christians
who are claiming in some sense to be Christ himself.  Many scholars are now assenting to this
conclusion in one form or another, but the question is: what evidence is there in Matthew for
such a conclusion?[2]  Matthew has followed closely

------

that particular community (Jeremias, "πολλοί,"
TDNT 6: 543).  We conclude that the πολλοί of
Matt. 24:5 are intra-community because the object
of their activity is the πολλούς (24:12).  Otherwise, if they are from outside of the community,
one would have to conclude that πολλοί and πολλούς
are two different groups, and there seems to be
little justification for that conclusion (cf.
Schweizer, Matthew, p. 186).

[1]Theodore J. Weeden, Mark--Traditions in
Conflict (Philadelphia: Fortress Press, 1971),
p. 79; cf. Bietenhard, "ὄνομα," pp. 270-282.

[2]Schweizer, Matthew, p. 268; Kelber, Kingdom in Mark, p. 115; Weeden, Traditions in Conflict, pp. 79-81; and Pesch, Naherwartungen, p.
111.  It is possible that ὁ Χριστός in 24:5 could
be simply "Messiah."  However, the phrase "in my
name" becomes more enigmatic in that case.
Furthermore, it has long been recognized that the
term "Christ," which appears at least sixteen
times in Matthew (only five of which can be
attributed to his sources), is an important term
for him by which he attempts to prove that Jesus
is the Jewish Messiah.  The term retains its

238

his Markan source in 24:4-5. In order to see what
is distinctive about the Matthean portrait of the
false prophets, let us first investigate his
treatment of this theme elsewhere in his gospel
(7:22-23 cf. 7:15-21). Then we can proceed to
what we feel is his redactional emphasis concerning the false prophets, namely, the theme that the
false prophets cause the increase of ἀνομία and
the decline of ἀγάπη within his community (cf.
24: 10-12).

## False prophecy and enthusiasm
## (Matthew 7:22-23)

E. Käsemann has portrayed the early Chris-

---

basic meaning for Matthew, but his use of it almost approaches that of a proper name: "Jesus, who
is called 'Christ'" (1:16; cf. 27:17, 22. See
Blair, Jesus in the Gospel of Matthew, pp. 54-55).
It is difficult to understand, if coming "in the
name of Jesus" (ἐπὶ τῷ ὀνόματί μου, 24:5) refers
to Christians as we have argued, how one could be
"Christian" and say: "I, instead of Jesus, am the
Christ (=Messiah)." Even if "in my name" only
means "with my power," it is still difficult to
understand the logic of their claim. If they are
claiming to be the Messiah, implying that Jesus
is not such, why would they need to appeal to his
authority?
It seems that in 24:5, at least, the claim
is an enthusiastic one: "I am Jesus." The absolute use of ὁ Χριστός in 23:10 is in a section
which implies that Christians will claim such
titles (even that of the Christ?) in order to
exalt themselves (cf. 23:8-12). Contrast, though,
the view of M'Neile, St. Matthew, p. 350, who
feels that the false christs and prophets are
allied but are not identical.

tian community as one in which enthusiasm was dominant. He points to Matt. 7:22-23 as "uncommonly instructive" in this regard. He contends that Matthew uses this polemic against false prophets within his community who, because they have been endowed with power from the exalted Christ, are enthusiasts with wonder-working power, the power of exorcism and prophecy. In short, they are enthusiasts who actually represent Christ on earth and administer his power. It is this group which cries "Lord, Lord" (7:21), but to whom the Risen Lord proclaims "depart from me, you evildoers" (7:23 cf. 7:15).[1]

It is quite possible that some kind of enthusiasm was prevalent in Matthew's church in which the participants were not only proclaiming Christ, nor simply drawing upon his authority, but were somehow claiming to be the κύριος incarnate. They are "false prophets" (7:15 cf. πολλοί, 7:22; 24:5) who prophesy, "cast out demons," and "do many mighty works" in Jesus' name (note the three-fold repetition in 7:22 of τῷ σῷ ὀνόματι). Judgment is pronounced against them in 7:23 because they are working "lawlessness" (ἀνομίαν cf. Luke 13:27, ἀδικίας). In their enthusiasm, that is, in their experience of Jesus' presence, they seemed to be saying not only that the Law is abrogated (cf. 5:17-20; 23:8-10), but also that the "epiphany of salvation" has appeared in the Christian prophet.[2]

_____

[1]Ernst Käsemann, "The Beginnings of Christian Theology," New Testament Questions of Today, trans. W. J. Montague (Philadelphia: Fortress Press, 1969), pp. 83-84 [hereafer cited as "Beginnings"]. See also Pesch, "Eschatologie und Ethik," p. 230 n. 25.

[2]Käsemann, "Beginnings," p. 103. Contrast

Such pneumatic activity differs from the same kind of charismatic activity which is approved elsewhere in Matthew (cf. 10:5-14) because the former is not according to "the will of the Father" (cf. 7:21). It is ἀνομία.[1]  G. Barth has also identified the false prophets of 7:21-23 as antinomians who have abrogated the Law and appeal instead to their χαρίσματα at the judgment. The distortion in the message of the false prophets is their understanding of Jesus' authoritative presence within the community.[2]

### The Presence of Jesus in Matthew's Community

One of the solid conclusions of Matthean scholarship is that Matthew's church believes that Jesus is present in and rules over them.[3]  In some sense the rule of Jesus began for Matthew after Jesus' exaltation (28:18). This point is so clear that C. H. Dodd can even say that Jesus' presence is a kind of "proleptic parousia."[4]  An

---

Cothenet, "Les prophètes chrétiens dans L'Évangile selon saint Matthieu," pp. 286-291.

[1]Weeden, Traditions in Conflict, p. 81 n. 23.

[2]Barth, "Matthew's Understanding of the Law," TI, pp. 73-75.

[3]Cf. Matt. 28:16-20; 1:22-23; 10:19-20; 18:20.

[4]C. H. Dodd, "Matthew and Paul," New Testament Studies (New York: Charles Scribner's Sons, 1952), p. 56; Barth, TI, p. 134 n. 2; and Hans-Werner Bartsch, "Zum Problem der Parusieverzögerung bei den Synoptikern," EvTh 19 (1959): 129.

enthusiastic church with such a sense of the
presence of the Risen Jesus, as well as the knowledge that they have been given his authority
(10:1 cf. 28:18), could certainly come "in his
name" and at the height of pneumatic experience
cry out: "I am the Christ!" (24:5 cf. 10:20). The
Parousia for them would not be simply "proleptic,"
it would be present.[1] Matthew 24:23 seems to say
virtually the same thing as Matt. 24:5, though
it might have a different meaning in the Markan
parallel (cf. Mark 13:21). If Matt. 24:23 does
have a meaning similar to 24:5, this would accord
with the disciples' question in 24:3 where they
ask specifically for clarification about Jesus'
Parousia. The question for Matthew's community
was not whether Jesus was present with them, but
how he was present.

## Jesus' presence as the Shekinah (18:20)

Matthew presents the presence of Jesus in
the community as an analogue to the presence of
the Shekinah when the Torah is studied. Pirke
Aboth 3:2 is quoted often in this regard:
" . . . when two sit and there are between them
words of Torah, the Shechinah rests between
them."[2] Matthew 18:20, a saying which is only in

---

[1]Cf. Beasley-Murray, Commentary on Mark
Thirteen, p. 33. This type of enthusiasm could
have resulted from such statements as Matt. 10:23
and 16:28 (Hill, Matthew, p. 191).

[2]R. T. Herford, Pirke Aboth: The Sayings of
The Fathers, in Apocrypha and Pseudepigrapha, ed.
R. H. Charles (Oxford: Clarendon Press, 1913),
p. 698. Herford adds that this refers not to the
place but to the act of dwelling.

in the First Gospel, and one which the evangelist
has placed within the framework of community
instructions (18:15-17), has virtually the same
concept. Jesus is present with the disciples when
they gather "in his name" (εἰς τὸ ἐμὸν ὄνομα). G.
Barth reflects the consensus of commentators in
his conclusion about this verse:

> The presence of Jesus in the congregation
> is here described as analogous to the
> presence of the Shekinah (cf. Aboth 3:2);
> the place of the Torah is taken by the
> ὄνομα of Jesus; the place of the Shekinah
> by Jesus himself. . . . In Jesus God
> himself is with the congregation, is
> present in the congregation.[1]

We have discussed already the presence of Jesus as
the Shekinah in Matthew, but here that presence
is bound up with Torah.[2]

Jesus' presence and Torah
(Matt. 11:28-30)

We have discussed already how Matthew identified Jesus with both Wisdom and with the Shekinah.[3] It is known commonly how Wisdom also was
identified with the Torah in the development of
the pre-Matthean Wisdom tradition. Wisdom was
somehow viewed as incarnate in Torah (cf. Sirach

---

[1]Barth, "Matthew's Understanding of the
Law," TI p. 135; cf. Bornkamm, "End-Expectation
and Church in Matthew," TI, p. 35 n. 2.

[2]See pages 72-75 above.

[3]See pages 49-72 above.

24:1, 8, 23; Baruch 3:37; 4:1).[1]  In light of this
background, some commentators have concluded that
in 11:28-30 Matthew has identified Jesus-Sophia
with Torah.  The "yoke" in 11:28-30 to which Jesus
invites persons is the yoke of Wisdom, and Jesus
himself becomes Wisdom-Torah.[2]  However, the yoke
of Jesus-Sophia is not a different yoke than the
yoke of Torah, but it is the Torah rightly interpreted by Jesus as Sophia.[3]

We are suggesting, then, that Jesus is
present for Matthew's church in the interim between his death and Parousia only in his "words,"
that is, in his interpretation of Torah.  Jesus'
presence as Torah is the only link between the
Jesus who ministered, was rejected, and bade farewell, and the Jesus who will come as the Son of
Man at the "consummation of the Age."[4]  If Jesus

---

[1]Suggs, Wisdom, pp. 103-108; Bultmann,
Gospel of John, p. 23 n. 2; Conzelmann, "The
Mother of Wisdom," The Future of Our Religious
Past, ed. James M. Robinson (New York: Harper and
Row, 1971), pp. 234-240; and Wilckens, "σοφία,"
pp. 465-528 passim.

[2]Suggs, Wisdom, pp. 100-108; Schweizer,
Matthew, pp. 272-274; Christ, Jesus Sophia,
p. 119 cf. pp. 81-118; Arvedson, Mysterium
Christi, pp. 207-215; cf. Barth, "Matthew's Under-
standing of the Law," TI, p. 103 n. 1; and Hans
Dieter Betz, "The Logion of the Easy Yoke and of
Rest (Matt. 11:28-30)," JBL 86 (1967): 22-23.

[3]Suggs, Wisdom, pp. 106, 107, 114; and
Barth, "Matthew's Understanding of the Law," TI,
p. 159.

[4]Notice that this phrase (cf. 28:20b) recalls the whole eschatological discourse (24:3b,

is present with Matthew's church only through his words, then this would make the interpretation of scripture the crucial issue in Matthew's church.[1] E. Schweizer's comment is relevant here:

> If God's Wisdom, Word, and Law have, so to speak, become flesh in Jesus, there can be no question of tossing the Law overboard (5:17-18); on the contrary, it is only in Jesus that the real purpose of the Law is revealed (5:20, 21-48; 11:28-30). In revealing this purpose, Jesus not only teaches the Law but fulfills it, i.e., carries it out. Thus his disciples are the true teachers of the Law in the time of fulfillment, teaching and doing God's will (5:13-16; 13:52; 23:34).[2]

---

6b, 13, 14b) as the phrases τοῦ υἱοῦ (28:19) and the emphatic ἐγώ (28:20b) recall 11:25-30 (τόν υἱόν) and 23:34-39 (ἰδοὺ ἐγώ). I agree with Hamerton-Kelly that the counterpart of 11:25-30 is 28:16-20 (see Hamerton-Kelly, Pre-Existence, pp. 68-71). This poses a solution to the implicit christology of 28:16-20. Some have posited only a Son of Man christology for this passage, while others have denied any Son of Man influence. Only the υἱός is mentioned (28:19) and ἰδοὺ ἐγώ (28:20b; cf. ʼΙησοῦς in 28:16 and μοι in 28:18). Both of these point us directly back to 11:25-30 and 23:34-39. In our opinion, the christology of 28:16-20 is to be understood in the πραΰς-ἐξουσία christological framework of Jesus as Wisdom and Son of Man (see chapter 4 below).

[1]Cf. Stendahl, School, p. 35.

[2]Schweizer, Matthew, p. 447 (italics mine).

To "call upon the name of Jesus" is to claim the authority to utter his words.[1] In light of this, it would seem that 24:5 is directed against enthusiasts who say in the name of Jesus that, in effect, "the Parousia has come, Jesus is with us totally; we _are_ Jesus!"[2] The point is made again and again in the eschatological discourse that "the end is not yet" (24:6, 8, 14c). Apocalyptic enthusiasm is thus toned down and "enduring until the end" is emphasized (cf. 24:13).[3] For Matthew, to redefine Jesus' words in any way other than Jesus-Sophia himself did (as the love-command) is

---

[1]See the discussion below of the persecution of the missionaries and of διὰ τὸ ὄνομά μου in Matt. 24:9 (pp. 277-283).

[2]Cf. W. Manson, "The ΕΓΩ ΕΙΜΙ of the Messianic Presence in the New Testament," _JThS_ 48 (1947): 139-145. Luke's form seems to provide the double focus: ἐγώ εἰμι, καί· ὁ καιρὸς ἤγγικεν (21:8). Whether the latter phrase is an interpretation of ἐγώ εἰμι and means "the Messiah has arrived," or whether it denotes two separate groups (false prophets--false christs) is uncertain (Beasley-Murray, _Commentary on Mark Thirteen_, p. 33 cf. Manson, _Sayings_, p. 325). Several commentators argue in one way or another for an early Christian "heresy" in which the Parousia was "realized" (see Kelber, _Kingdom in Mark_, p. 115 n. 18 for an extensive bibliography).

[3]Hill, _Matthew_, p. 317; and Fenton, _St. Matthew_, p. 383. The characteristics of the "false prophets" will be discussed further under Matt. 24:10-12 (see pp. 254-273).

to redefine community life itself.  If community
life were redefined in terms other than those of
Jesus himself, then the whole community would risk
the loss of salvation when Jesus returned.[1]  This
is precisely what the false prophets were doing,
and Matthew calls it ἀνομία.  The task of the true
disciple is to endure until the Parousia (24:13),
and to carry out his/her commission as an envoy of
the Wisdom of God (cf. 24:14).  Both the disciples' task and the nature of the prophets' ἀνομία
are clarified in Matthew's redaction of verses
10-12.

## Apostasy within the
## Community (24:10-12)

These verses are peculiar to Matthew and
they appear to be his own construction.[2]  The

---

[1]Cf. Schweizer, Matthew, p. 180.

[2]Bultmann, History of the Synoptic Tradition, p. 122, sees these verses as a Matthean
"substitute" for Mark 13:9-13, which Matthew
placed in 10:17-22.  Bultmann notes that 24:10-12
consists of parts of variants (24:10=10:21=Mark
13:12; Matt. 24:11=10:24=Mark 13:22), but he concludes that the Matthean composition of these
verses cannot be taken for granted (cf. Manson,
Sayings, pp. 240-241).
However, θλῖψις in 24:9 is a redactional
summary, and Matthew's substitution of 24:10-12
for Mark 13:9-13 is typical of his redactional
tendency to give a dual account of pieces which
he uses from Mark and Q (Marxsen, Mark the Evangelist, p. 201; Rigaux, St. Matthew, pp. 25-26;
and Werner G. Kümmel, Introduction to the New
Testament, 16th ed., trans. H. C. Kee [New York:
Abingdon Press, 1966], pp. 52-55).  It seems that
Matthew has also used words and ideas from the

thought of 24:5 is continued in 24:10-12.  In 24:5 "many" (πολλοί) are coming already "in the name" of Jesus (ἐπὶ τῷ ὀνόματί μου) claiming that Jesus, in effect, has arrived.  The πολλοί of 24:5 refers to the same group as the πολλοί of 7:22 who come prophesying (ἐπροφητεύσαμεν) and performing "mighty works" (δυνάμεις πολλὰς ἐποιήσαμεν) in the name of Jesus.  They are the "false prophets" (ψευδοπροφητῶν, 7:15) who can be recognized by their "conduct" (τῶν καρπῶν αὐτῶν, 7:20).  They prophesy, but they do not do the "will of the Father" (τὸ θέλημα τοῦ πατρός, 7:21).  A similar type of community concern about enthusiastic prophets is reflected in an interesting passage in the Didache, a document which many believe to be dependent upon Matthew: "Not every one that speaks in the spirit (ἐν πνεύματι) is a Prophet, but only if he has the behavior (the ways, τοὺς τρόπους) of the Lord.  By their behavior (τῶν τρόπων) then shall a false prophet and the [true] Prophet be known" (11:18 cf. 11:10-12).[1]  In Matthew the conduct of the false prophets is described as "lawlessness" (τὴν ἀνομίαν, 7:23).  Matthew 24:10-12 continues the same thought.  Apostasy (v. 10) is caused in part by false prophets (v. 11) who help "lawlessness" (τὴν ἀνομίαν) increase and the

---

context to form this piece rather than drawing from a source.  See Lambrecht, "Parousia Discourse," p. 320 n. 29 for a detailed discussion (cf. Kingsbury, Parables of Jesus in Matthew 13, p. 161 n. 67).

[1]Philip Schaff, The Oldest Church Manual Called the Teaching of the Twelve Apostles, 2nd ed. (New York: Funk and Wagnalls, Publishers, 1886), p. 201.  For the relation of the Didache to Matthew see Ibid., pp. 82-90, and Schweizer, Matthew, p. 182.

love of most to decrease (v. 12 cf. Didache 16:3-4).[1]

It is clear that the problem in these verses, just as in 7:15-23 and 24:5, is an intra-community one. The discourse is addressed to the community (οἱ μαθηταί, 24:3). The community members are the ones who are warned about being led astray (βλέπετε μή τις ὑμᾶς πλανήσῃ, 24:4b cf. αὐτοῖς, 4a). They are the target of the false prophets (24:5). The many who fall away in 24:10 (σκανδαλισθήσονται πολλοί) are within the community. They will fall away partly because of the hatred of the Gentiles (καὶ τότε, cf. 24:9b),[2] and partly because of the false prophets (24:11).[3] The warnings of 24:10-12, then, are addressed to the community in general in order to warn it about true and false discipleship.[4]

## Σκάνδαλον

Matthew's use of σκανδαλίζεσθαι (or σκάνδαλον) indicates that it is his favorite term

---

[1]Cf. Barth, "Matthew's Understanding of the Law," pp. 73-75; and Kingsbury, Parables of Jesus in Matthew 13, p. 104.

[2]See the discussion below, pp. 277-283.

[3]Lambrecht, "Parousia Discourse," pp. 319-321.

[4]Bornkamm, "End-Expectation and Church in Matthew," TI, p. 21; and Paul S. Minear, "False Prophecy and Hypocrisy in the Gospel of Matthew," Neues Testament und Kirche, ed. J. Gnilka (Freiburg: Herder, 1974), p. 80.

for "seduction and apostasy in the congregation
as phenomena associated with the end."[1]  Σκάνδαλον
in Matthew always deals with the obstacles to
faith or with the loss of faith, particularly
the kind of apostasy associated with persecution,
but it always has the eschatological connotation
that apostasy faces certain damnation.[2]  The cause
for σκάνδαλον can come from false prophets within
the church (cf. 13:41) or from persecution of
community members by outsiders,[3] but it is clear
that the actual matter of apostasy is an intra-
mural concern of Matthew's, that is, the concern
seems to be confined to the limits of his own
community.[4]

---

[1]Bornkamm, "End-Expectation and Church in
Matthew," TI, p. 47 n. 4; cf. p. 75 n. 2.  Cf.
Matt. 13:21, 41; 18:6, 7, 8, 9; 24:10; 26:31, 33.

[2]Cf. Matt. 5:29-30 to 11:6.  See Kingsbury,
Parables of Jesus in Matthew 13, pp. 59-60.  The
evangelist is drawing, perhaps, upon the theme of
false prophets to appear before the End, which was
a familiar theme in Judaism (cf. Str-Bill., 1:951)
and in the early Church (1 Tim. 4:1; 2 Tim. 3:1-8;
1 John 2:18-19; Jude 18).  There is much in the
Didache which is similar to the discussion of
false prophets in Matthew, as we have mentioned
(see Schweizer, Matthew, pp. 182-186; and
Bornkamm, "End-Expectation and Church in Matthew,"
TI, p. 17).

[3]Cf. Matt. 18:7; 13:21; 24:9b-10.

[4]Cf. Matt. 13:41; 16:23.  See Kingsbury,
Parables of Jesus in Matthew 13, p. 104; Senior,
Matthew: A Gospel for the Church, pp. 64-67;
Barth, "Matthew's Understanding of the Law," TI,
p. 75 n. 4; and Schweizer, Matthew, p. 451.

Matthew's use of σκάνδαλον as apostasy
means that the "many" who fall away, either
because of Gentile hatred (24:10) from the outside
or because of false prophets from within the community (24:11), constitute the majority of Matthew's church.[1] A similar concern for apostasy is
also reflected in Matthew's version of the lost
sheep (18:10-14). In the First Gospel the parable
occurs in the chapter which is usually said to
deal with community concerns (cf. Luke 15:3-7).[2]
In the Matthean version of the parable πλανάω occurs twice (18:12). The Lukan version of the
parable uses ἀπολέσας and ἀπολωλός (15:4). The
point in Luke is that the joy (χαρά, 15:7) is over
"one sinner (ἐνὶ ἀμαρτωλῷ) who repents." In the
Matthean version the owner of the sheep rejoices
(χαίρει) over finding the one who "went astray"
(πεπλανημένοις, 18:13). The application in the
Matthean context is made to <u>disciples</u>, not to
"sinners" as in Luke. The ones who can go
"astray" in Matthew's version are the "little
ones" (τῶν μικρῶν, 18:14 cf. v. 13), which the
evangelist applies to "disciples."[3] This parable

---

[1]Τῶν πολλῶν. See Barth, "Matthew's Understanding of the Law," <u>TI</u>, p. 75 n. 2; and Jeremias, "πολλοί," p. 540.

[2]E.g., Schweizer, <u>Matthew</u>, pp. 358-360;
Senior, <u>Matthew: A Gospel for the Church</u>, p. 63;
and Hill, <u>Matthew</u>, pp. 272-278. This concern
clearly appears in the introduction (προσῆλθον οἱ
μαθηταὶ τῷ Ἰησοῦ, 18:1), in the usage of "little
ones" (τῶν μικρῶν) as an expression of discipleship (cf. 18:6, 10, 14), and in the concern for
one's "brother" (ὁ ἀδελφός σου, 18:15) in the
"church" (ἐκκλησία, 18:17).

[3]Senior, <u>Matthew: A Gospel for the Church</u>,
pp. 63-64; and Schweizer, <u>Matthew</u>, pp. 358-9, 365.

in Matthew, then, is addressed to disciples, and
it " . . . is a call to faithful pastorship in the
community, to concern for those who are 'going
astray' into sin, and away from the Church."[1]
Similar community concerns appear in CD xiii:9-10
where the overseer of the community "is to bring
back all of them that stray, as does a shepherd
his flock. He is to loose all the bonds that con-
strain them, so that there be no one in his community who is oppressed or crushed" (cf. Matt.
18:18).[2] The warnings in Matt. 24:10-12, when
seen against this kind of background, become eschatological warnings not only about damnation,
but also about true and false discipleship. The
warnings reflect the concern of his community
about apostasy.[3]

The theme of intracommunity apostasy and
judgment is related intricately to Matthew's view
of the church as a "mixed body" which will be
judged at the τέλος (cf. 13:24-30, 36-43). It is
known commonly that the church in Matthew is
" . . . not a collection of the elect and eter-
nally secure, but a mixed body which has to face
the separation between good and evil at the final
judgment."[4] In other words, it is not easy to

---

[1]Hill, Matthew, p. 274.

[2]Theodor H. Gaster, The Dead Sea Scriptures,
3rd ed. (Garden City, New York: Anchor Books,
1976), p. 87. See Schweizer, Matthew, pp. 359-360
for a discussion of this passage and its relation
to Matthew.

[3]Ellis, Matthew: His Mind and His Message,
p. 78 n. 13; and Manson, Sayings, p. 240.

[4]Bornkamm, "End-Expectation and Church in
Matthew," TI, p. 19 cf. pp. 20, 23, 43; Barth,

distinguish between those within the community who
are true prophets and disciples and those who are
false ones.  All rational attempts to discern the
false prophets fail: they all confess Jesus (7:22;
24:5), prophesy, and even work miracles in Jesus'
name (7:22).  The one test by which to scrutinize
the prophets, namely, their "conduct" (καρπός,
7:16, 20), could itself be ambiguous.[1]  Although
it is clear in Matthew that a true prophet (or
disciple) is to follow Jesus in word and in deed
(ἀκούει καὶ ποιεῖ, 7:24), in the last analysis
only Jesus himself can separate the good disciple
from the evil one, the false prophet from the true
prophet.[2]

However, καρπός is not without focus completely in terms of what a disciple is to produce.
The true prophet and disciple of Jesus will not
only proclaim Jesus' words, that is, his interpretation of Torah, but his/her life will issue in
love for God and for neighbor.  Love is what Jesus
commanded (22:35-40), love constitutes the "higher
righteousness" of a true disciple,[3] and love is

---

"Matthew's Understanding of the Law," pp. 59, 73;
Ellis, Matthew: His Mind and His Message, p. 140;
Kingsbury, Structure, pp. 158-160; and Senior,
Matthew: A Gospel for the Church, pp. 54-55.

[1]See Barth, "Matthew's Understanding of the
Law," TI, p. 74; and Friedrich, "προφήτης,"
pp. 855-856.

[2]Cf. 7:23; 13:30, 37-43; 21:43.  See
Schweizer, "Observance of the Law and Charismatic
Activity in Matthew," p. 225.

[3]Cf. 5:17-20; 7:12; 9:13; 12:7.

the <u>only</u> criterion used by the Son of Man at the judgment (25:37-40).[1] In contrast to this, the false prophets and their disciples do not follow the words and the deeds of Jesus. By their ἀνομία, they cause the <u>love</u> of the majority to grow cold (24:12).

False prophets and their disciples, then, are those whose fruit is "lawlessness." They do not practice the love which Jesus commanded.[2] "Lawlessness" (ἀνομία) in this gospel is not just "sin" in general terms, nor is it simply breaking the rules of Torah, but ἀνομία for Matthew is (1) failing to follow the words and deeds of Jesus by which he (2) interpreted the Law (=the will of God) in terms of love.[3] To put it succinctly, ἀνομία is the loss of the love commanded by Jesus.[4] The close relation between ἀνομία and ἀγάπη in Matthew supports this interpretation.[5]

---

[1]Bornkamm, "End-Expectation and Church in Matthew," <u>TI</u>, pp. 23-32.

[2]Schweizer, "Observance of the Law and Charismatic Activity in Matthew," p. 224.

[3]Bornkamm, "End-Expectation and Church in Matthew," <u>TI</u>, pp. 31-38; Barth, "Matthew's Understanding of the Law," <u>TI</u>, pp. 78-105; Schweizer, <u>Matthew</u>, p. 108; and Minear, "False Prophecy and Hypocrisy in the Gospel of Matthew," p. 83.

[4]Barth, "Matthew's Understanding of the Law," <u>TI</u>, p. 75 n. 3.

[5]Cf. 24:12 to 7:12, 23. See Davies, <u>Sermon on the Mount</u>, p. 205.

The authoritative criterion in Matthew's community
is that Jesus' words and deeds interpret the will
of God. True discipleship, in fact, is obedience
to the Law as interpreted by Jesus.[1] Therefore,
the criterion which separates true discipleship
from false discipleship is the embodiment of
love as taught and lived by Jesus. Ἀνομία is thus
the opposite of love. It is apostasy itself.[2]
It is true that the Scribes and the Pharisees are
also accused of ἀνομία in the First Gospel
(23:28), but this accusation only enhances what
ἀνομία means for Matthew. Those who practice
ἀνομία can be extremely zealous for the outward
observance of the Law, or even for the words of
Jesus (7:15-23), but ἀνομία in Matthew refers to
an inner condition of the will rather than to outward conduct (cf. 24:12).[3] Ἀνομία is not practicing in communal life the essence of the Law,
which was defined as love by the words and deeds
of Jesus.[4] It is clear that Matthew's concern in

---

[1]Barth, "Matthew's Understanding of the
Law," TI, pp. 102-103.

[2]Schweizer, "Observance of the Law and
Charismatic Activity in Matthew," pp. 224, 227;
and Eduard Schweizer, "Matthew's View of the
Church in his 18th Chapter," Australian Biblical
Review 21 (1973): 10-14.

[3]Davies, Sermon on the Mount, pp. 202-205.

[4]Schweizer, Matthew, p. 178; Kingsbury,
Parables of Jesus in Matthew 13, pp. 105-106. To
reduce Matthew's concern about ἀνομία to the
Pharisees would make his Christianity only a
purified form of Pharisaism (Haenchen, "Matthäus
23," p. 61; cf. Barth, "Matthew's Understanding
of the Law," TI, p. 76; and, Kingsbury, Parables
of Jesus in Matthew 13, p. 161 n. 67).

24:12 is with <u>Christians</u> who call upon the name of
Jesus and cry "Lord, Lord," but who practice
ἀνομία.[1]  The evangelist interprets the increase
of ἀνομία and the decline of ἀγάπη <u>among Chris-
tians</u> as a clear sign of the End.[2]  The <u>Didache</u>,
again, provides an interesting and similar combination of both themes (the increase of ἀνομία and
the decrease of love): "For in the last days the
false prophets . . . shall be multiplied, . . .
and love shall be turned into hate.  For (γάρ)
when lawlessness (ἀνομίας) increases, they shall
hate and persecute, and deliver up one another"
(16:3-4a).[3]  The ἀνομία in Matt. 24:10-12 is the
evangelist's concern because the love which grows
cold is the love of <u>Christians</u> toward each other
(cf. Rev. 2:4).[4]

The Activity of False Prophets
Increases before the End
(24:23-25, 26-28)

Matthew warns against false prophets again
in the eschatological discourse in verses 23-25.
However, the question is: are these warnings directed against the same intracommunity false
prophets as depicted in 24:5, 10-12?  Are the

---

[1]Bornkamm, "The Risen Lord and the Earthly
Jesus: Matthew 28:16-20," p. 216.

[2]Davies, <u>Sermon on the Mount</u>, p. 206.

[3]Schaff, <u>The Teaching of the Twelve
Apostles</u>, p. 214.

[4]Manson, <u>Sayings</u>, p. 216.

false prophets (and false christs, v. 24) a real
and present danger, or, are these warnings directed to a generalized apocalyptic, future danger?  The context in which these verses occur must
be investigated in order to answer these questions.

The warnings in Matt. 24:23-25 occur between
the verses concerning the "great tribulation"[1] and
the ostensible advent of the Son of Man (vv.
26-27).  The tribulation will become more intense
the closer the τέλος draws.  In fact, it will be
so intense that if God allowed it to continue,
even the "elect" (τοὺς ἐκλεκτούς) would not be
saved (v. 22).  The sufferings will entail a
heightened anticipation of the Parousia (vv. 23,
26), and many false claims about the coming of the
Son of Man will be reported.  However, the coming
of Jesus as Son of Man will be so unmistakably
clear (v. 27) that one need not be led astray by
false claims (v. 26).  Several comments on the
context of 24:23-35 are in order.

First, it seems that 24:23-28 "intrudes"
into the context of 24:21-22 and 24:29.  Matthew
24:21-22 speaks of the "great tribulation," and
this thought is continued in 24:29 with "immediately after the tribulation of those days."  It
is clear from the insertion into this context that
Matthew intends verses 23-25 to be seen as part
of the context of the tribulation in verses 21-22.
The evangelist, of course, is following Mark where
the same thought intrudes into the apocalyptic
context (13:21-22).[2]  Mark apparently wanted to

---

[1] Θλίψις μεγάλη, 24:21 cf. Mark 13:19.

[2] Cf. Marxsen, Mark the Evangelist, pp. 161-
162 and Taylor, St. Mark, p. 516.  Luke seems to
sense the intrusion and deletes these verses (cf.

"tone down" a false apocalyptic speculation within
his community by breaking up the sense of imme-
diacy inherent in verses 19-20, 24.[1]  Whatever
Mark's motive was for inserting these verses, it
is clear that Matthew not only retains them, but
expands them with Q material![2]  This means that
the coming of the Son of Man, which should follow
immediately after verses 21-22, is not mentioned
until after verse 29.  Matthew makes it clear by
his redactional activity in verse 29 that the Son
of Man will not come until after the tribulation
(which includes the false prophets of verses 23-
25) is over.[3]  In other words, Matthew is not only
concerned to describe the false prophets (vv. 21-
23), he even adds greater detail about them (vv.
26-28).[4]  His expansion of Mark, as well as his

---

Schweizer, _Matthew_, p. 453).

[1]Pesch, _Naherwartungen_, pp. 154-166;
Schweizer, _Matthew_, pp. 263, 274; Hans Conzelmann,
"Geschichte und Eschaton nach Mc 13," _ZNW_ 3-4
(1959): 219-221; Howard Clark Kee, _Community of
the New Age. Studies in Mark's Gospel_ (Philadelphia: The Westminster Press, 1977), p. 159; and
Weeden, _Traditions in Conflict_, pp. 93-97.  Weeden
sees the intrusion of verses 21-23 not so much as
an attempt to tone down apocalyptic speculation
but to combat a θεῖος ἀνήρ heresy in the Markan
community.

[2]Cf. Luke 17:23-24, 37.

[3]Εὐθέως δὲ μετὰ τὴν θλῖψιν, v. 29 cf. v. 30.

[4]Matthew deletes Mark's πάντα (v. 25), and
ostensibly provides for his expansion in verses
26-28 (M'Neile, _St. Matthew_, p. 351).

addition of "great" (μεγάλη) to the tribulation and to the "signs and wonders" performed by these false prophets, shows how serious he considers the threat of false prophets to be.[1]

Matthew's redactional activity, then, suggests that he considers the threats of verses 23-25 to be a real (as opposed to a generalized future) danger to his community. The experience will occur during the great tribulation, and the implication is that the sufferings will be so intense (vv. 21-22) that they will lead to an enhanced anticipation of the Parousia within the community itself (cf. Didache 16:3-4).[2] Several other factors suggest that it is an intracommunity threat.

First, the threat posed is not only from false prophets but from false christs as well. The false christs should not be too quickly identified with the satanic antichrist who is to be in personal opposition against Jesus at his Parousia. The term ψευδόχριστοι occurs only here and in the Markan parallel verse (13:21) in the whole New Testament. It is not clear which "antichrist" tradition influences Matthew in this context. His tradition is not as highly developed as that in other texts.[3] One is left with the

---

[1]Matt. 24:21 cf. Mark 13:19; μεγάλα, Matt. 24:24 cf. Mark 13:22. See Schweizer, Matthew, p. 453.

[2]Fenton, St. Matthew, p. 388.

[3]E.g., T. Dan. 5:10-11; T. Levi 18:12; 1 QM 13; 16; Ascension of Isa. 3:13b-4:18; Rev. 13; 16:12-16; 17; 19:19-21.
    In contrast to the developed antichrist tradition (cf. 2 Thess. 2:10-14; Rev. 13; 16:12-

distinct impression that for Matthew these false
christs, unlike the AntiChrist, could arise only
within the Church.[1]  Secondly, all that can be
gleaned from Matthew about the false christs is
that they do exactly what the false prophets do:
perform miracles and wonders with the purpose of
leading even the elect astray.[2]  The false christs
are juxtaposed with the false prophets so that
Matthew makes no distinction between what they do
or their purpose for doing it.[3]  Thus, for Matthew
the false christs seem to be identical with those
persons in 24:5 who come in Jesus' name and say,
"I am the Christ."  The result of that group's

16; 17; 19:19-21) in which the AntiChrist and the
false christs seem to merge into one person, Matthew speaks of many false christs.  Furthermore,
in the AntiChrist tradition it is he who is responsible for the tribulation.  There is no hint
in Matthew that the false christs cause the great
tribulation.  In contrast to the other tradition,
in which Jesus as the Son of Man defeats the Anti-
Christ at the Parousia (cf. 2 Thess. 2:8; Rev.
19:19-21), Matthew says nothing at all about their
fate (M. Rist, "AntiChrist," IDB 1: 141).

[1]Davies, Sermon on the Mount, p. 201.

[2]I took ὥστε in the final sense, as in Mark
(cf. the πρὸς τό ἀποπλανᾶν, 13:22), rather than as
result (Bl-D §391.3; cf. M. Rist, "False Christs,"
IDB 2: 237).

[3]The reading ψευδόχριστοι is not in question
textually as it is in Mark.  Matthew's reading
makes ψευδόχριστοι almost a synonym for ψευδο-
προφῆται (see Beasley-Murray, Commentary on Mark
Thirteen, p. 83).

activity is also that they "lead many astray"
(24:5c), and they do it precisely by claiming in
their enthusiasm that Jesus, and all of his power,
is incarnate in them.  In other words, the false
christs or prophets are not saying "I, instead of
Jesus, am the Messiah," but "I am Jesus."[1]  The
divine epiphany, with all of its eschatological
glory, comes to perfection in the false prophet.
In him the "epiphany of salvation appears" and
" . . . he is, so to speak, personally the bearer
and embodiment of this salvation, in his capacity
as the emissary of his Lord."[2]  Thus, the false
prophets and false christs in 24:24 do not appear
to represent two different groups, but "one and
the same category of men" who arrogantly claim the
authority and identity of Jesus.[3]  They are
Christian prophets who claim falsely that the
Parousia has occurred already in its entirety.[4]
Matthew is saying, particularly in verse 27, that
Jesus will not be present as the Son of Man except
in universal and cosmic terms at the close of the

---

[1]It is possible, of course, that the false
prophets could allude to figures like Simon Magus
or Bar Kokba, but, if so, the allusions in Matthew
are simply too vague for speculation (cf. Davies,
Sermon on the Mount, pp. 200-208).  On the other
hand, the Matthean context (24:5, 10-12) provides
immediate referents for the figures in 24:24.

[2]Käsemann, "Beginnings of Christian
Theology," p. 103.

[3]Braun, "πλανάω," p. 246; cf. Kelber,
Kingdom in Mark, p. 115.

[4]Ibid., p. 116.

Age.  Any Christian who claims that Jesus is present in him/her in all of his glory as the Son of Man before his ostensible return as such is a "false prophet."[1]

Thirdly, the false prophets and false christs seek to seduce (πλανῆσαι) even the elect with "great signs and wonders."[2]  Matthew inserts that the false prophets will "give (δώσουσιν)[3] great signs and wonders" (v. 24).[4]  If, however, δώσουσιν is impersonal and refers circumspectly to the source rather than to the false prophets themselves, then the translation would be: "For false prophets and false christs will arise and there great signs and wonders will be given so as to lead astray, if possible, even the elect."[5]  The meaning would be that these false prophets had been granted the power to perform such miracles, and the implication is that it was granted by Jesus himself![6]

---

[1]Cf. Weeden, Traditions in Conflict, p. 111.

[2]Σημεῖα μεγάλα καὶ τέρατα, v. 24.

[3]Cf. ποιήσουσιν, Mark 13:22.

[4]Many commentators see Deut. 13:1-2 (LXX) as the influence in Matthew's tradition.

[5]Cf. Turner, Grammar of New Testament Greek, p. 293; and Bl-D §130.2.

[6]Bauer, Greek-English Lexicon, p. 192 #1β cf. Schweizer, Matthew, p. 188.  This use of δίδωμι in Matthew is not unlike that in the Fourth Gospel where God has given everything to Jesus (cf. John 3:35; 5:36; 6:37, 39; 17:11.  See Büchsel,"δίδωμι," p. 166).  It is clear in Matthew that Jesus has received authority from God

262

## The Community Situation

We would contend that the false prophets and false christs of Matt. 24:24 are Christians within Matthew's Church who are conscious of a commission from the Risen Lord to do works "in his name," that is, by the ἐξουσία which he has given them. They are the ones who cry out in 7:22: "Lord, Lord, did we not prophesy in your name, and cast out demons in your name, and do many mighty works in your name?"[1] The deception of the false prophets, along with the great tribulation, will eventually be too powerful even for the elect (vv. 21-22). The only hope is that God Himself/Herself, for the sake of the elect, will not allow the deception to reach fruition (24:24). The problem is not that their works are performed by the power of Jesus' name. The problem is that by arrogating to themselves the full eschatological power and identity of Jesus as Son of Man, their works lead to ἀνομία, that is, the diminution of the kind of love commanded by Jesus.[2] In fact, as we have seen, only the Lord Himself will be able to distinguish which exorcisms and mighty works constitute ἀνομία.[3]

The false prophets and false christs, then,

---

which Jesus, in turn, gives to his disciples (28:18 cf. 9:8; 10:1; 16:19; 18:18, 19, 20).

[1]Minear, "False Prophecy and Hypocrisy in the Gospel of Matthew," p. 82.

[2]Matt. 7:22-23 cf. 7:20-21; 24:5, 11-12.

[3]Matt. 7:21-23. Minear, "False Prophecy and Hypocrisy in the Gospel of Matthew," p. 82.

appear to be saying not only that Jesus as the
authoritative Son of Man is present with them, but
also that his presence is attested by miracles
which promise that eschatological deliverance is a
present reality.[1] Hence Matthew is concerned not
only to correct a false apocalyptic enthusiasm
which says that Jesus as the Son of Man has arrived, but he is also concerned to correct his community's understanding of the presence of Jesus.
Matthew is struggling to point out that the community still awaits Jesus as the Son of Man. In
other words, Jesus is not present with them in any
sense as Son of Man--neither in signs and wonders,
nor in any esoteric fashion (24:26).[2] On the con-

---

[1]See Kelber, Kingdom in Mark, p. 116; and
Braun, "πλανάω," p. 247. It is not certain that
the false prophets in Matthew consider themselves
"divine men/women" who have received their power
from Jesus as θεῖος ἀνήρ. However, it is possible
that they perceived themselves in θεῖος ἀνήρ
terms. If one followed Käsemann's argument too
far, then it would be possible to arrive at this
conclusion (cf. "Beginnings of Christian Theology," p. 103). Käsemann's analysis, though, is a
form-critical one which uses sayings in Matthew to
depict enthusiasm in primitive Christianity. It
seems that such enthusiasm was prevalent in Matthew's church, but, although it shares the same
general characteristics, we are not prepared to
agree that Matthew is opposing false prophets who
were interpreting Jesus in θεῖος ἀνήρ terms. On
the other hand, it is not entirely out of the
question that Matthew is fighting at least a θεῖος
ἀνήρ discipleship (cf. Bornkamm, TI, p. 37).

[2]Marxsen, Mark the Evangelist, p. 185;
Beare, "Apocalypse," p. 129; and Mauser, Christ
in the Wilderness, p. 146.

trary, his coming as Son of Man will be a spectacular, cosmic event (24:27) with a clear sign
(24:30).  His Parousia will be as evident as birds
of prey coming to a carcass (24:28).[1]  Jesus <u>is</u>

---

[1]Stendahl, "Matthew," p. 793.  In Matthew's
context the <u>mashal</u>-like saying in 24:28 (cf. Job
39:30) expresses a point similar to that of v. 27
(Bultmann, <u>History of the Synoptic Tradition</u>, pp.
81, 107).  The Matthean emphasis does not seem to
be upon the swiftness of the Parousia, though that
is a possible meaning (Manson, <u>Sayings</u>, p. 147;
and Fenton, <u>St. Matthew</u>, p. 388), but upon the
universality of the Parousia.  A carcass cannot
lie very long without attracting birds of prey (it
is debatable whether οἱ ἀετοί is best translated
by "eagles" or "vultures."  Surely the general
meaning is that of "birds of prey."  See Manson,
<u>Sayings</u>, p. 147; Dodd, <u>Parables of the Kingdom</u>, p.
65 n. 2; and Jeremias, <u>Parables of Jesus</u>, p. 162
n. 46.  This generalized meaning would argue
against the particularistic "eagles" as an allusion to the Roman armies about to descend upon
Jerusalem, at least as a meaning <u>for Matthew</u>).
The Parousia of the Son of Man will be just as
evident as the carcass is to the birds (or that
when birds of prey are gathered, there is a carcass).
     Perhaps the original meaning of this saying
can never be recovered (Dodd, <u>Parables of the
Kingdom</u>, pp. 65-66).  Surely the Matthean context
must determine the meaning of the saying for our
purposes (see Bultmann, <u>History of the Synoptic
Tradition</u>, pp. 99, 396; and Edwards, <u>Theology of
Q</u>, p. 142).  In Luke the saying answers the question of "Where, Lord?" (17:37), which does not
appear in Matthew.  Furthermore, Matthew has appended this saying to that about the lightning
flash (v. 27).  This seems to suggest that the
meaning in his context is similar to that of

present with Matthew's church as the Shekinah, but
not as the authoritative Son of Man.  Jesus as the
Son of Man is yet to come.[1]

---

quickness, or of being ostensible (Dodd, Parables
of the Kingdom, p. 65).  The Lukan emphasis seems
to be more upon the clarity of the signs which
accompany the Parousia (Jeremias, Parables of
Jesus, p. 162).  Some have also seen this as the
primary meaning in Matthew (Hill, Matthew, p.
322).  Others see the Lukan context as expressing
the inevitability of judgment, whereas in Matthew
the inevitability of the Parousia is emphasized
(A. W. Argyle, The Gospel According to Matthew,
The Cambridge Bible Commentary [Cambridge: University Press, 1963], p. 183).  All of these points
are possible in Matthew's context--the swiftness,
the inevitability, the judgment--and would be
implied.  But surely the primary emphasis in the
Matthean context is upon the Parousia of Jesus-Son
of Man as a universal manifestation (Beare,
"Apocalypse," p. 129 cf. Schweizer, Matthew,
pp. 454-455).

[1]Matthew's use of the Son of Man title
clearly shows that he conceives of Jesus as Son of
Man primarily in terms of Jesus' Parousia (cf.
10:23; 13:41, etc.).  For a detailed discussion of
this matter see Kingsbury, Structure, pp. 113-122.
Matthew still uses Son of Man sayings which refer
to the public ministry of Jesus (8:20; 9:6; etc.)
and to his passion and resurrection (12:40; 17:9;
etc.), but Matthew never refers to the activity
of Jesus as Son of Man between his resurrection
and Parousia (see Kingsbury, Parables of Jesus in
Matthew 13, p. 99; and Schweizer, Matthew, p. 309;
cf. p. 390 n. 3 below).

Therefore, the concern which is uppermost in Matthew's mind is that of correcting a false understanding of Jesus' Parousia. His discourse is concerned very clearly with the question he has posed redactionally for his community: "what will be the sign (τὸ σημεῖον) of your coming?" (24:3). The Son of Man will not appear with signs, wonders, and mighty works of the enthusiastic Parousia prophets (24:24 cf. 7:22), but his own sign will be clearly manifested (24:30) at his spectacular, cosmic Parousia (24:27).[1]

Matthew's concern is not simply to correct a false apocalyptic speculation, but his purpose is also to warn against it as a very serious threat to his community. His community is in danger of being led astray into ἀνομία, and, consequently, of losing the kind of love which Jesus commanded them to have (24:10-12). It is neither accidental that his discourse is introduced by a question about Jesus' Parousia (24:3), nor that it actually begins with a solemn warning from Jesus (ἀποκριθεὶς ὁ Ἰησοῦς): "Take heed that no one leads you astray" (πλανήσῃ, 24:4). Jesus' message to Matthew's church is clear: no matter how enticing the signs (24:5, 24) or the claims about his presence may be (24:23, 26), the End has not come.[2] His community has been forewarned

---

[1]The image of lightning in v. 27 not only refers to the suddenness of Jesus' coming but also to its universal clarity. His coming "is not the private concern of a few devout individuals" (Ibid., p. 454; cf. Hill, Matthew, p. 322; M'Neile, St. Matthew, p. 322; and Allen, St. Matthew, p. 257).

[2]Matt. 24:6c, 8, 13, 14c, 29, 30. Matthew explicitly identifies Jesus with the coming Son of Man again (note ἡ παρουσία [v. 27 cf. v. 3;

that these deceivers would come (24:25), and those
who remember and obey Jesus' words will not be
deceived. They will be the "elect."

The danger of false prophets, then, is a
present danger, for the false prophets have
already appeared in Matthew's community as a signal of the approaching End. Furthermore, the
false prophets and false christs of verses 23-25
have the same pedigree as the enthusiastic
prophets already working within the community.
Yet, on the other hand, verses 23-25 seem to speak
of a future time when the tribulation will become
so great that eschatological flight might become
necessary (cf. 24:20). This seems to allude, in
apocalyptic style, to a future situation rather
than to a past or a present one.[1]  In other words,
verses 23-25 refer to the same false prophets already working within Matthew's community, but the
reference is also to a time in the imminent future
when the tribulation will become so great that the
expectation and performances of the Parousia
prophets will be enhanced. The tribulation, together with the signs and wonders of the false
prophets, will be so potent that Matthew even
fears for the endurance of the elect.[2]

---

Luke 17:36]). See Klostermann, Matthäusevangelium, p. 195.

[1]See the detailed discussion of 24:15-22
below, especially the discussion of "a holy place"
in 24:15 (pp. 315-338).

[2]In fact, Matthew's use of the "elect" (τοὺς
ἐλεκτούς) in this context also suggests a future
situation. The elect in Matthew are not the "pre-
destined" whom God has foreordained as a special
class of people to pass the judgment (see Gottlob
Schrenk, "ἐκλέγομαι," TDNT 4:175; and Schweizer,

In summary, the tension between the present
and the future threat of the false prophets now
comes to light. The false prophets are already at
work in Matthew's community and the evangelist
warns the community not to be led astray into
ἀνομία, the violation of Jesus' love commandment,
by their enthusiastic proclamation (24:4, 10-12).
However, many are being deceived (24:5, 10-12),
and that is the present threat. But, if the majority of his community is being deceived now,
what will happen when the sufferings, which have
already begun (24:8), become unbearable and cause
the false prophets to increase their activities
and support their claims with even greater (μεγάλα,
v. 24) signs and wonders? The difference in time
between the false christs of 24:5, 10-12 and those
of verses 23-25 is not so radical, but Matthew's
emphasis is upon the difference in the degree of
of their activity.[1] Matthew sees no hope for his

---

Matthew, p. 540). In fact, Matthew omits Mark's
οὕς ἐξελέξατο (13:20) either to avoid such an
idea, or because he simply considers it pleonas-
tic. The "elect" in Matthew simply refers to that
eschatological group which will be gathered by the
angels at the coming of the Son of Man (24:31).
They are the "righteous ones" (οἱ δίκαιοι) who in-
herit eternal life at the last judgment (25:37,
46b) because they are the ones who have produced
the fruits of the kingdom (21:43 cf. 7:16-20).
In other words, their "election" is fulfilled in
their obedience and in their endurance until the
End (10:22; 24:9-13. See Kingsbury, Parables of
Jesus in Matthew 13, pp. 100-101; Bultmann,
"πιστεύω," TDNT 6:542; Schrenk, "ἐκλέγομαι," pp.
186-187; contrast Hare, Theme of Jewish Persecution, p. 161 n. 1).

[1]Lambrecht, "Parousia Discourse," p. 323.

community--even for those who steadfastly obey
Jesus (the "elect")--except that God in His/Her
mercy will shorten those days.[1]

In this short section, then, the evangelist
has two general emphases which continue the main
thrusts of 24:5 and 24:10-12. On the one hand,
he is warning against the false prophets who claim
that Christ has come already as the Son of Man,
and, on the other hand, he is trying to strengthen
the hope of those producing good "fruits" that
Jesus' coming will be soon.[2]

Conclusions about the False Prophets
(Matt. 24:4-8, 10-12, 23-25, 26-28)

Matthew's point in verses 4-8 is that "the
end is not yet" (v. 6). In verse 5 eschatological
"deceivers" are depicted. (1) They are Christians
(ἐπὶ τῷ ὀνόματί μου, v. 5), and they seem to be
intracommunity for the evangelist rather than
"outsiders."[3]  (2) The deceivers preach either

---

[1]Consistent with his usual style, Matthew
has κολοβωθήσονται (passive, 24:22) for Mark's
active (see Allen, St. Matthew, p. xxiii). This,
together with his deletion of κύριος, implies the
"keeping" action of God rather than of Jesus
(Pesch, Naherwartungen, p. 153). However, note
that Matthew has perhaps added αὐτοῦ to refer to
Jesus as the Son of Man in 24:31 (Schrenk,
"ἐκλέγομαι," p. 189).

[2]See Schweizer, Matthew, p. 455.

[3]Matthew's church seems to be a corpus
mixtum which will be separated only at the final
judgment (cf. 7:21-23; 13:36-43). See Kingsbury,
Structure, pp. 158-160, 166.

that they themselves are the Christ, or that
Jesus (as the Christ) has, in effect, already
returned. The latter message seems more probable
since the evangelist's church believed quite
strongly that the Risen Lord was present (1:23;
18:20; 28:20), had given them his authority (10:1
cf. 28:18b), and would lead them by the Spirit
(10:20). (3) The situation seems to have been an
enthusiastic one which said in effect that "the
Parousia has come and Jesus is totally present."
(4) The evangelist says that the upshot of this
proclamation is an ἀνομία which causes "love to
grow cold" (24:12).[1] The problem "in a nutshell,"
then, is not the "delay of the Parousia" per se,
but a false apocalyptic speculation which not only
distorted Jesus' teachings as understood by Matthew, but which also threatened the world-wide
mission of the church (24:14).

In the last analysis, however, whether there
is only one group, as we have proposed, or whether
there are two groups (false christs and false
prophets, 24:24) cannot be decided with precision.[2] The situation seems to be so complicated

---

[1]Cf. 7:21-23; 24:10-12. This is strikingly
similar to the situation depicted in 2 Thess. 2.
There the deceivers say that the Parousia has in
effect arrived (2:1-3a), but the writer cautions
that the Parousia is to be preceded by a period of
lawlessness (2:3-7). In Matthew Satan is the
"fountainhead of all 'lawlessness' (anomia cf.
13:38c-39a, 41)," the enemy of the exalted Son of
Man, and "he is at work to raise up 'sons' who
will do his bidding (cf. 13:37-39a)." (Ibid., p.
165; cf. Schweizer, Matthew, pp. 185-186, 189,
451; Taylor, St. Mark, p. 505; and Beare,
"Apocalypse," p. 128).

[2]See David Hill, for example, who sees the

that an oversimplification will not suffice.[1]
Matthew's general point, though, is clear. (5) He
is warning that Jesus as the Son of Man will not
reappear in this interim of world history--the
"end is not yet" (v. 6).[2] This warning is a certainty for Matthew because it was spoken by Jesus-
Sophia to his disciples as a secret revelation of
his own advent as the glorious Son of Man.   This
Word has been transmitted to Matthew's church, and
any disciples who hold fast to it will not be "led
astray" (24:4b) by a Parousia enthusiasm, or even
the apparent collapse of the social and natural
orders.   Jesus-Sophia himself has said that these
things are only the ἀρχή of difficulties for the
disciples (24:8).   The τέλος itself, which begins
with the Parousia, has not yet begun (24:6).
Jesus is present with Matthew's community through
his Word and in the love which they show for each
other.   His Word, his presence, and his love are

---

false prophets of 7:15 as a group from outside
the community which comes into the Church to de-
ceive, but those of 7:22-23 as charismatic
prophets within the Church (Hill, "False Prophets
and Charismatics: Structure and Interpretation in
Mt 7,15-23," Biblica 57 [1976]: 327-348).

[1]See Kingsbury, Structure, pp. 158-160.

[2]See Weeden, Traditions in Conflict, p. 135.
Σώζω in Matthew cannot be reduced to the physical
welfare of the "elect," or to any kind of well-
being promised by the false prophets, but it
implies their salvation at the final judgment
(W. C. van Unnik, "L'Usage de SŌZEIN 'Sauver' et
des Derives dans Les Evangiles Synoptiques,"
Sparsa Collecta [Leiden: E. J. Brill, 1973],
pp. 25-30).

inseparable.  By remaining obedient to the Word
of Jesus-Sophia, Matthew's community will prevent
love for each other from "growing cold" (cf.
24:10-12).  Those who try to remain obedient to
Jesus' Word will need that love in order to endure
the rejection which they are encountering in their
preaching mission as messengers of Jesus-Sophia.
This is the subject of the next section of the
testament of Jesus in Matthew.

### Part 4.   The Testament of Jesus-Sophia: the Church's Mission

Matthew's Redaction of
Mark 13:9-13

Matthew has made a major redactional move in
Matt. 24:9-14.  He has taken Mark 13:9-13 out of
the eschatological discourse and has put it in his
"missionary" discourse (10:17-21).  First, this
means that this preaching period is not contemporary for Matthew with the beginning of the
ὠδίνων which precede the End, as it is for Mark.
Matthew has "de-eschatologized" this preaching
mission by removing it from its eschatological
context.[1]  This preaching mission and its subsequent persecutions are for the evangelist "no
longer the pangs of the last day."[2]

Secondly, Matthew's rearrangement of this
material shows that for his community this kind of
persecution has become a way of life.  What Mark
describes as immediately preceding the Parousia
"has become for Matthew characteristic of a

---

[1]Hare, Theme of Jewish Persecution, p. 99.

[2]Donahue, Are You the Christ?, p. 215.

continuing situation."[1]  The evangelist has separated this particular "epoch" of mission with its
persecution from the "epoch" of the Parousia.[2]
Matthean redaction here shows that for Matthew's
community persecution is the result of witnessing
whereas for Mark persecution is the occasion for
witnessing.[3]  Thus, as Marxsen says: "This means
that what Mark says will happen just before the
Parousia has become a permanent state of affairs
for Matthew."[4]  The evangelist's community, therefore, needs instructions concerning persecution.
The so-called "missionary discourse," as Hare has
shown, is not concerned with any instructions
about preaching.  Its main concern is with the rejection and the hostility which the missionaries
will meet on their preaching tours.[5]  In chapter
10, then, the evangelist is not talking about the
mission of the Twelve in the life-situation of
Jesus, but it is clear that the concern of this
chapter is with his church's mission in the post-
resurrection period.[6]

---

[1]Hare, Theme of Jewish Persecution, p. 100.

[2]Marxsen, Mark the Evangelist, p. 203.

[3]Hare, Theme of Jewish Persecution, p. 100.

[4]Marxsen, Mark the Evangelist, p. 202.

[5]Hare, Theme of Jewish Persecution, p. 98.

[6]Ibid.  Cf. Donahue, Are You the Christ?,
p. 215; and Ellis, Matthew: His Mind and His
Message, p. 51.

Thirdly, Matthew's redaction of 24:9-14 shows that his concern in 10:17-21 is not with general persecution but with <u>Jewish</u> rejection. The παραδώσουσιν ὑμᾶς εἰς συνέδρια which is ambiguous in Mark (13:9) clearly becomes Jewish in Matthew by his additions of μαστιγώσουσιν (cf. Acts 22:19; 2 Cor. 11:23-24) and αὐτῶν (cf. 10:5-6). Αὐτῶν in particular suggests that Matthew's church has separated from the <u>Synagogenverband</u> and is in dispute with it.[1]

Our conclusion, then, is that the evangelist has shifted Mark 13:9-13 back to chapter 10 (the mission to Israel) because the rejection of the Gospel by the Jews, and the ensuing persecution, is in the distant past (the time of Jesus). This situation is not so much a contemporary one for Matthew's church as it is a prediction which has already been fulfilled. The rejection of Jesus' messengers to Israel is not part of the ὠδίνων of the End for Matthew. Therefore, he removes this reference from its eschatological context.[2]

---

[1]Ibid., p. 4; Hare, <u>Theme of Jewish Persecution</u>, pp. 101-105. The question of the relationship of Matthew's community to the Synagogue is not conclusively settled (see Hummel, <u>Auseinandersetzung</u>, pp. 28-30, 31-33; Strecker, <u>Weg</u>, p. 30 cf. pp. 16-17; Bornkamm, <u>TI</u>, pp. 20-22, 25-26, 39, 51 n. 5; Kilpatrick, <u>Origins of the Gospel of St. Matthew</u>, pp. 106-123; Davies, <u>Sermon on the Mount</u>, p. 332 cf. pp. 286-315; Kingsbury, <u>Structure</u>, pp. 153-157; Stendahl, <u>School</u>, pp. xi-xii; Ellis, <u>Matthew: His Mind and His Message</u>, p. 4; Blair, <u>Jesus in the Gospel of Matthew</u>, p. 113 n. 4; and Hare, <u>Theme of Jewish Persecution</u>, pp. 104-114, 127, 147-149).

[2]Ibid., p. 105.

However, it should be pointed out that the rejection of Jesus' messengers is "eschatological" even though it does not immediately precede the Parousia. In the evangelist's view, the judgment of Israel must be "filled up" (cf. 23:32). This judgment was fulfilled in Israel's rejection of Jesus-Sophia and his messengers, and in Jesus' reciprocal rejection of them.[1] Consequently, the evangelist turns his attention in 24:9 to the hatred exhibited by πάντων τῶν ἐθνῶν because from this point on they, not just the Jews per se, are the target of his missionary church.[2]

The function of this section (24:9-14) is to emphasize that Matthew and his community, as messengers of Jesus-Sophia, are not exempt from rejection. In fact, one could say that the rejection of their message actually proves to them that they are part of a long line of messengers sent out by the Wisdom of God (23:34). The difference for Matthew's community is that they know that the Wisdom of God is Jesus. They also know that Jesus had predicted their rejection, linked it with the fate of his former messengers, and even with his own rejection. This knowledge, passed down to them in Jesus-Sophia's testament, provides the encouragement they will need to "endure to the end" (24:13). A brief, but detailed, look at the evangelist's redaction in verses 9-14 will highlight these conclusions.

---

[1]23:37-39 cf. 24:1-2; 27:25. See above, pp. 94-112.

[2]24:14 cf. 28:19. We have already discussed our view that the mission to the Jews is over for Matthew's church (pp. 57-62, 98-132 above). The only evidence after 24:1 for a mission to the Jews is the word ἔθνος (24:14; 28:19 cf. appendix 4).

276

## Jesus promises persecution
## (Matt. 24:9a)

Matthew 24:9a is a redactional summary of
the general point made in Mark 13:9-13, and it
virtually repeats Matthew 10:22.[1]  Matthew, by his
use of παραδιδόναι, continues the same line of
thought which he finds in Mark.  The earliest use
of παραδιδόναι in the New Testament is as a technical term for the passion of Jesus, and, when it
is used with δεῖ, it emphasizes the divine necessity of Jesus' passion.[2]  The next development
of this παραδιδόναι tradition, a step taken by
Mark himself perhaps, seems to have been to apply
παραδιδόναι to the disciples who are to suffer the
same fate as their Lord.[3]  The παραδιδόναι in
Matt. 24:9a now refers to all of Matthew's community (οἱ μαθηταί, 24:3b).  It does not refer
just to Christian missionaries as does the persecution in Matt. 10.  The persecution in 24:9a is
generalized to include the whole community.
Further, it is not simply Jewish persecution as it
is in 10:17-21, but now Matthew adds τῶν ἐθνῶν,

---

[1]Marxsen, Mark the Evangelist, p. 201 n.
181; Taylor, St. Mark, p. 507; and Hare, Theme
of Jewish Persecution, p. 124.

[2]Norman Perrin, "The Use of (Para)didonai
in Connection with the Passion of Jesus in the
New Testament," A Modern Pilgrimage in New Testament Christology (Philadelphia: Fortress Press,
1974), pp. 98-103; Pesch, Naherwartungen, pp. 126-
128; and Taylor, St. Mark, p. 165.

[3]Perrin, "The Use of (Para)didonai . . . in
the New Testament," p. 100; cf. Donahue, Are You
the Christ?, p. 212.

which suggests that it is not <u>only</u> Gentile but is simply a period of universal hatred and includes the Gentile as well as Jewish persecutors.[1] The "delivering up" of the disciples, however, is still in accordance with the divine will (δεῖ γενέσθαι, 24:6).[2] The disciples in Matthew must suffer the same fate as their Lord.[3] As Jesus was "delivered up" (παραδίδοται) to crucifixion,[4] so his disciples (Matthew's church), as the evangelist's redactional summary in 24:9a warns, will be "delivered up" (παραδώσουσιν) to θλῖψις, that is, they will be "put to death" (ἀποκτενοῦσιν ὑμᾶς, v. 9b). The evangelist adds θλῖψις in 24:9a, an eschatological term which indicates tribulation before the Parousia, because the persecution in 24:9 is eschatological. Although the persecution

---

[1]24:9b cf. 10:22; Mark 9:13. See Hill, <u>Matthew</u>, p. 320; Lambrecht, "Parousia Discourse," p. 320; and Hare, <u>Theme of Jewish Persecution</u>, p. 124.

[2]Even if one does not want to connect παραδώσουσιν with δεῖ γενέσθαι of 24:6, the verb, even though it is a future <u>active</u> indicative, carries the idea of a divine passive, and should be placed under the "eschatological point of view" (see Jeremias, <u>New Testament Theology</u>, pp. 281-285). Παραδίδοσθαι, for example, in Mark 9:31 is a futuristic present for which both Matthew and Luke have μέλλει παραδίδοσθαι (Matt. 17:22-23 cf. Luke 9:44. See Taylor, <u>St. Mark</u>, p. 403).

[3]This is a well-established Matthean theme, and it will be discussed further in chapter 4 below (see, e.g., Senior, <u>Matthew: A Gospel for the Church</u>, pp. 53-67).

[4]Matt. 26:2 cf. 26:66; 27:23, 25.

278

of the disciples depicted in 10:17-21, as mentioned above, was "eschatological" in the sense
that Israel's judgment within salvation-history
was "filled up" (cf. 23:32), it does not immediately precede the Parousia as does that of 24:9a.
Matthew uses θλῖψις in 24:9 in order to distinguish it as that which immediately precedes the
coming of Jesus as Son of Man.  The Son of Man
comes (24:30) immediately after the tribulation
(εὐθέως δὲ μετὰ τὴν θλῖψιν, 24:29).

It is difficult to determine whether Matthew
regards the affliction at the hands of τῶν ἐθνῶν
as genuinely future or as contemporary.[1]  Since
the future tense is often interchangable with the
present tense in eschatological passages, it is
possible that the θλῖψις has begun already for
Matthew.[2]  The situation depicted in verses 10-12
at least, much like that of 24:5, seems to be a
present one.[3]  If this is true, then it is possible that the θλῖψις of verse 9 has begun in
Matthew's community.

However, verse 9 is correctly dealt with by
Hare as one of Matthew's "ambiguous references to
persecution."  It is simply impossible to detect
from the textual allusions who the agents of per-

---

[1]Hare, Theme of Jewish Persecution, p. 144.
Θλῖψις is a technical term which indicates general
apocalyptic tribulation (Conzelmann, Theology of
St. Luke, pp. 98-100; and Heinrich Schlier,
"θλίβω," TDNT 3:144-145).  In this context it most
likely echoes the judicial persecution of Mark
13:9, 11 (Hare, Jewish Persecution, p. 124; and
M'Neile, St. Matthew, p. 346).

[2]Bl-D §323.  [3]Hare, Jewish Persecution, 124.

secution were or who they were expected to be.[1]
The methodological problem with the text is the
same as that of Mark 13: the text itself is the
main entrée into the historical situation of the
gospel.[2] What is certain, as we have seen, is
that Matthew's community was undergoing persecution and expected the situation to become worse.

## The Church's mission results in persecution (διὰ τὸ ὄνομά μου)

The cause of the "hatred" (μισούμενοι) is
reflected in the phrase διὰ τὸ ὄνομά μου (v. 9b).
This phrase in Matthew occurs only here and in the
parallel verse (10:22). In each case in Matthew
where διὰ τὸ ὄνομά μου or its equivalent (ἕνεκεν
μου) occurs in relation to persecutors, the causal
phrase is used with the passive verb.[3] In every
other case where ἕνεκεν ἐμοῦ is used in Matthew,[4]
the verb is active and clearly denotes Christians
as the subject.[5] Thus, Hare is correct when he
claims that:

> In those instances in which the causal
> phrase is used with a passive verb
> (5:10; 10:18, 22; 24:9) it is best to
> take the causal phrase as indicating

---

[1]Ibid.

[2]Donahue, Are You the Christ?, pp. 216-217.

[3]Cf. 5:10; 10:18, 22; 24:9. The only exception is 5:11 where ἕνεκεν ἐμοῦ occurs with the
active verb and clearly denotes the persecutors
rather than those who are being persecuted.

[4]Except in 19:5.

[5]Cf. 10:39; 16:25; 19:29.

the motivation for Christian involvement
in the activity of being persecuted or
hated, not the motivation of the
persecutors or haters.[1]

The causal phrase makes it clear that Christians are being persecuted because of their relationship to Jesus, but what is that relationship
in this context? As we have suggested, it is the
motivation and the involvement of the disciples
which leads to the persecution. In this context
the character of their involvement is εἰς
μαρτύριον πᾶσιν τοῖς ἔθνεσιν (24:14). In Matt.
10:17-23 the persecution was caused by the Christian mission to Israel (cf. 10:17, 23) and it
involved only Christian missionaries. In 24:9 the
persecution is eschatological, involves the whole
church (the disciples), and the hatred comes from
πάντων τῶν ἐθνῶν. Thus, at the time Matthew
writes the failure of the Christian mission to
Israel is essentially a past event, and Matthew
"de-eschatologizes" it by shifting that material
back to chapter 10. The missionaries to Israel
were hated because of their preaching activity
(10:6-7, 17-18), and Israel constantly rejected
the messengers sent out by Jesus himself (23:34).
The relationship with Jesus (διὰ τὸ ὄνομά μου)
which leads to persecution is missionary involvement. In 24:9, then, Matthew is concerned with
the mission to πάντων τῶν ἐθνῶν and with their
rejection of that mission. This point is very
clear when 24:9 is read in conjunction with
24:14.[2] The hatred Matthew's church experiences

---

[1]Hare, Theme of Jewish Persecution, p. 133
n. 3; cf. Taylor, St. Mark, p. 510.

[2]Hare, Theme of Jewish Persecution,
pp. 163-164.

is not simply because they are Christians, nor is it unambiguously stated that the hatred is because of Jesus himself.[1] The subject of the causal phrase is the evangelist's church itself and its own motivation for involvement in the preaching mission. The phrase διὰ τὸ ὄνομά μου seems to express an implicit <u>Heilsgeschichte</u> which emphasizes the necessity of mission more than it does an explicit christology. The implicit view of history is that Jesus himself was rejected, his messengers to Israel were rejected (chap. 10), the preaching to πάντων τῶν ἐθνῶν (24:9, 14) must be carried out and rejected, and "then the End will come" (24:14).[2] This seems to be the implicit Wisdom view of the history of salvation which was discussed above. The same admonition which was given in the mission to Israel is given in the mission to all the ἐθνῶν, namely, "he who endures to the end will be saved" (10:22b; 24:13).

In summary, Matthew's shift of Mark 13:9-13 to Matt. 10:17-21 suggests that persecution, hatred, and rejection for Matthew are: (1) a normal and expected result of the church's mission, and (2) in chapter 10, as the evangelist suggests, "persecution arises <u>precisely on account of the Church's mission</u>."[3] In Mark persecution was the <u>occasion</u> for witnessing, but in Matthew persecution is the <u>result</u> of missionary activity.[4]

---

[1]Ibid., p. 133.

[2]We will discuss this view of salvation-history further in chapter 4 below.

[3]Hare, <u>Theme of Jewish Persecution</u>, p. 100.

[4]Ibid.

In Matt. 24:9-14 the evangelist clearly sees the persecution, hatred, and rejection continuing and becoming more intense until the End. The cause of the persecution is the Church's mission (διὰ τὸ ὄνομά μου, cf. 24:14). He makes the same general point in 24:9-14 as he did in 10:17-23, but now the mission is to πάντων τῶν ἐθνῶν. This mission, rather than the one to Israel, will immediately precede the Parousia.

### The Message of the
### Church (24:14)

Matthew 24:14 says that "this gospel of the kingdom will be preached throughout the whole world, as a testimony (εἰς μαρτύριον) to all nations (ἔθνεσιν); and then the end will come." What is "this gospel of the kingdom" (τοῦτο τὸ εὐαγγέλιον) which is to be proclaimed? The evangelist leaves it undefined here, but he is clear in other places about it. He uses the phrase "the gospel of the kingdom" (τὸ εὐαγγέλιον τῆς βασιλείας) twice (4:23; 9:35), "this gospel of the kingdom" (τοῦτο τὸ εὐαγγέλιον τῆς βασιλείας) once (24:14), and the phrase "this gospel" (τὸ εὐαγγέλιον τοῦτο) once (26:13). The phrase occurs at strategic places in his gospel. The first occurrence (4:23) summarizes the beginning of Jesus' preaching in Galilee. At the same time, it serves as an introduction to the Sermon on the Mount where Jesus' teaching is presented.[1] The second point at which the phrase occurs (9:35) summarizes Jesus' authoritative deeds in almost identical terms as 4:23. It is clear from these two summaries that the "gospel of the kingdom" cannot be separated from what Jesus <u>does</u> or teaches.

---

[1]Schweizer, <u>Matthew</u>, p. 180.

The evangelist omits the word "gospel" twice, ostensibly because he does not want "gospel" to refer only to Jesus or to his name.[1]  "Gospel" for Matthew cannot be thought of apart from what Jesus taught _and_ did; it is not enough just to claim Jesus or his name (7:21-23; 24:5).[2]  This concept of εὐαγγέλιον reflects Matthew's "word-deed" christology, namely, that Jesus' deeds confirm his teaching of the higher righteousness (5:20).[3]  The evangelist's redactional activity reveals, then, that "the gospel of the kingdom" is the one proclaimed in word and deed by Jesus himself.  Matthew adds "_this_ (τοῦτο) gospel [of the kingdom]" twice (24:14; 26:13) to emphasize that there is no gospel other than the one proclaimed by the earthly Jesus.[4]

Consequently, if Matthew's community is to preach "this gospel of the kingdom," then it must proclaim the same message which Jesus preached.

---

[1]16:25; 19:29 cf. Mark 8:35; 10:29.

[2]Schweizer, _Matthew_, p. 180.

[3]Bornkamm, "End-Expectation and Church in Matthew," _TI_, p. 53; Held, "Matthew as Interpreter of the Miracle Stories," pp. 179, 246, 255; Blair, _Jesus in the Gospel of Matthew_, p. 9; Fenton, _St. Matthew_, p. 15; and Senior, _Matthew: A Gospel for the Church_, pp. 45-53.

[4]Strecker, _Weg_, p. 128 says: ". . . τὸ εὐαγγέλιον τοῦτο bezeichnet die Botschaft Jesu." Cf. Schweizer, _Matthew_, p. 180; and Lambrecht, "Parousia Discourse," p. 320 n. 26.

If they are to remain true disciples, then the
community can proclaim no other εὐαγγέλιον than
that proclaimed by Jesus himself.  Indeed, Jesus
himself has entrusted this gospel to them.  Jesus
calls his twelve disciples and gives them the same
authority as he had over "unclean spirits, to cast
them out, and to heal every disease and every in-
firmity" (10:1).  This is virtually the same summary of Jesus' own proclamation of the "gospel of
the kingdom" (9:35 cf. 4:23).  The Twelve are also
instructed to "preach" as they go that "the kingdom of heaven is at hand" (10:17), which essentially means that the "rule of God" has "come
near" (ἤγγικεν, 4:17).[1]  This is the identical
proclamation of Jesus himself (4:17).[2]  The
Twelve, then, are recognized as the first disciples of Jesus who are entrusted with the gospel of
the kingdom.  The Twelve are promised a special
place in the kingdom (19:28).  Peter is even
granted authority to "bind and loose" (16:19).

---

[1]See Norman Perrin, Jesus and the Language
of the Kingdom (Philadelphia: Fortress Press,
1976), pp. 20-21; Perrin, Rediscovering, pp. 55-
60; and Jeremias, New Testament Theology, p. 102.
On ἤγγικεν see Herbert Preisker, "ἐγγύς," TDNT
2:330-332.

[2]Jesus' activity is summarized as
"Teaching . . . preaching . . . healing."  The
disciples are to heal (10:1), to preach (10:7),
and to teach (28:20).  See Kingsbury, Structure,
pp. 57, 60, 63.
    "This gospel" in 26:13 should not, then, be
reduced to mean "the passion of Jesus," as
Strecker rightly concludes (Weg, p. 129).  "This
gospel" is an "absolute" expression here (as in
4:23; 9:35; 24:14), and is not explicitly connected with Jesus' passion in the text (Kingsbury,
Structure, p. 130 n. 2).

However, it must be remembered that the Twelve for
Matthew are only examples of all disciples who are
commissioned by Jesus.[1] Furthermore, Peter in the
First Gospel is representative of any disciple of
Jesus, and the authority which is granted to him
"to bind and to loose" (16:19) is granted to all
members of Matthew's community (18:18).[2] It is
the community, then, which is to proclaim the
gospel of the kingdom, or the same message which
Jesus proclaimed. The phrase "the gospel of the
kingdom" is the means by which Matthew summarizes
"in the same terms both the pre-Easter message of
Jesus and the post-Easter message of his church."[3]

Matthew's community, however, is not simply
to proclaim the same message which Jesus proclaimed, it is to proclaim him and his presence
among them. What gives the gospel of the kingdom
its uniqueness and authority is not only the past
instruction of Jesus, but his continuing presence
as well.[4] Jesus has instructed his disciples on

--------

[1]See the discussion on οἱ μαθηταί in
Matthew on pp. 132-143 above.

[2]Schweizer, Matthew, pp. 178-179; and
Strecker, Weg, p. 175.

[3]Kingsbury, Structure, p. 10 cf. p. 129.

[4]Matthew borrows the noun τὸ εὐαγγέλιον
from Mark (Strecker, Weg, p. 128), yet for
Matthew Jesus is still the subject of the
proclamation (Marxsen, Mark the Evangelist,
pp. 148-150; and Kingsbury, Structure, p. 133).

"the law and the prophets" (5:17), and has instructed them on the righteousness required for
the "kingdom of heaven" (5:20), a righteousness
which they must teach (5:19b). He has also given
them the authority (10:1) to proclaim this gospel.
However, this gospel and the authority to proclaim
it are bound up with the presence of Jesus.[1]  This
means, succinctly, that Matthew's community is not
simply to proclaim the gospel as content which has
been passed down to them, but they are also to
live the gospel. The continual presence of Jesus
calls for a redefinition of life as well as a redefinition of the "law and the prophets."[2]  The
disciples have been "trained for the kingdom of
heaven" (13:52), but they are not only to interpret correctly Jesus' teachings. They, in contrast to the false prophets (24:10-12), are to
follow Jesus' teachings.

The one criterion in Matthew by which false
prophets can be identified is by "their fruits"
(7:20), that is, by what they do. In Matthew's
view any post-Easter disciple is deceived if that
disciple proclaims the name or the authority of
Jesus but no longer lives by his commandments.[3]
A true disciple hears and does the "words" of
Jesus (7:24). He/she lives by the commandments
as reinterpreted by Jesus (5:19 cf. 7:12). A true
disciple will not simply call on the name of
Jesus, nor will he/she simply invoke the authority
of Jesus to do "many mighty works" in his name,
but he/she, in contrast to the false prophet, will
do the will of God (7:21-22).[4]  The true follower

---

[1]Schweizer, Matthew, p. 180; and Bornkamm,
"The Risen Lord and the Earthly Jesus," pp. 216,
218, 221.

[2]Schweizer, Matthew, p. 180.  [3]Ibid.

[4]Bornkamm, "End-Expectation," TI, p. 26.

of Jesus, then, is the one who interprets author-
itatively the words of Jesus for others, but
he/she is also the one who follows those teachings
and lives by Jesus' model.[1]

In the First Gospel if one is a true follower
of Jesus, then that disciple's life will issue in
love for God and neighbor. All of the commandments literally "hang"(κρέμαται, 22:40) upon this
commandment to love God and neighbor (22:35-40).
The life of love is the higher righteousness
demanded by Jesus.[2]  In fact, the fulfillment of
the love command is the only criterion by which
one will be pronounced righteous at the last judgment (25:37-40 cf. 23:23).[3]  Therefore, the proclamation of the gospel of the kingdom is, in
essence, the preaching of love for one's neighbor,
for that is the standard by which they will be
judged.[4]  In contrast to this the false prophets
work "lawlessness" (7:23; 24:12a), they have
"relaxed" the commandments (5:18), and, consequently, cause many disciples' love to "grow cold"
(24:12b).  Indeed, many will even "hate one

---

[1]Schweizer, Matthew, p. 180; and Hill,
Matthew, p. 107.

[2]Matt. 5:17-20; 7:12; 9:13; 12:7. Bornkamm,
"End-Expectation and Church in Matthew," TI, pp.
24-32; Barth, "Matthew's Understanding of the
Law," TI, pp. 78-89; and Schweizer, Matthew,
pp. 425-426.

[3]Bornkamm, "End-Expectation and Church in
Matthew," TI, pp. 23-24.

[4]Schweizer, Matthew, p. 452.

another" (24:10c).

The true disciple, then, not only teaches but does what Jesus commands. Jesus' commandment, as understood by Matthew, forbids the diminution of one's love for neighbor as a result of ἀνομία. Anyone in the community is deceived who believes that prophesying, performing exorcisms and miracles, or even confessing Jesus as Lord is only what Jesus commanded. It is necessary to note that these actions as such are not condemned by Matthew, but they are of no effect if the love commandment is neglected. If Jesus' command to love one's neighbor is neglected, then one alienates himself from Jesus at the last judgment. The Pharisees too, even though they obey the commandments, are full of ἀνομία (23:28) because they do not understand that the demand of God is "mercy, not sacrifice" (cf. 9:13; 12:7).[1] The true disciple will be saved, as the "hinge" verse 24:13 shows, by proclaiming the gospel of the kingdom until the End (24:14), and by embodying the love which Jesus requires of his followers (24:12).

In summary, the gospel of the kingdom which Matthew's community is to propagate involves: (1) the proclamation that "the kingdom of heaven is near" (10:7); and, (2) the proclamation of Jesus' authority and his presence with them, an authority which is especially evident in exorcisms and healings. Κηρύσσειν in Matthew is not just preaching and teaching, but it is proclamation with the full authority and power of Jesus--indeed of God--himself (cf. 1:23; 28:18). Consequently, the disciples' proclamation of the reality of God's rule and of Jesus' presence among them is

_____

[1]Ibid., p. 189; and Bornkamm, "End-Expectation and Church in Matthew," TI, p. 26.

accomplished by signs and wonders.1 Finally,
(3) the gospel of the kingdom entails teaching
men and women to observe all that Jesus has commanded them (28:20), which is summarized in the
love commandment.2 Kingsbury has an excellent
summary of Matthew's understanding of the entire
phrase "the gospel of the kingdom." He says that:

> . . . "the Gospel of the Kingdom" is the
> news, which saves or condemns, that is
> revealed in and through Jesus Messiah . . .
> and is proclaimed to Israel and the nations
> alike to the effect that in him the Rule
> of God has drawn near to humankind.3

The "gospel of the kingdom" is Matthew's
summary phrase for the content of his whole work
as well as his summary of his community's understanding of its mission.4 However, one senses
from the repeated warnings throughout the work
about false prophets leading many astray that the

---

1Gerhard Friedrich, "κῆρυξ," TDNT 3: 714;
Gerhard Friedrich, "εὐαγγελίζομαι," TDNT 2: 720;
Strecker, Weg, pp. 128, 175; and Bornkamm, "End-
Expectation and Church in Matthew," TI, p. 18.

2We cannot agree with M'Neile that "this
gospel of the kingdom" can be reduced to mean
"the good tidings that the Kingdom is near"
(M'Neile, St. Matthew, p. 347 cf. Hill, Matthew,
pp. 107, 182).

3Kingsbury, Structure, pp. 136-137 cf.
pp. 132-137.

4Ibid., pp. 5, 129. This "gospel of the
kingdom" includes discourse and narrative
materials--in short, the entire document Matthew
has written (Ibid., p. 131).

word of the kingdom has almost been "choked" by
the "cares of the world" (13:22) and by the weeds
sown by the devil (13:39). The gospel of the
kingdom is a "narrow gate" which few in Matthew's
time can seem to find (7:14). Many in Matthew's
church are following the "many" (πολλοί, 7:13 cf.
24:5, 10, 11) through the wide gate that "leads to
destruction" (7:13), and Matthew only expects the
lawlessness to get worse before the Parousia
(24:10-12). Where would Matthew have his community look to discover the gospel they are to cling
to and to proclaim until the end? "Obviously,"
says Kingsbury, "[Matthew would have them look] to
the document he has written, for it is, again,
coterminous with the Word, or Gospel, of the
Kingdom."[1]

## Ἐν ὅλῃ τῇ οἰκουμένῃ

Matthew next tells to whom this gospel is to
be proclaimed (ἐν ὅλῃ τῇ οἰκουμένῃ) and why (εἰς
μαρτύριον πᾶσιν τοῖς ἔθνεσιν). At first glance
this statement seems to contradict other statements in the gospel (10:5, 23).[2] However, as we
have seen, Matthew presents Jesus and the disciples as having preached the gospel of the kingdom
to Israel first, but they soundly rejected it.
The kingdom, God's rule and presence (1:23; 18:20;

---

[1]Ibid., p. 131. See Kingsbury's discussion
of the phrase the "gospel of the kingdom" as being synonymous with the "word of the kingdom"
(Ibid. Cf. Lambrecht, "Parousia Discourse," p.
320 n. 26; Bornkamm, "End-Expectation and Church
in Matthew," TI, pp. 20-21; and Strecker, Weg,
pp. 128-129).

[2]Marxsen, Mark the Evangelist, p. 202 n.
183.

28:20), therefore, was taken away from Israel and given "to a nation (ἔθνει) producing the fruits of it" (21:43). The kingdom confronted Israel, as we have seen, in the person of Jesus-Sophia, and, in the post-Easter setting, in the proclamation of his messengers (the church). God's rule and presence leaves Israel in a definitive way when Jesus, who is "God with us" (1:23), turns his back on the temple and pronounces judgment upon it (24:1-2). The ἔθνει to which the presence of God goes, of course, is Matthew's community, and from 24:3 on Jesus never preaches or teaches to "Israel" again.[1]

The result of Israel's rejection of the proclamation of Jesus and of the church was not only the loss of God's kingdom. Their rejection also meant that the proclamation of the gospel of the kingdom would no longer be directed to Israel per se, but now (in Matthew's time) the proclamation would go to the nations.[2] Matthew, of

---

[1]Cf. 16:18 to 18:17. Actually Jesus, for all practical purposes, does not preach or teach to the Jews after 11:1 in Matthew (Kingsbury, Parables of Jesus in Matthew 13, pp. 29-31). However, Matthew reveals his own stance as far back as the first summary of Jesus' preaching in 4:23. While Mark has Jesus going through Galilee and "preaching in their synagogues" (1:39), Matthew seems to distinguish between Jesus' "teaching in their synagogues" and his "preaching the gospel of the kingdom . . . among the people" (4:23 cf. 9:35). It is interesting that in Matthew none of Jesus' discourses have their setting in a synagogue (cf. Luke 4:16; Schweizer, Matthew, p. 77).

[2]This is the main reason why we feel Matthew "de-eschatologizes" Mark 13:9-13 and shifts it back to chapter 10.

course, sees that the proclamation also will be rejected for the most part by the nations (24:9). They, like Israel, will be judged for their rejection.[1] But still, the gospel must be proclaimed "as a testimony" (εἰς μαρτύριον) until the End.[2] Proclaiming the gospel in word and in deed, and refusing to be led astray in either aspect, is what the disciple of Matthew's community must "endure until the End." If he/she does endure, then he/she will be "saved" (24:13).

Matthew 24:14, then, is to be understood as the counterpart of the missionary command in 28:19-20 rather than as the counterpart of 10:5 and 10:23.[3] The evangelist has placed 24:14 here because his community exists in the time of the world-wide preaching mission to "all the nations" (πάντα τὰ ἔθνη, 28:19) rather than in the time

---

[1]See the excellent summary by Kingsbury, Structure, pp. 155-157.

[2]The interpretation of εἰς μαρτύριον here is extremely difficult (see Marxsen, Mark the Evangelist, pp. 174-178; H. Strathmann, "μάρτυς," TDNT 4: 502-503; Beasley-Murray, Commentary on Mark Thirteen, pp. 40-45; Hare, Theme of Jewish Persecution, p. 107; Trilling, Wahre, p. 128; and Strecker, Weg, p. 240).

[3]Trilling, Wahre, p. 128. The very phrase ἐν ὅλῃ τῇ οἰκουμένῃ, as contrasted with εἰς ὁδὸν ἐθνῶν μὴ ἀπέλθητε (10:5b), indicates that 24:14 should be read in light of 28:19-20. Further, οἰκουμένη itself, which occurs only here in Matthew and as his redaction, has the "universal-hellenistic" tone of 28:19-20 rather than the "particularistic" tone of 10:5 (Otto Michel, "οἰκουμένη," TDNT 5: 158).

when the preaching mission was only to the Jews
(10:5-6).[1] The positive aspect of the mission is
that the gospel is presented to the ἔθνη. They,
unlike the Jews, have not yet totally rejected
the proclamation. They are in the crisis of the
decision which will determine whether or not the
gospel will be a "testimony against" them.[2]

Matthew's church is involved, then, in a
mission to proclaim the gospel of the kingdom as
a witness to the whole world. However, the church
must understand that it is only <u>after</u> the completion of this mission that the end will come (καὶ
τότε ἥξει τὸ τέλος, v. 14). The "end," which is
inaugurated at the Parousia of Jesus as the Son
of Man and is consummated with the judgment (24:3
cf. 25:31-46), has not yet arrived (ἀλλ' οὔπω
ἐστὶν τὸ τέλος, 24:6d). Even though at times it
appears that Jesus is present with them in all
glory so that some worshippers can cry "I myself
am the Christ" (24:5b), and others can cry "'Lo,
here is the Christ!' or 'There he is!'" (24:23),
Matthew's church must remember that Jesus'
Parousia has not occurred. Jesus' true disciples
(οἱ μαθηταί, 24:3) are not to be led astray,[3]
nor are they to believe them (24:23, 26). Even
if the social and natural orders appear to be
breaking up (24:6, 7), this is still only the
"beginning of the sufferings" (24:8). The End
(τὸ τέλος), Jesus' Parousia and the judgment, will
not come until the mission to the Gentiles is
complete (24:14). The true disciple will endure

---

[1]Pesch, "Eschatologie und Ethik," p. 230.

[2]Εἰς μαρτύριον, 24:14. This means that
ἔθνη <u>in this context</u> does not include the Jews.

[3]24:4b cf. 24:5c, 6b, 6c, 8, 10-12.

in his/her task of mission, will resist the temptation to believe that Jesus' Parousia has already occurred, and will resist the ἀνομία which goes with that false belief. The true disciple will not allow the love Jesus commanded (22:37-40) to grow cold (24:12). To put it succinctly, the true disciple will remain obedient to the words presented here in the testament of Jesus-Sophia. The disciple is not merely to "persevere" (ὑπομείνας, v. 13), but he/she is to persevere just as Jesus himself did--in love. Indeed, for Matthew love can help one endure (cf. 1 Cor. 13:7) because it focuses one's gaze upon the future (τὸ τέλος, 24:13) and its reward (5:43-48; 25:37-40, 46) rather than only upon the suffering of the present (24:8-12).[1] For Matthew the phrase "until the end of the world" always carries with it the experience of the constant nearness of the Risen Lord. The train of thought "endure to the End" carries inseparably with it words of promise: "lo, I am with you always, to the close of the Age" (28:20b). If the disciple endures all of this until Jesus' Parousia (τὸ τέλος), then he/she (οὗτος) will be saved in the judgment (24:13 cf. 25:34-39, 46b).[2]

---

[1]Trilling, Wahre, p. 43. In this context ὑπομείνας (v. 13 cf. 10:22b) does not mean simply "suffer with patience" the ὠδίνων (v. 8). The "endurance" required here is not "mere continuance to the end of the age," but it includes endurance in the preaching task as well as endurance in ἀγάπη (Beasley-Murray, Commentary on Mark Thirteen, p. 52 cf. Hill, Matthew, pp. 189, 321). When used in relation to εἰς τέλος and σωθήσεται, ὑπομείνας is very close to ἐλπίς itself (Friedrich Hauck, "μένω," TDNT 4: 587).

[2]Pesch, Naherwartungen, p. 136. On the possible meanings of εἰς τέλος in 24:13 see:

In summary, it is clear that one of Matthew's main purposes in this discourse is not to discuss the punishment of the Jews or the destruction of the temple, but it is, as Hare says, " . . . to prepare Christians for enduring faithfulness during the indefinite period that remains."[1] The message which has been passed down to Matthew's community, as well as the "hope" which it inspires for the true disciple, is in keeping with the character of the discourse as a "testament" of Jesus.[2] In short, the true disciple is the one who remains obedient to the words presented here in the testament of Jesus-Sophia.

This passage does not tell us whether Matthew envisions the τέλος as distant or as close at hand, but it does reveal something of how he perceives the place of his community within the scheme of salvation-history.[3] Matthew's church is a mission church which is conscious of living in

---

Hill, Matthew, p. 321; Allen, St. Matthew, p. 255; Fenton, St. Matthew, pp. 384-385; and Beasley-Murray, Commentary on Mark Thirteen, pp. 52-53.

[1]Hare, Theme of Jewish Persecution, p. 178; cf. Ellis, Matthew: His Mind and His Message, p. 89.

[2]Ibid., p. 83.

[3]Hill, Matthew, p. 231; cf. Trilling, Wahre, p. 43. The question is not whether a "Delay of the Parousia" is implied in Matthew (24:48; 24:45-51; 25:5), but the question is: was the delay a problem for Matthew's community? (See Bornkamm, "End-Expectation and Church in Matthew," TI, pp. 23, 42; Trilling, Wahre, pp. 43-45; Strecker, Weg, p. 45; and Hare, Jewish Persecution, p. 144 n. 4).

the time of the Gentile mission. The mission to
Israel by both Jesus and his disciples, which includes Matthew's church, has ended in rejection
(23:34-39) and persecution (10:17-21). The
Heidenmission is also meeting with rejection
(24:9), but this is the last preaching mission
before the End comes (24:14).

It seems, then, that one can distinguish at
least two epochs in Matthew's Heilsgeschichte:
the time of Israel and the time of Jesus. The
time of Israel is preparatory and prophetic for
the time of Jesus. The time of Jesus begins,
it seems, with the preaching of John (3:1),[1] or
with the preaching of Jesus (4:17).[2] The time of

---

[1]Kingsbury, "Structure of Matthew's Gospel,"
p. 471; and Strecker, "Concept of History in Matthew," pp. 223-230. Kingsbury argues that the
phrase "in those days" is an eschatological phrase
for Matthew which denotes the period of time to
precede Jesus' Parousia and the consummation of
the age. Therefore, "in those days" in 3:1
" . . . designates that eschatological period of
time that was inaugurated by the public ministry
of John the Baptist and will continue until the
parousia of Jesus son of Man" (Kingsbury, "Structure of Matthew's Gospel," p. 470).

[2]The function of ἀπὸ τότε is generally
agreed upon "to indicate the beginning of a new
period of time" (Ibid., p. 453). However, whereas
Kingsbury contends that the time of Jesus begins
with John (3:1), Strecker places the preaching of
John within the time of Israel and says that ἀπὸ
τότε at 4:17 marks the beginning of the time of
Jesus (Strecker, "Concept of History in Matthew,"
p. 220). Others contend that Jesus' ministry begins with his public baptism (Fenton, St. Matthew, pp. 59-60; Allen, St. Matthew, p. 28; and

Jesus extends from the beginning of his preaching (4:17) until his Parousia.[1]  The central feature of the time of Jesus is that he proclaims the gospel exclusively to Israel only to have it completely rejected.[2]  Israel consequently loses her place in the scheme of salvation-history, as we have seen, and the preaching mission turns to the Gentiles.  This is the time of world mission, and the time of Matthew's church, which will last until the Eschaton.[3]  However, as we have seen, Matthew's church is conscious of the fact that its mission is a continuation of the proclamation of Jesus and of the historical Twelve (10:1).  Thus, Matthew's church still lives in the "time of Jesus" because of Jesus' presence with them until the Eschaton (28:20).[4]  In encouraging his church

---

Hill, _Matthew_, p. 97).

[1]Kingsbury, "Structure of Matthew's Gospel," pp. 473-474.  Contrast Strecker, "Concept of History in Matthew," pp. 222-223 in which he extends the time of Jesus from his birth to his resurrection.

[2]Ibid., p. 222.  Kingsbury, "Structure of Matthew's Gospel," pp. 460-474, basically agrees with this point.

[3]Ibid., pp. 461-465; and Strecker, "Concept of History in Matthew," p. 223.

[4]Kingsbury subsumes the "time of the church," rightly we think, under the "time of Jesus," and makes the mission of Matthew's church coalesce with that of Jesus and the historical Twelve (Kingsbury, "Structure of Matthew's Gospel," pp. 473-474).  On the other hand, Strecker separates the time of Matthew's church from that of Jesus and the Twelve (Strecker,

to faithful endurance until the Eschaton.  Matthew
draws upon the consciousness of his church that
they live in the time of Jesus when he is still
present with them.

One further note of encouragement is implied
by Matthean redaction.  By deleting πρῶτον, and by
changing Mark's δεῖ κηρυχθῆναι to κηρυχθήσεται
(24:14 cf. Mark 13:10), the evangelist implies
that the End to come is an event independent of
their own missionary efforts.[1]  The preaching is
human activity, but the End to come is a divine,
apocalyptic act of Jesus himself which will bring
his own epoch to a close.[2]  Matthew's idea is not
simply that "the gospel must first be preached to
all nations" (Mark 13:10), but the idea is that
the gospel of the kingdom would be preached εἰς
μαρτύριον πᾶσιν τοῖς ἔθνεσιν, καὶ τότε ἥξει τὸ
τέλος.  The evangelist has coalesced the mission
to all the nations with the idea of the presence
of the exalted Jesus by deleting the typical
apocalyptic concepts of πρῶτον and δεῖ.  In this
way Matthew has taken up and transformed a
strictly apocalyptic christology of Jesus as
coming Son of Man, and has combined it and comple-
mented it with his exaltation christology.  The
disciples are sent into the world with the promise
of the Risen Jesus' presence until the End.  In
other words, Matthew holds together the eschatological tension of the disciples' existence
between the presence of the Risen Jesus and the

"Concept of History in Matthew," pp. 223-230; cf.
Walker, Heilsgeschichte, p. 115).

[1]Marxsen, Mark the Evangelist, p. 201.

[2]Bornkamm, "Risen Lord and the Earthly
Jesus," p. 209; and Hill, Matthew, pp. 320-321.

coming Son of Man.[1]  The members of the evangelist's community are conscious of the fact that
they are messengers of Jesus-Sophia.  They are
conscious of his presence as the Shekinah, but
they know also that he is still to come in a
definitive way as the Son of Man.

## Part 5.  The Testament of
Jesus-Sophia: Warnings
about the Desolating
Sacrilege

The Risen Lord will be present with the
community in the period between the resurrection
and the Parousia, but this period also will be a
time of "great tribulation" (θλῖψις μεγάλη, 24:2)
initiated by the "desolating sacrilege" (τὸ
βδέλυγμα τῆς ἐρημώσεως, 24:15).  The evangelist
joins the period of world mission (24:9-14) together with the time of the "great tribulation"
(24:15-22).  His addition of οὖν shows that
verses 15-22 are an explication of what has preceded, and "when you see" (ὅταν οὖν ἴδητε, v. 15)
defines the θλῖψις (v. 9a cf. v. 14) of those
days (v. 29) as "great."[2]

However, while it is fairly clear that the
evangelist intends verses 9-14 to be read together with verses 15-22, it is not at all clear
what he means by the "desolating sacrilege" and
the "great tribulation."  In fact, there is such
a divergence of opinion as to Matthew's meaning
here that one hesitates to attempt any interpre-

---

[1]Bornkamm, "Risen Lord and the Earthly
Jesus," pp. 209, 211-212; cf. Strecker, Weg,
p. 225; and Lange, Erscheinen, p. 301.

[2]24:21 cf. vv. 19, 22.  Bacon, Studies in
Matthew, pp. 68, 77; M'Neile, St. Matthew, p.

tation of these verses at all.  Fortunately, our
investigation--the <u>function</u> of the eschatological
discourse in Matthew--does not depend upon an explicit historical identification of the "desolating sacrilege."  Thus , we will not engage in
speculation concerning any referent outside of the
text itself, but we will take only the meanings
which the Matthean text will give, vague though
they are, and determine the function of these
verses within the eschatological discourse as a
whole.[1]

We discussed earlier how one's interpretation of 24:1-2 and 24:3 would determine one's
interpretation of 24:15-22.[2]  Our conclusion was
that Matthew has placed a caesura between 24:2 and
24:3.  The upshot of this conclusion is that vv.
15-22 seem to refer to an <u>eschatological</u> abomination rather than to an event of the past <u>only</u>
(e.g., Antiochus IV, Caligula, or C.E. 70).  We
concluded that the evangelist was using "scripture" (Mark as well as Daniel?) in an apocalyptic
fashion.  Consequently, while past events such as
the desecration by Antiochus IV provide the empirical evidence for the <u>nature</u> of the End-time abomination, those events <u>were not</u> the End-time abomination itself for Matthew.

This "apocalyptic" use of Daniel means that
for Matthew's readers the "abomination" which

---

347; Johnson, <u>St. Matthew</u>, p. 546; and Pesch,
<u>Naherwartungen</u>, p. 232.

[1]On the history of the interpretation of τὸ
βδέλυγμα τῆς ἐρημώσεως see the excellent summary
by Beasley-Murray, <u>Commentary on Mark Thirteen</u>,
pp. 59-72.

[2]See the discussion on pp. 198-209.

immediately precedes the End <u>is still outstanding</u>.
It did not occur at 167-163 B.C.E. nor at C.E. 70.
Although those events were "abominations," they
obviously were not the End-time abominations when
God would intervene and establish the kingdom.
When a first century Christian like Matthew read
the book of Daniel, he/she did not do so with
critical scholarship's conclusions about apocalyptic at his/her disposal. He/she read apocalyptic texts like any Christian today might who
is unacquainted with critical scholarship: current
events are scrutinized in order to see if they
might possibly be the events alluded to in the
text.  It was this "relevance" of apocalyptic
literature which seemed to account for its popu-
larity.  Apocalyptic literature was always contemporary.[1]  Therefore, when Matthew and his
readers read phrases like "the abomination of
desolation," they did not think of an event which
occurred almost two hundred years earlier in the
age of Antiochus IV.  When Matthew read: "But you,
Daniel, shut up the words, and seal the book,
until the time of the end" (Dan. 12:4), he would
naturally believe that the "abomination" belonged
to the time of the End.  He would begin to survey
his own times to see if an "abomination" was occurring which would suggest that <u>his time</u> was the
End-time prophesied in Daniel.

Admittedly, this line of interpretation,
since it grows out of Matthean redaction itself
rather than some referent outside of the text,
will yield the exegetical minimum when applied to
verses 15-22.[2]  It will not allow us to identify

---

[1]See H. H. Rowley, <u>The Relevance of Apoca-
lyptic</u> (London: Lutterworth Press, 1963); and
Russell, <u>Method and Message of Jewish Apocalyptic</u>,
p. 29 cf. p. 190.

[2]We are following the excellent discussion

the abomination explicitly with a person or with
an event, but it will allow Matthew's general
meaning and purpose for this section to surface.

## Τὸ Βδέλυγμα τῆς Ἐρημώσεως

The phrase τὸ βδέλυγμα τῆς ἐρημώσεως, for
which the evangelist explicitly alludes to Daniel
(τὸ ῥηθὲν διὰ Δανιὴλ τοῦ προφήτου), is derived
from the Septuagint (Theodotian[A]) and most likely
should be translated: "the Appalling Abomination,"
or, "the Abomination that causes horror."[1]    In

---

of F. W. Beare, "Apocalypse," p. 129 cf. pp. 124-
129.  See also Walter Schmithals, The Apocalyptic
Movement, trans. John E. Steely (New York:  Ab-
ingdon Press, 1975), p. 17; Hare, Theme of Jewish
Persecution, p. 163; and Marxsen, Mark the
Evangelist, p. 203.

[1]Beasley-Murray, Commentary on Mark Thirteen, p. 54.  We take ἐρημώσεως, then, as an
epexegetic genitive (see Maximillan Zerwick, A
Grammatical Analysis of the Greek New Testament,
vol. 1, trans. Mary Grosvenor [Rome: Biblical
Institute Press, 1974], p. 78; hereafter cited as
AGNT).  The LXX translates two abstract nouns
(haššiqqûṣ mᵉšōmēm, Dan. 11:31 cf. Dan. 8:31;
12:11).  Shiqqûṣ is a term used in the tanak
"almost exclusively for idolatrous objects and
practices, and means 'a detested thing.'"  (S. B.
Frost, "Abomination that Makes Desolate," IDB 1:
13; cf. M. H. Lovelace, "Abomination," IDB 1: 13;
Werner Foerster, "βδελύσσομαι," TDNT 1:598; Béda
Rigaux, "ΒΔΕΛΥΓΜΑ ΤΗΣ ΕΡΗΜΩΣΕΩΣ Mc 13,14; Mt 24,
15," Biblica 40 (1959): 675-676; and C. H. Dodd,
"The Fall of Jerusalem and the 'Abomination of
Desolation,'" More New Testament Studies [Man-
chester University Press, 1968], p. 81).  The
phrase should probably be translated then as "the

other words, the phrase refers primarily to the
<u>horror</u> caused by desecration associated with idol-
atry and heathen gods.  It does not necessarily
refer to "desolation" in the sense of physical
destruction.[1]  In Daniel the phrase clearly refers
to Antiochus IV who "desecrated" the sanctity of
the Jewish temple[2] with an idol of Zeus, or of
himself, or of both.[3]  As Beasley-Murray says:

> In view of this meaning in Dan. 9.27,
> etc., it is clear that the expression
> has by itself no thought of the temple's
> destruction but purely of its desecration.
> The Abomination horrifies. . . . But it
> still stands as a building.[4]

---

appalling abomination."

[1]However, this is not ruled out totally
since the root š̌mm can mean: "to be appalled,
overwhelmed with astonishment and dread," or "to
be desolated, emptied of inhabitants" (Frost,
"Abomination that Makes Desolate," p. 13; cf.
Beasley-Murray, <u>Commentary on Mark Thirteen</u>,
pp. 54-55).

[2]It is the consensus of commentators that
Antiochus IV is alluded to in Daniel.  This identification rests upon a comparison of Daniel with
1-2 Maccabees.  See Rigaux, "ΒΔΕΛΥΓΜΑ ΤΗΣ
ΕΡΗΜΩΣΕΩΣ," pp. 677-678 for an exhaustive comparison of the texts.

[3]See Beasley-Murray's discussion of Dan.
8:13 (LXX) and 1 Macc. 1:54-64 (Beasley-Murray,
<u>Commentary on Mark Thirteen</u>, pp. 54-55).

[4]Ibid., p. 55; cf. Gerhard Kittel, "ἔρημος,"
<u>TDNT</u> 2: 660; and Taylor, <u>St. Mark</u>, p. 511.

In Daniel, then, the emphasis seems to be upon the fact that the temple had been profaned, and that that profanation "laid waste" ("made desolate") Israel's worship.[1] The question now is: what does the "abomination" mean in Matthew?

There is no question that Matthew points specifically to Daniel (τὸ ῥηθὲν διὰ Δανιήλ), but it does not follow from this that the evangelist takes over every element of the Danielic meaning. The concept of the βδέλυγμα is a fluid one which takes its meaning from any author's contemporary perspective.[2] This means that Daniel (LXX) lies before Matthew as a commentary, but it does not follow that Daniel determines the specific historical meaning of the phrase for Matthew.

---

[1] M'Neile, St. Matthew, p. 347.

[2] One has only to glance at the tradition to see its fluidity. The βδέλυγμα in Daniel, as discussed above, refers to the abominable object placed in the temple sanctuary by Antiochus. In Luke, or in the pre-Lukan tradition, the βδέλυγμα is thought of in terms of armies (21:20). And, if the AntiChrist concept can be seen as a form of the βδέλυγμα concept, then 2 Thess. 2 interprets it as the AntiChrist. As Schrenk says: "The new application of βδέλυγμα underlies the Christian prophecy" (Schrenk, "ἱερόν," p. 245). Beasley-Murray is even more to the point: " . . . it would be possible to align the βδέλυγμα with the Anti-Christ doctrine if, with Althaus, it be recognized that in the N.T. this doctrine is fluid, possessing a variety of forms and above all has what he terms 'immediate actuality' . . . . That is, the concept of a power at work against God is applied to forces operative in the contemporary situation; the idea illumines the present, it does not impose on it a programme (Mark Thirteen, pp. 68-9).

In fact, Matthew tells us that he is reading Daniel (LXX) as prophecy. The evangelist refers specifically to what is written in Daniel the prophet (τοῦ προφήτου).[1] It seems that for Matthew " . . . the book of Daniel was regarded as a prophecy of future events, and so the passage in Daniel was looked upon as not yet fulfilled."[2]

Matthew's "fulfillment texts," in which he appeals to Old Testament prophecy to highlight his point, seem to suggest that the abomination in 24:15 is a future event. The more or less stereo-typed formula by which the evangelist introduces these texts from Old Testament prophecy is "in order to fulfill what the Lord had spoken by the prophet."[3] Matthew 24:15 has a form very similar to the Reflexionszitate (τὸ ῥηθὲν διὰ Δανιὴλ τοῦ προφήτου), yet it does not contain the complete formula. For this reason, and also because it is only an allusion to Daniel rather than an explicit quotation, Matt. 24:15 is not usually reckoned among the Reflexionszitate. It is our contention that Matthew refers apocalyptically to "Daniel the prophet" and intentionally does not want this text, even though it is a text from the prophets, to be understood as fulfilled.[4]

---

[1]Daniel is included among the prophets in the LXX, and Matthew is certainly using the LXX text for Daniel. The decisive thing, though, is Matthew's use of his characteristic formula for the prophets (τὸ ῥηθὲν ὑπὸ κυρίου διὰ τοῦ προφήτου λέγοντες). See Friedrich, "προφήτης," p. 831.

[2]Fenton, St. Matthew, p. 387.

[3]See 1:22; 2:15, 17, 23; 4:14; 8:17; 12:17; 13:35; 21:4; 26:56; 27:9-10.

[4]This point was suggested to me in private

There are several factors which seem to suggest this conclusion is correct. First, all of the fulfillment texts are introduced by some form of πληρόω (usually the aorist passive).[1] Matthew 24:15 has all of the essentials of a fulfillment formula <u>except</u> an explicit reference to any fulfillment of the Danielic text. Secondly, every fulfillment text in Matthew refers to a particular prophet by name or by allusion. Matthew 24:15 is the only reference in the entire gospel to the text of a prophet, either by name or by allusion, which has no indication that the prophecy has been fulfilled. It would be highly unusual for Matthew to leave this important prophecy unfulfilled when, as Stendahl has clearly shown, his <u>pesher</u> tendency in all of the formula quotations is that of an "actualizing nature" which is "closely associated with the context in the gospel."[2] The eschatological context of Matt. 24:15 makes it inconceivable that the evangelist would not allude to the fulfillment of "the desolating sacrilege spoken of by the prophet Daniel" if he considered that event to be past. The clear implication is that he regards the "desolating sacrilege" as a

---

conversation by Father John R. Donahue.

[1]John J. O'Rourke, "The Fulfillment Texts in Matthew," <u>CBQ</u> 24 (1962): 395.

[2]Stendahl, <u>School</u>, pp. 200-201. Stendahl moves from this to the conclusion that "Matthew's formula quotations seem . . . to be a decisive indication that we must postulate a School of Matthew." Although Stendahl has been criticized for this conclusion, his point about the "actualizing nature" of the quotations still stands (see Gärtner, "The Habakkuk Commentary [DSH] and the Gospel of Matthew," pp. 1-24; and Davies, <u>Sermon on the Mount</u>, pp. 208-216).

future event.

Thus, the evangelist could take Daniel's general meaning--the profanation of a holy place--and apply it apocalyptically to the specifics of his contemporary situation without necessarily taking all of the details of Daniel's text along with it.[1] The βδέλυγμα for Matthew does not have to be in the temple at Jerusalem. The βδέλυγμα can be simply the profanation of a holy place, and the evangelist (and his readers) can define both concepts ("profanation" and "holy place") in terms different from the text in Daniel. At any rate, it is clear from Matthew's specific reference to Daniel (τὸ ῥηθὲν διὰ Δανιήλ) and from his retention of the cryptic, apocalyptic note to the reader (ὁ ἀναγινώσκων νοείτω) that "Matthew's version is . . . an early exegesis of this passage."[2]

Secondly, the fluidity of the βδέλυγμα con-

---

[1]J. A. Montgomery says that in Matt. 24:15 we find "a patently apocalyptic use of the Danielic prophecy" (J. A. Montgomery, A Critical and Exegetical Commentary on the Book of Daniel, [New York: Charles Scribner's Sons, 1927], p. 396).

[2]Marxsen, Mark the Evangelist, p. 163; cf. Beasley-Murray, Commentary on Mark Thirteen, p. 57. Cf. also Mark 13:14; 2 Thess. 2:5-6; Rev. 13:18. The note to the reader, we feel, refers primarily to the reader of Matthew's section (24:15-22) as a commentary on Daniel, and not just to the reader of Daniel only, or of a pre-synoptic apocalypse. Contrast R. H. Gundry, The Use of the Old Testament in St. Matthew's Gospel (Leiden: E. J. Brill, 1967), p. 49.

cept means that none of the prevailing meanings
should be read too quickly into Matthew. The
βδέλυγμα in Matthew does not necessarily mean the
destruction of the Jerusalem temple in C.E. 70, or
for that matter the threat of Caligula in C.E. 40,
even if it did mean one of those for Mark.[1] First
of all, there is simply no explicit evidence in
the text (even if one dates Matthew after 70) to
indicate that the evangelist understood the
βδέλυγμα as the destruction of the Jerusalem
temple--especially after C.E. 70.[2] This is true
even if one could show that Mark 13 understands
the βδέλυγμα as the destruction of 70.[3] Secondly,
if Matthew understands the βδέλυγμα as the destruction of the Jerusalem temple, then one must
ask how 24:15-22 is related to the prophecy of the
temple's destruction (24:1-2). Several commentators have distinguished between the prophecy of
destruction in 24:1-2 (=Mark 13:1-2) and the desecration in 24:15 (=Mark 13:14). Their contention
is that Matt. 24:15 actually implies the inde-
structibility of the temple, its preservation, and
its deliverance by the returning Messiah.[4]

---

[1]Strecker, Weg, p. 239 n. 8.

[2]J. A. T. Robinson makes this silence of the
Matthean text the crux of his argument that Matthew is to be dated before 70 (see J. A. T.
Robinson, Redating the New Testament [Philadel-
phia: Westminster Press, 1976], pp. 13-20). However, an argument from silence can go in the other
direction as well (see Beare, "Apocalypse,"
pp. 121-133).

[3]This silence, of course, is one of the
reasons why Mark cannot be dated with precision.

[4]See the summary in Beasley-Murray, Commentary on Mark Thirteen, pp. 60-61.

Whether or not one accepts this line of argument, it is true that if one attempts to hold 24:1-2 in congruence with 24:15, then one is compelled to argue that even though desecration is the dominant idea in 24:15, the destruction is still implied.[1] However, as we have seen, 24:1-2 does not relate directly to 24:15-22. Matthew 24:1-2 climaxes the reciprocal theme of Israel's rejection of Jesus and Jesus' rejection of Israel. For Matthew, when Jesus leaves the temple (24:1) as the Shekinah, then the Jerusalem temple is profane and "desolate" (ἀφίεται, ἔρημος, 23:38).[2] For Matthew the loss of Jesus' presence <u>was</u> the desecration of the Jerusalem temple. Jesus' implicit rejection of Israel in his departure from the temple is made explicitly clear to his disciples (Matthew's community) by his prophecy of its destruction (24:2). Matthean redaction at 24:3 creates a new scene in which Jesus-Sophia centers upon the question of his return as Son of Man. The theme of the Jerusalem temple is not discussed

---

[1]Ibid., p. 61.

[2]Matthew only speaks explicitly of the profanation of the temple in one place (12:5, βεβηλοῦσιν). The point of the passage, however, is that "something greater than the temple is here" (v. 6), in which μεῖζον undoubtedly means Jesus because "in him the Messianic fulfillment and consummation has come and he is therefore more than the Temple" (Barth, "Matthew's Understanding of the Law," <u>TI</u>, p. 82. Contrast Hill, <u>Matthew</u>, p. 211). The contrast here is between Jesus as the Shekinah and the <u>temple</u>, not the Law (Bornkamm, "End-Expectation and Church in Matthew," <u>TI</u>, p. 35 n. 2). Thus, when Jesus announces in 23:38 that the temple is left desolate, it is when his presence leaves it definitively in 24:1 that it becomes desolate.

again in the eschatological discourse—even in
24:15-22.

A third factor which makes it difficult to
believe that 24:15 alludes to the Jerusalem temple
(or to C.E. 70) is the Lukan parallel. Luke 21:20
specifically interprets the "desolation" of Jerusalem (ἡ ἐρήμωσις αὐτῆς) by armies which surround
it. Whether one sees Luke 21:20 as an ex eventu
interpretation of Mark 13:14,[1] or as a pre-Lukan
tradition (which is independent of Mark) which
presents a generalized picture of Jerusalem's fall
drawn imaginatively from the prophets,[2] the point
is that Matthew does not picture the βδέλυγμα in
terms of armies or of destruction at all. Matthew, as far as we can discern, alludes to the
βδέλυγμα only as desecration.

Fourthly, Matthew's addition of ἐν τόπῳ ἁγίῳ
might not refer to the temple at Jerusalem. Several commentators are quite certain that the
phrase refers to the Jerusalem temple,[3] while
others equally contend that the allusion is not

---

[1]E.g., Marxsen, Mark the Evangelist,
pp. 191-192.

[2]Dodd, "The Fall of Jerusalem and the
'Abomination of Desolation,'" p. 79; cf. Robinson,
Redating the New Testament, p. 27.

[3]Dodd, "The Fall of Jerusalem and the
'Abomination of Desolation,'" p. 81; Hill,
Matthew, p. 321; and Helmut Koester, "τόπος,"
TDNT 8: 204 who says: "Matthew relates the
mysterious allusion of Mark (ἐστηκότα ὅπου οὐ
δεῖ, Mk. 13:14) unequivocally to the temple."

to the temple.[1] The latter support their position in several ways. (1) If the evangelist is following Dan. 9:27, as most interpreters contend who say that the Matthean reference is to the temple, then Matthew differs from Dan. 9:27. The LXX (and ϑ) reads: ἐπὶ τὸ ἱερὸν βδέλυγμα τῶν ἐρημώσεων, and it is clear from the context that the βδέλυγμα is in the temple (cf. Dan. 9:27; 11:31).[2] Those who argue that Matthew's phrase alludes to the Jerusalem temple do so on the premise that the evangelist is seeking to bring Mark's vague ὅπου οὐ δεῖ into a closer relation with Dan. 9:27. It is extremely difficult to understand why then he does not do precisely that.[3] It is even more difficult to understand why Matthew deletes τὸ ἱερόν from the LXX text if he wanted to bring 24:15, which refers to the Jerusalem temple, into a relation with 24:1-2 where he does use τὸ ἱερόν. This redactional ambiguity seems very strange indeed unless it is Matthew's intention to avoid an allusion to the Jerusalem temple in 24:15.[4]

(2) A second argument that Matt. 24:15 does

---

[1]E.g., Marxsen, Mark the Evangelist, p. 203 n. 191; Johnson, St. Matthew, p. 547; and Strecker, Weg, p. 239 n. 8.

[2]Hartman, Prophecy Interpreted, p. 162 and n. 58.

[3]Contrast Gundry, The Use of the Old Testament in Matthew's Gospel, pp. 48-49.

[4]Indeed, Matthew seems to distance himself from that cultus altogether (see Strecker, Weg, p. 239 n. 8; and Schrenk, "ἱερόν," p. 235).

not allude to the Jerusalem temple is that Matthew's phrase is anarthrous, and, thus, seems to be indefinite.[1] The anarthrous construction is quite out of line with the fact that every explicit reference to the Jerusalem temple in Matthew carries the definite article, and that elsewhere in the New Testament where the Jerusalem temple is referred to in this manner, it is definite.[2] In contrast, if 24:15 is excluded, the Jerusalem temple is never called ὁ ἅγιος τόπος in Matthew.

(3) Lastly, the phrase in 2 Macc. 2:18, even with the article, most likely refers to "the Holy Land" (τὸν ἅγιον τόπον), and, to complicate matters even more, the temple is referred to simply as τὸν τόπον.[3] As discussed earlier, the βδέλυγμα in Daniel was not a destruction as much as a desecration. It was a "desecration" (or "desolation") because a pagan force had profaned the land of Israel by evicting YHWH from the sanctuary.[4] All of the sanctuaries of Israel were

---

[1]Contrast Stendahl, "Matthew," p. 793.

[2]Matt. 4:5; 12:5, 6; 21:12, 14, 15, 23; 24:1; 26:55. In fact, every reference to Jerusalem as a city (πόλις) is definite except one (5:35). Twice it is called τὴν ἁγίαν πόλιν (4:5; 27:53 cf. 21:10, 17, 18; 22:7 [?]; 26:18; 28:11). Compare these Matthean texts with Acts 6:13; and 21:28. Cf. also Acts 6:14; 7:7; and John 4:20.

[3]2 Macc. 5:17, 19. Allen, St. Matthew, p. 256.

[4]Dan. 9:26-27 cf. 1 Macc. 1:41-64; 2 Macc. 2:17-18; Matt. 23:38.

defiled (1 Macc. 1:51, 54), not just the temple at Jerusalem. The same thing could be said about the βδέλυγμα of C.E. 66-70. According to Josephus,[1] the desecration of 66-70 began in a Caesarean synagogue. These facts point to the conclusion that Matthew is, like Daniel, emphasizing that the βδέλυγμα is primarily a desecration, and that he is supposing that another desecration will occur in "a holy place," but not necessarily in "<u>the</u> holy place" at Jerusalem.[2]

---

[1]<u>Jewish War</u> II.14.5.

[2]See Nikolaus Walter, "Tempelzerstörung und synoptische Apokalypse," <u>ZNW</u> 57 (1966): 43; and Johnson, <u>St. Matthew</u>, p. 547. Streeter, arguing in favor of the Syriac tradition, contends that ἑστὸς ἐν τόπῳ ἁγίῳ in Matt. 24:15 is a marginal gloss. He bases his argument upon the anarthrous construction of the phrase (Streeter, <u>Four Gospels</u>, pp. 519-520). Beasley-Murray, building upon Streeter's argument, contends that the "original" referent of βδέλυγμα then was to "the Roman army approaching Jerusalem" (<u>Commentary on Mark Thirteen</u>, p. 70). This argument does not have good textual support, as Beasley-Murray himself acknowledges (Ibid., p. 71), but even more than this, it shows how vague the history of tradition is for this verse. The textual evidence for the received text is overwhelming, and we do not feel that speculation on a reconstructed "original" helps in the interpretation of this verse <u>in its Matthean context</u>.

The Holy Place as a Cryptic
Allusion to the Church

## Tradition and redaction
## in Matt. 24:15

It might be helpful if we would pause at
this point and summarize how interpreters have
understood Matthew's redaction of his traditional
material. In this way the options available for
interpreting ἐν τόπῳ ἁγίῳ might become clearer.

If we knew the date of the final redaction
of Matthew's gospel, and at what point the author
could be located in the sequence of fulfilled and
unfulfilled events, then interpretation of the
discourse would be easier. The consensus of opinion is that Matthew was written after the destruction of Jerusalem.[1] Because of this opinion, most
interpreters have understood ἐν τόπῳ ἁγίῳ and its
desecration to refer clearly to the destruction of
the Jerusalem temple. This conclusion has a direct bearing upon how one understands the evangelist's redaction of the tradition.

In Matthew's tradition the speech is one of
Jesus concerning the future.[2] In Mark 13, as
discussed earlier, Jesus clearly seems to predict
the destruction of the temple and to connect that
event with the Parousia. In other words, in
Mark's account, whether it was written shortly
before or after 70, the destruction is the sign

---

[1]See Feine-Behm-Kümmel, Introduction to the
New Testament, 17th ed., pp. 119-120.

[2]We are not arguing that the speech as it
stands in Matthew was actually delivered by Jesus
during his ministry.

to precede the End. Matthew, who according to
most interpreters was written <u>after</u> the destruction <u>and</u> using Mark, had a problem of unfulfilled
prophecy: Jesus had predicted that the fall of
Jerusalem would usher in the End. The End, of
course, did not come. Interpreters, then, have
understood Matthew's redaction of the tradition as
an attempt to answer <u>their</u> question: "How could
Matthew, writing after 70, transmit a prophecy of
Jesus which seemed to be erroneous, since Jesus
had connected the temple's destruction with the
time of the End?" Interpreters have taken three
positions in an attempt to answer this question.

A. Feuillet argues that Matthew redacted the
tradition in order to eliminate any reference by
Jesus to the End of the world. He argues that the
evangelist redacted Mark 13:4 so that both the
word Parousia and the phrase συντελείας τοῦ αἰῶνος
referred to the destruction of 70. Matthew, in
other words, has reconciled the apparent contra-
diction in Jesus' prophecy by interpreting it to
mean that Jesus never alluded to the End in 24:3.[1]

F. W. Beare, who believes that Matthew was
writing at least fifteen years after the temple's
destruction, also finds it " . . . most remarkable
that it should still be possible for a Christian
writer to link it [the temple's destruction] so
closely with the Parousia of Jesus as Son of Man
and with the end of the age."[2] Yet, Beare concludes, that is precisely what Matthew has done.
He has redacted Mark 13:4 so that although a distinction is made in 24:3 between the destruction

───────────────

[1]Feuillet, "Le Sens Du Mot Parousie dans
L'Évangile de Matthieu," pp. 261-280.

[2]Beare, "Apocalypse," p. 125.

316

and the Parousia, the evangelist assumes no temporal division between the two events.[1]  Beare
then notes that Matthew's redaction in 24:15-22
includes "only minor changes" of Mark 13:14-20.
The "minor changes" include specifying the source
of Mark's "abomination of desolation" as Daniel,
and Mark's " . . . vague ὅπου οὐ δεῖ is changed to
the interpretative ἐν τόπῳ ἁγίῳ (v. 15)."[2]  Beare
then curiously argues that Matthew has only retained the phrase "the abomination of desolation"
as a traditional element.  It does not refer to
the destruction of 70 for Matthew, but to a _future_
event.  In other words, Matthew has separated in
this section (24:15-22) what he had held together
in 24:3, namely, the destruction of 70 and the
End.  According to Beare, the traditional picture,
in which readers are warned to "flee to the moun-
tains" (v. 16) in anticipation of the End, would
make little sense to readers fifteen or more years
after the event which was supposed to initiate the
End.  He concludes, therefore, that for Matthew:

> . . . "the abomination of desolation"
> will not be a statue of Zeus or Jupiter--or
> of the emperor--to be set up in the temple.
> Christian readers of the second generation
> would not be deeply concerned with a pagan
> profanation of a temple which had been
> more deeply profaned by the impiety of
> its own worshipers and had now (in the
> time of Matthew if not already of Mark)
> been reduced to ruins . . . _such an
> interpretation would make nonsense of
> the whole passage._[3]

Beare argues that the "abomination" for Matthew

---

[1]Ibid.    [2]Ibid., p. 127.

[3]Ibid., p. 128 (italics are mine).

is the threat of organized state pressure which could force Christians anywhere in the Empire into apostasy.[1]

W. Marxsen offers a third solution. He too contends that Matthew is writing after 70 and that he has carefully redacted Mark 13:14, in which Mark reckons the temple's destruction among the last things. Marxsen argues that Matthew has redacted Mark 13:14 in order to separate topically (not temporally) the Parousia from the destruction.[2] Marxsen can then conclude that for Matthew the " . . . βδέλυγμα τῆς ἐρημώσεως (24:15) is no longer connected with Jerusalem's destruction; it is a prophecy once more and with express reference to Daniel."[3] Marxsen does not interpret ἐν τόπῳ ἁγίῳ (v. 15). He only asks in a footnote: "For Matthew (as a Jewish Christian?), is the temple a holy place even after Jerusalem's destruction?"[4]

In summary, one has several options. One could argue (with Feuillet) that Matthew has redacted the tradition so that the destruction of Jerusalem and the "abomination of desolation" in the "holy place" are equivalent to the Parousia and the "consummation of the age." Or, one could

---

[1]Ibid.

[2]Marxsen, Mark the Evangelist, p. 199. Marxsen has to qualify this statement, although he does not clarify his position. He says that Matthew offers a discourse which leads step by step to the Parousia. This means that " . . . Matthew too creates a temporal sequence, but in such a way as to juxtapose groups of related material" (Ibid., p. 204 cf. p. 203).

[3]Ibid., p. 203.    [4]Ibid., p. 203 n. 191.

contend (with Beare) that even though Matthew has not clearly separated the destruction from the Parousia, he only retains the phrases "abomination of desolation" and "a holy place" as traditional imagery in order to express his concern over a future desecration of Christian sanctuaries. Finally, one could argue (with Marxsen) that Matthew has separated, topically at least, the Parousia from the temple's destruction and really does not address the latter in his discourse at all. In relation to Matthew's understanding of the "abomination of desolation" and "a holy place," it seems that one can say that "Matthew either looks back to that war or supposes that still another desecration will occur in 'a holy place', not necessarily the holy place [the Jerusalem temple]."[1]

Feuillet, Beare, and Marxsen argue partially from their perspective that Matthew was written after 70. Perhaps this has posed the wrong question in some cases, namely, Matthew's concern with Jesus' incorrect prophecy. However, it would not clarify anything to argue from the position that Matthew was written before 70. It would not be helpful not only because a pre-70 date for Matthew is impossible to prove, but also because Matthew's allusions in 24:15 would be just as historically and geographically vague. For example, the "abomination of desolation" in Mark 13:14 could allude to the threats of Caligula to erect his statue in the temple.[2] Matthew, assuming that he uses Mark, could be trying to

_____

[1]Johnson, St. Matthew, p. 547.

[2]Cf. Josephus' remarks in Antiquities, vol. 18,8.8 about the attempt of Caligula, or at least his threat, to erect a statue in the temple.

enhance Caligula's threats to suggest an impending crisis.[1]  Or, quite differently, one could
argue with Hare, even though he does not hold a
pre-70 date for Matthew, that: "Although this
appears to have been Mark's understanding of the
'abomination of desolation' [that is, as an allusion to a desecration of the Jerusalem temple],
there is no positive evidence that Matthew understood it in this way."[2]  Matthew's allusions are
just as vague whether one assumes a pre-70 or a
post-70 date for his gospel.

Thus far we have intentionally tried to
argue only on the literary basis of Matthew's redactional activity because we feel that no certain
date can be posited for the First Gospel, though
we ourselves lean towards a post-70 date.  Method-
ologically, we feel that this is still the best
way to proceed.  Therefore, while we are discussing the problem of tradition and redaction in
Matt. 24:15, it might be helpful to summarize
briefly our conclusions about Matthew's use of his
traditions, and then we can proceed to discuss for
the first time an element in his tradition--the
relation of βδέλυγμα and ἀνομία--which could help
us understand better his allusions in 24:15.

The evidence seems to suggest that Matthew
is not alluding to the desecration of the Jerusalem temple but to the Church, which includes,
but is not limited to, his own community.[3]

---

[1]Cf. ἐστός, 24:15; εὐθέως, 24:29.  See
Robinson, Redating the New Testament, pp. 17, 21-
25, whose argument could easily be carried in this
direction.

[2]Hare, Jewish Perseuction, p. 177 (italics
mine).

[3]Pierre Bonnard, L'Évangile selon Saint

Several factors point to the fact that Matthew's
language in 24:15 is a cryptic allusion to the
Church--the "holy place" of Jesus-Sophia'
presence.

First, Matthew's redaction has created a
caesura between the discussion about the temple
(24:2) and the eschatological discourse (24:3-31).
The evangelist's work has created a new scene in
24:3. Jesus definitively left the temple (24:1)
and prophesied its destruction (24:2). Matthew
deletes "opposite the temple" in 24:3 (cf. Mark
13:3) ostensibly to focus this introductory verse
on the Parousia. He sharpens Mark's question,
which connects the last things and the predicted
destruction, by defining "these things" (ταῦτα) as
"your Parousia and the consummation of the Age."
Matthew's καί explicative redacts the disciples'
question to read: "Tell us, when will these things
be, that is (καί), what will be the sign of your
coming and of the consummation of the Age?" The
effect of Matthew's redaction in 24:3 is to continue the tradition that this is a discourse of
Jesus about the future, but the discourse does not
concern Jesus' prediction of the temple's destruction. This conclusion is attested in the immediate context of 24:15. Matthew does not make <u>his
redaction</u> of a "holy place" (cf. Mark 13:14) <u>re-</u>
fer explicitly to the temple. Although the evangelist adds an explicit allusion to "the prophet
Daniel," he does not bring ἐν τόπῳ ἀγίῳ into a
closer relation with Dan. 9:27 (cf. Dan. 11:31).
He seems to delete τὸ ἱερόν from the LXX text, a
deletion which could have connected easily with
τὸ ἱερόν in Matt. 24:2. The best explanation for
the evangelist's redactional ambiguity is that he
wanted to use and allude to the "prophet Daniel,"

---

Matthieu. Commentaire du Nouveau Testament, vol.
1 (Paris: Delachaux et Niestlé, 1970), p. 351.

but to avoid a specific reference to the temple.

Secondly, Matthew specifically alludes to "the prophet Daniel" because he wants the desecration of "a holy place" to be understood as a future, that is, unfulfilled, prophecy. This is clearly demonstrated by the fact that this is the only place in the First Gospel where a prophetic text is used without the characteristic fulfillment formula. We have shown already that this unfulfilled event for Matthew does not refer to the prophecy about the temple's destruction (24:2). The only redactional clue which Matthew gives about the event in 24:15 occurs in his change of Mark's masculine ἑστηκότα (13:14) to the neuter ἑστός. The change to ἑστός makes the prophecy from Daniel a general " . . . 'sign' to be awaited, a sign of which men can read (in Daniel!)."[1]

Thirdly, this cryptic sign to be awaited (ὁ ἀναγινώσκων νοείτω) seems to allude to the Church in the time of its world-wide mission. Within the immediate context of 24:15 only Matthew has emphasized a world-wide preaching mission.[2] This world-wide mission will involve hatred from "all the nations,"[3] as opposed to only the Jews (Matt. 10:17-21 cf. Mark 13:9-13). Hatred comes from ὅλη τῇ οἰκουμένῃ as part of the End-time tribulation.[4] Surely, Matthew does not see his

---

[1]Marxsen, Mark the Evangelist, p. 203.

[2]24:14 cf. Mark 13:13; Luke 21:17-19.

[3]Cf. ὑπὸ πάντων, Mark 13:13a.

[4]θλῖψις, 24:9a. Marxsen, Mark the Evangelist, p. 203.

particular community as literally preaching into all the world. He, rather, sees his particular church as part of the Church's world-wide mission, and as sharing the θλῖψις which he feels accompanies that mission. God's presence in Jesus-Sophia is not, for Matthew, confined to one particular place. God is, of course, present in Matthew's community through Jesus (18:20), but the Risen Jesus, who promises his presence to the disciples as they go to make disciples of "all nations" (πάντα τὰ ἔθνη, 28:19), is also for Matthew the eschatological ruler of the whole world. "All authority" has been given to him (28:18), and he is present wherever the Gospel is proclaimed.[1] The evangelist's emphasis upon the world-wide scope of the preaching effort within the same context as the "abomination of desolation" (24:14, 15) suggests that Matthew retains and modifies traditional imagery in order to express his concern about the potential desecration of Christian communities anywhere in the world (that is, the Empire).

Finally, Matthew's redaction of the traditional imagery of the "flight" also suggests this concern. Although 24:15-22 seems to be derived from a Jewish apocalypse with little or no "Christian" content, in Matthew this piece is addressed to the same disciples presented to the readers in 24:3.[2] The eschatological "flight" (φευγέτωσαν) of "those who are in Judea" (24:16) becomes "your flight" in Matthew.[3] Matthew sees

---

[1]Barth, "Matthew's Understanding of the Law," TI, pp. 133, 136-137; cf. Schweizer, Matthew, p. 535; and Hill, Matthew, pp. 360-362.

[2]See Pesch, Naherwartungen, p. 231; and Bultmann, Synoptic Tradition, pp. 402-403.

[3]ἡ φυγὴ ὑμῶν, 24:20 cf. Mark 13:19.

these verses about the βδέλυγμα and the flight as part of the answer to the question with which this discourse began--the question his community (the disciples) has about Jesus' Parousia ("Tell us, when will this be?").[1]

Many interpret the flight of Matt. 24:15-16 by the traditions of either the flight of Mattathias (1 Macc. 2:28) or by the general motif of the "day of the Lord."[2] In light of these traditions, and in view of the fact that "Judea" (Ἰουδαίᾳ) is mentioned in verse 16, some interpret the warning as an allusion to the inhabitants of Judea in general. Other interpreters, however, see in Ἰουδαίᾳ a warning to the Jerusalem Church.[3] Either of these views is possible for

---

[1]Lambrecht, "Parousia Discourse," p. 322 and n. 35.

[2]E.g., Amos 5:18-20 cf. Ezek. 7:16.

[3]For a summary of the views see Beasley-Murray, Commentary on Mark Thirteen, pp. 57-58. Pesch contends that μηδὲ σαββάτῳ (24:20) accords with a warning for the Jerusalem Church (Pesch, "Eschatologie und Ethik," p. 232). However, according to Eusebius (HE 3.5,3) they fled to Pella, not to the hills. Further, if the flight were connected with "the End," as most contend, what meaning would such a flight have? (Bo Reicke, "Synoptic Prophecies on the Destruction of Jerusalem," Studies in New Testament and Early Christian Literature, ed. David E. Aune [Leiden: E. J. Brill, 1972], p. 125).
Others think that the addition means that Matthew's church is still related to the synagogue, while still others contend that the phrase is meaningless to Matthew's community (see Walker, Heilsgeschichte, p. 86). The addition by itself

the pre-Matthean traditions of this warning. However, for the evangelist not only does the warning to flee become a personal one for his readers (ἡ φυγὴ ὑμῶν, 24:20), but there is also the question of does Matthew intend "Judea" to be understood literally?

Pesch, for example, contends that "Judea" is to be understood in a literal sense.[1] However, geographical places often have a symbolic meaning. For example, recent research on "Galilee" in the Gospel of Mark suggests that Galilee has not only a literal and a symbolic meaning, but that it has a theological meaning as well.[2] It is possible, of course, to read too much into this and to see theological connotations which were not really Matthew's. On the other hand, exegesis dare not return to a pre-redactional state and maintain that the only meanings that a geographical name has for an evangelist are the literal or those in the tradition before him. It must always be recognized that the evangelist interprets the tradi-

---

tells nothing about whether Matthew's community is still related to the synagogue. It could mean that his community, which is separate, keeps the sabbath law but not as strictly as the Rabbinate does (Barth, "Matthew's Understanding of the Law," TI, pp. 91-92; and Schweizer, Matthew, p. 452). This suggestion seems most likely, not to mention that it probably recalls the flight of those who were zealous for the law in the days of Mattathias, a flight which is paradigmatic for Matthew.

[1]Pesch, "Eschatologie und Ethik," p. 232.

[2]Marxsen, Mark the Evangelist, pp. 84-92; and Kelber, Kingdom in Mark, p. 139.

tion and "steers it in a certain direction." The
recognition that the evangelist's tradition has
already provided him with an orientation to the
significance of any material will keep interpretation from unnecessary flight into fantasy about
the symbolic or theological meaning of the material.[1]  In other words, the exegete will seek to
discover how the evangelist has interpreted--in
agreement or disagreement--his traditional material by his redaction of it.[2]  In the case of the
warning to the inhabitants of Judea to flee in
Matthew 24:15-16, the tradition which Matthew is
interpreting must be investigated, and, since
verse 16 is tradition and not redaction in the
narrow sense,[3] the context in which Matthew has
placed this material must also be analyzed.

The problem with taking "Judea" literally
in the Matthean context is that verses 15-22 address the same audience (the disciples) as do
verses 4-14, yet verses 15-22 sound so "Jewish" in
comparison with 4-14.  Any reference to the Jews
is avoided in verses 4-14, and the church is depicted as a mission church among the Gentiles.[4]
F. W. Beare, sensing the dilemma, argues that

---

[1]Marxsen, Mark the Evangelist, pp. 93-95;
cf. Kelber, Kingdom in Mark, pp. 45-48.

[2]Marxsen is arguing on the basis of the
secondary and redactional nature of Mark 16:7
(Marxsen, Mark the Evangelist, pp. 84-92) whereas
we are arguing primarily on the basis of the new
context which Matthew has given 24:15.

[3]Cf. Mark 13:14; Luke 21:21.

[4]Lambrecht, "Parousia Discourse,"
pp. 322-323.

Judea "is not to be taken literally, as a geographical expression," but he goes on to conclude
that "The dwellers in 'Judea' of the oracle will
then be Christians who live anywhere in the world
(i.e., in the Roman Empire)."[1] We think that
Beare is essentially correct. We contend, though,
that the clue to Matthew's understanding of this
oracle is in his tradition and in the context of
the oracle in his gospel.

## Βδέλυγμα and ἀνομία in Matthew's tradition

Looking first of all at the tradition, Matthew, as we have seen, points specifically to the
prophet Daniel for the background of the βδέλυγμα
concept. There the βδέλυγμα was the Seleucid
desecration of both the temple and the land of
Judah. There are several elements in that tradition, but Matthew seems to enhance one in parti-
cular--the concept of βδέλυγμα as ἀνομία.

The relation of βδέλυγμα and ἀνομία is already found in the tradition with the prophets.
Broadly speaking, the relation of βδέλυγμα and
ἀνομία seems to have developed from things which
were cultically, and perhaps aesthetically, unclean in the legal parts of the Old Testament. It
ranges to the idols themselves.[2] In the writing
prophets βδέλυγμα becomes a parallel expression to
ἀνομία.[3] Finally, the LXX gives the relation a

---

[1]Beare, "Apocalypse," pp. 127-128.

[2]LXX: Jer. 13:27; 39:35; 51:22; Ezek. 5:9,
11; 6:9.

[3]LXX: Ezek. 11:18; 20:30; Pss. 52:1; 118:163
cf. Jer. 4:1; Pss. 5:7; 13:1; Job 15:16.

new orientation altogther by extending βδέλυγμα
beyond the natural, cultic, and aesthetic connotations to equate it with ἀνομία as an ethical
concept.  In the LXX πᾶν βδέλυγμα becomes an "expression of the dualistic antithesis between the
will of God and that of man,"[1] and it can also
"denote the repugnance of the ungodly to the will
of God (Prv. 29:27; Sir. 1:25; 13:20)."[2]

The relation of βδέλυγμα and ἀνομία is
rarely discussed when considering the tradition
behind Matt. 24:15, but the relation occurs explicitly in Daniel itself.  Daniel's prayer (9:3-
19) is preceded by an allusion to Jeremiah's prediction[3] that the entire land of Judah "shall become a ruin and a waste" (Jer. 25:11) because the
people have not obeyed the words of the Lord
(25:8).  The sanctuary[4] is already "desolate"
(ἔρημον) because all Israel has transgressed the
Law and has sinned against God (9:11).[5]  The

---

[1]Foerster, "βδελύσσομαι," p. 599 cf.
Sirach 15:13-15.

[2]Foerster, "βδελύσσομαι," p. 599.  Foerster,
who traces the development of βδέλυγμα and ἀνομία
says: "The word group βδελυκ- in the LXX is a
regular translation of the word group tʿb. . . .
ἀνομέω and derivatives are used in 24 of these"
(Ibid.).

[3]Dan. 9:2 cf. Jer. 25:8-12.

[4]τὸ ἁγίασμά σου, Dan. 9:17 ϑ'.

[5]The same theme appears in 1 Macc. 1:63-64
where the divine wrath falls upon Israel because
of "lawlessness" (cf. 3:5-6; J. R. Bartlett, The
First and Second Books of the Maccabees [Cam-
bridge: The University Press, 1973], pp. 33, 46;

"desolation"[1] has been brought upon Israel because she has not obeyed God (9:14). Israel's "lawlessness" provides the context for the βδέλυγμα τῶν ἐρημώσεων in 9:27, the verse which is cited as the background for Matt. 24:15 by virtually every interpreter.

The same theme is continued in the context of another passage adduced as a <u>Vorlage</u> for Matthew. Βδέλυγμα ἐρημώσεως occurs in Dan. 11:31, but the point there is that the one who sets up the abomination will lead the lawless ones <u>within</u> the covenant community astray with "flatteries" (11:32).[2] The meaning here seems to be that "The renegades proceeded from technical wickedness to apostasy."[3] Furthermore, in the last Danielic <u>Vorlage</u> (12:11) adduced for Matthew, Daniel is told to seal his book up "until the time of the End"[4] when the "abomination that makes desolate" (βδέλυγμα ἐρημώσεως) is to be set up (12:11 ϑ'). Here the theme of ἀνομία and βδέλυγμα is explicitly stated in the Theodotian text: καί

---

and J. A. Goldstein, <u>I Maccabees</u>, The Anchor Bible, vol. 41 [Garden City, New York: Doubleday, 1976], pp. 228, 245).

[1]Cf. 9:13, τὰ κακά.

[2]Brown-Driver-Briggs, <u>Hebrew Lexicon</u>, p. 325 give baḥᵃlqqôt. Cf. LXX (ϑ'): οἱ ἀνομοῦντες διαθήκην.

[3]Montgomery, <u>Book of Daniel</u>, p. 458; cf. Norman W. Porteous, <u>Daniel</u> (London: SCM Press, Ltd., 1965), p. 168.

[4]ἕως καιροῦ συντελείας, 12:4.

ἀνομήσωσιν ἄνομοι· καὶ οὐ συνήσουσιν πάντες ἄνομοι
(12:10b-c).  The implication is that the last act
in the drama before the desecration occurs is that
those working ἀνομία will persist in it and increase it right up to the End.  Notice here also
the theme of the endurance of the faithful who
know God and who refuse to be led astray by the
ἀνομία and apostasy of the others (12:10 cf. Rev.
12:10).  The same theme occurs in Dan. 11:32b.[1]
Daniel asks for further information about the time
of the End (12:8 cf. 12:4), but all that he is
told is that " . . . the distinction between the
saints who are purified and the wicked who continue in wickedness will be maintained right up
to the end."[2]

## Matthew's redaction of
## βδέλυγμα and ἀνομία

The similarities between the emphases of
ἀνομία, apostasy, and βδέλυγμα in Daniel and Matthew are apparent.  We have seen already that
within the context of our discourse Matthew is
concerned with the danger that his community (the
disciples, 24:3) will be "led astray" by false
prophets.[3]  Matthew's chief concern about this
apostasy is that it is characterized by ἀνομία,
which, for him, means that they are forsaking the
words of Jesus-Sophia himself.  The upshot is that
apostasy is causing the very love which Jesus
commanded to "grow cold" (ψυγήσεται, 24:12).  The

---

[1]Montgomery, Book of Daniel, p. 477.

[2]Porteous, Daniel, p. 172.

[3]βλέπετε μή τις ὑμᾶς πλανήσῃ, 24:4b cf.
24:5, 11, 23-25; 7:15-23.

apostasy will become so bad during the "great tribulation" that even the elect, those who would
be faithful ordinarily to the End, might be led
astray (24:21-26 cf. 24:29). It is quite clear
that Matthew's concern is with apostasy--ἀνομία
and loss of the love Jesus commanded. Schweizer's
comment on 24:22 is instructive:

> The reference to God's merciful shortening
> of the days of affliction is borrowed
> from Mark. The Matthean interpretation
> in verse 13 lends it new weight: the
> most dangerous temptation is the loss
> of love [italics mine]. At this very
> point men must rely on God's mercy to
> see them through.[1]

Our contention, then, is that Matthew's concept of βδέλυγμα in 24:15 is concerned primarily,
as it is in Daniel, with desecration as an upshot
of apostasy--the forsaking of God's law (for
Daniel) as interpreted by Jesus (for Matthew).
Call to mind that for Matthew the holy place at
Jerusalem--indeed all of Israel--was left "forsaken and desolate" (23:38) when Jesus' presence
as Sophia-Shekinah left that sanctuary forever
(24:1). The loss of Jesus' presence was the prelude to the destruction he predicted (24:2). The
temple at Jerusalem for Matthew had become already
desolate and profane because of ἀνομία (cf.
23:28). The Jews had rejected Jesus-Sophia
(23:34-39).

Jesus' presence was now with the Church, not
in all of Israel.[2] Jesus as the Shekinah is
present in Christian communities when Jesus'
words, his interpretation of Torah, are enacted

---

[1]Schweizer, Matthew, p. 453.

[2]Ibid., p. 448.

331

(18:20) and proclaimed (28:20).[1]  But, what if
the same rejection of Jesus-Sophia's commands, in
other words ἀνομία, overtook the Church in general
and Matthew's community in particular?  The implication for the evangelist seems to be that his
community would lose the presence of Jesus just as
Israel had lost it.  Certainly, Jesus had promised
to be with his true followers, his disciples,
until the "consummation of the Age" (28:20 cf.
28:16), but the ἀνομία, which could forfeit the
presence of Jesus, was multiplying so rapidly that
even the endurance of the most faithful to the End
was in question (24:12, 22, 24 cf. 24:13).  The
ἀνομία of Matthew's own community was desecrating
the sanctuary of Jesus just as the "iniquities of
the Fathers" had left Jerusalem and all of Israel
desolate before Antiochus erected the idol itself
(Dan. 9:3-19, 26-27).  In Daniel the upshot of
Israel's own iniquity was the abomination by
Antiochus.

The ἀνομία of Matthew's community, though,
is only part of the βδέλυγμα.[2]  Matthew seems to
expect the same kind of phenomenon within the
Church generally as that related in Daniel.  Part
of the reason for apostasy in the time of world-
wide mission was the increased hatred of "all the
nations" (24:9, 10).  Gentile persecution (θλῖψις)
would help cause "most persons' love to grow
cold" (24:12).  For the evangelist the multipli-
cation of ἀνομία was not just a community phenomenon, but it was a phenomenon associated with the

---

[1]Hill, Matthew, pp. 276-277.

[2]J. Barr, "Daniel," Peake's Commentary on
the Bible, ed. M. Black and H. H. Rowley (London:
Thomas Nelson and Sons, Ltd., 1962), p. 600.

End-time itself.[1]  The hatred of the Gentiles itself would increase until it became so great that
it would threaten the elect.[2]  Thus, two parallel
phenomena--ἀνομία from Christians themselves and
θλῖψις from the outside--threatened the whole
Church and the very pillars of the Matthean community.  The "elect" were being threatened by
intra-community ἀνομία,[3] but this was only an ex-
tension of the rejection of Jesus by the world at
large.  The latter was exhibited by hatred and
persecution of Jesus' messengers (24:9a), and the
former was distinguished by an erroneous view of
Jesus' Parousia (24:5, 23-26).  One could conjec-
ture that Matthew envisioned the apostasy to culminate in an even greater desecration by the
Gentiles.  Perhaps it would be the erection of an
idol just as Antiochus had done, but more likely
Matthew uses Daniel's reference as a "sign" to be
awaited.

Ἐστὸς ἐν τόπῳ ἁγίῳ

Desecration by an idol is suggested not only
by Matthew's explicit allusion to Daniel, but also
by his change of Mark's masculine ἐστηκότα to the
neuter ἐστός (24:15).  Mark's allusion seems to be
to a person.[4]  Matthew does not seem to understand

---

[1]Cf. 2 Thess. 2:3; Rev. 2:4.

[2]θλῖψις μεγάλη, 24:21 cf. 24:22.

[3]24:5, 10-12, 23-25.

[4]See Bl-D §134(3).  Some have conjectured
that Mark's reference is to the attempt of Gaius
to erect his image in the temple in C.E. 40
(Dodd, "Fall of Jerusalem and the 'Abomination of
Desolation,'" p. 81) while others have said that
it alludes to an AntiChrist figure such as the

Mark's personal allusion, and he probably edits ἐστηκότα out to accord better with the Jewish understanding, and with the text of Daniel in particular, of the idol erected by Antiochus.[1] To put it succinctly, it appears that the desecration by Antiochus is functioning as a prototype for Matthew by which he envisions a new desecration of a new "holy place," the sanctuaries of Jesus-Sophia.[2] The apostasy of Israel and the desecration of Antiochus have become a symbol for Matthew of the holy place "forsaken and desolate" (23:38). The desecration is a "sign" for which all can watch.[3] As the desecration happened then, so it will happen again.

We dare not push this too far and contend that Matthew expects a new Antiochus and that the Church communities become the new Maccabees,[4] but the flight, which seems to recall the flight of Mattathias, does become a personal one for the readers.[5] The alternative to reading "Judea"

---

the one depicted in 2 Thess. 2 (e.g., Rigaux, "ΒΔΕΛΥΓΜΑ ΤΗΣ ΕΡΗΜΩΣΕΩΣ," pp. 679-680). Ἐστός could be a gloss. However, that contention is supported only by Sy$^S$ and one minuscule (1010).

[1]Marxsen, Mark the Evangelist, p, 181; cf. Stendahl, School, pp. 79-80.

[2]Dodd, "The Fall of Jerusalem and the 'Abomination of Desolation,'" p. 82.

[3]Marxsen, Mark the Evangelist, p. 203.

[4]Cf. Dodd, "The Fall of Jerusalem and the 'Abomination of Desolation,'" p. 82.

[5]ἡ φυγὴ ὑμῶν, 24:20. It is interesting to note that Mattathias' flight was made not only

literally is to contend that the flight to the Judean hills most likely recalls the flight of the Judean rebels. But surely Matthew's readers are not bidden to "understand" that as followers of Jesus they should become armed guerilla warriors and escape as such. The nature of Mattathias' flight, namely, of how the State could force apostasy and flight, speaks to the nature of the pressure Matthew's church and the Church in general could face. The evangelist retains the cryptic setting in Judea only as part of the imagery which is necessary to grasp the nature of the situation.[1]

    <u>In the Matthean context</u>, then, the "dwellers in Judea" are members of the Church at large and of Matthew's own community who are being warned that apostasy will increase side by side with Gentile persecution until both intersect in τὸ βδέλυγμα τῆς ἐρημώσεως, the essence of which can be seen in Antiochus' desecration of long ago. When that happens, then the flight of the dwellers in Judea becomes "your flight," and the "Law" for which they are to be zealous consists of the words and deeds of Jesus-Sophia, the essence of which is the love commandment (cf. 1 Macc. 2:27-28).

    Succinctly, the evangelist's chief understanding of the βδέλυγμα concept is in its relation with ἀνομία. Ἀνομία within his community

---

because he killed a Jewish apostate and an officer (1 Macc. 2:23-25), but he fled also out of zeal for the Law and seemingly out of a desire to keep a remnant community from becoming apostate (1 Macc. 2:27-28 cf. 2:50, 64, 68; 1:48-50, 52-53). See Bartlett, <u>First and Second Books of the Maccabees</u>, pp. 42-45.

    [1]Beare, "Apocalypse," pp. 127-128.

is already leading to apostasy. 'Ανομία from
without, reflected in rejection and persecution of
his community's prophets, is also a cause of apostasy. Matthew expects ἀνομία on both fronts to
increase until his community's worship, and that
of the Church generally, is desecrated totally by
the Gentiles themselves. This desecration could
be an idol, as his use of ἑστός suggests, or it
could be a generalized "sign."[1] The only hint
which Matthew gives us about his meaning of
βδέλυγμα is from the context: he is concerned
about the ἀνομία, the apostasy, and the tribulation which threaten to destroy the community of
Jesus. What contemporary political situation, if
any, sparked these fears cannot be ascertained
from this passage alone. However, as Beare points
out, for Matthew to entertain such fears about the
Church " . . . it is not necessary that they
should be justified by anything on the contemporary political horizon. The Book of Daniel provided all the justification that was needed."[2]
It seems that we must conclude that ἐν τόπῳ ἁγίῳ
is a veiled allusion to the Church, including
Matthew's community, and that in it the "abomination of desolation" characterized by ἀνομία and
θλῖψις will be manifested in a form which only
his readers would understand.[3]

Let us summarize. In seeking to determine
the meaning of βδέλυγμα for Matthew we have tried
to stay only within the Matthean literary context.
This procedure, as expected, yielded only the
exegetical minimum. The minimum, though, consists

---

[1]Ibid.    [2]Ibid.

[3]ὁ ἀναγινώσκων νοείτω, 24:15.  Bonnard,
L'Évangile selon Saint Matthieu, p. 351.

of several conclusions which are pertinent for determining the function of the eschatological discourse in this gospel. (1) Matthew is using the Danielic tradition of the βδέλυγμα. (2) The βδέλυγμα in Daniel and in Matthew primarily emphasizes a desecration of a sanctuary, not its destruction. (3) The evangelist uses the Danielic text apocalyptically. For him the prediction of the βδέλυγμα in Daniel is prophecy to be fulfilled in the evangelist's own time. (4) The βδέλυγμα for Matthew is primarily associated with ἀνομία. The relation of ἀνομία and βδέλυγμα is probably suggested to him by their relation in Daniel. (5) Ἀνομία in the First Gospel involves the forsaking of the commandments of Jesus-Sophia by those within his community (and the Church at large). Total rejection of Jesus' commandments could lead to the consequent loss of Jesus-Sophia's presence just as it did for the Jews (24:1). Ἀνομία also alludes to the Gentile rejection of the "gospel of the kingdom." (6) Matthew expects the ἀνομία on both fronts to increase until it issues in the wholesale desecration of the Church at large. (7) Matthew's apocalyptic style brings his readers up to the time of his writing. The sanctuary of Israel was left desolate in Jesus' time because the Jews rejected him. Jesus' presence has forsaken the temple (23:38; 24:1-2). For the evangelist it is still desolate in his time because of Israel's rejection of the Gospel (cf. 10:17-21). Matthew's church has already begun a mission to the Gentiles which is also meeting with rejection (24:9). Coupled with that, antinomians within the community are already leading many astray.[1] Matthew's apocalyptic survey brings his readers up to the present, and they understand the situation which he describes as

---

[1]See Lambrecht's discussion, "Parousia Discourse," p. 323.

their situation. (8) Matthew then tells them that
the upshot of their present situation will be the
βδέλυγμα τῆς ἐρημώσεως, which his readers will
recognize when they see it. (9) When they do see
the obvious βδέλυγμα, then they, like the inhabitants of Judea long ago, are to flee. (10) The
intensity of the βδέλυγμα will be so great (24:21)
that antinomian activity will be enhanced (24:23-
26). (11) However, they have been warned before-
hand (24:25) that the βδέλυγμα is not the End (cf.
24:29) and that Jesus' Parousia, which will usher
in the consummation of the age, will be evident to
all (24:27-28). (12) This section (24:15-28),
then, directly takes up again the disciples' question from verse 3. It describes the climax of
apostasy and tribulation immediately before the
Parousia of Jesus as the Son of Man.[1] The Parousia itself becomes the explicit subject of the
subsequent section.

## Part 6. The Testament of
## Jesus-Sophia: The Sign of
## the Son of Man

Matthew moves immediately to the Parousia
of the Son of Man which he says follows εὐθέως δὲ
μετὰ τὴν θλῖψιν τῶν ἡμερῶν ἐκείνων (v. 29), that
is, the θλῖψις μεγάλη just described in verses
15-25.[2] Matthew follows Mark in alluding to the

---

[1]Cf. Pesch' discussion, "Eschatologie und
Ethik," p. 233.

[2] The θλῖψις of 24:15-25 is, as we have
said, the culmination of that in 24:9-14. Εὐθέως
is surely due to Matthean redaction. Εὐθέως is a
favorite Markan word (ca. 41 times) which Matthew
consistently edits out (Allen, St. Matthew, pp.
xix-xx). It is clear that Matthew understands
the θλῖψις of 24:15-25 to be that just preceding

cosmic upheaval which will precede the Parousia,[1]
but it is recognized generally that Matthew develops Mark 13:24-27 by two significant additions.
First, to Mark 13:26 the evangelist adds φανήσεται
τὸ σημεῖον τοῦ υἱοῦ τοῦ ἀνθρώπου ἐν οὐρανῷ,[2] καὶ
τότε κόψονται πᾶσαι αἱ φυλαὶ τῆς γῆς (24:30).
Matthew then adds μετὰ σάλπιγγος μεγάλης to Mark
13:27. These two additions form the <u>crux inter-
pretum</u> for these verses, and should be considered
together.[3] The first question is: what does the

---

the Parousia by his use of τῶν ἡμερῶν ἐκείνων. As
Kingsbury has shown, this is a Matthean phrase
which "denotes the time that precedes the Parousia
and the Final Judgment" (Kingsbury, <u>Structure</u>, p.
139; cf. also Matt. 24:22: αἱ ἡμέραι ἐκεῖναι with
Mark 13:20: τὰς ἡμέρας).

[1]Cf. Isa. 13:9-10; 34:4.

[2]Butler, who argues for the priority of
Matthew, contends that Mark has deleted this
material (B. C. Butler, <u>The Originality of St.
Matthew</u> [Cambridge: The University Press, 1951],
p. 78). As we shall see, the consensus of
interpreters is that Matthew has developed Mark
13:26, not vice versa.

[3]T. Francis Glasson, <u>The Second Advent. The
Origin of the New Testament Doctrine</u> (London: The
Epworth Press, 1942), p. 189; cf. Hill, <u>Matthew</u>,
p. 322; Schweizer, <u>Matthew</u>, pp. 455-457; and
Beare, "Apocalypse," pp. 129-130.
The history of tradition for these verses is
extremely complicated and has been discussed extensively. Some would argue that this Son of Man
saying stems ultimately from Jesus himself (e.g.,
Beasley-Murray, <u>Jesus and the Future</u>, pp. 172-250;
and Frederick H. Borsch, <u>The Son of Man in Myth
and History</u> [Philadelphia: Westminster Press,

339

"sign" mean for Matthew?[1]

1967], p. 360 [hereafter cited as Borsch, Son of
Man]). Others are hesitant to attempt to trace
the origin of this saying to Jesus, yet they will
not totally disregard that possibility. They
simply conclude that the saying clouds any understanding of the Son of Man which Jesus might have
had (e.g., Taylor, St. Mark, pp. 643-644; Morna D.
Hooker, The Son of Man in Mark [London: SPCK,
1967], p. 157; and K. H. Rengstorf, "σημεῖον,"
TDNT 7: 237 n. 264). Still others see the origin
of this saying in a setting of Jewish apocalyptic
which has undergone Christian editing (e.g.,
Manson, Sayings, p. 242; Bultmann, History of the
Synoptic Tradition, pp. 402-403 and the literature
cited there; Kümmel, Promise and Fulfillment, pp.
97-98; and H. E. Tödt, The Son of Man in the
Synoptic Tradition, trans. D. M. Barton [Phila-
delphia: Westminster Press, 1965], p. 36 [cited
hereafter as Tödt, Son of Man]). Perrin has
carried this argument one step further and argues,
correctly in our opinion, that this Son of Man
saying is the product of Christian exegetical
traditions (Perrin, Rediscovering the Teaching of
of Jesus, p. 183; and Norman Perrin, "The Son of
Man in Ancient Judaism and Primitive Christianity:
A Suggestion," A Modern Pilgrimage in New Testament Christology [Philadelphia: Fortress Press,
1974], pp. 23-40).
    The important point to note for our purposes
is that although Matthew is drawing out of a
common fund of Christian exegetical traditions
(cf. Rev. 1:7; John 1:51; Luke 21:27), our major
task is not so much to pinpoint Matt. 24:30 on the
pesherim continuum as it is to interpret this
verse within its immediate Matthean context.

    [1]The "sign of the Son of Man" has received
four basic interpretations. (1) The oldest in-

340

## The Sign of the Son of Man

First, Matt. 24:30 directly answers the
question of the disciples in 24:3: τί τὸ σημεῖον
τῆς σῆς παρουσίας καὶ συντελείας τοῦ αἰῶνος; This
means that τὸ σημεῖον of 24:30 is brought into
relation with 24:3, not with 12:39-40. The key to
the interpretation of τὸ σημεῖον in 24:30 is
within the immediate context of the eschatological
discourse itself.[1] Several redactional factors

---

terpretation, perhaps, is that the "sign" is the
cross which was taken up into heaven at the Ascension. It was believed that the cross would reappear in the sky at Jesus' Parousia (cf. Gospel
of Peter 10:39; Didache 16:6; Epistula Apostolorum
16:6). A. B. J. Higgins has put forth a vigorous
argument that the sign is the cross (Higgins,
Jesus and the Son of Man [Philadelphia: Fortress
Press, 1964], pp. 108-114; cf. A. B. J. Higgins,
"The Sign of the Son of Man [Matt. xxiv.30]," NTS
9 [1963]: 380-382). Or, (2) the sign is the Son
of Man himself. This interpretation is based upon
a formal correspondence between "the sign of
Jonah" (Matt. 12:39) and the "sign of the Son of
Man" (24:30; see Bultmann, History of the Synoptic
Tradition, p. 118; and Tödt, Son of Man, p. 153).
(3) The sign is the ensign of the Messiah to be
exhibited when he comes to establish God's kingdom
(see T. F. Glasson, "The Ensign of the Son of Man
[Matt. XXIV.30]," JThS 15 [1964]: 299-300; and
Schweizer, Matthew, p. 456). (4) No one knows
what the "sign" will be (perhaps even Matthew),
only that it will be a certainty at the time of
its appearance (e.g., Fenton, St. Matthew, p. 389;
and Borsch, Son of Man, p. 361 n. 3).

[1]Fenton, St. Matthew, p. 389; and Higgins,
Jesus and the Son of Man, p. 109.

point to this conclusion. The first is that in 24:3 the disciples clearly ask Jesus about <u>his</u> Parousia (τῆς σῆς παρουσίας). In 24:27 Matthew has ἡ παρουσία τοῦ υἱοῦ τοῦ ἀνθρώπου while Luke seems to preserve the earlier reading of ὁ υἱὸς τοῦ ἀνθρώπου ἐν τῇ ἡμέρᾳ αὐτοῦ.[1] This change makes it clear that "To Matthew and his readers 'Son of man' is another name for Jesus."[2] It means also that the "sign" of the Son of Man in 24:30 is a direct reference to the Parousia <u>of Jesus</u> as the Son of Man, which was the precise focus of the disciples' question in 24:3. As L. Cope concludes: "The center of attention through-out the discourse [that is, chapters 24-25] is the future 'return of Jesus and the end of the age' (xxiv.3)."[3]

Secondly, Matthew uses Zech. 12:10 and Dan. 7:13 in this saying.[4] Matthew, in comparison with other New Testament writers, does three interest-ing things with these texts. (1) He omits any

---

[1]Cf. Perrin's remark: "The explicit parousia reference in the 'coming of the Son of man', is certainly Matthaean, which makes 'the Son of man in his day' the more original of the two" (Perrin, <u>Rediscovering the Teaching of Jesus</u>, p. 196).

[2]Higgins, <u>Jesus and the Son of Man</u>, p. 109; cf. L. Cope, "Matthew XXV:31-46 'The Sheep and the Goats' Reinterpreted," p. 43.

[3]Ibid., p. 33.

[4]Gundry, <u>Use of the Old Testament in St. Matthew's Gospel</u>, pp. 53-54; Tödt, <u>Son of Man</u>, pp. 33-34; and Hooker, <u>Son of Man in Mark</u>, p. 158. Contrast Borsch, <u>Son of Man</u>, p. 362 n. 2.

reference to "piercing" (cf. Zech. 12:10). It
seems that the evangelist does not want the primary reference to be to the Passion of Jesus as,
for example, does John 19:37.[1]  (2) He omits ἐπ'
αὐτόν from Zech. 12:10 (LXX). Both John 19:37
and Rev. 1:7 include this detail, which seems to
have been part of early Christian Passion apologetic.  In Rev. 1:7 it seems to be implied clearly
that the moment of vindication for the crucified
Son of Man is his Parousia, that is, when those
who rejected him will see his wounds and mourn.
Matthew, however, does not enhance the traditional
motif.  Any Passion apologetic is subordinated to
his interest in Jesus' Parousia.[2]  (3) When compared to Rev. 1:7, Matt. 24:30 uses Dan. 7:13 and
Zech. 12:10 in reverse order.  This use of these
texts, along with the two redactional uses already
mentioned, shows two things.  It shows, first of
all, that Matthew is independently adapting these
Old Testament texts to his apocalyptic framework.
"This all," to use Rengstorf's words, "amounts to
the fact that in Mt 24:30 . . . the Evangelist is
using traditional material to make his own
point."[3]  It also shows that Matthew has adapted

---

[1]Higgins, Jesus and the Son of Man, p. 381.

[2]Barnabas Lindars, New Testament Apologetic
(Philadelphia: Westminster Press, 1961), p. 126
cf. p. 125.  It must be kept in mind that the
meaning of apocalyptic writings cannot be pressed
too far since they employ great literary freedom
(cf. Stendahl, School, pp. 213-214).  Even
granted that caveat, it is still clear that Matthew does not use Zech. 12:10 as a basis for a
Passion apologetic in Matt. 24:30.

[3]Rengstorf, "σημεῖον," p. 237; cf. Tödt,
Son of Man, p. 80 n. 2.

the traditional material for the express purpose
of introducing another element (whether it is a
fixed traditional phrase or his own), namely, τὸ
σημεῖον τοῦ υἱοῦ τοῦ ἀνθρώπου.[1] To pick up our
primary point, we maintain that the evangelist has
adapted the traditional material in order to bring
it directly into line with his redactional question in 24:3. It is our conclusion that Matt.
24:30 directly answers the disciples' question in
24:3.

Matthew's interest seems to be primarily in
the sign and its function as opposed to the person
of the Son of Man.[2] The context of the whole discourse makes it clear that the problem Matthew's
church has is a false understanding of the Parousia. The community understands that Jesus is the
Son of Man, but it does not understand Jesus'
Parousia as the Son of Man. The community is
being led astray by false prophets who perform all
kinds of signs supposedly related to his Parousia.[3] What Matthew wants his community to understand is that "the παρουσία will not come directly

---

[1]Rengstorf, "σημεῖον," p. 237.

[2]Cf. Rengstorf's remark: " . . . the reference is less to the person of the Son of Man
than to His apocalyptic function" (Ibid). This is
shown in the deletion of ἐπ' αὐτόν from Zech.
12:10, if indeed that is Matthew's hand at work
(cf. Rev. 1:7). The tribes mourn at the appearance of the sign, not at the Son of Man; when he
appears, it will be too late for mourning (particularly if one takes κόψονται as connoting conversion) because he comes in judgment (Higgins,
"The Sign of the Son of Man," p. 381).

[3]Cf. Matt. 24:4, 5, 10-12, 13, 14c, 23-25,
26-27.

but will announce itself first" by a sign which will be clear to everyone (24:27); no doubt at all will be possible about the Parousia when it occurs.[1] The "sign" will be clearly of a different character than the other cosmic and natural signs of the End-time (24:29 cf. 24:6-7) because this sign is linked directly to the Parousia itself. This still does not identify the sign, and it should not be assumed too quickly that Matthew's community understood what the sign would be either. All that can be assumed is that the community believed it would be a clear, cosmic sign.[2]

But Matthew's interest is not only in the appearance of the sign, he is more interested, perhaps, in the fact that "seeing" the sign would lead to understanding about Jesus as the Son of Man and about one's relationship to him. Glasson contends that the sign would signal salvation for "all the tribes of the earth." He argues that σάλπιγγος (v. 31) is the crucial element in this text, and that it should be construed with σημεῖον. The translation of σημεῖον, when used with σάλπιγγος, should be the "standard" (nēs) of the Messiah. He points out that the "standard" and the "trumpet" frequently occur together[3] and usually imply the eschatological gathering of God's people.[4] One of the difficulties with

---

[1]Rengstorf, "σημεῖον," p. 237; cf. Hill, Matthew, p. 322.

[2]Matthew's use of φανήσεται (passive) almost suggests that the sign is "veiled" until the appropriate time for its disclosure (Allen, St. Matthew, p. 258).

[3]Cf. Isa. 18:3; Jer. 4:21; 6:1; 51:27.

[4]Isa. 11:12; 27:13; 49:22; Glasson, "Ensign

345

Glasson's view is that nowhere in the New Testament does σημεῖον mean "standard."  E. Schweizer, who follows Glasson's argument, connects Matthew's "great trumpet" call with 1 Thess. 4:16.[1]  However, if the trumpet in Matt. 24:31 has a meaning similar to that of 1 Thessalonians, it is surely strange that he does not mention a resurrection (cf. 1 Thess. 4:16), nor a physical transformation of any kind (cf. 1 Cor. 15:52), and nothing is said about a gathering place for the elect (cf. 1 Thess. 4:17).[2]  The "great trumpet" of verse 31 seems to be pro forma apocalyptic imagery which Matthew has utilized from the general stock in order to signal the Parousia of Jesus.[3]  The "sign" should be connected in its immediate context with the mourning of the tribes rather than with the trumpet.[4]  The great trumpet in verse 31, if not used as a convention only, is related to the gathering of the elect for salvation rather than with the tribes of the earth.[5]  This connection would mean for Matthew that it is only at Jesus' Parousia that all of those who have rejected Jesus--Israel, the Gentiles, and members of Matthew's own community--will really recognize

---

of the Son of Man," pp. 299-300.

[1]Schweizer, Matthew, p. 455 cf. p. 456.

[2]M'Neile, St. Matthew, p. 353; and Stendahl, "Matthew," p. 692.

[3]Cf. 1 Cor. 15:52; 1 Thess. 4:16; Psa. Sol. 11:1-3; 2 Esd. 6:23.  Beare, "Apocalypse," p. 130; and Caird, Revelation of St. John, p. 107.

[4]Cf. 2 Esd. 6:23.  Higgins, Jesus and the Son of Man, p. 114 n. 1.

[5]Hill, Matthew, p. 323.

Jesus and understand their situation.[1]  Jesus'
statement to the Jews in the transition pericope
to this discourse (23:37-39) is balanced beautifully by the statement at the end of the discourse
(24:30-31).  The solemn statement to the Jews in
23:39 is programmatic for all who reject Jesus:
λέγω γὰρ ὑμῖν, οὐ μή με ἴδητε ἀπ' ἄρτι ἕως ἂν
εἴπητε· εὐλογημένος ὁ ἐρχόμενος ἐν ὀνόματι κυρίου.
They will ὄψονται τὸν υἱὸν τοῦ ἀνθρώπου ἐρχόμενον
ἐπὶ τῶν νεφελῶν . . . μετὰ δυνάμεως καὶ δόξης
πολλῆς (24:30).  The "sign," though, will make it
clear to them that it is Jesus-Sophia, whom they
have rejected,  who is coming as the glorious Son
of Man, and that he is coming to them in judgment
(καὶ τότε κόψονται πᾶσαι αἱ φυλαὶ τῆς γῆς).[2]

---

[1]Note the element of surprise in Matthew's
judgment scene (25:31-46).  It is only after the
Parousia that either group--righteous or un-
righteous--recognize their true status before
Jesus as the Son of Man.

[2]L. Cope says, e.g., that: "The Son of Man
divides the . . . nations on the basis of their
reception or rejection of Him through his agents,
the disciples" (Cope, "Matthew XXV: 31-46 'The
Sheep and the Goats' Reinterpreted," p. 43).
    The expression κόψονται πᾶσαι αἱ φυλαὶ τῆς
γῆς in its original context (Zech. 12:10-12) means
that the Jews will mourn in repentance.  However,
in view of Matthew's judgment scene, which includes πάντα τὰ ἔθνη (25:32), and in light of the
contrast here between αἱ φυλαὶ τῆς γῆς and τοὺς
ἐκλεκτοὺς αὐτοῦ (24:31), Manson is surely correct
when he states that the "original sense [of Zech.
12:10-12] has been abandoned; and the text of
Mt., as it stands, shows the standpoint of . . .
prophecies of woe for the Gentile nations"
(Manson, Sayings, p. 242; contrast Fenton, St.
Matthew, p. 389).  The mourning here is one of

On the other hand, just as Jesus turned
away from the Jews and toward his true followers
(the disciples) in 24:1, so at the sign of his
coming his followers will understand that the time
of their salvation has come.1

For Matthew, what was true in a limited way
of Jesus' "historical" ministry in Palestine will
be true in a universal sense at the Parousia.
Jesus' ministry through the witness of the Church,
ἐν ὅλῃ τῇ οἰκουμένῃ . . . πᾶσιν τοῖς ἔθνεσιν, will
precede the End (καὶ τότε ἥξει τὸ τέλος, 24:14),
that is, the Parousia, at which time Jesus-Sophia
as the Son of Man (25:31) will judge πάντα τὰ ἔθνη

---

judgment and it includes Matthew's church (cf.
Kingsbury, Structure, pp. 144, 158, 164).  It
means that all who have rejected the "gospel of
the kingdom" proclaimed by Jesus' disciples
(24:14) or by Jesus (cf. 4:17; 9:35) will have no
hope of repentance when the sign appears (Tödt,
Son of Man, pp. 81-82; Higgins, Jesus and the Son
of Man, p. 114; Lindars, New Testament Apologetic,
pp. 123-126; and Schweizer, Matthew, pp. 456-457).

1ἀποστελεῖ τοὺς ἀγγέλους αὐτοῦ . . . τοὺς
ἐκλεκτοὺς αὐτοῦ, v. 31 cf. 19:28.  The addition
of τοὺς ἀγγέλους αὐτοῦ in this context, as opposed
to 13:41, is to "gather all that is good"
(M'Neile, St. Matthew, p. 353; cf. Kingsbury,
Parables of Jesus in Matthew 13, p. 68).  The
addition of αὐτοῦ also shows that it is Jesus as
the Son of Man who is gathering his elect (Kingsbury, Structure, p. 120).  The picture implies
that the "kingdom of the Son of Man" is ultimately
cosmic in scope (Ibid., pp. 120-121, 147).  Matthew's alteration of Mark's ἐκ τῶν τεσσάρων
ἀνέμων ἀπ' ἄκρου γῆς, etc. to ἐκ τῶν . . . ἄκρων
οὐρανῶν ἕως τῶν ἄκρων αὐτῶν (24:31) could also
suggest this.

348

(25:32).[1]  At the appearance of the sign, all will
understand that Jesus is the Son of Man and Judge,
and the further implication is that in some sense
they will understand whether their destiny is the
"right hand" or the "left" (25:33).[2]  "Historically" speaking, Matthew has Jesus-Sophia deliver
this discourse while he "sits" (καθημένου) upon
the Mount of Olives (24:3a), but the same Jesus
who sits there will "sit (καθίσει) on his glorious
throne" at the time of his coming (25:31).[3]  For
his disciples the words of Jesus-Sophia here are
words of comfort and hope, yet, at the same time,
they reveal to the disciples, since they are the
only audience here, that his coming will also mean
distress and judgment for most groups.[4]  It has a
note of warning, though, for Matthew's community:
Jesus' coming will be also the time of the separation of the "wheat from the tares" in the Church.[5]
Matthew seeks to show his community that the
future harvest is continuous with what is sown in

---

[1]Cope, "Matthew XXV: 31-46 'The Sheep and
the Goats' Reinterpreted," p. 43.

[2]This seems to be true even if there is an
element of "surprise" in Matthew's judgment scene.
The judgment takes place when the Son of Man
comes (25:31).

[3]The Matthean addition of his angels (24:31)
underlines Jesus' sovereignty (Tödt, Son of Man,
p. 82).

[4]Cope, "Matthew XXV: 31-46 'The Sheep and
the Goats' Reinterpreted," p. 33; cf. Stendahl,
"Matthew," p. 692.

[5]13:36-43.  Bornkamm, "End-Expectation and
Church in Matthew," TI, p. 43.

the community in the present.[1]

In summary, the "sign of the Son of Man" is distinct from the Son of Man himself. The "sign" announces the coming of Jesus-Sophia as Son of Man. The order of events in verses 29-31 seems to be: cosmic disturbances (v. 29), the manifestation of the "sign of the Son of Man" in heaven, the mourning of all the tribes, then the coming of the Son of Man (v. 30) and the gathering of the elect (v. 31).[2] The sign cannot be identified from our standpoint, but its significance for Matthew is that it clearly announces the End of this epoch and ushers in the judgment.[3] At the appearance of the sign persons will know who Jesus-Sophia really is--the glorious Son of Man and Judge--and the status of their relationship with him.[4] The "sign

---

[1]Kingsbury, Structure, p. 144 cf. pp. 158-159.

[2]Higgins, "The Sign of the Son of Man," p. 381. This is indicated by Matthew's καὶ τότε . . . καὶ τότε . . . καὶ by which he has structured v. 30 (Rengstorf, "σημεῖον," p. 237; and Higgins, Jesus and the Son of Man, p. 109).

[3]Rengstorf, "σημεῖον," pp. 236-237.

[4]Probably the sign for Matthew would be literally seen in the heavens. But, even granted this, the significance of the sign is not just its appearance but the understanding which it brings. The literal and figurative meanings of ὄψονται come into play here, and an artificial distinction cannot be made between them.
It is true that Matthew uses a different word for "see" than does Dan. 7:13 (ἐθεώρουν), but this is probably due to a pesher wordplay (κόψονται-ὄψονται). (See Perrin, Rediscovering

350

of the Son of Man" clearly concludes Jesus-
Sophia's answer to the question of the disciples
in 24:3; they now know what to expect right up to
the "consummation of the age." The function of
such teaching from Jesus-Sophia for Matthew's
community clearly has the double aspects of warning and hope. It is the warning of judgment and
the hope that they will be among the gathered
elect.[1] In these words Matthew's community has a
"testament" from Jesus-Sophia which should protect
them from the confusion of signs offered by the
false prophets within the community. It should
also keep them from ἀνομία and loss of love
(24:10-12).[2] "On the one hand," says Schweizer,
"Matthew is warning against the false prophets who
state that Christ has already come; on the other,
he is strenghtening men's hope that the coming

---

the Teaching of Jesus, p. 182; and Schweizer,
Matthew, pp. 456-457.)
    On the other hand, the significance of ὁράω,
which is regularly associated with the Parousia
and future events, cannot be reduced either to a
mere word-play or to only an inner spiritual
vision (cf. Donahue's discussion with Perrin's.
See Donahue, Are You the Christ?, pp. 93, 94 and
n. 1. See also F. Hahn, The Titles of Jesus in
Christology, trans. Harold Knight [New York:
World, 1969], pp. 163-164).
    To put it succinctly, both the literal and
the revelational aspects of ὄψονται should be kept
in mind in this passage, but it would be difficult
to deny that the latter aspect is the more significant in Matthew (Michaelis, "ὁράω," TDNT 5:361).

[1]Beare, "Apocalypse," pp. 120-130; cf. Tödt,
Son of Man, p. 34; Manson, Sayings, p. 241; and
Kingsbury, Structure, pp. 145-146.

[2]Stendahl, "Matthew," p. 692.

351

will be soon."[1]  This is the testamental function
of the eschatological revelation which has been
passed down to Matthew's community (the disciples)
from Jesus-Sophia.

## Conclusion

In this chapter we have seen that although
the eschatological discourse in Matthew shares
characteristics with both the apocalypse and the
farewell discourse, the position in which Matthew
has placed this discourse causes it to function
primarily as a testament within the gospel.  He
has deleted the story of the Widow's penny (cf.
Mark 13:41-44) in order to position the eschatological discourse just after Jesus' definitive
departure from the temple and the allusion in
23:39 to his final departure from his historical
ministry.  The evangelist redacts the introduction
(24:3) in such a way that the discourse becomes a
private revelation of Jesus-Sophia to his successors of what is to occur before his return as Son
of Man.  The revelation does not deal with the destruction of the temple (24:2), but with the
events which will precede the appearance of the
sign which will herald the Parousia of Jesus as
the Son of Man.  The question about the sign in
24:3 is answered definitively in 24:30-31, and
these verses form the brackets for the testament
per se.  Matthew's expansion of Mark in 24:32-
25:46 seems to form a unified section of seven
Parousia parables.  They reinforce parenetically
the injunctions given in 24:3-31.  However, it
must be noted that the debate over the extent of
the discourse makes it clear that one could extend the testament through 25:46.  If one chooses
that option, though, it is still clear that verses

---

[1]Schweizer, _Matthew_, p. 455.

3-31 constitute a major independent unit within the discourse.

One major concern of the discourse is with false prophets. They are Christians and seem to be intracommunity figures for Matthew. Their message is an enthusiastic one which says that Jesus' Parousia has already occurred. They seem to believe that he is present totally in them and through their works. The effect of their activity is "lawlessness" (ἀνομία), that is, a forsaking of Jesus' interpretation of the Law by the love command. The warning in the discourse is that Jesus as the Son of Man has not yet appeared (24:6). Thus, one must not be led astray from obedience to the Word of Jesus-Sophia, and all disciples must continue to love each other.

Obedience to Jesus-Sophia also means endurance in the world-wide preaching mission (24:9-14). The disciples of Matthew's community are to preach and to live the "gospel of the kingdom" as proclaimed and lived by Jesus. In essence, they are to proclaim the life of love as the higher righteousness. The higher righteousness was fulfilled in Jesus' life, and is demanded of all his true followers. As a result of their proclamation (διὰ τὸ ὄνομά μου), the disciples will encounter the hatred of "all the nations" (24:9). The disciple will be saved, though, if he/she endures in proclaiming the gospel in word and deed until the End (24:13). The evangelist is conscious that the Church still lives in the "time of Jesus" and that his presence with them will help them endure until his Parousia (28:20).

The time of world-wide proclamation, that is, between Jesus' resurrection and his Parousia, will be one of "great tribulation" for the disciples (24:21). The "great tribulation" will be initiated by the "desolating sacrilege" (24:15).

353

Matthew interprets Daniel (LXX) apocalyptically to indicate that this phrase in his gospel denotes an impending desecration of the entire Church. The evangelist uses the traditional imagery from Daniel and Mark of the temple's desecration in order to show that the Church's desecration will be similar in nature to that prior event, that is, the desecration of Antiochus IV. The "abomination" which will stand in "a holy place" thus becomes a "sign" for Matthew's readers. Although the sign itself is too cryptic for us to identify, Matthew intends his readers to understand that the nature of the "abomination" (βδέλυγμα) is "lawlessness" (ἀνομία), that is, the forsaking of God's Law as interpreted by Jesus. The lawlessness will increase to the point where even the elect will be in danger of apostasy. The "desolating sacrilege" of "a holy place" thus becomes a disguised allusion to the Church, and functions as a sign for which Matthew's readers can watch.

The sign of the Son of Man will appear immediately after the great tribulation which is initiated by the desolating sacrilege. The sign will clearly announce the Parousia of Jesus so that no doubt at all will be possible about his advent. The disciples, while awaiting the sign, should not be led astray by signs and wonders performed by the false prophets. The function of the sign is to announce the Parousia, but it will also clarify one's relation to Jesus. The sign will clarify that the Jesus who is returning as glorified Son of Man is the same Jesus who was accepted or rejected as Sophia.

We have not yet shown how the eschatological discourse is related to the gospel as a whole. We would like to suggest the significance of our interpretation for understanding Matthew's christology and discipleship. This discussion will be the focus of the final chapter.

## Excursus: the End-Time
## Scenario in Matthew

We are now in a position to summarize the scenario of events which lead up to the Parousia according to Matthew's eschatological discourse. As we have seen, in 24:3 the evangelist redacts the disciples' question in order to relate it topically to the Parousia rather than to the destruction of the temple. There is little question that Matthew offers a Parousia discourse which leads step by step topically to that event, but in his organization of the material he has also created what appears to be a temporal sequence for the signs to precede the Parousia.[1] Kingsbury has shown that it is characteristic of Matthean redaction to combine temporal expressions with traditional material in order to give movement to the text. He has also suggested that Matthew's temporal expressions can indicate an eschatological period of time.[2] The evangelist's redactional arrangement of the testament in this way is apparent.

First, there is the traditional material which warns about the beginning of sufferings:

---

[1]Marxsen, Mark the Evangelist, pp. 203-204.

[2]Kingsbury, Structure, pp. 27-31. It is not entirely clear whether Matthew's "temporal" expressions mean chronological sequence as we ordinarily think of it, or whether it is some kind of "eschatological" reckoning of time in terms of "epochs," however long, within salvation-history. It is most likely the latter, but, as we shall see, Matthew does give the epochs a temporal, or better, a sequential order by his use of expressions such as καὶ τότε.

πάντα δὲ ταῦτα ἀρχὴ ὠδίνων (24:8). The sufferings
entail disturbances of the social and natural
orders: μελλήσετε δὲ ἀκούειν πολέμους καὶ ἀκοὰς
πολέμων· ὁρᾶτε, μὴ θροεῖσθε· δεῖ γὰρ γενέσθαι,
ἀλλ' οὔπω ἐστὶν τὸ τέλος. Ἐγερθήσεται γὰρ ἔθνος
ἐπὶ ἔθνος καὶ βασιλεία ἐπὶ βασιλεῖαν, καὶ ἔσονται
λιμοὶ καὶ σεισμοὶ κατὰ τόπους (24:6-7). The sufferings also bring the appearance of eschatological deceivers: πολλοὶ γὰρ ἐλεύσονται ἐπὶ τῷ
ὀνόματί μου λέγοντες·Ἐγώ εἰμι ὁ Χριστός, καὶ
πολλοὺς πλανήσουσιν (24:5). It is difficult to
ascertain in pro forma apocalyptic passages like
these whether or not the evangelist really intends
for his readers to think of actual events to occur
before the End, or whether he simply is using
stock imagery. Part of his point in this section
is that surely hardships (ὠδίνων) will come before
the End, and one must not be surprised by them
when they do arrive. They are part of the necessary plan (δεῖ γὰρ γενέσθαι) which will ultimately lead to the End and to redemption for the
community. The major point is that these sufferings are not the End itself. These disturbances are only the preliminaries to the End; they
are not the End (ἀλλ' οὔπω ἐστὶν τὸ τέλος, v. 6),
nor are they the time of crisis immediately before
the Parousia (24:29). Matthew's use of τότε in
verse 9a could denote temporal sequence, but it
most likely means that the period of sufferings
will encompass the affliction of the disciples
(θλῖψις, v. 9a), that is, they will be hated by
"all the nations" (v. 9b).[1] This clearly suggests
that the affliction is to occur during the time of
the world-wide mission (v. 14), which means that
it is probably contemporary for Matthew's church.
After the disciples begin to experience affliction
from all the nations (καὶ τότε, v. 10), the community itself will begin to experience division

---

[1]Pesch, "Eschatologie und Ethik," p. 230.

356

and hatred (vv. 10-12). The τέλος, though, will not come until the world-wide mission is completed (v. 14).

Matthew's addition of οὖν (v. 15 cf. Mark 13:14) shows that he considers the traditional material concerning the "desolating sacrilege" as part of the time of world-wide mission. Verses 15-28 are an explication of the θλῖψις warned about in verse 9a. The time of the world-wide mission will be one of "great tribulation" (v. 21). The θλῖψις intensifies after the "desolating sacrilege" occurs (v. 15), and it could even necessitate flight (v. 20). After the desolating sacrilege appears (τότε, v. 23), Matthew expects the activity of the false prophets to increase (cf. μεγάλα, v. 24) during the period of great tribulation (vv. 23-28). The expectation of the Parousia will be enhanced and the false prophets will intensify their claim that the Son of Man has come (v. 26). Matthew's redaction, though, in verse 29 makes it perfectly clear that the Parousia comes after the great tribulation of verses 15-28.[1]

Although Matthew is using traditional material in verses 29-31, he does add two significant occurrences which will precede the Parousia. The first is the universal appearance of the sign which announces the Parousia (καὶ τότε, v. 30). After the appearance of the sign, the Son of Man will come (v. 30), but Matthew has inserted a trumpet call in verse 31 which is distinct from the sign of the Son of Man. The sign of the Son of Man announces the appearance of the Son of Man and the implied judgment for the tribes of the earth.[2] The trumpet signals the angels to gather

---

[1]εὐθέως δὲ μετὰ τὴν θλῖψιν τῶν ἡμερῶν ἐκείνων.

[2]καὶ τότε κόψονται πᾶσαι αἱ φυλαὶ τῆς γῆς.

the elect for salvation.

There is a break in Matthew's sequential arrangement of the material at verse 32. The evangelist structures a parenetical section in 24:32-25:46. However, it is clear that Matthew expects the Son of Man to act as judge after his Parousia (25:31). The evangelist's characteristic phrase συντελείας τοῦ αἰῶνος is clearly connected with the Parousia and the judgment of the Son of Man earlier in the gospel (13:39, 40, 49), and one would naturally expect Matthew's eschatological discourse, which begins with that connection (24:3), to have the judgment immediately after the Parousia in 24:30-31.

What Matthew has done in this section, though, is characteristic of his style. He consistently uses the themes of pericopae which end a section as transitional material to another section. We have seen, for example, that Matthew used the concluding pericope of the discourse in chapter 23 to effect a transition to the eschatological discourse.[1] Similarly, he uses the concluding pericope of the testament (24:39-41), which speaks of the Parousia of the Son of Man to judge the status of all the nations in relation to him, as an introduction to his parenetical section of seven parables,[2] all of which emphasize the need to be prepared for the Son of Man's judgment.[3] The judgment scene in 25:31-46

---

[1]23:37-39; 24:1-2. See the detailed discussion in Ellis, Matthew, pp. 17-19, and in each exegetical section of his book.

[2]Ibid., pp. 90-91.

[3]Bornkamm, "End-Expectation and Church in Matthew," TI, pp. 22-24.

functions not only as the close of the parenetical section, but also, as Matthew has clearly told his readers earlier (13:39 cf. 13:36-43), as the final event at the "close of the age."

In summary, the redaction of the eschatological discourse provides a step by step presentation of the signs Matthew expects to precede the Parousia and the consummation of the age. The discourse has several elements in common with other New Testament traditions concerning the Parousia, but some important elements are also missing in Matthew. The "lawlessness" which Matthew expects to increase until the Parousia is very similar to the situation depicted in 2 Thess. 2. In 2 Thessalonians the deceivers, as we also argued for Matthew's discourse, say that the Parousia has arrived (2:1-3a). The writer cautions that the Parousia has not arrived, but will be preceded by a period of lawlessness (2:3-12). In contrast to that tradition, Matthew does not depict the period of lawlessness as the activity of "the man of lawlessness" (2 Thess. 2:3). Matthew does, however, depict Satan as the cause of all lawlessness,[1] and this includes the time of lawlessness as characterized by "signs and wonders" from the false prophets.[2] The "man of lawlessness" in 2 Thessalonians will take "his seat in the Temple of God, proclaiming himself to be God" (2:4). It is interesting to speculate about whether or not this tradition is related to

---

[1]13:37-39, 41 cf. 2 Thess. 2:9.

[2]24:24 cf. 2 Thess. 2:9; 1 Tim. 4:1, 2; 2 Tim. 3:1-8, 12-13; 1 John 2:18-19; Jude 18. See the discussions in Kingsbury, Structure, p. 165 cf. pp. 142, 164-167; and Schweizer, Matthew, pp. 185-186, 189, 451.

the "desolating sacrilege" of Matt. 24:15. If the two traditions are related, then it is difficult to understand Matthew's redaction of Mark's personal reference (ἑστηκότα) to an impersonal one (ἑστός cf. Mark 13:14; Rev. 13:18). Matthew seems to want the nature of the "desolating sacrilege" to be understood in terms of Daniel's prophecy and Antiochus' action, as his specific allusion to Daniel indicates, rather than in terms of another figure.

Although Matthew is the only evangelist who emphasizes the "great trumpet" (24:31), which is also emphasized in other parts of the New Testament,[1] he seems to do so only in _pro forma_ fashion to signal the gathering of the elect. The use of the trumpet as a convention is suggested by the fact that Matthew has neither a resurrection follow the trumpet blast (cf. 1 Thess. 4:16) nor a physical transformation (cf. 1 Cor. 15:52). For the time of "great affliction" (24:21) and apostasy (24:5, 10-12) Matthew has no literal or symbolic reference to how long it will last (cf. Rev. 20:7-9). The evangelist also has the time of apostasy and affliction occur before Jesus' Parousia (24:29-31 cf. Rev. 19:11-16), and there is no hint in Matthew of an interval between the Parousia and the final judgment exercised by the Son of Man.[2]

---

[1] 1 Cor. 15:52; 1 Thess. 4:16; Rev. 1:10; 4:1; 8:2, 6, 13; 9:14.

[2] 25:31 cf. 13:40-43; Rev. 20:1-3, 7-8, 11-15. The "sequence" of eschatological events in the Apocalypse is not entirely clear. The Seer could be presenting his eschatological themes in serial fashion so that any attempt at understanding his scenario is a precarious venture (see Caird, The Revelation of St. John, pp. 239-260).

# CHAPTER IV

# THE SIGNIFICANCE OF THE ESCHATOLOGICAL
# DISCOURSE FOR INTERPRETING
# THE GOSPEL OF MATTHEW

## Introduction

In the last chapter we saw how Matthean
redaction, particularly at 24:3, set the stage for
Jesus to reveal secrets of the End-time to his
disciples (Matthew's community) in private. The
apocalyptic character of the discourse was evident
because it is clearly a "Parousia discourse" (τῆς
σῆς παρουσίας) which deals with the cataclysmic
"consummation of the Age" (συντελείας τοῦ αἰῶνος).
The farewell character of the discourse was also
apparent in the evangelist's redaction. Jesus,
who is obviously an authoritative figure (κάθημαι)
worthy of reverence (προσέρχομαι), imparts information and encouragement to his followers and
successors (οἱ μαθηταί) which will help them
"endure until the end" (24:13). Jesus has also
passed on to them his task of proclaiming the
"gospel of the kingdom" (24:14 cf. 4:23; 9:35;
28:19-20). Both the encouragement to "endure
until the end" and the task of preaching the
"gospel of the kingdom" (=Jesus' Word) constitute
the testament which Jesus leaves with his disciples. The testament is his last discourse with
them before his public ministry ends and he goes
on to his death (23:39 cf. 26:1-2). This is the
function of the discourse in its immediate context, but the question of the function of Jesus'
testament within the context of the whole gospel
is still unanswered. As we pointed out at the
beginning of our study, the question of the purpose and function of Matthew 24:1-31 within the

361

whole gospel continues to resist an adequate explanation.[1] In this chapter we will suggest what purpose and function the testament has within the larger framework of Matthew's christology and view of discipleship.

We have seen that Matthew's Son of Man and Wisdom christologies coalesce in the testament. Jesus speaks as Sophia about his future advent as the Son of Man. The consensus clearly is that a Son of Man christology plays an important part in the theology of the Matthean community. There is not a consensus, however, that a Wisdom christology plays a prominent role in the evangelist's theology. We, of course, have argued that a Wisdom christology is an important aspect of Matthew's understanding of Jesus in the testament. Suggs concludes his presentation with this question:

> How is Matthew's understanding of Jesus as Wisdom incarnate to be integrated with the whole of his Christology, for example? It is perfectly clear that the Son of Man concept is open to more extensive exploration from this perspective.[2]

The first stage of our discussion in this chapter will attempt to answer this question: how are the Son of Man and Wisdom christologies related to each other in the whole gospel? Our exegesis of 24:1-31, a context where Matthew has Jesus-Son of Man speak as Jesus-Sophia, suggests that the two christologies are complementary. We will attempt

---

[1]See the quotation from P. Ellis on p. 1 above.

[2]Suggs, Wisdom, p. 129.

362

to show that they are complementary within Matthew's christological framework as a whole. We will first discuss his christological framework, and then proceed to a discussion of 11:25-30, a passage which we will argue exemplifies Matthew's christological schema.

We have also seen that 24:1-31 is a testament which Jesus leaves with his disciples. In it Jesus encourages them to "endure until the end" in their preaching task. This raises the question: how do the mission and the fate of the disciples relate to Jesus as Sophia and as Son of Man? Thus, in the second stage of our discussion we will discuss how the evangelist's christological schema influences his understanding of discipleship. We will see that not only is christology the basis for understanding discipleship in Matthew, but that the evangelist has an understanding of discipleship which is parallel to his overall christological framework. First, a survey of Matthew's christological framework will be presented, and areas of consensus among commentators will be noted as we proceed. We will then attempt to draw the various elements of our discussion together into a coherent presentation of christology and discipleship in the First Gospel.

### Matthew's Christological Framework

In his seminal essay on "The Stilling of the Storm in Matthew," G. Bornkamm gives this conclusion about Matthean christology:

> Thus the nature miracle of the stilling of the storm is taken out of a biographical context and placed in a series which consists predominantly, though not exclusively, of healing miracles which set forth the "Messiah of deed" after the presentation of the "Messiah of the

word" has already occurred in chapters
5-7.[1]

Bornkamm's point is that the compositional structure of Matthew's christology in chapters 5-9
presents Jesus as the Messiah of Word and Deed.[2]
In other words, Jesus is not only a teaching
Messiah for the evangelist, but Jesus' actions
confirm his "Word" about the higher righteousness
which he came to reveal (5:17-20). Jesus' Word in
the Sermon on the Mount (chaps. 5-7) is confirmed
by his subsequent miraculous deeds in the First
Gospel (chaps. 8-10).[3] The mode and content of
Jesus' revelation takes a definite structure in
Matthew's "Word-Deed" christology.

As virtually every redaction critic agrees,
Matthew has structured his presentation in this
way so that it becomes clear at the beginning of
his gospel that Jesus is the fulfillment of the
Old Testament promises. It is commonly known that
the evangelist frequently appeals to the Old Testament in order to confirm the Messianic status
of Jesus. The usual formula by which he attaches
an Old Testament quotation to Jesus' life is
roughly "this took place to fulfill what the Lord
had spoken by the prophet" (1:22; 2:5, 17, etc.).

---

[1]Bornkamm, "The Stilling of the Storm in
Matthew," _TI_, p. 53.

[2]See the discussion by Held, Bornkamm's
student, on how Matthew works this christological
presentation out in the miracle stories. See
Held, "Matthew as Interpreter of the Miracle
Stories," _TI_, pp. 165-300.

[3]Ibid., p. 246 and the literature cited
there.

Our own investigation has confirmed what appears to be the consensus among redaction critics about Matthew's "Word-Deed" christological structure. Therefore, we will simply give a representative quotation of that consensus. Donald Senior, in a section entitled "Jesus, Messiah in Word and Deed," says:

> If Matthew's sensitivity to the Old Testament helps us appreciate his understanding of the authority of Jesus as Messiah, it is the very outline of the body of his gospel that gives Jesus' Messianic mission its form and content. In other words, links with the Old Testament alert us to the fact that Jesus is the fulfillment of the promise; the gospel material tells us how.[1]

## Jesus as the Revealer of God's Will

A second area of consensus concerning Matthean christology is that Jesus reveals the will of God through his Words and Deeds. One could say that revelation in the First Gospel equals the Words plus the Deeds of Jesus.[2]

---

[1]Senior, Matthew: A Gospel for the Church, pp. 45-46. See also Rigaux, Testimony of St. Matthew, pp. 41-50; Ellis, Matthew: His Mind and His Message, pp. 31-40 (=Messiah in Word), pp. 40-46 (=Messiah in Deed); Blair, Jesus in the Gospel of Matthew, p. 9; Schweizer, Matthew, pp. 78-254 cf. p. 109; Hill, Matthew, pp. 165-167; Fenton, St. Matthew, pp. 119-121; and Kingsbury, Structure, p. 48.

[2]Blair, Jesus in the Gospel of Matthew, p. 9.

Matthew, as Schweizer says, " . . . does not
speak simply of Jesus' new teaching, but of fulfillment of the Law.  He means that Jesus himself
does what he teaches, and thus makes it possible
for his disciples to do God's will, learning by
his example."[1]  Just before Jesus begins his
public ministry of preaching (4:17), Matthew
implies that Jesus and his message will be a light
to those in darkness (4:16).  As this theme unfolds in the First Gospel, Jesus is seen as the
one who comes to reveal what has been previously
hidden (cf. 13:35).[2]  Although there is dis-
agreement concerning the primary christological
title by which the evangelist expresses this
function, the function of Jesus as the Revealer
is conceded by almost every commentator to be
important for Matthew.[3]

## The character of Jesus'
## revelation

It is important to note the character of

---

[1]Schweizer, Matthew, p. 109.

[2]Stendahl, School, p. 117 cf. pp. 104, 116,
141-142.

[3]Suggs, Wisdom, pp. 48-58, 101, 129;
Hamerton-Kelly, Pre-Existence, p. 83; Davies,
Sermon on the Mount, pp. 140-156, 214, 235;
Stendahl, School, pp. 104, 116-117; Rigaux,
Testimony of St. Matthew, pp. 39-45, 163, 193;
Held, "Matthew as Interpreter of the Miracle
Stories," TI, p. 292; Hare, Theme of Jewish
Persecution, p. 136; Kingsbury, Parables of Jesus
in Matthew 13, pp. 41, 43, 44, 99; and Beardslee,
"The Wisdom Tradition in the Synoptic Gospels,"
p. 235.

Jesus' Words and Deeds. On the one hand, Jesus reveals God's will with "authority," (ἐξουσία) while, on the other hand, he is humble, modest, and becomes the exemplar of his own teachings.[1] Both aspects--authority and humility (πραΰς)--are recognized by almost all commentators to form an integral part of Matthean christology.

Jesus' ἐξουσία

E. P. Blair, for example, says that ἐξουσία is the chief means by which Matthew presents Jesus as the Revealer of God's will (28:18). Blair's thesis is that "Matthew's portrait of Jesus centers in his representation of Jesus' authority."[2] This is, again, an area which is generally conceded by commentators, but they differ about which title Matthew primarily uses to present Jesus' ἐξουσία. Blair is convinced that the main title used by the evangelist to express Jesus' ἐξουσία is "Son of Man." J. D. Kingsbury agrees that "If we survey the whole of Jesus' ministry as sketched by Matthew, we discover that its distinguishing mark is the 'authority' (exousia) with which he speaks and acts." However, Kingsbury contends that Matthew primarily expresses this through the title "Son of God."[3] In other words, commentators agree on the source and the basis of Jesus' authority; it is God, Jesus' "Father" (11:25-30).[4] Disagree-

---

[1]Senior, Matthew: A Gospel for the Church, p. 47.

[2]Blair, Jesus in the Gospel of Matthew, p. 14.

[3]Kingsbury, Structure, p. 58; cf. Ellis, Matthew: His Mind and His Message, pp. 40-53.

[4]E.g., Blair, Jesus in the Gospel of Mat-

ment ensues as commentators try to work out how they think <u>Matthew</u> understood the relationship between Jesus and the Father, but there is little doubt that the evangelist connects Jesus' ἐξουσία with his Sonship.

## Jesus as the humble one

Although Matthew presents Jesus as the possessor of all authority (28:18), he is also presented as the humble one (πραΰς). This general christological theme is also recognized by almost all commentators. In Matt. 12:17-21, for example, Jesus is presented as the servant of God (παῖς, 12:18) who, by virtue of his humility and lowliness, will neither wrangle nor cry out in the streets (12:19). For Matthew Jesus' humility, as a fulfillment of Isa. 42:1-4, becomes an act of obedience.[1] In fact, one could say that:

> . . . <u>the unobtrusiveness of Jesus</u> depicted in 12:16, which is the thematic link that binds the Isaianic quotation (cf. 12:19) to its context, <u>is a trait that is typical of the Matthaean Jesus almost across the board</u>.[2]

In a summary at 8:17 Matthew seems to see Jesus' humility as a fulfillment of Isa. 53:4: "He took

---

thew, pp. 95-96; and Rigaux, <u>Testimony of St. Matthew</u>, p. 163.

[1]Barth, "Matthew's Understanding of the Law," <u>TI</u>, pp. 125-128.

[2]Kingsbury, <u>Structure</u>, p. 94 (italics mine). Kingsbury connects this with Matthew's presentation of Jesus as the Son of God.

our infirmities and bore our diseases." Jesus'
humility, <u>precisely in the setting of his miracles</u>
<u>where his authority is most evident</u>, gives
Matthew's portrait of Jesus a certain balance.

Matthew presents Jesus in the miracle
stories as the authoritative one who is able to
heal, but Jesus does so in obedience to God's
will.  The humiliation, or lowliness, of the
mighty one who is obedient to God's will is only
one part of Matthew's presentation of Jesus.  The
other side is that Jesus as the obedient one does
not lose his authority; he uses it to effect God's
purpose.  One could entitle Matthew's portrait of
the miracle-working Jesus as "the obedient
humiliation of the mighty one."[1]

Once again in 21:4-5 Jesus is presented by
the evangelist as the βασιλεὺς πραΰς.  The meaning
for Matthew seems to be clear:

> The decisive thing for Matthew in
> reproducing Zech. 9.9 is that Jesus is
> πραΰς, he is the βασιλεὺς πραΰς.  What
> is meant by that?  Obviously above all
> his lowliness, his humiliation, the
> fact that the One who is destined to be
> the eschatological judge of the world,
> disclaiming his power and glory, enters
> here in lowliness on the way to the
> cross.[2]

To put it succinctly, in the First Gospel Jesus

---

[1]Held, "Matthew as Interpreter of the
Miracle Stories," <u>TI</u>, pp. 262-263; cf. Barth,
"Matthew's Understanding of the Law," <u>TI</u>,
pp. 128-129.

[2]Ibid., p. 130.

proves himself and fulfills the obedience to the
Law, in the sense of the piety of the <u>Anawim</u>, as
the one who is "gentle (πραΰς) and lowly in heart
(ταπεινὸς τῇ καρδίᾳ)" (11:29).[1]  It is no accident
that Matthew associates the "yoke" (of the Law)
which Jesus offers with the πραΰς and ταπεινός of
Jesus (11:29).[2]

In summary, it is agreed in very general
terms that Jesus in Matthew is the Revealer of
God's "higher righteousness" (5:20).  He reveals
God's righteousness through his words and deeds
with authority (ἐξουσία) and yet with humility
(πραΰς).  On the one hand, this "lowliness-
exaltation" christology in the First Gospel is
usually interpreted in terms of Jesus as the humble Servant (παῖς) of God, and, on the other hand,
in terms of Jesus as the exalted, apocalyptic Son
of Man after the fashion of Dan. 7:13 (cf. Matt.
28:16-20).  We would like to suggest that these
themes of Matthew's πραΰς-ἐξουσία christology are
more aptly explained by the fact that Matthew complements his presentation of Jesus as the apocalyptic, exalted Son of Man with his presentation
of Jesus as the humble Wisdom of God.  Jesus as
the Son of Man in the First Gospel is not only the
exalted one who will return as judge of all nations, but Jesus <u>as the Son of Man</u> also functions
as the Revealer of God's ultimate will.  We are
suggesting that the function of Revealer, which
Matthew applies to Jesus as the Son of Man, is due
to the influence of one kind of Wisdom tradition
upon Matthew's christology.

---

[1]Bornkamm, "End-Expectation and Church in
Matthew," <u>TI</u>, p. 36.

[2]Barth, "Matthew's Understanding of the
Law," <u>TI</u>, pp. 131-137.

## Wisdom and apocalyptic

It is commonly known that the Son of Man concept is closely associated with both the Wisdom and apocalyptic traditions. The two traditions are not mutually exclusive, yet, as we have seen, commentators have interpreted Matthew's concept of Jesus as the Son of Man almost exclusively in terms of the latter tradition. The apocalyptist, though, worked with many diverse streams of tradition.[1] One of those streams was undoubtedly the Wisdom tradition. It is undeniable that apocalyptic works such as Daniel, 1 Enoch, and 4 Ezra have been influenced, among other things, by the Wisdom tradition.[2]

The confluence of these traditions is evident in both pre-Matthean texts and in texts which are roughly contemporary with the First Gospel. Consequently, we will not attempt to trace the confluence of the traditions back to their roots.[3] We will simply give some commonly accepted examples of the confluence, namely, 1 Enoch and Q, and then bring these to bear upon Matthew.

1 Enoch

The Similitudes of 1 Enoch (chaps. 37-71)

---

[1] James Muilenburg, "The Son of Man in Daniel and the Ethiopic Apocalypse of Enoch," JBL 79 (1960): 208-209 (cited hereafter as Muilenburg, "Son of Man").

[2] Paul D. Hanson, The Dawn of Apocalyptic, Philadelphia: Fortress Press, 1975), p. 9.

[3] Hanson points out the dilemma in any such attempt. He points out (in 1975) that a compre-

are usually taken as an example of how the Son of
Man is interpreted in terms of Wisdom.[1]  Like Wisdom, the Son of Man in 1 Enoch is pre-existent,
and it is Wisdom who reveals the Son of Man as the
holy and righteous one (48:1-7).  The Son of Man
is inexhaustibly filled with Wisdom (49:3 cf.
48:1), and God has committed all judgment to the
Son of Man (69:27).[2]  When they see the Son of Man
sitting on his glorious throne, all the mighty of
the earth shall recognize him and be as women in
travail.[3]  In other words, in 1 Enoch, " . . . the

---

hensive study of the confluence is needed (Ibid.).

[1] Enoch provides the clearest example of a
tradition which presents Wisdom and the Son of Man
as kindred figures.  There seems to be some evidence, although it is being debated, that there
was a propensity in the Palestinian Wisdom tradition to see Wisdom and the "primal man" (geber),
a concept which seems to have influenced 1 Enoch,
as kindred figures.  See William H. Brownlee,
"Jesus and Qumran," Jesus and the Historian, ed.
F. Thomas Trotter (Philadelphia: Westminster
Press, 1968), pp. 52-81; and G. Vermes, Scripture
and Tradition in Judaism: Haggadic Studies, Studia
Post-Biblica, vol. 4 (Leiden: E. J. Brill, 1961),
pp. 56-67.

[2] The Son of Man in 1 Enoch appears in chapters 46-48 and 62-71.  Although these chapters
could be a source which is separate from chapter
49, where the Elect One appears, " . . . the final
author of the Similitudes appears to regard the
two [the Son of Man and the Elect One] as identical" (S. E. Johnson, "Son of Man," IDB 4: 414).

[3] 62:5 cf. 62:1-4; 69:27-29; Matt. 25:31.

judgment of God in its significance for the just is thus personified in the wisdom of the Son of Man."[1]  This is not to suggest that the figures of the Son of Man and Sophia were identified in 1 Enoch, but the parallels are striking enough to suggest that the Son of Man is a kindred figure to Wisdom.[2]

The Son of Man as Revealer

One of the functions of the Son of Man in an apocalyptic tradition influenced by Wisdom speculation is that of Revealer.  The Son of Man is the bearer of God's Wisdom.  It is particularly emphasized in 1 Enoch that the eschatological character of the Son of Man is to reveal all the secrets of Wisdom.  The Son of Man will reveal all of the hidden things about the order of creation; he will also reveal secrets about the End-time (46:3 cf. 48:1-2; 52-55).[3]  The Son of Man can also fulfill

---

[1]Wilckens, "σοφία," p. 504.  The date of the Similitudes does not really affect this argument in relation to Matthew since we are not arguing for direct literary dependence of one upon the other (cf. the remarks by Suggs, Wisdom, p. 49 n. 30).  Tödt argues that pre-existence is not in any of the Synoptic Son of Man passages (Tödt, Son of Man, pp. 284-285; contrast Hamerton-Kelly, Pre-Existence, p. 19; and Muilenburg, "Son of Man," pp. 203-209).

[2]Ibid., pp. 208-209.

[3]Sigmund Mowinckel, He That Cometh, trans. G. W. Anderson (New York: Abingdon Press, 1951), p. 376.

all righteousness because the spirit of righteousness dwells in him.[1] The Son of Man knows all the secrets of the righteousness of God (62:6), and he will reveal them to the Elect (48:7). In other words, the Son of Man reveals the righteousness of God to the Elect who, in contrast to the "sinners," understand the revelation.[2] As we shall see, understanding the revelation of Jesus is an important theme of Matthean discipleship.

It would only be stating the obvious if we continued discussing the fact that the Wisdom and apocalyptic traditions influenced one another in such a way that the Son of Man and Wisdom became kindred figures.[3] Our purpose in discussing 1 Enoch was to show the existence of a tradition in which the Son of Man as eschatological judge is interpreted in terms which are usually considered to be characteristic of Wisdom. Matthew's presentation of Jesus as the Son of Man, the eschatological judge, within the same context as Jesus as Wisdom is very similar to, if not dependent upon, the tradition in 1 Enoch.[4] We will discuss the

---

[1]Ibid., p. 377.    [2]Ibid., p. 387.

[3]Davies, Sermon on the Mount, pp. 140-156; Suggs, Wisdom, pp. 49-55; Norman Perrin, The Kingdom of God in the Teaching of Jesus (Philadelphia: Westminster Press, 1963), pp. 97-100; and Jeremias, New Testament Theology, pp. 268-275.

[4]See the discussion in Hamerton-Kelly, Pre-Existence, p. 83. Once again, the question of the date of the Similitudes really does not affect the discussion of the kind of tradition in 1 Enoch. If the Similitudes are post-Matthean, then one could argue that the editor of the Similitudes was dependent upon Matthew! The date of the Similitudes is admittedly controversial,

relation of Jesus as Wisdom to Jesus as the Son of Man in Matthew in our analysis of Matt. 11:25-30 below, but first let us look at the relation of these two figures in the Q tradition.

Son of Man and Sophia in Q

The Wisdom and apocalyptic traditions are too diverse and amorphous to discuss in general terms. It seems that a more productive approach would be to discuss Matthew's particular tradition. At this point research into Matthew's Wisdom background is still in its infancy, but, as indicated above, the present state of research suggests that Matthew was influenced by a diversity of Wisdom traditions similar to those in Sirach 24 and 1 Enoch. As we also discussed, though, more fruitful research is being done on Matthew's redaction of Wisdom influence in Q.[1]

The present state of Q research seems to suggest that Jesus as the Son of Man belongs with the picture in Q of Jesus as the last and greatest envoy of Wisdom.[2] Jesus as the Son of Man in Q is

---

but one could plausibly argue for a pre-Christian date. (See Suggs, Wisdom, p. 49 n. 30; Johnson, "Son of Man," p. 414; contrast J. C. Hindley, "Towards a Date for the Similitudes of Enoch: An Historical Approach," NTS 14 (1968): 551-565.) Our argument is not based upon a literary dependence between the First Gospel and the Similitudes. All that we are suggesting is that Matthew represents the same kind of tradition as the Similitudes.

[1]See the discussion on pp. 49-67, 81-92 above.

[2]Suggs, Wisdom, pp. 48-55. We will not

unquestionably the eschatological judge, but it seems probable that the Q community added present Son of Man sayings to the future Son of Man sayings in order to present Jesus in his lifetime as the Son of Man.[1] In an article which sketches the Wisdom trajectory through Jewish and primitive Christian apocalyptic traditions (including the stages of the Q traditions), James M. Robinson summarizes the present state of research on the Son of Man and Sophia in Q:

> By this time [i.e., at the last stages of the Q tradition] the identification of the apocalyptic Son of man with Jesus applied not only to the future but already to his public ministry. This called for some theological category for comprehending his public ministry as a positive category in its own right. The final emissary of Sophia becomes this category. . . . The association of this final emissary of Sophia with the unique apocalyptic Son of Man made it easy to heighten the

---

discuss the debate about whether Jesus appears in Q as the pre-existent Son of Man, or, for that matter, in any Synoptic passage (see Tödt, Son of Man, pp. 284-290; Leivestad, "Exit the Apocalyptic Son of Man," NTS 18 [1972]: 243-267; and B. Lindars, "Re-Enter the Apocalyptic Son of Man," NTS 22 [1975]: 52-72).

[1]This seems probable if (1) Jesus himself either spoke of the future Son of Man as a figure distinct from himself (Tödt, Son of Man, chap. 2), or (2) if the future Son of Man sayings were the product of an early Christian pesher tradition (Perrin, Rediscovering the Teaching of Jesus, pp. 164-170 cf. Edwards, Theology of Q, pp. 35-36).

christology in the wisdom sayings of Q
by according to the Son Sophia's unique
relation to the Father, in effect
identifying Jesus with Sophia herself.
This Sophia christology was then further
developed in Matthew, and in the first
half of the second century became common,
in the Gospel of the Hebrews, the Gospel
of Thomas, Justin Martyr, and so on, and
thus became a permanent if minor ingredient
in all subsequent christology.[1]

Matt. 11:25-30

The question to which this discussion has
led us is: do the themes of Jesus as Wisdom, Jesus
as the Revealer, and Jesus as the authoritative
one who humbles himself in obedience, intersect
in Matthew?  We believe that they do intersect in
Matt. 11:25-30.

We discussed earlier how the evangelist has
appended 11:28-30 to a Q saying (11:25-27) which
has long been recognized to have affinities with
the Wisdom tradition.[2]  We also discussed how
Matthew moved beyond the meaning of the saying in
Q by identifying the content of the revelation
(ταῦτα, 11:25) with the "deeds of Wisdom," that
is, with the deeds of Jesus (11:2, 19).  Then the
evangelist, by his addition of 11:28-30 to 11:25-
27, built upon the identification of Wisdom and
Torah in order to identify Jesus-Sophia with

---

[1]Robinson, "Jesus as Sophos and Sophia:
Wisdom Tradition and The Gospels," pp. 14-15 cf.
p. 6.

[2]See the discussions on pp. 34-37, 72-75,
and 241-243 above.

Torah. In this passage Matthew has identified
Jesus with Wisdom-Torah who invites persons to
take his "yoke" upon them because he is "gentle"
(πραΰς) and lowly (ταπεινός) in heart (11:29).1
This pole (πραΰς) of Matthew's πραΰς-ἐξουσία
christological framework appears clearly in this
passage.2

On the other hand, there is little doubt
that Matthew connects the authority of Jesus with
his Sonship.3 As we have seen, almost every

---

1Cf. our point with the discussion in
Suggs, Wisdom, pp. 95-97.

2Even Bornkamm's students, who do not
emphasize a Wisdom christology in Matthew, acknowledge the wisdom influence upon Matthew's concept of πραΰς in this passage (e.g., Barth,
"Matthew's Understanding of the Law," p. 103
n. 1).

3Jeremias' contention that ὁ υἱός is never
used in pre-Christian Judaism as a title for the
Messiah certainly does not apply to the stage of
christological development at which Matthew writes
(see Jeremias, New Testament Theology, p. 58).
The use of "Son" as a Messianic title in pre-
Christian Judaism occurs possibly as early as the
midrash on 2 Sam. 7:10-14 in 4QFlorilegium. In
that text the son promised to David, that is, the
promised Messiah, is called God's "Son" (Donald
Juel, Messiah and Temple. The Trial of Jesus in
the Gospel of Mark, SBL Dissertation Series, no.
31 [Missoula, Montana: Scholars Press, 1977], pp.
172-181; Patte, Early Jewish Hermeneutic in Palestine, pp. 297-298; and Hill, Matthew, p. 207).
Matthew's absolute use of "Son" in a titular
sense clearly stands as a later application of
that title to Jesus (Reginald Fuller, The Founda-

commentator agrees that Jesus' relationship to God, his Father, is the source of his ἐξουσία.[1] This is stressed in 11:27 by the phrase "all things (πάντα) have been delivered (παρεδόθη) to me by my Father." The aorist παρεδόθη primarily denotes the authority which the Father has given to the Son. Consequently, the following statement, "and no one knows the Son except the Father, and no one knows the Father except the Son and any one to whom the Son chooses to reveal him" (11:27), refers primarily to the mysterious ἐξουσία of the Son. It is primarily, though not exclusively, the <u>authority</u> of the Son which has been hidden from the wise and revealed to babes according to the Father's will (11:25-26).[2] In the Matthean con-

---

tions of New Testament Christology [New York: Charles Scribner's Sons, 1965], pp. 114-115).

[1]See the discussion in Kingsbury, <u>Structure</u>, pp. 58-67.

[2]Büchsel, "δίδωμι," <u>TDNT</u> 2: 171. Contrast Jeremias who argues that παραδιδόναι " . . . is a technical term for the transmission of doctrine, knowledge, and holy lore. Thus πάντα, like ταῦτα in v. 25, designates the mystery of revelation, and the first line means: 'My Father has given me a full revelation'" (Jeremias, <u>New Testament Theology</u>, p. 59). The revelation in Matt. 11:27 certainly does not exclude the idea of "content." The Qumran community, for example, knew that the revelation of eschatological secrets meant election by God (W. D. Davies, "'Knowledge' in the Dead Sea Scrolls," <u>HThR</u> 46 [1953]: 122-125). The Matthean context, however, speaks of an unrestricted revelation in the next verse (11:28, πάντες). As we have seen, the revelation which Jesus gives in Matthew is the love command, which is his fulfillment of the Torah in Word and

text "these things" (ταῦτα) which have been hidden
from the wise and revealed to babes (v. 25) are
the "mighty deeds" (δυνάμεις) to which the Gali-
lean cities failed to respond (11:20-24). But,
as we have seen, these "mighty deeds" (11:20) have
been interpreted by Matthew as the "deeds of the
Christ" (11:2) and, in turn, as the deeds of Wisdom incarnate (11:19).[1] The confluence of Jesus'
Sonship, which is the basis of his authority
(11:27), with the idea of lowliness (πραΰς,
ταπεινός), as obedience to the will of the Father,
occurs in this passage (11:26, 29).

In view of the discussion of the Son of Man
and Wisdom as kindred figures, and in light of
Matthew's christological schema, our suggestion is
that Jesus as the "Son" in 11:25-30 should be seen
within the perspective of Matthew's πραΰς-ἐξουσία
christological schema. Jesus as the "Son" in
11:25-30 expresses for Matthew both the humility,
the obedience, and the rejection of Jesus as Wisdom and the authority of Jesus as the Son of Man,
whose future appearance will manifest the hidden
ἐξουσία of the earthly Jesus.[2] E. Schweizer has

---

Deed. This is the revelation which the disciples
are to proclaim and the "yoke" they are invited to
take upon themselves (=the "gospel of the kingdom," 4:23; 24:14 cf. 10:1, 26-27; 28:20). See
the discussion in Schweizer, Matthew, pp. 269-270.

[1]See the discussion in Suggs, Wisdom, p. 95;
and Davies, "'Knowledge' in the Dead Sea Scrolls,"
p. 137.

[2]Cf. the conclusion of Bornkamm on the relation of christology and Torah in Matthew: "All
these passages, in which Matthew . . . interprets
theologically the received tradition, aim at the
distinction between the earthly lowliness of Jesus

argued convincingly that the pattern of humility and obedience, which results in exaltation and glory, was a traditional one in Judaism, that it was used by the early Church as an essential component of its christology, and that it appears in virtually every developmental phase of New Testament christology.[1] In relation to Matthew, H. Koester has argued that the evangelist's christological pattern is part of a general "humiliation-glorification" schema of Jesus as rejected Wisdom. For Koester the theme of rejection-humiliation is how Wisdom mythologies are connected with the earthly Jesus.[2] If Schweizer and Koester are correct, then Matt. 11:25-30 seems to be a passage in which Matthew expresses the humble incarnation of the authoritative Son as Wisdom.[3] On the other hand, many commentators have just as quickly identified the "Son christology" of 11:25-27 as a Son of Man christology.[4] The identification of the "Son" with the Son of Man is not to be sought primarily in the idea of humility, though that is

---

and his future appearance in glory for judgment" (Bornkamm, "End-Expectation and Church in Matthew," TI, p. 35).

[1]Eduard Schweizer, Lordship and Discipleship, SBT (Naperville, Illinois: Alec R. Allenson, Inc., 1960).

[2]Helmut Koester, "The Structure and Criteria of Early Christian Beliefs," Trajectories through Early Christianity (Philadelphia: Fortress Press, 1971), p. 222.

[3]Beardslee, "The Wisdom Tradition in the Synoptic Gospels," p. 235; cf. Arvedson, Das Mysterium Christi, pp. 165-170.

[4]S. Schultz, e.g., contends that πάντα μοι

possible,[1] as it is in the apocalyptic idea that the revelation of the glorious Son of Man is hidden until his full disclosure at the End (Luke 17:30 par. Matt. 24:39).[2] The use of "Son" for an original "Son of Man" in the Synoptic tradition's apocalyptic contexts has also suggested to commentators that the "Son" in 11:27 should be identified with the "Son of Man."[3]

In light of our exegesis of the testament in Matt. 24:1-31, we would suggest that the evangelist is presenting Jesus as the "Son" within the traditional christological pattern of humiliation-exaltation, but with his redactional emphasis upon

---

παρεδόθη ὑπὸ τοῦ πατρός μου is to be connected directly with the Son of Man traditions (S. Schultz, Untersuchungen zur Menschensohn-Christologie im Johannesevangelium [Göttingen: Vandenhoeck and Ruprecht, 1957], pp. 124-130). See the discussions also in J. Schniewind, Das Evangelium nach Matthäus, 2nd ed. (Göttingen: Vandenhoeck and Ruprecht, 1963), p. 154; L. Cerfaux, "Les sources scripturaires de Mt 11,25-30," EThL 31 (1955): 336; and Blair, Jesus in the Gospel of Matthew, p. 47.

[1]Schweizer, Lordship and Discipleship, p. 31; cf. Mowinckel, He That Cometh, pp. 410-415.

[2]Paul Hoffmann, "Die Offenbarung des Sohnes. Die apokalyptischen Voraussetzungen und ihre Verarbeitung im Q-Logien Mt 11,27 par Lk 10,22," Kairos 12 (1970): 281-286.

[3]Matt. 24:36 par. Mark 13:32. Fuller, Foundations of New Testament Christology, p. 114.

Jesus as humble Wisdom and authoritative Son of
Man.  Matthew never explicitly says within the
same context that Jesus is Wisdom and the Son of
Man.  The middle factor in the equation is the
Sonship of Jesus.[1]  Jesus as the Son is humble
Wisdom, and Jesus as the Son is authoritative Son
of Man.  Therefore, humble and incarnate Wisdom
will be revealed as the authoritative Son of Man
at his Parousia.[2]  Matthew's interest is in the
Sonship of Jesus as the basis of his humiliation
and authority.  He expresses that in his gospel in
two major ways, namely, Jesus as Wisdom and Jesus
as Son of Man.  Jesus as Wisdom has authority and
performs deeds on the basis of that authority, but

---

[1]Several backgrounds have been posited for
the intimate relation of Father to Son in Matt.
11:27.  Several commentators see the "Son" in
11:27 in terms of a Hellenistic Redeemer figure
(Martin Dibelius, From Tradition to Gospel, trans.
B. T. Woolf [New York: Charles Scribner's Sons,
n.d.], pp. 279-286; Bultmann, History of the
Synoptic Tradition, pp. 159-160, 166; and
Arvedson, Das Mysterium Christi, pp. 154-157).  In
opposition to this view Hunter has suggested the
Old Testament concept of da'ath Elohim as the
background of the relationship in Matt. 11:27
(A. M. Hunter, "Crux Criticorum--Matt. XI.25-30--
A Critical Re-Appraisal," NTS 8 [1962]: 245).
Davies has shown that an intimate dependence upon
God, even for knowledge of His/Her eschatological
plans, existed at Qumran (Davies, "'Knowledge' in
the Dead Sea Scrolls," pp. 122-126).  The Wisdom
tradition, though, could provide the eschatological background for the "Son" christology in Matt.
11:27 (Suggs, Wisdom, pp. 89-97; cf. Schweizer,
Matthew, pp. 271-274; and Christ, Jesus Sophia,
p. 87).

[2]Hamerton-Kelly, Pre-Existence, p. 98.

it is the will of the Father that Wisdom's ἐξουσία be hidden until his Parousia as Son of Man (11:25-26; 13:10-15, 36-43). The christological pattern of humiliation (=Jesus as Sophia) and exaltation (=Jesus as Son of Man) appeared in both Matthew's redaction of the testament and its immediate context. The relation of christological elements in the testament becomes clear when seen in terms of this christological pattern.

As we have seen, in Matt. 23:34 Jesus is identified with Sophia. In 23:39 Jesus as Sophia speaks <u>eschatologically</u> of "the coming one." Matthean redaction (ἀπ' ἄρτι) clearly identifies the "coming one" as Jesus the Son of Man (τῆς σῆς παρουσίας, 24:3 cf. 24:30-31; 26:29, 64). In 23:39 Jesus as Sophia is speaking also as humiliated Wisdom (23:37) whose rejection fulfilled the plan of salvation-history (23:32 cf. 21:33-43). Jesus as Wisdom, whose authority has been rejected, can promise that he (με) will not be seen again until his Parousia, a time when all will acknowledge his authority (23:39 cf. 24:30). The relation which Matthean redaction has effected in 23:37-39 (together with 23:32-36) suggests the humiliation-glorification schema in which Jesus' Parousia as Son of Man will reveal and vindicate his authoritative deeds as incarnate Sophia (cf. 11:19c).

This same christological pattern is evident in Matthew's redaction of the testament (24:1-31). In the evangelist's redaction of 24:3 Jesus sits (κάθημαι) as authoritative, yet rejected, Sophia. He encourages his followers to endure until the Parousia when his appearance as Son of Man will confirm universally his authority (24:30-31). The parenetical section, which reinforces the instructions given in the testament, closes with an explicit reference to the Parousia. Jesus as Son of Man will come "in his glory" (ἐν τῇ δόξῃ

384

αὐτοῦ) and "sit (καθίσει) upon his glorious throne (ἐπὶ θρόνου δόξης αὐτοῦ, 25:31)." The authoritative posture of Jesus as rejected Sophia, which began the testament (κάθημαι, 24:3), is thus balanced at the end of the parenetical section with the eschatological sitting of Jesus as the glorified Son of Man. Thus, the two poles of Matthew's christological presentation appear within the testament and its immediate context. In a pattern like that of 11:25-30, Jesus, as the humiliated and glorified Son, appears as rejected Sophia and as the glorified Son of Man.

If this is the correct interpretation of Matthew's christological pattern, then it also explains how the christology in the whole gospel should perhaps be understood. The phrase of the Son in 11:27 that "All things have been delivered (παρεδόθη) to me by my Father" immediately calls to mind the finale of Matthew's gospel. There the Risen Jesus as the Son proclaims: "All <u>authority</u> (ἐξουσία) in heaven and <u>on earth</u> has been given (ἐδόθη) to me" (28:18 cf. 28:19). The statement in 28:18 is the best commentary on 11:27.[1] On the one hand, 28:18 elucidates the meaning of "all things" (πάντα) which the Father delivered to the Son in 11:27. The Son received ἐξουσία which, as we have seen, was exercised on earth in the deeds of rejected Wisdom (11:2, 19, 20). The point of Matt. 11:27 is that as the unrecognized Son, Jesus is still the Lord of the universe, but only God knows this. On the other hand, the point of Matt. 28:18-20 is that it is only through the Risen Son that persons can have insight into what God has done. The Risen Son reveals his authority to those who follow him, and his followers,

---

[1]Cf. Büchsel's remark on 11:27: "To deny that Mt. 28:18 offers the closest parallel is an example of 'critical' prejudice"("δίδωμι," 171).

in turn, proclaim what the Son has revealed to them.[1]  Matthew 28:18, then, reveals the authority of the Risen Son which Matthew expects to be vindicated universally at the Parousia of the Son of Man.  The relation of the two passages (11:25-30 and 28:18-20) has been stated succinctly by Hamerton-Kelly:

> If one reads the pericope 11:25-30 as a whole—the Q section plus Matthew's addition—as Matthew obviously intended it to be read, a counterpart appears in Matt. 28:18-20.  In 11:25-30 Jesus is the pre-existent Wisdom-figure, in humility praying to the Lord of heaven and earth, and inviting men to come to him, the source of knowledge; in 28:18-20 he is the one who has all authority in heaven and earth, sending men out to teach the world. . . .
>      11:25-30, when read in conjunction with 28:18-20, expresses the fact that the one who is gentle and lowly is really the one who has all authority in heaven and on earth. . . . In the juxtaposition of 11:25-30 and 28:18-20 there is a hint of the Son of Man—associated with Wisdom/Torah—humiliated and exalted.[2]

---

[1]11:29; 28:19-20 cf. 10:26-27.  See the discussions in Schweizer, _Matthew_, p. 272, and Blair, _Jesus in the Gospel of Matthew_, p. 96.

[2]Hamerton-Kelly, _Pre-Existence_, pp. 68-70; see also Schweizer, _Matthew_, pp. 273-274.  It seems that however the "Son" in 11:25-27 is interpreted will determine how one interprets "Son" in 28:19.  Kingsbury, for example, interprets "Son" in 11:27 as the "Son _of God_," and he consistently does so with "Son" in 28:19 (Kings-

In summary, in the First Gospel Jesus fulfills the Old Testament prophecies in Word and in
Deed. Jesus' words and deeds <u>reveal</u> the will of
God. The mode and character of Jesus' Word-Deed
revelation occur within Matthew's lowliness-
exaltation (πραΰς-ἐξουσία) christological framework. This framework is best understood as a
Wisdom-Son of Man schema. We feel that an analysis of Matthew's Son of Man and Wisdom christologies provides a basis for the assertion that these

---

bury, <u>Structure</u>, pp. 58-61). Kingsbury's exegesis, though, does show the larger relation which
we feel exists between the two passages (cf. the
discussion in Blair, <u>Jesus in the Gospel of Mat-
thew</u>, pp. 108-109; and Betz, "The Logion of the
Easy Yoke and of Rest [Matt 11:28-30]," p. 24).
    It has been argued vigorously that 11:27 is
an authentic saying of the historical Jesus and,
therefore, is not to be construed as a saying of
the Risen Jesus which is "put onto the lips of the
historical Jesus" (Jeremias, <u>New Testament Theol-
ogy</u>, pp. 56-68; I. H. Marshall, "The Divine Sonship of Jesus," <u>Interpretation</u> 21 [1967]: 87-103;
and Hunter, "Crux Criticorum--Matt. XI.25-30--A
Re-Appraisal," pp. 241-249; contrast Bultmann,
<u>History of the Synoptic Tradition</u>, pp. 166, 328;
and Dibelius, <u>From Tradition to Gospel</u>, pp. 264,
279-286). However, there is little doubt that the
saying in its Matthean context is a dominical
saying of the Risen Jesus (Schweizer, <u>Matthew</u>,
pp. 271-272; Hill, <u>Matthew</u>, p. 207; and Blair,
<u>Jesus in the Gospel of Matthew</u>, pp. 66-68). For
Matthean christology in general it must be recognized that "He who is always with his own even
to the close of the age is speaking. And what he
says is for Matthew identical to what the 'historical Jesus' said" (Marxsen, <u>Mark the Evange-
list</u>, p. 206).

two christologies are complementary in the First
Gospel. The earthly Jesus is the Wisdom of God
who reveals the higher righteousness by Word (his
interpretation of Torah by the love command), and
he is also the authoritative Son who authenticates
his revelation by his Deeds (miracles). In his
lifetime the earthly Jesus was glorified in those
who understood and believed his revelation (the
disciples). In the same way, the Risen Jesus is
to be glorified in Matthew's church until the
"close of the age" (28:20).[1] Jesus' Parousia at
the close of the age (24:3) will indisputably
vindicate his revelation--even to those who rejected it--and he will be glorified by all.[2]

It seems that Matthean christology can almost be put on a continuum of ἐξουσία which ranges
from humiliation at one pole to glorification at
the other pole. At the pole of humiliation
stands the earthly Jesus as incarnate Wisdom,
while at the other pole stands Jesus' glorification as he presents the kingdom to the Father
after the Parousia and the judgment. In between
the two poles stands the authority of the Risen
Jesus whose ἐξουσία is still hidden in a universal
sense.

Matthew's redaction in 26:63 (par. Mark
14:61), for example, suggests that the future,
triumphant Son of Man is the Risen Lord to whom
all authority has been given (28:18). Matthew's
characteristic "from this time on" (ἀπ' ἄρτι) in

---

[1]Koester, "Jesus as Wisdom's Envoy and as
Wisdom," Trajectories through Early Christianity,
(Philadelphia: Fortress Press, 1971), p. 221.

[2]24:30-31 cf. 13:41-43; 23:39. See the
discussion in Hamerton-Kelly, Pre-Existence,
p. 83.

26:63 unites the humiliation of the earthly Jesus
with the Son of Man, who sits on the throne of
power and who will come as judge,[1] in such a way
that the humiliation of Jesus becomes part of his
universal enthronement as Son of Man.[2]  Exaltation
and Parousia christologies are not necessarily
mutually exclusive, and, as Donahue has shown,
they co-existed in the tradition before Matthew.[3]
The combination of the allusions to Psa. 110:1 and
to Dan. 7:13 clearly suggests that the humiliation
associated with the Passion is the way to Jesus'
enthronement as the Son of Man.[4]

The christology of Matt. 28:18-20 depicts
the Risen and exalted Son whose authority is revealed only to his disciples (28:16).  They, in
turn, are to reveal the Son to all people (28:19-
20).  The christology of 28:18-20, though, is
still part of Matthew's Sonship christology and
still falls within his humiliation-glorification
schema.  Jesus' exaltation as Risen Lord is the
evangelist's understanding of the Son's authority
during the time of the world-wide mission.  During
this time the authority of the Son is revealed

---

[1]24:30-31; 25:31 cf. 11:27; 28:18.

[2]Schweizer, Matthew, pp. 499-500; cf. John
H. Hayes, "The Resurrection as Enthronement and
the Earliest Church Christology," Interpretation
22 (1968): 333-345; and Bornkamm, "The Risen Lord
and the Earthly Jesus: Matthew 28.16-20," pp.
203-229.

[3]Donahue, Are You the Christ?, pp. 142-162.

[4]Hans Conzelmann, "History and Theology in
the Passion Narratives of the Synoptic Gospels,"
Interpretation 24 (1970): 178-197.

only to those who worship him as the Risen Lord,[1]
but his authority will be proclaimed universally
at his Parousia as the glorious Son of Man. After
his Parousia, Jesus will function as the eschatological judge (25:31-46). At that time, he will
separate out of his kingdom all those who practice
lawlessness (13:41 cf. 13:36-43). His judgment
will bring the "close of the age" (13:40, 49 cf.
24:3; 25:31-46), that is, the end of the world-
wide preaching effort and the time of the Risen
Son's presence with his disciples (24:14; 28:20).
The glorification of the Son will be fulfilled
ultimately when he delivers his eschatological
reign to the Father[2] and is seated in the
Father's kingdom.[3]

---

[1]προσεκύνησαν, 28:17 cf. 8:25; 14:32-33.

[2]13:41-42; 16:28 par. Mark 9:1; Matt. 20:21;
cf. 1 Cor. 15:24-28.

[3]Matt. 16:21, 23 par.; 26:64 par. See
Schweizer, Matthew, pp. 309-311. Matthew never
uses the Son of Man title to refer to the activity
of Jesus as Son of Man between his resurrection
and his Parousia, although he does use Son of Man
sayings to refer to the public ministry of Jesus
(e.g., 8:20; 9:6) and to his Passion and resurrection (e.g., 12:40; 17:9, 12). Matthew's use of
"Son of Man" as a title for Jesus shows that he
conceives of Jesus as Son of Man primarily in
terms of his Parousia (e.g., 10:23; 13:41; see
Kingsbury, Structure, pp. 113-122 for an extensive
discussion). The only passage which could be
construed as an allusion to Jesus' activity as
Son of Man during the interval between Easter and
the Parousia is 13:36b-43. J. D. Kingsbury, who
has investigated thoroughly the redactional functions of the christological titles in Matthew,
graciously has pointed out (continued on p. 392)

At the risk of over-simplification and possible distortion, Matthew's christological schema might be diagramed thusly:

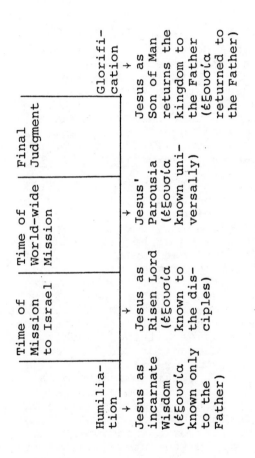

If this schema is correct, then one can see that Matthew's Wisdom christology complements his Son of Man christology. Jesus as incarnate Wisdom is not the only component of Matthew's christology, but it certainly seems to play more of a role within his total christological framework than is usually acknowledged.

---

(continued from p. 390) in private correspondence that a modification has occurred in his understanding of the relationship between the κύριος and Son of Man titles in Matthew. Although Kingsbury still argues that the Son of Man in 13:37 seems to refer to post-Easter activity, he does not want to contend that the Son of Man title there has the confessional overtones of Jesus as the Risen κύριος (Ibid., pp. 113-122 cf. pp. 105-107; Kingsbury, Parables of Jesus in Matthew 13, p. 99).

While Matthew's use of Son of Man in 13:37 could refer to post-Easter activity, it seems to me that it would be out of character to do so. The contrast in 13:37-43 seems to be between Jesus' public ministry in which he "sowed the seed" (13:37) and the "harvest" at the "close of the age" (13:39), i.e., the activity of Jesus as judge at his Parousia (13:41-43). Matthew's interpretation of the judgment in this passage is that it is the last judgment. This means that the βασιλεία of the Son of Man (13:41b), in which the righteous and unrighteous are living together, cannot mean simply the Church for Matthew (contrast Tödt, Son of Man, pp. 69-75). If, as Schweizer contends, " . . . this passage deals with the final Kingdom that will be established when the Son of Man returns, it is impossible to distinguish a 'Kingdom of the Son of Man' belonging to the present world from a 'Kingdom of the Father' (v. 43) to come in the future" (Schweizer, Matthew, p. 310 cf. W. O. Walker, "The Kingdom of

Christology and Discipleship
in Matthew

Matthew's Word-Deed
Discipleship

## The disciples' understanding

It is commonly agreed that the disciples in the First Gospel are those who <u>understand</u> the word and work of Jesus. As we have seen, the words plus the deeds of Jesus constitute the revelation from the Father. One could say that understanding the revelation of Jesus, that is, his authoritative fulfillment of the Law as the love command, is <u>the</u> theme of Matthean discipleship.[1] Understanding is not just the use of their intellectual faculties, but, as we shall see, it is the disciples' recognition of God's revelation through Jesus and their response to it in word and deed. To put it succinctly, one could say that " . . . according to Matthew the concept of understanding describes the nature of the Christian man."[2]

The disciples have a privileged status because they have been made the recipients of divine

---

the Son of Man and the Kingdom of the Father in Matthew," <u>CBQ</u> 30 [1968]: 579).

[1]Barth, "Matthew's Understanding of the Law," <u>TI</u>, p. 109. For a discussion of this theme see pp. 288-291 above.

[2]Kingsbury, <u>Parables of Jesus in Matthew 13</u>, p. 62. See also Barth, <u>TI</u>, pp. 110-112 cf. pp. 105-112 for a full discussion of understanding in Matthew. See also Davies, <u>Sermon on the Mount</u>, pp. 214-220.

insight and revelation (13:10-17). The revelation is the gift of God to the disciples because they have been chosen by the Son to be its recipients (11:27). The revelation consists of the "secrets of the kingdom of heaven" (13:11b) which have "been hidden since the foundation of the world."[1] The revelation has been hidden from Israel (13:11c), but the Son has been granted (δέδοται) authority to reveal knowledge (γνῶναι) of the kingdom's secrets to the privileged disciples (13:11b).[2]

## The content of the Revelation

The words and deeds of Jesus reveal the "higher righteousness," that is, God's will. The disciples, if they truly understand Jesus' words and work, will obey Jesus' words just as Jesus obeyed the Father. The words and work of Jesus were bound up with the Torah. Jesus interpreted the Law by the love command, and then he fulfilled it in his deeds. This means that for Matthew the " . . . following of Christ and radical fulfillment of the law are one and the same. . . . Imitation [of Jesus] is expressed in obedience to the law as interpreted by Jesus."[3] The function of

---

[1]ἀπὸ καταβολῆς, 13:35. See the discussions in Stendahl, School, p. 117; and Koester, "The Structure and Criteria of Early Christian Beliefs," p. 222.

[2]We have basically agreed with and summarized the exegesis of Kingsbury in Parables of Jesus in Matthew 13, pp. 41-62.

[3]Barth, "Matthew's Understanding of the Law," TI, pp. 102-103 cf. Hare, Theme of Jewish Persecution, pp. 142-143; Rigaux, Testimony of

the earthly Jesus for the evangelist was to interpret the Law.[1]

As we discussed above, Jesus' interpretation of the Law issued in the love command. Love constitutes the "higher righteousness,"[2] and it is the only criterion invoked by Jesus-Son of Man at the judgment (cf. 25:37-40). In contrast, lawlessness is to neglect or lose sight of the love which Jesus commanded. For Matthew the criterion which separates true from false discipleship is whether or not one practices the love command as taught and lived by Jesus.[3] The love command, which constitutes the righteousness of God, is the content of Jesus' Word-Deed revelation. In other words, for Matthew the content of God's will has a christological basis. Discipleship for the evangelist is not simply the elevation of one hermeneutical principle over another one. For Matthew " . . . what is involved here is not merely a principle of interpretation but the issue of authority, and Matthew's identification of Christ and Wisdom is central to that issue."[4]

---

St. Matthew, pp. 161, 164-165, 192, 208; Davies, Sermon on the Mount, pp. 94-99, 106-107, 187-190, 203, 205; and Bornkamm, "End-Expectation and Church in Matthew," TI, pp. 30-31, 60, 69, 71, 102 n. 1, 125, 137, 141.

[1]Ibid., p. 35.

[2]5:17-20; 7:12; 9:13; 12:7.

[3]See the discussion above, pp. 288-291.

[4]Suggs, Wisdom, p. 120 (italics mine).

Love is the revelation from God because Jesus-
Sophia, as the authoritative interpreter of Torah
(cf. 7:29), commanded and lived it.[1]

## The disciples proclaim
## the revelation

Jesus sends those who understand his revelation out to proclaim it. As we have seen, part
of Matthew's redactional purpose in his portrait
of the disciples' understanding was to point out
that they understood the message which they were
sent to proclaim.[2] The disciples are commissioned
to preach the "gospel of the kingdom."[3] This is
the same message which Jesus proclaimed in Word
and Deed.[4] Jesus did not simply pass down content; he lived the revelation. Consequently, for

---

[1]Perhaps Matthew has given such a positive
picture of the historical Twelve's understanding
of Jesus' revelation in order to hold up the ideal
of brotherhood and sisterhood (18:15, 21-22, 35;
22:36-40; 23:8-12) to his own community which was
threatened by lawlessness and division (24:10-12
cf. 10:21; 18:16-17).

[2]Cf. the discussion in Ellis, Matthew: His
Mind and His Message, p. 65.

[3]10:5-7 cf. 4:23; 9:35; 28:20.

[4]See the discussions in Kingsbury, Structure, pp. 129-137; Fenton, St. Matthew, pp. 75,
120; Barth, "Matthew's Understanding of the Law,"
TI, p. 162 n. 3; Held, "Matthew as Interpreter of
the Miracle Stories," TI, pp. 250-253; Bornkamm,
"End-Expectation and Church in Matthew," TI, p.
40; Stendahl, School, p. 26 n. 5; Rigaux, Testimony of St. Matthew, pp. 91, 190; and Davies,
Sermon on the Mount, pp. 97-99, 197.

the disciples "proclaiming the gospel" also
involves living it.[1] The proclamation of the gospel of the kingdom is, in essence, preaching and
practicing the love which Jesus commanded. The
disciples become Jesus' personal envoys who are
commissioned to proclaim his message (10:40;
23:34; 28:18-20). The identification of Jesus
with his disciples is so close that their word
becomes his word.[2]

Jesus gave the disciples the same ἐξουσία
which he possessed in his proclamation of the
gospel of the kingdom,[3] but the gospel and the
authority to proclaim it are bound up with the
presence of Jesus (28:16-20). The disciples (Matthew's community) are not simply to proclaim the

---

[1]5:20, 48; 7:12, 21, 24; 10:24-25; 28:19-20.

[2]10:40 cf. 5:11-12; 10:22, 24-25, 38, 39;
23:34; 24:9. Cf. Suggs' statement: "The language
that describes Wisdom's relation to her representatives has a great deal in common with that
of mysticism. It is easy, therefore, to apply
to this relationship such terms as synousia,
incarnation, and identification" (Suggs, Wisdom,
p. 41). In other words, the message of Wisdom's
representatives is identical with the message
of Wisdom herself (Ibid.).

[3]10:1 cf. 4:23; 9:35; 28:18. Cf. the
discussion in J. M. Reese, "How Matthew Portrays
the Communication of Christ's Authority," Biblical
Theology Bulletin 7 (1977): 139-144. In Matt.
10:1 they are μαθηταί, but in 10:2 they have
become ἀποστόλων. The difference implied is that
as ἀπόστολοι they have the full ἐξουσία of the
Sender (Rengstorf, "ἀπόστολος," TDNT 1: 421,
427).

same _message_ which Jesus proclaimed, but they are
to proclaim _him_ and his presence among them.
Their task, as we have seen, is to proclaim to all
persons the unrecognized authority of the Risen
Lord (28:18-20 cf. 11:27).  On the one hand, the
disciples are Jesus' appointed interpreters of
Torah, but, on the other hand, when they proclaim
Jesus' _presence_ and authority, they are the personal envoys of Jesus (23:34) who is Sophia-Torah-
Shekinah.[1]  To summarize: the disciples are Jesus'
personal envoys, and his mission becomes their
mission.  They are given Jesus' ἐξουσία and his
Word to proclaim, namely, the love command.  Thus,
Matthew has a Word-Deed discipleship which is
parallel to his Word-Deed christology.

## The rejection of
## the disciples

Jesus' disciples have his authority and proclaim the same message.  Consequently, their fate
is like his fate.  As we discussed in the redaction of Matt. 24:9-14, rejection and persecution
seem to be a way of life for the envoys from Matthew's community.  Their rejection is a direct
result of their proclamation of Jesus' message.[2]
The disciples, that is, the Twelve and Matthew's
community, stand in continuity with the long line
of envoys sent by Jesus-Sophia; their rejection
is the age-old rejection of Jesus' envoys by

---

[1]Suggs, _Wisdom_, pp. 126-127.  Cf. Barth's
statement: "For Matthew the love-commandment became the principle of interpretation for the law.
Alongside it is the imitation of Christ, which
obviously also carries with it an interpretation
of the law" (Barth, "Matthew's Understanding of
the Law," _TI_, p. 104).

[2]See the discussion on pp. 273-283 above.

Israel.[1]  The upshot of rejection--both for Jesus and his envoys--is death.[2]  Their fate and their humiliation are similar to his fate and humiliation.

Therefore, the humility (πραΰτης) which characterized Jesus himself is also demanded of his disciples.[3]  As G. Barth has put it:

The link between the two [the πραΰτης of Jesus and that demanded of his disciples] is seen in 11:28-30, when Jesus as the πραΰς καὶ ταπεινὸς τῇ καρδίᾳ calls men to himself and invites them to take his yoke upon them.  It is hardly likely that an ideal of meekness already in the evangelist's mind led him to portray Jesus according to it, for Matthew is not influenced in this emphasis by the traditions he received.  The reverse is more probable: the demand for lowliness in the disciples was influenced by the lowliness of the Son of man.[4]

---

[1]23:32 cf. 5:11-12; 10:16-23; 24:9-14.

[2]23:34-36 cf. 26:2, 66; 27:23, 25.

[3]5:5; 18:1-10; 19:13-15; 20:20-28; 23:8-12.

[4]Barth, "Matthew's Understanding of the Law," TI, p. 104.  Cf. the statement of Rigaux: "The Church thus appears to be closely joined with Jesus.  She will continue to be humble and in this state of struggle, a state identical with that of Jesus himself" (Rigaux, Testimony of St. Matthew, p. 191).

The disciples will be "delivered up" (παραδιδόναι, 24:9a) and suffer the same fate as their Lord in accordance with the divine will (δεῖ γενέσθαι, 24:6). As Jesus was "delivered up" (παραδίδοται) to crucifixion (26:2), so his disciples will be "delivered up" (παραδώσουσιν) to be killed (ἀποκτενοῦσιν ὑμᾶς, 24:9). In the First Gospel, as Barth says, "To be persecuted for righteousness' sake means the same as to be persecuted for Jesus' sake" (5:10, 11).[1] The disciples are persecuted <u>because</u> of their proclamation in the name of Jesus (διὰ τὸ ὄνομά μου, 24:9b cf. 10:22).

This causal link between the disciples' suffering and that of Jesus, however, means that they will not only share his humiliation but also his <u>exaltation</u> (18:14; 23:12). They share Jesus' πραΰς, but they also share the ἐξουσία which ultimately led to his exaltation. The humiliation of the disciples is the rejection of their message and the persecution they experience because of their message. They proclaim Jesus as the authoritative Son who fulfilled Torah, and they contend that he is present among them as the Risen Lord who commands all persons to obey his teachings (28:19-20). Their humiliation is the rejection of their attempt to reveal the presence of the Risen Lord among them and the validity of his command, the only evidence of which, until his Parousia, is their own words and deeds. But the disciples know that their commission is from the Risen Lord, whose own words and deeds were vindicated at his resurrection by the Father (cf. 27:43). Jesus told them that the same Father wills that no dis-

---

[1]Barth, "Matthew's Understanding of the Law," p. 105. Notice how Matthew has "Christianized" the saying in 23:34 (par. Luke 11:49) by his allusion to the crucifixion (Friedrich, "προφή-της," p. 835 cf. Haenchen, "Matthäus 23," p. 54).

ciple should perish (18:14). It is the Risen
Lord, vindicated by the Father, whom they worship
(28:9, 17), and for Matthew's community it is He
who has promised to be present with them until the
end of their preaching mission (28:20 cf. 18:20)
just as He was present with his historical disciples in times of great distress.[1] The historical
Twelve could cry out to Jesus "Save Lord; we are
perishing" (8:25), and he calmed their fears with
"Take heart, it is I; have no fear" (14:27 cf.
8:26; 14:26). It was He, as Jesus-Sophia, who
told them not to fear the sufferings which must
occur before the End (24:6), and for Matthew's
community it is still He, as Risen Lord, whose
continuous presence calms the fears of those who
worship Him (28:9-10, 20). In the First Gospel it
is this same Risen Lord and exalted Son, to whom
the Father has given all authority (28:18 cf.
11:27), who will return as Son of Man and universally acknowledge their obedience in the face of
humiliation and rejection. In other words,
" . . . the disciples who continue Jesus' ministry
are promised a share in his suffering, but they
are also assured of his victory: 'Whoever acknowledges me before men I will acknowledge before my
Father in heaven' (10:32)."[2] The glorification
and exaltation of Jesus, which has heretofore occurred only in the life of the believer, will become definitive salvation for the disciples at
Jesus' Parousia. After the Parousia and the judgment, the true disciples "will shine like the sun"
in the Kingdom which Jesus will deliver to his
Father (13:43).

---

[1]σεισμὸς μέγας, 8:24 cf. 8:23; 14:24, 32.
Bornkamm, "Stilling of the Storm in Matthew,"
TI, pp. 53-57.

[2]Senior, Matthew: A Gospel for the Church,
p. 57; cf. Barth, TI, p. 105.

In summary, Matthew has a Word-Deed discipleship to parallel his Word-Deed christology.
The disciples are given the task of continuing the
mission of Jesus in both Word and Deed.  The disciples, like Jesus, first go to Israel with their
message (10:6), but Israel soundly rejects the
proclamation.  The Kingdom, God's presence in
Jesus, is finally taken away from Israel because
they rejected the gospel of the kingdom (cf.
21:43).  The disciples, in turn, are given a new
commission in which they are told to go to "all
nations" (28:19 cf. 24:14), but it appears that
the message still, for the most part, will be rejected (24:14 cf. 24:9).  The implicit Heilsgeschichte of rejection, so strong in the First
Gospel, provides the framework for the parallel
presentation of Jesus as Sophia-Son of Man and the
disciples as his envoys who share his task and
fate.[1]  For Matthew, the parallelism of their
task, calling, and fate with that of Jesus is
based upon the general picture of Wisdom and her
envoys.

However, it should be kept in mind that the
"disciples" in Matthew include Matthew's community.  The disciples are not just "the prophets of
old," or the original Twelve, but they are all
messengers of Jesus, Wisdom of God and Son of Man.
Speaking as the Wisdom of God in Matt. 24:3-31,
Jesus reminds his messengers that his message has
been passed down to them.  His discourse is a
"testament" in which he forecasts their fate and
exhorts them to hold fast to the commission and
revelation which they have received.  Jesus'
testament reminds Matthew's church that their
suffering is in continuity with all of Jesus'
envoys--the prophets of old, the Twelve, and even

----

[1]Hare, Theme of Jewish Persecution,
pp. 139-140.

Jesus himself--but that on the other side of this
humiliation, if they endure until the End (24:13),
is exaltation. Jesus is present with Matthew's
church as the Shekinah when they study his Words,
and his authority is present with them when they
glorify him in their words and deeds. Jesus has
promised, though, that his presence with them
during the interim (between the time in which
Matthew's church lives and the Parousia), which
entails suffering and humiliation, will soon end
and he will come as Son of Man. Jesus' Parousia
as Son of Man will bring an end to their humiliation. And this, Jesus promises them, will take
place immediately (εὐθέως, 24:29) after the
interim in which Matthew's church is living.
Their task is to endure until then (24:13) and to
carry out their mission as envoys of the Wisdom
of God. Jesus' testament, which Matthew presents
as passed down from the Twelve to his church,
serves as a constant reminder of their task and
gives them the hope which they need to fulfill it.

## Ὄχλος IN MATTHEW

The discourse in Matthew 23 moves from "crowds" and "disciples" (23:1) to "Scribes, Pharisees, hypocrites" (23:13), and finally to "Jerusalem, Jerusalem" (=the "crowds," 23:37).[1] This change of audience makes it clear that the warning of Jesus in Matthew is not directed only against the leaders of the people, nor against the temple only, but it is against all of the people (the ὄχλος).

The "crowd" (ὄχλος, ὄχλοι)[2] is one of several groups which commentators have distinguished in the First Gospel, and it seems to be one of the primary terms by which the evangelist alludes to the Jewish masses.[3] Trilling has convincingly

---

[1]Fenton, St. Matthew, p. 377. Τὰ τέκνα σου, that is, "sons of Jerusalem," could refer to Jewish people in any part of the land (Hill, Matthew, p. 315), and, as we have seen, ὁ οἶκος ὑμῶν symbolizes the people as a whole.

[2]The word ὄχλος (ὄχλοι) occurs 49 times in Matthew, 38 in Mark, and 16 times in Luke.

[3]Hummel, Auseinandersetzung, pp. 136-137. Some commentators, however, think that ὄχλος can include Gentiles as well as Jews (e.g., M'Neile, St. Matthew, p. 47). In his historical ministry Jesus undoubtedly met Gentiles as part of the "crowd." In terms of Matthean redaction, though, ὄχλος seems to refer to the Jewish masses. One might contrast the view of van Tilborg who believes that the ὄχλοι represent Matthew's "environment," that is, the universalistic missionary target of Matthew's church (van Tilborg, Jewish

shown that the theater of Jesus' activity in Matthew is always within the confines of Israel.[1] However, Matthew is careful to distinguish the ὄχλοι from their leaders. As far as Matthean redaction is concerned, it can generally be said that the ὄχλοι, in stark contrast to their leaders, respond favorably to Jesus.[2] There is one place in the First Gospel, though, and perhaps two, where the "crowd" does not appear in a favorable light, namely, Matt. 27:20.

This whole section (27:15-26) appears to be one which is constructed by Matthew himself,[3] and this presents difficulties for commentators who contend that the evangelist views the ὄχλοι in a favorable light all through his gospel.[4] Sjef van Tilborg, for example, argues that the total redactional strength of the gospel should receive

---

Leaders in Matthew, pp. 168-172 cf. Fenton, St. Matthew, p. 197).

[1]Trilling, Wahre, pp. 131-138.

[2]van Tilborg, Jewish Leaders in Matthew, chap. 6 cf. Matt. 7:28-29; 9:1-8, 32-34; 12:22-24; 21:9-17; 22:23-33. Also see the excellent summaries in Blair, Jesus in the Gospel of Matthew, pp. 101-107; and Kingsbury, Parables of Jesus in Matthew 13, pp. 25-26.

[3]Schweizer, Matthew, pp. 506-507; Hill, Matthew, p. 349; Dahl, Passionsgeschichte bei Matthäus," p. 26; and Fitzmyer, "Anti-Semitism and the Cry of 'All the People' (Mt 27:25)," pp. 677-681.

[4]See the discussion in Kingsbury, Parables of Jesus in Matthew 13, p. 26.

priority over one verse.  He concludes that the
total view of the ὄχλοι in Matthew, other than
27:20 (cf. 27:25), is a very favorable one.  His
contention is that:

> It does not seem justified to me to
> attribute the same redactional strength
> to this verse [27:20] as to Mt 9,33; 12,23
> and 21,9.15.  In these last verses it is
> Mt himself who speaks [italics mine] but
> what he says in Mt 27,20 has been defined
> by his tradition.  It is therefore not
> permissible to harmonize the ὄχλοι
> mentioned in Mt 9,33; 12,23; 21,9 with the
> ὄχλοι of Mt 27,20 and then continue to
> assume a certain development or to believe
> that Mt eventually condemns the ὄχλοι.[1]

But, is it likely that Matthew, who, according to
van Tilborg, seemingly structured this whole narrative himself and who is definitely speaking in
27:20, would allow such a blatant inconsistency
to exist at a crucial place in his gospel?

It is true that 27:20 depends heavily upon
Mark 15:11, but it does not follow that "the datum
has been determined by tradition."[2]  A comparison
of the two verses shows significant differences:

| Mark 15:11 | Matt. 27:20 (cf. Luke 23:18) |
|---|---|
| οἱ δὲ ἀρχιερεῖς ἀνέσεισαν τὸν ὄχλον ἵνα μᾶλλον τὸν Βαραββᾶν ἀπολύσῃ αυτοῖς | οἱ δὲ ἀρχιερεῖς καὶ οἱ πρεσβύτεροι ἔπεισαν τοὺς ὄχλους ἵνα αἰτήσωνται τὸν Βαραββᾶν, τὸν δὲ Ἰησοῦν ἀπολέσωσιν |

---

[1]van Tilborg, Jewish Leaders, p. 159.

[2]Ibid., p. 149.

(1) In Mark the "chief priests stir up (ἀνέσεισαν) the crowd" (ὄχλον, singular) so that (ἵνα) Barabbas might be released. In Matthew, however, the chief priests (and "elders") <u>persuade</u> (ἔπεισαν) the crowds (ὄχλους, plural) to ask for Barabbas, as in Mark, but then Matthew adds that the intent of the leaders also was to get the ὄχλοι to "destroy" (ἀπολέσωσιν) Jesus. Matthew brings out the contrast between Barabbas and Jesus more emphatically than Mark does: the "crowds" give Barabbas his freedom, but they decide to destroy Jesus. As Schweizer says, "The contrast with Barabbas has been consciously expanded."[1] It is certainly true, as van Tilborg says, that "Mt 27,20 says that οἱ ὄχλοι were not the chief culprits in the tragedy" because "they are led astray and make the wrong choice" at the urging of their leaders.[2] But, the ὄχλοι in Matthew were not duped by the leaders, nor were they "stirred up" as in Mark, they were <u>persuaded</u>. Up to this point it is true that the ὄχλοι have followed Jesus in the First Gospel just as the true disciples have done, but in 27:20 the ὄχλοι are persuaded and consciously decide to destroy Jesus. In stark contrast to the "disciples," they do not follow Jesus again, in the sense of discipleship, after 26:55 (τοῖς ὄχλοις).[3] Thus, we find it difficult to agree with van Tilborg that "Mt 27,20, in spite of everything, once again reveals the contrasts

---

[1]Schweizer, <u>Matthew</u>, p. 506.

[2]van Tilborg, <u>Jewish Leaders</u>, p. 164.

[3]See the discussion immediately below for the explanation that Matthew adds in 26:56 that οἱ μαθηταὶ πάντες ἀφέντες αὐτὸν ἔφυγον (cf. Mark 14:50, ἔφυγον πάντες).

between οἱ ὄχλοι and the Jewish leaders."[1]  Matthew 27:20 reveals precisely the opposite: the
ὄχλοι are of the same stamp as their leaders.
Matthew presents the ὄχλοι as following their
leaders now instead of Jesus, and the responsibility for Jesus' death belongs to both groups.[2]  It
is no small matter that only Matthew has Pilate
say to the ὄχλοι: "It is your responsibility" (or,
"this is your doing").[3]  Matthew then has the

---

[1]van Tilborg, Jewish Leaders, p. 164.

[2]Strecker, Weg, p. 107 cf. pp. 116-117.

[3]Matthew uses πᾶς ὁ λαός here instead of
ὄχλοι.  Sjef van Tilborg uses this in the discussion of 27:20 to point out that this is a
different group than the ὄχλοι and that the ὄχλοι
remain in a favorable light with Matthew.  He
says: "Finally, from Mt 27,25 it appears that Mt
does not speak of οἱ ὄχλοι at the decisive moment,
but of πᾶς ὁ λαός and that he gives a concrete
form to the crowds and narrows its meaning down to
the Jewish people itself" (Jewish Leaders, p.
149).  This is a logical explanation if one holds,
as van Tilborg does, that ὄχλοι really represents
"how Mt saw the reception of Jesus in his own
world" (Ibid., p. 160).  However, if one accepts
ὄχλος as synonymous with λαός, as we do, then
ὄχλοι means the Jewish masses also, and it does
not represent the universalistic target of Matthew's church (cf. Hummel, Auseinandersetzung, pp.
136-137).  There is not much question that λαός
is a technical term meaning "the people of God"
(Kingsbury, Parables of Jesus in Matthew 13, p.
26; and Fenton, St. Matthew, p. 76).  However, we
fail to see how this puts the ὄχλοι in a favorable
light in Matthew unless ὄχλοι includes Gentiles
and is equivalent to or included in "all the
nations" (πάντα τὰ ἔθνη, 28:19).  If so, then

important declaration in verse 25: "(Let) his blood be on us and on our children."

Perhaps Matthew's view of the ὄχλοι is seen more clearly in his comparison of the ὄχλοι with the "disciples" than with the Jewish leaders. The ὄχλοι follow Jesus as the disciples have done,[1]

---

the ὄχλοι would have to be included in the judgment of πάντα τὰ ἔθνη in 25:32 also. The real issue is whether ὄχλος in Matthew refers to believing Jews <u>and</u> Gentiles, in which case the ὄχλοι would be included in the missionary command.

Certainly it seems to be an untenable position to hold that no Jews are included in the missionary target and command of 28:19. However, we do not see the real issue as whether or not Matthew envisions the future conversion of some Jews. The real issue for Matthew is: are the Jews the people of God any longer, that is, is God <u>present</u> among the Jews (here λαός=Judaism; see Kingsbury, <u>Parables of Jesus in Matthew 13</u>, p. 26) or among the disciples (=Matthew's church)? We contend that in Matthew's view Jesus' rejection of Israel is the end of Israel as the people of God (ὁ λαός), among whom He is present, and that this includes the ὄχλοι. Cf. Strathmann's comment: "In Mt. 27:25: πᾶς ὁ λαός . . . λαός is to be equated with the ὄχλος of v. 24" (H. Strathmann, "μάρτυς," <u>TDNT</u> 4: 51). That is, ὄχλοι is, for all practical purposes, synonymous with ὁ λαός. Jesus is not present among the ὄχλοι, the Jewish masses, nor among the official religion of the Jews (ὁ λαός, 27:25). In Jesus' departure from the temple (24:1), God has abandoned both groups and is now present only with the disciples (the "Church"), the new people of God.

[1]4:20, 22; 8:22, 23; 9:9; 19:27, 28.

and this "following" is for Matthew the essence of
being a disciple.[1]  However, the ὄχλοι do not
really "follow" Jesus after 23:1, and after 24:1
only the disciples are the objects of Jesus'
teaching and presence.  Up to this point in his
gospel, Matthew has presented the disciples as a
special group around Jesus which is to provide a
model of obedience for the ὄχλοι.[2]  The pattern is
always, so to speak, that Jesus gives the "bread"
to the disciples and they give it to the crowd.[3]
When Jesus leaves the temple in 24:1, he has not
only turned his back upon the Jewish leaders, but
his presence is also no longer with the ὄχλοι.
Matthew's point seems to be that the ὄχλοι might
not be as incorrigible as their leaders, but at
the crucial moment they have chosen to identify
themselves with Judaism in its official capacity
(27:25) rather than with Jesus.[4]  Futhermore,
whether or not Matthew envisions a mission to the
Jewish ὄχλοι, it is certainly clear that they
stand beyond the boundary of the church.  Although
they flee (26:56), follow Jesus from a distance
(26:58), and even deny him (26:74), the disciples

---

[1]van Tilborg, Jewish Leaders in Matthew,
p. 164.

[2]5:1-2; 12:46-50; 13:2, 34-36; 14:13-21.
Ibid., pp. 160-163 cf. Kingsbury, Parables of
Jesus in Matthew 13, pp. 26-28.

[3]οἱ δὲ μαθηταὶ τοῖς ὄχλοις, 14:19b cf.
Mark 6:14.

[4]Minear makes the opposite point in "False
Prophecy and Hypocrisy in the Gospel of Matthew,"
pp. 76-77, 79.  See also David E. Garland, The
Intention of Matthew 23 (Leiden: E. J. Brill,
1979), pp. 34-41.  Garland and I reached the same
redactional conclusion independently on ὁ ὄχλος.

still have no part in his death as did the ὄχλοι. The disciples are not rejected by Jesus (28:7 cf. 10:32-33), and they ultimately obey Jesus' command (28:16) and receive his missionary instructions (28:18-20a). Their lack of understanding is a temporary lapse.[1] Most importantly, Jesus promises the disciples that he will be present with them until the completion of the Age (28:20b cf. 18:20). This promise is not made to the Jewish officials or to the ὄχλοι. Matthew's purpose, then, is two-fold: (1) it is to show that the Jews, including the ὄχλοι, have been rejected and are no longer the people of God,[2] and (2) to tell his church that a disciple is one who constantly follows Jesus, not just for a short while as the ὄχλοι did. A true disciple is one who does the will of God as Jesus interpreted it "until the end of the age."[3]

---

[1]Cf. Barth's remark on the ὄχλος with the temporary lapse of the disciples: "Hence Matthew cannot completely carry through the thought that the Jewish multitude does not recognise anything . . . but the intention to portray the multitude as obdurate as a whole is clear" (Barth, TI, p. 108 n. 2).

[2]See the succinct discussion of this point in Hare, Theme of Jewish Persecution, pp. 150-152. See also Johannes Munck, Christ and Israel. An Interpretation of Romans 9-11, trans. Ingeborg Nixon (Philadelphia: Fortress Press, 1967), p. 65; and Karl H. Schelkle, "Die 'Selbstverfluchung' Israels nach Matthäus 27,23-25," Antijudaismus im Neues Testament?, ed. W. P. Eckert (München: Chr. Kaiser, 1967), pp. 152-153.

[3]12:48-49 cf. 5:11-12, 17-20; 7:21-22, 24-28; 10:32-33; 12:46-50; etc. See Schweizer, Matthew, p. 509.

## APPENDIX II

## Πορεύομαι IN MATTHEW

Like ἐξέρχομαι, πορεύομαι seems to imply more in Matthew 24:1 than the fact that Jesus simply walked out of the temple.[1] A brief look at the evangelist's redactional use of πορεύομαι suggests that he uses it as a technical term in some instances for a commission, or as a theological term for the mission of Jesus.[2]

Πορεύομαι occurs quite frequently in the

---

[1]See appendix 5 on ἐξέρχομαι. According to the syntax in 24:1, it is uncertain whether ἐπορεύετο is to be linked directly to ἀπὸ τοῦ ἱεροῦ (Klostermann, Matthäusevangelium, p. 191). The imperfect here could describe Jesus in the act of walking through the temple complex and, in that case, the aorist participle (ἐξελθών) would indicate simultaneous action rather than antecedent action (cf. Moulton-Turner, Grammar of New Testament Greek, vol. 3, p. 79). If the participle indicates simultaneous action, then the meaning would be that Jesus definitely left the temple (aorist ptc.), and, when he was going through the courts (imperfect), his disciples came to him (Zerwick, Biblical Greek, § 275). On the other hand, the aorist could denote antecedent action, and could be translated as we prefer: "And Jesus left the Temple and went away" (Schweizer, Matthew, p. 448; and Klostermann, Matthäusevangelium, p. 191). Simultaneous action is indicated without question in Mark: καὶ ἐκπορευομένου αὐτοῦ ἐκ τοῦ ἱεροῦ.

[2]These uses of πορεύομαι are frequent in the LXX. See Hauck and Schultz, "πορεύομαι," TDNT 6: 570-572.

First Gospel as a term for "sending out" someone
with a purpose. Herod sends the Magi out to find
Jesus (πορευθέντες, 2:8), and they obediently "go"
(ἐπορεύθησαν, 2:9).[1] In Matt. 2:20 the angel commands Joseph to "go" into Egypt (πορεύου). In
9:13 Jesus commands the Pharisees to go and learn
the meaning of the Law (πορευθέντες). There are
numerous examples of this general use of πορεύομαι
in the First Gospel,[2] but most noteworthy is where
Jesus sends his disciples out on a missionary
journey (10:6). Here, as B. J. Hubbard has shown,
πορεύομαι could be a technical term as used in
Hebrew commissioning Gattungen.[3] The disciples
are commissioned in 28:19a (πορευθέντες) in a
fashion similar to 10:6, and, as Hubbard says:

> . . . the sense of mission is emphasized
> by πορευθέντες in a way which parallels
> the participial use of this verb in the
> commissioning of the Twelve in 10:7:

---

[1]The participle is used for the imperative
quite consistently in Matthew, and in almost
every case Matthean redaction is evident (2:8;
9:13; 10:7; 11:4; 28:7).

[2]Jesus commands John's disciples to report
what they have seen to John (11:4, πορευθέντες cf.
11:7; Luke 7:22); Simon is commanded to fish for
the Shekel (17:27, πορευθείς); Jesus' disciples
are commanded to get the colt and the ass (21:2,
πορεύεσθε cf. 21:6, πορευθέντες); the King commands his servants to invite everyone to the
marriage feast (22:9, πορεύεσθε cf. 10:6; 21:2);
the foolish maidens are commanded to go and buy
oil (25:9, πορεύεσθε); and the angel commands the
women to go and tell the disciples that Jesus has
risen (28:7, πορευθεῖσαι cf. 28:11, πορευομένων).

[3]Hubbard, 28:16-20, p. 67.

πορευόμενοι δὲ κηρύσσετε ("and preach
as you go").[1]

In these instances, it is very clear that πορεύομαι is a commission, that is, a "sending out" to
accomplish a mission.[2]

Πορεύομαι is also used theologically in the
First Gospel to indicate the mission of Jesus or
of someone else.  In 18:12 "a man" (τινι ἀνθρώπῳ)
goes out to seek (πορευθεὶς ζητεῖ) the wandering
sheep; in 19:15 ἐπορεύθη indicates that Jesus continues on his way of ministry; in 22:15 the Pharisees go (πορευθέντες) and plan to entrap Jesus;
in 26:14 Judas goes (πορευθεὶς) to ask for money
in the plot to take Jesus; and, in 28:16 the disciples go to the mountain which Jesus has appointed and there they receive their commission
from him (28:16-20).  In all of these cases,
πορεύομαι expresses purposive action in carrying
out a divinely appointed mission.

In particular, we are concerned with the
implications of πορεύομαι for the mission of Jesus
in Matthew.  This use of πορεύομαι is already
foreshadowed when John the Baptist (3:5) proclaims
the message of the kingdom (and of judgment) to
all who go to hear it (ἐξεπορεύετο).  The ministry
and mission of Jesus are depicted from the outset
as a movement toward his people.  Hauck's comment
is pertinent here: "If, then, πορεύομαι is often
used in relation to His [Jesus'] travels, this is

--------------------

[1]Ibid., p. 83 cf. Lange, Erscheinen, p. 306.

[2]Πορεύομαι is also used literally in Matthew (12:1, 45[?]; 25:16).

414

no mere description. The word expresses His mission."[1] Πορεύομαι is used when Jesus continues his mission (19:15), and it is used when others plot to abort it (22:15; 26:14). Jesus' mission becomes a model for his followers. As the shepherd, he goes out and seeks the lost (18:12); his followers must do the same thing (10:6). As a wandering preacher himself, Jesus commissions the disciples to become travelling preachers who carry his message (10:7 cf. 4:17) to the lost sheep of the house of Israel (10:6), and, finally, to the whole world (28:19 cf. 24:14).[2]

An important use of πορεύομαι in the Septuagint, and in the New Testament, is to denote one's "going to death."[3] This meaning of πορεύομαι is not explicit in Matthew, but it is certainly implied. The Pharisees go and plan to entrap Jesus (22:15), an entrapment which eventually issues in his death.[4] Judas "goes" to enter the plot against Jesus (26:14), a plot which leads to Jesus' _and_ Judas' deaths.[5] In 24:1 Jesus "goes"

---

[1] Hauck, "πορεύομαι," p. 574.

[2] Ibid., pp. 574-575.

[3] Hosea 13:3; 1 Kings 2:2; Luke 22:22.

[4] 26:66; 27:22, 23, 25, 26, etc.

[5] 26:47-50; 27:3-5. Ὑπάγω, which is a synonym for πορεύομαι, is used in the Synoptic Gospels to depict the movement of Jesus toward his death (Bauer, _Greek-English Lexicon_, p. 844 cf. Matt. 26:64 par.). However, Matthew specifically connects the movement of Jesus towards his death (ὑπάγω) with Judas and his movements to betray Jesus (26:25 cf. 26:23), for which he has used πορεύομαι (26:14). "In this respect," says

on his way (ἐπορεύετο) which is, first, to deliver
his final sermon (chaps. 24-25), and, secondly, to
announce his impending death (26:1-2). It is
noteworthy in this regard that in the Fourth Gospel Jesus speaks several times of "going" to the
Father.[1] It has already been noted that the
eschatological discourse in Matthew is a testament,
perhaps a farewell discourse of Jesus as Wisdom,
and the use of πορεύομαι before Jesus delivers
this discourse alludes to the fact that this is
his last teaching to the disciples before his
death. The whole discourse is bracketed by πορεύομαι, which indicates movement toward his death,
and by his explicit announcement of his death
immediately when the discourse concludes.[2]

A final use of πορεύομαι which could be
applicable to Matt. 24:1 is its meaning in the
Septuagint of obediently following God or someone
else (Deut. 13:5; 3 Kings 18:21, etc.). Πορεύομαι
is used in this sense as the moral or religious
"walk" of obedience. Although this use does not
occur explicitly in the Matthean text, the image
does occur of Jesus going on his way and of the
disciples following him in this way.[3] The disciples "come to" (προσῆλθον) him immediately after

---

Hauck, "it should not be overlooked that πορεύομαι
alternates with ὑπάγω" (Hauck, "πορεύομαι,"
p. 575).

[1]14:2, 3, 12; 16:28 cf. 14:28; 16:7.

[2]The "discourse" here is defined as 24:3-31
plus the parenetical section in 23:32-25:46.

[3]Hauck, "πορεύομαι," pp. 571, 575.

416

he leaves the temple and proceeds on his way to
death (24:1). The call to discipleship in Matthew
is "come after me,"[1] and the disciples are portrayed throughout the gospel as "following"
Jesus.[2] In Matthew whoever does not take his/her
cross and "follow after" (ἀκολουθεῖ ὀπίσω) Jesus
is not worthy of him (10:38 cf. Luke 14:27). The
theme of discipleship as "following Jesus on the
Way" is a prominent one in Mark, but Matthew enhances it.[3] The disciples not only follow Jesus
but they are also given his authority (ἐξουσία,
10:1), his message (10:28; 28:16-20), and they are
rejected just as he was rejected (23:34-39 cf.
cf. 10:17-21, 24-25). The disciples also share
Jesus' task and his fate. The image, then, of
the disciples "following" Jesus in the religious
sense of obedience is certainly present in Matt.
24:1. The disciples follow Jesus-Sophia as he
"turns his back" (ἐξελθών) on Israel and "goes on
his way" (ἐπορεύετο) to fulfill his mission as
the Wisdom of God, namely, rejection and death.

---

[1]4:19 cf. 8:19, 22; 9:9a; 16:24; 19:21.

[2]4:20, 22; 8:23. Cf. the "crowds" in 4:25;
8:1, 10; 12:15, etc. As Schweizer remarks on
Matt. 8:23: "Unlike Mark, Matthew describes the
boarding of the ship as the 'following' of the
'disciples'; as in 14:24, the ship has become a
symbol for the band of disciples, the community
of Jesus" (Schweizer, Matthew, p. 221 cf. Matt.
9:9b, 19; 19:27-28; 26:58).

[3]Cf. the discussions in Perrin, What is
Redaction Criticism?, pp. 44-60; and Best,
"Discipleship in Mark: Mark 8:22-10:52," Scottish
Journal of Theology 23 (1970): p. 326.

## APPENDIX III

## Οἱ μαθηταί IN MATTHEW

E. Martinez has argued that οἱ μαθηταί αὐτοῦ in Matthew is distinctly different from οἱ μαθηταί.[1] The expression "his disciples" does not denote any definite group of disciples, but, says Martinez, "only some followers of Christ."[2] The expression "his disciples," he contends, is indefinite in Matthew. Because of the definite article, he contends that οἱ μαθηταί quite clearly refers only to the Twelve who, for Matthew, are the leaders of the Christian community.[3] If this distinction holds up throughout the entire gospel, then the discourse in 24:3-31 (οἱ μαθηταί, 24:3) is addressed only to the Christian leaders and not to the community as a whole. Matthew 24:1-2 would then be addressed to an indefinite group of Jesus' followers which would include, perhaps, even the ὄχλος.

First, it seems that Martinez does a word study in which too much emphasis is placed upon the use of the definite article with οἱ μαθηταί. As Matt. 10:1 and 11:1 clearly show, the rigorous distinction which he finds throughout the gospel between οἱ μαθηταί and οἱ μαθηταί αὐτοῦ is not consistently followed by Matthew.[4]

---

[1]Ernest R. Martinez, "The Interpretation of HOI MATHĒTAI in Matthew 18," CBQ 23 (1961): 281-292.

[2]Ibid., p. 286.    [3]Ibid., pp. 286-292.

[4]Cf. Kingsbury's remark: "Martinez advances the thesis that Matthew distinguishes in his Gospel between 'his disciples (=an indefinite group of Jesus' followers) and 'the disciples'

Secondly, Martinez does not discuss Matthew's use of possible synonyms for οἱ μαθηταί (αὐτοῦ) such as οἱ ὀλιγόπιστοι. In the classical passage of the "Stilling of the Storm," ὀλιγόπιστοι (cf. 8:26) quite clearly is synonymous with οἱ μαθηταὶ αὐτοῦ (8:23) and means Matthew's church community[1] while in 14:31 it is synonymous with οἱ μαθηταί (14:26) and is used of a "church leader," Peter. In 14:31, though, it is clear that the whole church community is meant (cf. v. 33) and not just the leaders of the community.[2]

Thirdly, Matt. 18:1, which perhaps is addressed to community leaders only, is too quickly read into other parts of the gospel.[3] This, in

_____

(=the Twelve). However, Matthew's text at 10.1 and 11.1 alone makes such a differentiation untenable" (Kingsbury, Parables of Jesus in Matthew 13, p. 146 n. 67). It is interesting that Pesch, however, sees οἱ μαθηταὶ αὐτοῦ as the Twelve (Pesch, "Eschatologie und Ethik," p. 226).

[1]Bornkamm, "Stilling of the Storm in Matthew," TI, pp. 55-56. Cf. Barth's statement: "Matthew sees the Church in general embodied in the μαθηταί" ("Matthew's Understanding of the Law," TI, p. 100 n. 2). See also Senior, Matthew: A Gospel for the Church, pp. 60-62; and Held, "Matthew as Interpreter of the Miracle Stories," TI, pp. 293-296.

[2]Οἱ μαθηταί in Matt. 15:36-37, whom Martinez argues equal church leaders only, are called ὀλιγόπιστοι in 16:8 (Martinez, "HOI MATHĒTAI," p. 288 cf. also 17:19-20).

[3]See the discussion in Ellis, Matthew: His Mind and His Message, pp. 68-72.

419

turn, is based upon a questionable assumption about "the early Christians," namely, that they appear as a homogeneous group. For example, Martinez says:

> Furthermore, the words "the disciples" in Matthew would surely have been as well known to the early Christians as "the Twelve" or "the Apostles," and could easily have been understood as equivalent. Certainly the early Christians [italics mine] did not question the fact that only the bishops, the rulers of the different churches, possessed the power granted in 18,18. The Christian community as a whole assumed no such power because the faithful knew that "the disciples" in 18,1 referred only to the twelve disciples.[1]

Fourthly, Martinez does not discuss how οἱ μαθηταί αὐτοῦ as an indefinite group differs from the ὄχλος in Matthew. As we have seen concerning ὁ ὄχλος in Matthew,[2] the two groups cannot be equated and function quite differently for Matthew—especially in 24:1 after Jesus has rejected Israel and the "crowds."

Fifthly, προσέρχομαι, a cultic term of reverence and worship, is used as regularly with οἱ μαθηταί αὐτοῦ as it is with οἱ μαθηταί. There appears to be no distinction, and both phrases point to a worshipping community rather than to

---

[1]Martinez, "HOI MATHĒTAI," p. 287 cf. Rengstorf, "μανθάνω," TDNT 4: 450.

[2]See appendix 1.

only its leaders.[1]

Finally, it is possible to identify οἱ μαθηταί with the Twelve only if one assumes that Matthew's chief interest is a "historicizing" one. That is, if one assumes that Matthew is primarily interested in presenting the "disciples" in their time (the time of Jesus' ministry), then this would clearly set them apart from the time of Matthew's church (chronologically speaking). Strecker is perhaps the leading proponent of the view that Matthew has structured his gospel in linear terms: the time of preparation (the Old Testament, the prophets), the time of Jesus (and οἱ μαθηταί), and the time of the Church.[2] While it is correct to say that Matthew has a view of salvation-history, it might not be correct to assert that he has structured his whole gospel in terms of such a scheme as opposed to a topical or a geographical outline. In the First Gospel, the "disciples" are not historicized to the degree that they, along with Jesus, are past figures who are encapsulated into the "time of Jesus." As passages like 28:20 suggest (cf. 1:23; 18:20), Jesus is always present with "the disciples." If one were going to put forth a salvation-historical scheme for Matthew at all, it seems that in light of Matt. 1:23 and 18:20 the "time of Jesus" and "the time of the Church" would have to be coalesced into one. Kingsbury has done this, and

---

[1]E.g., 5:1; 13:10, 36; 14:12, 15; 15:12, 23; 17:19; 18:1; 24:1, 3. See Barth, "Matthew's Understanding of the Law," TI, p. 100 n. 2.

[2]Strecker, "The Concept of History in Matthew," pp. 219-230 cf. Strecker, Weg, pp. 185-188, 191; and Walker, Heilsgeschichte, p. 115.

his conclusion is most convincing that the time of the Church and the time of Jesus coalesce so that the disciples become representative Christians.[1]

We conclude, then, that the distinction between οἱ μαθηταί and οἱ μαθηταί αὐτοῦ advanced by Martinez does not hold up under redactional scrutiny.

---

[1]Kingsbury, "The Structure of Matthew's Gospel and His Concept of Salvation-History," CBQ 35 (1973): 472-473. See also pp. 132-142 above.

## APPENDIX IV

## Ἔθνη IN MATTHEW

Ἔθνος, in any of its forms, occurs fifteen times in the First Gospel.[1] It is generally agreed that any use of ἔθνη, particularly as the object of missionary preaching, must be understood in light of Matt. 28:19. Thus, ἔθνη in 28:19 becomes the crucial point for interpreters.

W. Trilling argues that πάντα τὰ ἔθνη in 28:19 includes the Jews. He contends that Matthew uses ἔθνη in a universal sense in 24:9 (πάντων τῶν ἐθνῶν), in 24:14 (ἐν ὅλῃ τῇ οἰκουμένῃ . . . τοῖς ἔθνεσιν), and in 25:32 (πάντα τὰ ἔθνη).[2] However, none of these passages suggest that Matthew's church is still engaged in a mission to Israel even if ἔθνη in them includes Israel.[3] If ἐθνῶν includes the Jews, all that it means is that the persecution and hatred brought about by the Jews is still going on for Matthew's church during the time of world-wide mission. In 24:14 the point is that the gospel must be preached ἐν ὅλῃ τῇ οἰκουμένῃ before the τέλος. The gospel of the kingdom has already been proclaimed to Israel (10:5-7). In 10:7 Jesus explicitly commanded the

---

[1]4:15; 6:32; 10:5, 18; 12:18, 21; 20:19, 25; 21:40; 24:7(twice), 9, 14; 25:32; 28:19.

[2]Trilling, Wahre, pp. 26-35; see also John P. Meier, "Nations or Gentiles in Matthew 28:19?" CBQ 39 (1977): 94-102.

[3]See the discussion in Walker, Heilsgeschichte, pp. 85-90 and the discussion of the rejection theme in Matthew on pp. 98-112 above.

disciples not to go to the ἐθνῶν,[1] but before the ἐθνῶν the proclamation must proceed to the whole world, as opposed only to Israel (cf. 10:6).[2]

In this regard, Hare contends that τὰ ἔθνη in 28:19 must be taken as "Gentiles" rather than "nations." In view of βαπτίζοντες αὐτούς, ἔθνη must mean <u>individuals</u> and "can therefore refer only to non-Jews."[3] There is no <u>a priori</u> reason, of course, that <u>Jewish</u> individuals could not also be included in the phrase "baptizing them." It is difficult to believe that an <u>individual</u> Jew would be excluded from the missionary command or from Matthew's community. The individual Jew who accepted the "Gospel of the Kingdom" would belong to the <u>new</u> people of God.[4] Matthew's presentation concerning Israel is a salvation-historical one, namely, that Israel <u>as a nation</u> has been definitively rejected by God. As a nation, Israel no longer has God's rule and presence. The presence of God, which Matthew believes to be in Jesus-Sophia-Shekinah, has passed to another "people" (ἔθνει), that is, the true disciples (=Matthew's church) who "produce the fruits of it" (21:43).

As we have attempted to show, Matthew makes

---

[1]εἰς ὁδὸν ἐθνῶν μὴ ἀπέλθητε.

[2]εἰς μαρτύριον πᾶσιν τοῖς ἔθνεσιν (24:14).

[3]Hare, <u>Theme of Jewish Persecution</u>, p. 148 n. 3.

[4]See the discussion in Hill, <u>Matthew</u>, p. 72, and Dahl, "The Passion Narrative in Matthew," pp. 49-50 (ET).

this point clear in three ways.  First, <u>literarily</u>
he has structured the theme of Israel's rejection
so that God's presence leaves Israel when Jesus
departs from the temple (24:1).  Secondly, Matthew
makes the point <u>theologically</u> when he contends
that the Church, which includes his community, has
been given the kingdom (21:43), the presence of
the Risen Lord (1:23; 18:20; 28:20), and the task
of proclaiming the gospel of the kingdom in word
and deed (10:1, 7; 24:14).  Finally, this implies
<u>historically</u> how Matthew's church had arrived at
these conclusions.  Israel decidedly rejected and
crucified Jesus (27:25), and they have rejected
the proclamation of Matthew's church (and the
Church in general).  Israel's rejection of Jesus
and the Gospel implies historically that Matthew's
church is separate from the Synagogue and that an
organized mission to Israel is a thing of the past
(cf. 10:17-22).[1]  Thus, we agree with Hare's
general conclusion that ἔθνη in 28:19 does not
include a mission to Israel.  He says:

> In the future converts from Israel will
> not be refused, but their conversion
> will not be sought.  Henceforward the
> mission is not to Israel and the Gentiles
> but only to the Gentiles.[2]

For Matthew, the judgment upon Israel for
their rejection of Jesus and the Gospel was the
loss of their status as God's people.  This judgment, as we have said, precluded any organized

---

[1]See the discussion of Matthew's redaction
of Mark 13:9-13 (pp. 273-283 above) where we
argue that the evangelist "de-eschatologizes" the
Markan material.

[2]Hare, <u>Theme of Jewish Persecution</u>, p. 148;
cf. Schweizer, <u>Matthew</u>, p. 148; and Kingsbury,

mission to them as a nation. Therefore, we can
find no hint in the First Gospel " . . . that
after the full number of the Gentiles have been
admitted to the Kingdom the resistance of Israel
will be supernaturally overcome, as in Romans
11:25f. For Israel the future holds only Judgment."[1]

Trilling, then, seems to be correct when he
argues that πάντα τὰ ἔθνη in 25:32 includes the
Jews. The context in 25:32 is one of judgment
after the Parousia and not of mission before the
"consummation of the age" (28:20) as in 28:19.
In Matthew's scheme of salvation-history, the
"gospel of the kingdom" has been proclaimed to
Israel and is being proclaimed to the Gentiles as
a "witness against" them.[2] The Parousia, the
τέλος, and the judgment, come after the proclamation to both groups is finished (24:14). Matthew
deleted Mark 13:10 from the context of preaching
to the Jews because that preaching mission, which
was a "testimony against" them, is past. He
shifts Mark 13:10 to 24:14 because his church is
currently involved in the mission to the "Gentiles." However, the evangelist still includes
the same catchword in 24:9a as in 10:17-22 (παρα-
δίδωμι). He indicates that the mission to the

Parables of Jesus in Matthew 13, p. 29.

[1]Hare, Theme of Jewish Persecution, pp.
148-149. Matthew's deletion of Mark's πρῶτον
(24:14 cf. Mark 13:10), which in Mark seems to
have the eschatological meaning that Israel will
be converted after the full number of Gentiles
have "come in," seems to make the point of
Israel's rejection by Jesus and their judgment
very clear (cf. Marxsen, Mark the Evangelist,
p. 176).

[2]εἰς μαρτύριον, 24:14 cf. 10:18.

ἔθνεσιν will be met with the same "hatred" as the mission to the Jews,[1] and that the disciples will still be "delivered up" by "all the nations"[2] just as they were "delivered up" during the Jewish mission.[3]  To put it succinctly, the proclamation of the Gospel and their <u>present</u> acceptance or rejection of it will serve as a "witness against" πάντα τὰ ἔθνη (both Israel and the Gentiles) at the final Judgment.[4]  The Son of Man at the judgment will make it clear to all persons what their (earthly) response to the Gospel was.  The only criterion used at the judgment is their acceptance or rejection of the "gospel of the kingdom,"[5] which for Matthew meant Jesus' Word-Deed interpretation of the love command.[6]  For Israel <u>as a nation</u> this means that the Son of Man can only pass the judgment which they rendered as a final judgment against themselves when they rejected Jesus-Sophia--they are no longer the sons and daughters of the kingdom.

---

[1]μισούμενοι, 24:9 cf. 10:22.

[2]πάντων τῶν ἐθνῶν, 24:9b cf. ὑπὸ πάντων in Mark 13:13.

[3]παραδώσουσιν, 10:17 cf. 10:19, 21.

[4]25:32 cf. 10:32-33.  See the discussion in Kingsbury, <u>Structure</u>, pp. 148-149.

[5]24:14 cf. 4:17; 9:35.

[6]22:34-40 cf. 25:35-40, 42-45.

# APPENDIX V

## Ἐξέρχομαι IN MATTHEW

We have seen that the aorist participle in Matt. 24:1 is characteristic of the evangelist's style,[1] but further investigation suggests that Matthew uses ἐξέρχομαι to denote the beginning or the termination of some activity. When it is used in reference to Jesus and his disciples, the connotation of ἐξέρχομαι is that the activity is occurring according to God's plan. Thus, ἐξέρχομαι does not seem to be just a stylistic device of the evangelist, but in some cases it is also theologically important for him. This seems to be particularly true when he uses ἐξέρχομαι of Jesus and his activities.

Ἐξέρχομαι in the First Gospel can denote a good or evil intention. When it is used of Jesus, ἐξέρχομαι usually denotes a turning point in his teaching or his ministry. In light of its use to describe Jesus' work, ἐξέρχομαι is theologically significant for Matthew because it indicates the beginning or the ending of his preaching. It is also used of those who go out to hear Jesus' preaching. Therefore, ἐξέρχομαι quite often has the significance of salvation or of judgment in the First Gospel.

Ἐξέρχομαι is used for the intentions which proceed from the hearts of men and women: "But what comes out of the mouth proceeds (ἐξέρχεται) from the heart, and this defiles a man" (Matt. 15:18 cf. Mark 7:20). The intentions can be evil: "But the Pharisees went out (ἐξελθόντες) and took counsel against him, how to destroy him."[2] The

---

[1] See pp. 116-118 above.

[2] Matt. 12:14 cf. 18:28, ἐξελθών.

428

same word is used to describe the fulfillment of the intentions to destroy Jesus as they "were marching out" (ἐξερχόμενοι) to crucify him.[1]  The word also ends the Eucharist with Jesus' prediction that the disciples would fall away (26:30-31 cf. vv. 26-29).

On the other hand, persons come out to Jesus and humbly seek his help (15:22 cf. Mark 7:25). They also "go out" to hear a prophetic message from John,[2] or they could be drawn out to hear a false message.[3]  Ἐξέρχομαι is used of those who "go out" spreading news about Jesus' deeds (9:26, 31).  It is used of Jesus' disciples on their missionary journeys--particularly when they end their mission in a given place (10:11, 14).  Ἐξέρχομαι also denotes Jesus' change of locale for his own ministry, that is, when he terminates his message in one place and begins it in another (15:21 cf. Mark 7:24).  It can denote when he is about to change the subject of his teaching (13:1 cf. Mark 4:1).  Ἐξέρχομαι is used when people desire to be separated from Jesus (8:34), and it is used of Jesus when he separates himself from his adversaries (21:17 cf. 24:1).

Ἐξέρχομαι is used to prophesy Jesus' first advent according to the plan of God (2:6), and it is used as an analogy of his Parousia as Son of Man (24:27 cf. Luke 17:24).  It also describes those who will go out to meet the Son of Man when he comes (25:1, 6) and the angels as they go out

---

[1]27:32 cf. 26:55; Mark 15:21; Luke 23:26.

[2]11:7, 8, 9 par. Luke 7:24-26.

[3]24:26 cf. Luke 17:23.

to separate those for judgment (13:49). The evangelist also uses ἐξέρχομαι as a synonym for the resurrection of the dead (27:53).

This survey of Matthew's use of ἐξέρχομαι is not to suggest that every use of ἐξέρχομαι in the First Gospel is theologically pregnant and has a meaning other than the literal meaning of "to come out" or "to go away" (cf. 12:44). None of the word studies which we have offered in the appendices should be taken in this way because such word studies are quite inconclusive. Although word studies are necessary and can indicate the range of possible meanings of a word in a gospel, at best they only offer suggestions concerning the meaning of the word in any given context. However, ἐξέρχομαι is used many times in Matthew to suggest the beginning or the termination of some action--teaching, preaching, healing, judgment--according to the divine plan, particularly in relation to Jesus and his disciples.[1] The question which must be asked is: what significance does ἐξέρχομαι have in relation to Jesus' departure from the temple in 24:1?

The theological significance of ἐξέρχομαι in Matthew

As Trilling points out, the evangelist uses ἐξέρχομαι forty-three times, and he uses a whole cluster of verbs which are almost synonymous--ἀποστέλλειν (22 times), πέμπειν (4 times), and ἔρχεσθαι (111 times, especially ἦλθον).[2] The whole cluster of verbs is used 180 times in Matthew. Although this is statistically impressive, it does not necessarily follow that ἐξέρχομαι is

---

[1]Trilling, Wahre, pp. 171-172.

[2]Ibid.

part of a verbal cluster which is <u>theologically</u> important for Matthew.

There seems to be more to the use of ἐξ-έρχομαι in the First Gospel, though, than its statistical importance.  E. Arens, who alludes to the cluster of verbs already mentioned, concludes that ἐξέρχομαι in the whole Synoptic tradition " . . . bears the particular nuance of coming FROM (ἐξ--), and in fact it is used almost exclusively to refer to Jesus' divine origin."[1]   In view of the fact that ἐξέρχομαι in the Synoptic tradition denotes Jesus' origin, it seems that Trilling is on secure ground when he concludes that ἐξέρχομαι (and the related cluster of verbs) suggests that Jesus' commission and vocation are given by God and that Matthew's use of ἐξέρχομαι is his <u>characteristic way</u> of expressing this connotation.[2]   Trilling's conclusion seems to be the theological minimum for Matthew's use of ἐξ-έρχομαι.  Can the discussion be carried any further?

As we mentioned above, one way ἐξέρχομαι functions in Matthew is to suggest the beginning or the termination of some activity according to the divine plan.  Emissaries are sent out and called back by using ἐξέρχομαι.  Jesus and the disciples move about very boldly in the First Gospel, usually in relation to the term ἐξέρχομαι.

Probing the possible theological connotations of ἐξέρχομαι more deeply, we find that it is often used in the Septuagint to depict operations which proceed from God.  For example, the

---

[1]Arens, <u>ELTHON-Sayings</u>, p. 309.

[2]Trilling, <u>Wahre</u>, pp. 171-172.

431

Law will "go forth" from God,[1] as will salvation.[2]
God's "word" (ῥῆμα) and God's commandments proceed
from His/Her mouth.[3] God's wrath (ὀργή) can also
"proceed" (ἐξῆλθεν) from Him/Her,[4] as can judgment
(Hosea 6:6) and righteousness (Isa. 45:23). God's
spirit also proceeds from God (Isa. 57:16) and
God Himself/Herself "goes out" before the people
of God.[5] The Messiah "comes out"[6] just as the
people "came out" of Egypt.[7] The Remnant is said
to "come out" (Isa. 37:32). Ἐξέρχομαι is also
significant in cultic and sacral use--particularly
because it expresses the epiphany of God.[8]

The Fourth Gospel seems to use ἐξέρχομαι in
terms similar to the Septuagint. In that gospel,
Jesus "comes forth" (ἐξῆλθον) from God the Father.[9] Bultmann has posited a connection between
Jesus as λόγος in John and Jesus as σοφία. Λόγος

---

[1]ἐξελεύσεται, Isa. 51:4 cf. 2:3; Micah 4:2b.

[2]Isa. 51:5 cf. Zech. 14:8.

[3]Isa. 55:11; πρόσταγμα, Gen. 24:50.

[4]Num. 17:11 cf. Jer. 4:4; 37:23.

[5]Micah 2:13 cf. Hab. 3:13; Isa. 52:12;
Zech. 9:14; 14:3.

[6]Micah 5:2; Isa. 11:1.

[7]Isa. 11:16; Jer. 7:25.

[8]Isa. 42:13; Zech. 14:3 cf. 5:5. For other
references see J. Schneider, "ἔρχομαι," TDNT
2: 679.

[9]8:42; 13:3; 16:27, 28 cf. 16:30; 17:8. Cf.
Bultmann, Gospel of John, pp. 45 n. 1 cf. pp. 22f.

and σοφία are used synonymously in Wisdom of Sol.
9:1, and Bultmann contends that Jesus as λόγος,
particularly in his function as Revealer, corresponds with σοφία.[1] How much Wisdom speculation
has influenced the Fourth Gospel is a disputed
question, but the use of ἐξέρχομαι in that gospel
to say that Jesus proceeded from God is interesting. Regardless of how one might interpret
ἐξέρχομαι in the Fourth Gospel, Schneider is certainly correct when he states:

> In Jn. the Messianic self-witness of
> Jesus can take the form: ἐκ θεοῦ ἐξῆλθον
> (Jn. 8:42; 16:27f.; 17:8 cf. 13:3). The
> aim of this self-witness is achieved when
> the disciples reply to it with the con-
> fession: πιστεύομεν ὅτι ἀπὸ θεοῦ ἐξῆλθες
> (Jn. 16:30).[2]

This speculation about the use of ἐξέρχομαι
in the Fourth Gospel is particularly interesting
when it is recalled that one of the uses of ἐξέρχομαι in the Septuagint is to show that Sophia
proceeds from God. The <u>locus classicus</u> is Sirach
24:3 where Sophia says: "I came forth (ἐξῆλθον)
from the mouth of the Most High." Several other
passages in the Septuagint imply that Wisdom proceeded from God.[3] This is not surprising, however, when it is recalled that in Judaism everything, including Wisdom, was believed to proceed

---

[1]Ibid., pp. 22-25, 46 n. 1.

[2]Schneider, "ἔρχομαι," p. 680.

[3]Cf. Prov. 8:22-31; ἐξαπόστειλον, Wisdom of
Sol. 9:10; Sirach 1:11; 11:15; 24:30.

from God.[1]  It is also said that Wisdom (of YHWH?) goes out (ἐξῆλθον) with a seductive appeal, and in Sirach 14:22 one is to "go out after" Wisdom.[2]

Several commentators have suggested that Matthew's Sophia christology stands in connection with a tradition like Sirach 24.[3]  Many have emphasized, however, that Matthew's Sophia tradition is more complex and seems to be the upshot of several traditions.  In any case, whatever the background of Matthew's Sophia christology might be, it does appear that ἐξέρχομαι in Matt. 24:1 suggests the termination of Jesus' activity to Israel as God's people, and it is possible that the word has Wisdom overtones as well.

---

[1]Cf. Isa. 48:3; Lam. 3:38.  I simply cannot agree with Arens' restrictive statement that "The coming of Wisdom (σοφία), to which Wis. 7,7; Sir. 24,8.10b.11 and 4 En. 42,2 refer, is so rarely mentioned that--in spite of its personalization-- it cannot be said that behind the New Testament ἦλθον lies the coming of Wisdom" (Arens, ELTHON-Sayings, p. 280 n. 15).

[2]ἔξελθε; cf. Sirach 14:20.

[3]See Lange, Erscheinen, p. 333 n. 14; Steck, Geschick der Propheten, p. 232; and Christ, Jesus Sophia, pp. 35-36, 140-145.  Sirach 24 is very suggestive.  Wisdom "glories" in the midst of her "people" (λαοῦ, 24:1).  Sophia comes forth from the mouth of God (ἐξῆλθον) to "tabernacle" in "high places" and her throne is ἐν στύλῳ νεφέλης (24:2, i.e., the Shekinah).  Her dwelling place in Israel (24:8) is the holy tabernacle in Jerusalem (24:10, 11).  There Wisdom pleads for those who will obey her (24:19-22 cf. Prov. 8:32-36). Cf. Snaith, Ecclesiasticus, p. 120.

# INDEXES

## SCRIPTURE INDEX

### OLD TESTAMENT LITERATURE

Genesis
|  |  |
|---|---|
| 15:16 | 60 |
| 24:50 | 432n3 |
| 47:29-50:14 | 188n2 |

Exodus
|  |  |
|---|---|
| 13:24-25 | 68 |
| 19:4 | 65 |
| 33:9-10 | 68,95 |

Numbers
|  |  |
|---|---|
| 17:11 | 432n4 |
| 18:14 | 143-144 |

Deuteronomy
|  |  |
|---|---|
| 13:1-2 | 262n4 |
| 13:5 | 416 |
| 32:11 | 65 |

Joshua
|  |  |
|---|---|
| 23:1-24:32 | 188n2 |

Ruth
|  |  |
|---|---|
| 2:12 | 65 |

I Samuel
|  |  |
|---|---|
| ch. 12 | 188n2 |

II Samuel
|  |  |
|---|---|
| 15:30 | 212 |

I Kings
|  |  |
|---|---|
| 2:1-9 | 188n2 |
| 2:2 | 415n3 |
| 9:7f. | 74n1 |

I Kings (cont.)
|  |  |
|---|---|
| 14:6 | 173 |

Job
|  |  |
|---|---|
| 15:16 | 327n3 |
| ch. 28 | 96,170 |
| 39:30 | 265n1 |

Psalms
|  |  |
|---|---|
| 5:7 | 327n3 |
| 13:1 | 327n3 |
| 17:8 | 65 |
| 36:7 | 65 |
| 47:8 | 210n2 |
| 52:1 | 327n3 |
| 57:1 | 65 |
| 61:4 | 65 |
| 63:7 | 65 |
| 118:26 | 78,114,115,116 |
| 118:163 | 327n3 |

Proverbs
|  |  |
|---|---|
| 1:20 | 28,95 |
| 1:28 | 95,96 |
| ch. 8 | 66 |
| 8:22-30 | 170 |
| 8:22-31 | 433n3 |
| 8:22-32 | 96 |
| 8:32-36 | 144n2, 434n3 |
| 9:1-6 | 144n2 |
| 29:27 | 328 |

435

441

447

448

449

451

457

## INDEX OF NAMES

Ellis, P.F. (cont.), 139,
140,142,143,186,190,191,
193,194,195,196,197,200,
201,202,203,205,252,274,
275,296,358,362,365,367,
396,419
Farmer, W.R., 6
Fenton, J.C., 110,210,211,
221,234,236,246,259,265,
284,296,297,306,341,347,
365,396,404,405,408
Feuillet, A., 8,9,199,
200,205,224,230,316,319
Fiorenza, E.S., 170
Fitzmyer, J.A., 102,110,
405
Flückiger, F., 161
Foerster, W., 303,328
Friedrich, G., 45,49,79,
173,253,290,306,400
Frost, S.B., 303,304
Fuller, R., 378,382
Funk, R.W., 27
Gärtner, B., 174,307
Garland, D., 410n4
Gaster, T.H., 252
Gaston, L., 12,28,162,
186,192
Ginzberg, L., 191
Glasson, T.F., 339,341,
345
Gnilka, J., 177,178
Goldstein, J.A., 329
Gould, E.P., 121,207
Goulder, M.D., 38,54
Grant, R.M., 42
Grundmann, W., 230
Gundry, R.H., 308,312,
342
Haenchen, E., 20,58,60,
74,79,124,173,255,400

Hahn, F., 351
Hamerton-Kelly, R.G.,
37,46,52,61,170,171,
245,366,373,374,383,
386,388
Hanson, P.D., 371,372
Hare, D.R.A., 10,46,
49,56,57,59,61,62,
64,78,79,99,102,105,
107,108,109,110,119,
128,129,130,158,164,
165,172,193,194,200,
202,203,204,205,223,
228,269,273,274,275,
277,278,279,280,281,
282,293,296,303,320,
366,394,402,411,424,
425,426
Harnack, A. See von
Harnack.
Hartman, L., 162,223,
312
Hauck, F., 295,412,
415,416
Hayes, J.H., 389
Held, H.J., 90,138,139,
140,284,364,366,369,
396,419
Herford, R.T., 242
Higgins, A.B.J., 341,
342,343,344,346,348,
350
Hill, D., 17,20,64,78,
83,87,88,89,90,114,
115,124,172,176,197,
217,220,222,224,228,
231,234,236,242,246,
251,252,266,267,271,
272,278,288,290,295,
296,298,299,310,323,
332,339,346,365,378,

460

# ABSTRACT

The rise of Redaction Criticism has enhanced interest in the theologies of the communities which produced the Gospels. Significant conclusions about Matthean theology have been reached by redaction critics, but one part of Matthew's Gospel which has not been extensively investigated with this method is the "eschatological discourse" (Matt. 24:3-31). This book is a redaction-critical investigation of the eschatological discourse in Matthew.

No study of the eschatological discourse in Matthew has produced a statement which has gained a consensus about the theological reasons for Matthew's composition of the discourse. This book uses Redaction Criticism in both its narrower sense, in which tradition and redaction are distinguished, and its broader sense, in which redactional themes are investigated in terms of the whole Gospel, in order to reveal the Evangelist's theological motivations in the composition of the discourse.

The thesis of this work is that Jesus delivers the discourse in its Matthean context as the Wisdom of God. The discourse, delineated as 24:3-31, functions within the whole Gospel as a testament of Jesus-Sophia to his followers, which includes Matthew's community. It is concluded in chapter two that the Evangelist has presented the discourse in a context which culminates his compositional theme of Israel's rejection of Jesus. It is concluded further that Matthew's theological motivation is to suggest that Israel's rejection of Jesus is the culmination of Israel's continual rejection of Sophia, who has become incarnate in Jesus. The eschatological discourse of Jesus-Sophia, then, is delivered in a context in which he definitively withdraws his presence from

465

Israel and delivers his last words to the disciples before he goes to his death. Chapter three is a detailed investigation of the content of Jesus-Sophia's discourse. Suggestions are then made in chapter four for understanding christology and discipleship in Matthew in light of the eschatological discourse. The general conclusions are that Wisdom christology is a major component within Matthew's christological framework, and that one understanding of discipleship for Matthew's community was that they were envoys of Jesus-Sophia.

## ABOUT THE AUTHOR

Fred Burnett completed his graduate work in New Testament Studies at Vanderbilt University in 1979. He is currently associate professor of Religious Studies at Anderson College, Anderson, Indiana.